The Era of the

American Revolution

The Era of the
American Revolution

STUDIES INSCRIBED TO
EVARTS BOUTELL GREENE

Edited by

RICHARD B. MORRIS *ed*

NEW YORK : MORNINGSIDE HEIGHTS

COLUMBIA UNIVERSITY PRESS

1939

The William A. Dunning Fund

The publication of this volume was made possible by assistance from the fund for the encouragement of historical studies bequeathed to Columbia University by the late Professor William A. Dunning.

COLUMBIA UNIVERSITY PRESS, NEW YORK

Foreign Agents: OXFORD UNIVERSITY PRESS, *Humphrey Milford, Amen House, London, E.C. 4, England,* AND *B. I. Building, Nicol Road, Bombay, India;* MARUZEN COMPANY, LTD., *6 Nihonbashi, Tori-Nichome, Tokyo, Japan*

MANUFACTURED IN THE UNITED STATES OF AMERICA

Foreword

IN ASSAYING western civilization in the time between Sedan and Warsaw we may, under stress of the tragic contemporary trend, unduly emphasize the negative and destructive side. The humane and liberal concepts which flourished in the last century are still cherished in American society despite the competition of current ideologies. The field of historical scholarship affords evidence to support this view. The perpetuation of standards of objectivity and fairmindedness in the writing of history in America is in no small measure due to the precepts and example of recent generations of American scholars. Prominent among these scholars has long stood Evarts Boutell Greene.

Before the perilous view became fashionable that the historian is controlled by a personal frame of reference from which he cannot escape, scholars such as Greene, educated in the latter part of the nineteenth century, wrote in self-dedication to the then prevailing concept of history as a description of the past as it actually was. In his distinguished Harvard doctoral monograph, *The Provincial Governor in the English Colonies of North America,* published in 1898—a study of constitutional relations in the colonies—Greene embodied this fair-mindedness and impartiality, buttressed by evidence drawn from the primary sources. In a guide to the manuscript sources for American history available in New York City and in a study of population estimates before the first Federal census, he endeavored to make available to other scholars the primary sources for the pursuit of further original investigations.

The career of Evarts Greene illustrates that New England dispersion which, as he indicates in his biography of his father, Daniel Crosby Greene, he regards as so important a phase of American history. Born in Kobe, Japan, July 8, 1870, of New England parentage, educated successively at Northwestern, Harvard, and Berlin, he held posts in the history faculties at Harvard (1890–93), at the University of Illinois (1894–1923), where for seven years he was Dean of the College of Liberal Arts, and at Columbia University, from 1923 until his recent retirement. Because of advantages of background and rich experience, Greene has always been free, in his writings and teaching, of the narrow provincialism so often associated with the American intellectual activity that is nurtured in the universities. His scholarly interests have not been circumscribed by the thirteen seaboard colonies, but embrace Middle Western history, his studies in which are perhaps best exemplified by an edition of the letter books of early Illinois governors, and the history and culture of Japan. His father's pioneer missionary activities in the Far East and his family background also serve to explain Professor Greene's deep interest in the problems of the relationship between Church and State, not alone in colonial times, although in this field he has rendered some of his most important contributions, but in contemporary life as well. While sympathetic with modern emphases, he has not permitted his writing or teaching to be shackled to any monistic determinism. This is apparent both in his students' research in economic, legal, and social history and in his own works—his pioneer treatment of provincial society, 1690–1740, in the "American Nation" series and his current investigation of the social history of the Revolutionary generation. Although he recognizes the fact that the thirteen colonies were part of a larger imperial system and therefore may be considered rightly as a phase of British colonial history, Professor Greene has very properly sought to emphasize the gradual differentiation in viewpoint and interest between colonies and mother country. The development of our distinguishing characteristics is carefully traced in his *Foundations of American Nationality*. In this work, considerable emphasis is placed also upon the conflict in political thought between Great Britain and her colonies by the time of the Revolution.

Those who have joined in the present volume to pay tribute to the scholar also pay homage to the teacher and the man. The contributors are recipients of the doctorate, at either the University of Illinois or Columbia, under his immediate supervision, but the limitations of space have prevented representation of all his doctoral students. One signal omission should be mentioned, however:

the late Clarence W. Alvord, whose notable investigations of the role of the frontier and the Mississippi Valley in the American Revolution were begun under Greene's direction.

Even those whose studies with Professor Greene were of a more transient character have been at times profoundly influenced. Carl Van Doren's experience may be accepted as representative:

The nearest I came to thinking about it [scholarship] was in the feeling I arrived at in the year when I had Evarts Greene as my teacher in American history. His tall shyness touched me. A kind of courtliness—I can think of no other word—in his intellect moved me. Seeing and admiring the conscience with which he hunted for the truth and the justice with which he tried to make it clear, I felt that I had been helter-skelter and sluttish. Exactness in learning, I told myself, was as satisfying as in verse. Scrupulous truth was beautiful, careless error was ugly. Ugly and dirty. I told myself that it would be cheap and mean ever to pretend to know anything I was not sure of, or not to know anything I had had chance or reason to find out.[1]

Students and colleagues who have penetrated the shy and retiring exterior have discovered a Puritan conscience manifesting itself in an emphasis upon thoroughness, impartiality, meticulous attention to detail, and moral and intellectual integrity. These old New England virtues are associated in Evarts Greene with sympathetic understanding, genuine concern with the problems of the student, quiet forcefulness and determination, and exemplary modesty. And with this rare combination of qualities he has won the deep affection and respect of those who have come to know him well.

The contributors of these studies have striven to formulate a coherent point of view with regard to the era of the American Revolution, the period, 1760–90, of their teacher's principal scholarly activity. Lawrence A. Harper's study serves to correct the prevailing misconception, associated with George Louis Beer, that the old colonial system was so nicely balanced that economic burdens and advantages fell evenly on colonies and mother country. His statistical analysis demonstrates that the burdens on the colonies outweighed the benefits and that the Acts of Trade retarded colonial economic expansion. It is clear, as regards both the enforcement of the Acts and the presence of a standing army, that if the American

[1] *Three Worlds* (New York, 1936), pp. 79–80.

Revolution had not interposed, constitutional changes would have been introduced to limit colonial self-government. The struggle against the writs of assistance, which O. M. Dickerson establishes as not confined to a single colony, brings out very forcefully the desire of the British government to curb the judiciary. From the widespread colonial resistance to such curbs Dickerson dates the determination in this country to keep the courts free from executive control. Clarence E. Carter's study of the position of the military commander in chief emphasizes an important constitutional innovation and focuses attention upon the fear, widespread in the colonies, that ultimately they would be consolidated under a military regime. The rise of the military commander was accompanied by a corresponding decline in the prestige of the governors. Louise Dunbar, concentrating on the role of the executive in the six royal provinces of the middle and southern sections on the eve of the Revolution, emphasizes the growing weakness and isolation of their position. Their failure to give the military commander genuine coöperation, the prevailing hostility to the military, and an insufficiency of funds and men serve to explain why Major General Thomas Gage was unable to achieve any real measure of unified control.

Mercantilism manifested itself in the life of the colonies not only in such external regulations as the Acts of Trade but also in internal economic policies, such as wage and price controls, introduced in the early years of settlement and dramatically revived during the American Revolution. This challenge to *laissez faire* theories of free markets and the natural rate of wages is examined in the study entitled "Labor and Mercantilism." To the experience with such regulations may be attributed in large measure the desire of the Founding Fathers to avoid such internal controls in the future but at the same time to provide adequate tariff protection. The view that the American Revolution was a phase of the struggle to maintain a colonial balance of power fitted well into the philosophic framework of mercantilist nationalism. As Max Savelle demonstrates, the position of France, whose aid in the Revolution was decisive, was determined by a desire to rebuild this balance, which had been completely destroyed by the Seven Years' War.

While in the American Revolution there was no hard-and-fast

alignment of class against class, the Sons of Liberty, as Herbert Morais demonstrates, played an important role in directing mass activities of mechanics and artisans and in counteracting, in the direction of democracy, the conservatism of the merchants and lawyers. From this situation one should not conclude that the propertyless were arrayed against the propertied. The tobacco planters, the large investors in western lands, and many other men of substance supported the Revolutionary cause. Typical of the propertied group who espoused the Revolution was Eliphalet Dyer of Connecticut. George Groce makes it quite clear that the treatment by the home authorities of Dyer's land claims and those of his colony served to swing him over to the radical position. The Revolution was not fought merely to correct injustices to seaboard mercantile interests; speculative as well as legitimate interests in frontier expansion found their activities sharply curbed by the imperial program. The Connecticut-Pennsylvania land dispute serves to remind students of this period that it was necessary for the colonies to surmount regional differences, even conflicts of economic and class interest, in order to redress the greater economic grievances against Britain.

In an era when public opinion in many countries is molded by government-controlled systems of news dissemination, a study of newspaper propaganda during the American Revolution assumes special interest. Though atrocity stories were fed by newspapers in those days as today, the distinctive feature of the patriot press in that contest, according to Sidney Pomerantz, was its integrity. In New York and New Jersey, for example, the Whig press in the Revolution maintained canons of journalistic conduct all too often forgotten in wartime. The press abroad also reflected the events transpiring on the Atlantic seaboard. The impact of the Revolution on France has already been well established; and now a still closer relationship in Ireland has been demonstrated by Michael Kraus. The American Revolution kindled a spirit of resistance in Ireland; but the reforms which were won in that country were ultimately buried under the reaction brought on by the French Revolution.

In the concluding study Robert East shows that the insurrections in back-country Massachusetts in the Critical Period were aggra vated by the conservative fiscal and social policies pursued in that state after 1780, and that these disturbances played into the hands of the strong nationalists, who were enabled thereby to bring divergent conservative groups to accept a Federal union.

The editor was assisted by Professors John A. Krout and Allan Nevins in the preparation of this volume for the press. Grateful acknowledgment should be made also to Professor Carlton J. H. Hayes of Columbia University for his sympathetic interest and coöperation in this enterprise and to the staff of the Columbia University Press for valued technical assistance.

RICHARD B. MORRIS

New York City
October 4, 1939

Contents

The Era of the
American Revolution

The Effect of the Navigation
Acts on the Thirteen Colonies

~~~ LAWRENCE A. HARPER

THE ENGLISH Navigation Acts have long been a topic of great interest to both British and American historians, but there has been no agreement as to their effect upon the colonies. The opposite extremes are represented by George Bancroft, who viewed the Acts as horrible instruments of English tyranny against which the colonies nobly arose to throw off the oppressive yoke, and George Louis Beer, who veered to the other extreme in pointing out that the measures were not unfair and who maintained that the old colonial system was so nicely balanced that both the colonies and the mother country bore burdens for the good of the Empire and shared in the general advantages.

The ultimate answer to the question must be deferred until more detailed knowledge of colonial trade and commerce is available. Work which has been done and research now in progress make it possible at this time to outline the factors involved in the problems and to formulate tentative hypotheses.[1] The difficulties are many, but most critics of attempts to solve the problem empha-

[1] For many years George Louis Beer's excellent volumes *The Old Colonial System* (2 vols., New York, 1912) and *British Colonial Policy, 1754-1765* (New York, 1907) have supplied our best account of the Acts. No modern work has been devoted to the laws themselves except the fourth volume of C. M. Andrews's *The Colonial Period of American History* (New Haven, 1938), which only recently appeared, and L. A. Harper's *The English Navigation Laws* (in press). Neither, however, treats at length the effect of the laws upon the colonies, each examining the legislation primarily from the point of view of English administration and policies. The present study has been facilitated by the use of basic data now being compiled by WPA Project No. 10482-A-10, which has been supplemented for present purposes by student help supplied by the National Youth Administration. Thanks are also due to the Social Science Research Council of the University of California for financial assistance and to Miss Frances Burke and Dr. Gerald White for help in collecting and analyzing statistics and laws.

size two points: that the existence of smuggling renders it impossible for us to determine what happened when the laws were in force and that any conclusions which we may reach will be mere conjecture, since we cannot reorder the past to determine what would have happened if the laws had never been enacted. Neither objection, however, should prove insuperable.

Although the exact extent of smuggling cannot be determined with accuracy because of the nature of the smugglers' activities, we can establish its limits. We know that great quantities of European goods, of tobacco, and of rice, the three most important items regulated, passed through England as the law required. In comparison with the volume of such trade, the amount of goods smuggled was necessarily small because by far the greater percentage of colonial shipping is known to have been engaged in legal trades, and, however illicit their intentions, the smugglers could not find sufficient cargo capacity to present formidable competition. Moreover, the very existence of so great a legal commerce discloses that the community was not a unit in violating the laws. There were "fair traders" whose own financial interests led them to oppose smuggling, which if unchecked might have driven them out of business. Most important of all, the continued existence of legal trade implies either that smuggling was negligible or that it encountered sufficient hazards to equalize the burdens that the laws placed upon legal commerce. As a consequence we can concentrate our attention upon legal trade in the belief that indirectly the English commercial system exercised a similar influence over illicit trade.[2]

Although we cannot state with absolute certainty "what might have been" if there had been no Navigation Acts, we can attain a degree of probability far beyond mere conjecture by comparing what actually happened when the laws were in force with conditions which existed when their restraints were removed. Lack of data for the seventeenth century prevents much comparison of

---

[2] The extent of colonial smuggling is discussed more fully in L. A. Harper, *The English Navigation Laws*, pp. 247–71. It should be noted that the argument presented applies only to the trans-Atlantic trade, not to violations of the Molasses Act of 1733. There it was possible for the continental colonists, in part at least, to force the British West Indies to accept competitive prices; and as the provisions shipped to the Caribbean were more bulky than sugar, there was always plenty of room for returning cargoes, whether licit or illicit.

conditions before and after the enactment of the laws, but we do have adequate figures which permit us to compare the course of trade before and after the Revolution freed the thirteen colonies from British commercial regulations.[3] The fact that in the nineteenth century the former thirteen colonies were economically much more developed than in the seventeenth century, when they did not even number thirteen, is not fatal to our proposed analysis. The Britain of 1776 also had far outstripped the England of 1660 in commercial importance. At the earlier date Holland was the acknowledged commercial, industrial, and financial center of Europe. It was the Dutch who paid most, sold cheapest, carried goods most economically, and extended the most liberal terms of credit.[4] Under a system of free economy American trade would naturally have gravitated to the Netherlands. Dutch capital would have sought investment in the colonies. In fact both developments occurred and were the principal reasons for legislative restraints.[5] By 1776 Britain had taken Holland's place as the predominant trading center. The commercial ties which would thus naturally

[3] Unless otherwise noted, in the statistics cited hereafter the figures for 1770 for the continental colonies are those prepared by Thomas Irving, Inspector General of Imports and Exports of North America, and printed in Timothy Pitkin, *A Statistical View of the Commerce of the United States* (Hartford, 1816), and in Lord Sheffield, *Observations on the Commerce of the American States* (London, 1784); those for 1773 for England are from Customs 3/73, for Scotland from Customs 14/1B; those for the United States in 1790, 1799, and 1821 are from American State Papers, Class IV, *Commerce and Navigation*, and in 1840 are in U.S. 26th Congress, second session, *Senate Documents*, No. 238. Statements as to duties and bounties are based upon material set forth in Henry Crouch, *A Complete View of the British Customs* (London, 1730), S. Baldwin, *Survey of the British Customs* (London, 1770), and William Sims and Richard Frewin, *Rates of Merchandize* (London, 1782), so corrected by the references therein cited as to apply to the dates under discussion. For statutes prior to 1714 the citations are those given in the *Statutes of the Realm* (London, 1810–28).

[4] Violet Barbour, "Dutch and English Merchant Shipping in the Seventeenth Century," *Econ. Hist. Rev.*, II, 261–90 (1929–30); G. L. Beer, *Origins of the British Colonial System, 1578–1660* (New York, 1908), pp. 209, 389, 392; *The Advocate* (London, 1651), p. 4; Sir Josiah Child, *A Short Reply to a Treatise, Entitled Interest of Money Mistaken*, p. 22.

[5] *The Advocate*, p. 6; *Calendar of State Papers, Venetian (1647–52)*, pp. 230–31, 234; *(1653–54)*, p. 103; Edmund Ludlow, *Memoirs, 1625–1672* (Oxford, 1894), I, 266–67; John Thurloe, *A Collection of the State Papers* (London, 1742), III, 494; *Maryland Archives*, XLIX, 299, 323–24, 341–42, 388, 391–93; *Documents Relative to the Colonial History of the State of New York*, XIV, 126–28; Andrews, *Colonial Period*, II, 263–64; V. T. Harlow, *A History of Barbados, 1628–1685* (Oxford, 1926), pp. 37–43, 65–68, 85–93; C. S. S. Higham, *Development of the Leeward Islands under the Restoration* (Cambridge, 1921), pp. 37, 143; A. P. Newton, *Colonizing Activities of the English Puritans* (New Haven, 1914), pp. 221, 261–62.

develop between Britain and the United States were strengthened
after cotton became the South's chief crop and the Industrial Revolution made Britain the chief cotton manufacturer. Thus conclusions based upon evidence that America's trade turned to countries other than Britain after 1776 should underestimate rather
than overstate the tendency which existed in 1660.

The general history of the acts is too well known to require a
chronological account of their development or any extended introduction concerning their provisions. We will do best to pass
directly to an analysis of the regulations, proceeding from the
simplest to the most complex, from those dealing with manufacturing and shipbuilding to those concerning shipping and trade.

The rule forbidding shipment of colonial wool or woolen manufactures outside the borders of a colony appears to have been
passed primarily as a precautionary measure [6] and to have had
no material restraint upon colonial activity. Although there are
few records of shipping for the seventeenth century, those which we
do have for Massachusetts from 1686 to 1688 disclose no shipments
of such products when they would still have been legal, and the
statistics of American exports following the Revolution fail to
disclose any potential foreign market from which the colonists
were excluded. Regardless of legislation the colonial woolen industry would probably have been confined primarily to the
production of homespun garments. The exigencies of frontier life
did not provide the labor to establish the industry on a broader
scale.[7]

The restraints on the colonial manufacture of hats, however,
present another story. The labor problem here did not offer so
great an obstacle, and the local supply of furs acted as a stimulus.
By 1732, when the company of felt makers in London prevailed
upon Parliament to forbid any colonial exportations of hats, to require a seven-year apprenticeship, to exclude Negroes from the
industry, and to limit each manufacturer to two apprentices,[8] a
flourishing industry had developed, especially in New England

---

[6] 10 Gul. III, c. 16, sec. 19 (effective Dec. 1, 1699).

[7] C.O. 5/848; J. L. Bishop, *History of American Manufactures* (Philadelphia, 1861),
I, 326–30, 344–45; V. S. Clark, *History of Manufactures in the United States* (New
York, 1929), I, 22, 81–82, 204–9.

[8] 5 Geo. II, c. 22 (1732).

and New York, which were exporting hats to neighboring colonies, the West Indies, and southern Europe. The law doubtless was not perfectly enforced, but there is reason to suspect that it hindered colonial activity. Before its passage England exported only 2,650 dozen beaver hats to all her colonies in 1698 out of a total of 5,761 dozen, while in 1773 her total exports were 13,000 dozen, of which 9,562 dozen went to the colonies. Moreover, the importation of hats from Britain declined sharply after the Revolution, and the United States once again began to export them to southern Europe, the West Indies, and South America.[9]

The regulations governing iron represented a clash between conflicting English interests, the natural result of which was legislation that on the one hand granted colonial pig and bar iron preferential treatment when entering England and on the other forbade the erection of any additional slitting mills in the colonies or the exportation of colonial iron outside the Empire.[10] Studies of the subject by Bining suggest that the preferential duties had little effect upon the colonial development, since the American market was much the greater factor in its growth, and that the prohibition of the erection of new mills was openly defied—the most flagrant instance being that of the Pennsylvania colonial assembly which gave financial aid to Whitehead Humphries in developing his steel mill.[11] But it seems unwise to dismiss the law as immaterial. Although some investors undoubtedly were willing to assume the risk, capital is notoriously timid, and many investors probably directed their funds into other channels where there was not added to the customary hazards of starting a new industry the danger that their competitors in England might ruin it merely by

[9] C.O. 5/1224 and 1225. The value of fur and felt hats imported from Britain declined from £44,769 in 1773 to $11,027 in 1821 and $4,246 in 1840. Exports rose from nothing in 1773 to $63,363 in 1821 and $103,398 in 1840. There were 68 hatters in Philadelphia City and County in 1791 (Tench Coxe, *A View of the United States* [London, 1794], p. 158; J. T. Scharf and Thompson Westcott, *History of Philadelphia* [Philadelphia, 1884], III, 2336). Earlier figures from the tax lists are not altogether satisfactory because of gaps in the record and failures to list occupations in some years. Correcting the figures as best we can by interpolation, it appears that there were 24 hatters in 1769 and 43 in 1774 and 1780 (*Pennsylvania Archives,* 3d ser., Vols. XIV, XV).

[10] 23 Geo. II, c. 29 (1750); 30 Geo. II, c. 16 (1757).

[11] A. C. Bining, *British Regulation of the Colonial Iron Industry* (Philadelphia, 1933), pp. 82–83, and *Pennsylvania Iron Manufacture in the Eighteenth Century* (Harrisburg, 1938), pp. 154–59.

persuading colonial officials to enforce the law. In this connection it is interesting to note that during the twenty-five years from 1750 to 1775 only thirty-eight iron-producing establishments were founded in Pennsylvania and Delaware, whereas the number was almost doubled in the ten years from 1790 to 1800.[12] The multiplicity of other factors which intervened forbid any dogmatic conclusions, but the statistics tend to support rather than to confute the theory that the Iron Act had some restraining influence.

In the field of colonial shipbuilding, we find that the industry benefited from the English legislation, but the gain was probably not great. Although the Navigation Acts discouraged use of foreign-built vessels in the English merchant marine, they did not forbid it until 1786, except in the colonial trade, and in the seventeenth century, when protection afforded by the laws would have been of the greatest aid to the colonial industry, the frequent grant of dispensations lessened their effect.[13] Moreover, the colonists apparently could hold their own in free competition with foreign builders, such as the Dutch, because colonial shipbuilding had attained respectable proportions before 1660, and American ships found a market abroad without the benefit of protection after the Revolution.[14] Certainly as far as the English builders were concerned the colonists proved formidable rivals. In 1724, the Thames shipbuilders sought unsuccessfully to procure protection against their competition,[15] and in 1739, when permission was granted to ship West Indian sugar to ports south of Cape Finisterre without

[12] Bining, *Pennsylvania Iron Manufacture*, pp. 188–92. It is not clear how many of the furnaces, forges, etc., established between 1750 and 1775 were legal under the provisions of the Iron Act. It also should be noted that there may have been illegal mills set up of which we now have no record.

[13] 12 Car. II, c. 18 (1660); 15 Car. II, c. 7 (1663); 7 and 8 Gul. III, c. 22 (1696); 26 Geo. III, c. 60 (1786); Barbour, "Dutch and English Merchant Shipping," *Econ. Hist. Rev.*, II, 289. The provision in the Act of 1662 (14 Car. II, c. 11) that thereafter foreign-built ships should be deemed to be foreign vessels was held merely to require that they pay certain alien duties charged on goods imported in foreign vessels.

[14] In the 34 years between 1815 and 1848 the United States sold an average of 10,584 tons of sailing vessels each year (Hans Keiler, *American Shipping* [Jena, 1913], p. 62). It should be remembered that the two principal markets for ships, Great Britain and France, were closed to the American shipbuilders (Coxe, *A View of the United States*, p. 184). The tonnage built for sale abroad jumped to 60,033 when the British shippers were allowed to purchase American-built bottoms in 1854 (Keiler, *loc. cit.*).

[15] W. B. Weeden, *Economic and Social History of New England, 1620–1789* (Boston, 1891), II, 573.

going to England, the privilege was at first confined to English-built vessels although later amended to include the cheaper, colonial-built vessels.[16] It has been said that by the time of the American Revolution one-third of the British merchant marine was colonial-built, and the thirteen colonies were building 28,747 tons per year.[17] Yet American shipbuilding was not dependent upon sales to Britain, because after independence closed that outlet the tonnage built in the United States was at least 29,606 tons by 1790 and 154,624 tons in 1815.[18] Apparently the benefits conferred by opening the English market for the sale of ships were offset by the limitation of the American market which resulted from the restrictions placed upon colonial shipping.

For most practical purposes, colonial-owned ships were entitled to the same privileges as British-owned vessels, in contradistinction to foreign vessels, which were excluded from the plantation trade. Yet the protection thereby afforded does not appear to be very important. In the early stages of American maritime development navigation would naturally be limited to the coasting trade, in which small colonial vessels would actually have an advantage over their greatest potential rivals, the larger, ocean-going Dutch flyboats. Later, when the colonies had developed to such an extent that one might expect their shipping to branch out into broader fields, we find it mostly confined to the coasting and West Indian trade, four-fifths of the traffic crossing the Atlantic in 1769–71 being carried in British bottoms.[19] Although we cannot conclusively demonstrate the connection between this phenomenon and the laws, it probably resulted from the natural tendency of the British merchant, who controlled the disposal of the goods, to use his own or his friend's shipping. Certainly there seems to be significance in the fact that after control over colonial trade passed from British hands the situation was reversed, and four-fifths of

[16] 12 Geo. II, c. 30 (1739); 15 Geo. II, c. 33 (1742); F. W. Pitman, *The Development of the British West Indies* (New Haven, 1917), p. 184.

[17] Richard Champion, *Considerations on the Present Situation of Great Britain and the United States* (London, 1784), p. 13; R. G. Albion, *Forests and Sea Power* (Cambridge, 1926), p. 246. The figure represents an average of the three years 1769 to 1771 (Pitkin, *Statistical View*, p. 17) to which has been added one-third for understatements of tonnage; see Sheffield, *Observations*, p. 96.

[18] Coxe, *A View of the United States*, pp. 217–18; Keiler, *American Shipping*, p. 62.

[19] Champion, *Considerations*, pp. 27–28, 65, 66.

the trans-Atlantic trade in 1821 was carried by American rather than British vessels.[20]

The rules governing shipping were simple as compared with the complex maze of restrictions, duties, preferential rates, drawbacks, penalties, and charter monopolies which governed trade. Anyone desiring to make order out of the confusion must proceed warily, step by step.

Trade with Africa and in America was subjected to few regulations of importance. Until 1698 colonists who wished to go to Africa ran afoul of the Royal African Company's privileges,[21] but thereafter they met no important hindrances in trading with that continent. Except for the assessment in 1673 of the so-called "plantation duties" upon the transshipment between colonies of the enumerated commodities,[22] trade in nonenumerated American products was free until the Molasses Act of 1733.[23] It can be disregarded as not being enforced, but the acts of 1764 and 1765 cannot.[24] The resentment aroused by the attempts to collect duties upon foreign molasses and sugar demonstrates beyond question the importance placed upon trade with the foreign West Indies; but there is room for argument as to whether this trade would have been deemed so important if England had not restrained American commerce with Europe.

The legislation governing colonial importations from Europe and Asia required that with a few exceptions, such as Madeira wine, salt for the fisheries, and provisions and servants from Scotland and Ireland, all goods be procured in England or, after 1707, in Britain. Bounties were granted on the export of certain commodities, including gunpowder, linen, sailcloth, silk, and refined sugar,[25] but these bounties were not special favors to the colonies, being granted on exportations to all countries and designed to develop British manufactures. Merchants reëxporting goods during the greater part of the colonial period were repaid all the duties on most commodities which had been paid upon importation to

---

[20] Immediately after the Revolution the carriage was still in British hands, for their Navigation Acts were still in force and the United States had not yet built up her own shipping. The year 1821 was chosen as offering a sounder basis of comparison, since it was typical of conditions following the Reciprocity Treaty with Great Britain.
[21] 9 Gul. III, c. 26 (1697–98).   [22] 25 Car. II, c. 7 (1673).   [23] 6 Geo. II, c. 13.
[24] 4 Geo. III, c. 15; 6 Geo. III, c. 52.   [25] Champion, *Considerations*, p. 40.

England, except one-half of the Old Subsidy. Yet the fact that drawbacks were usually allowed must not cause us to forget that the duties had been assessed and that when England wished extra revenue she could decrease the drawback as she did in 1764,[26] or that she could withhold it entirely when she wished to protect her industries, as she did in the case of unwrought iron or steel, cordage, sailcloth, unwrought hemp, paper, and oysters.[27]

The artificiality of the indirect routing of European goods is revealed clearly by the sharp decline of goods shipped in that manner after the Revolution. During the colonial period such goods averaged almost one-quarter of the value of the thirteen colonies' imports of British, European, and Asian goods (excepting such imports as Madeira wine and salt, which were not covered by the laws), but they represented less than two percent in the nineteenth century.[28] The effect of these burdens upon the colonists' purchases of European goods was to increase the proportion of British manufactures which they acquired, a tendency which was reversed after independence. Despite the influence of established consumer habits, commercial connections, and long-time credits, Britain, which had produced almost 73 percent of the goods imported by the thirteen colonies from elsewhere than Africa or America in 1773, supplied only 54 percent in 1799, 55 percent in 1821, and 45 percent in 1840.[29]

In turning to the legislation governing exportations from the colonies, we find that only the enumerated commodities were regulated, but they constituted one-half of the total shipments from

[26] 4 Geo. III, c. 15.

[27] 2 & 3 Anne, c. 18, xii (1703, iron and steel); 6 Anne, c. 73, xiii (1707, cordage); 4 Geo. II, c. 27 (1731, sailcloth and cordage); 10 Geo. II, c. 27, iv (1737, paper); 10 Geo. II, c. 30, iv (1737, oysters). The denial of drawback was general except in the case of unwrought iron, steel, and hemp, when it was denied only in the case of reëxportation to the British colonies in America.

[28] Reëxported goods constituted only 2.8 percent of the goods shipped to the United States from Great Britain from 1806 to 1808 (Pitkin, *Statistical View*, p. 223); 1.5 percent in 1821 (Great Britain, House of Commons Sessional Papers [1822], XXI, No. 274); and 4.4 percent in 1828 (*ibid.* [1830], XXVII, No. 292). At that time Britain supplied only slightly more than one-half of the total of British, European, and Asian goods imported into the United States.

[29] Statistics in César Moreau (*Chronological Records of the British Royal and Commercial Navy* [London, 1827], pp. 13, 15, 17–18) show that British goods had constituted 75 percent of such colonial imports in 1698–1701; 73 percent in 1713–17; 64 percent in 1722–38; 86 percent in 1749–55; and 83 percent in 1763–74.

the continental colonies in 1770 and much more of those from the British West Indies.[30] Since such goods had to be marketed through Britain, we must endeavor to understand the British customs system. As Parliament confessed when reconstructing it in 1787, the manner of charging and computing the duties was "in many instances intricate and complicated, and productive of much embarrassment to the persons who are to pay the same, as well of great perplexity on the accounts of the public revenue,"[31] an acknowledgment which historians will agree to be a masterpiece of understatement. It will only add to the confusion if we attempt to trace the evolution of the various provisions, which frequently changed in matters of detail. Our best chance to obtain a working knowledge of the rules is to analyze them at the eve of the Revolution when British mercantilism had attained its maturity. In the case of the British West Indies an analysis discloses that the benefits they received outweighed the burdens incurred (see Table 1, page 13).

The great bulk of the shipments to Britain in both quantity and value consisted of sugar. All except 10.46 percent was consumed in England, and 98.7 percent of the small portion reëxported was shipped to Ireland, which cannot really be classed as a foreign country for the purposes of this discussion. Originally, the enumeration of sugar had inconvenienced the West Indian planters, but by 1773 the greater fertility of the foreign islands enabled their rivals to undersell them by at least five shillings per hundredweight.[32] Thus, the preferential duty of 13s. 0d.$\frac{18}{20}$ per hundredweight was a real boon since it virtually excluded foreign competition from the English market. Calculated on the conservative basis of five shillings a hundred, it appears that the West Indies benefited to the extent of £446,125 a year and were assessed very little in duties retained on reëxported West Indian products, the £1,382 collected on Jamaican pimento being the largest item, except for the discriminating duties against Dominican products, which were charged the same rate as French goods.

When we turn to the regulations governing the products of the

---

[30] In this calculation shipments of enumerated products to the other colonies have been disregarded as negligible.   [31] 27 Geo. III, c. 13.

[32] Beer, *The Old Colonial System*, II, 1–30; Pitman, *Development of the British West Indies*, pp. 160–67; Sheffield, *Observations*, p. 121.

TABLE 1. ENUMERATED GOODS PRODUCED CHIEFLY IN THE WEST INDIES

ARTICLE AND UNIT OF MEASUREMENT	BOUNTY AND PREFERENCE	IMPORT DUTY	DUTY RETAINED, EXPORT TAX, AND BOUNTY REPAID	QUANTITY IMPORTED AND TOTAL ESTIMATED VALUE	PERCENTAGE REEXPORTED
ACT OF 1660					
Cotton wool (lb.)	$\frac{15\%(\text{P})}{20}$	free	5%(E)	2,386,509 / £78,576	1.11
Ginger (cwt.)	£2 os. 8d. $\frac{7\frac{1}{2}(\text{P})}{20}$	9s. 6d. $\frac{4}{20}$	5d. $14\frac{1}{20}$(D)	8,280 / £7,153	69.87
Sugar (white) (cwt.)	14s. 5d. $1\frac{9}{20}$(P)	£1 1s. 1d.		none / none	none
Sugar (brown) (cwt.)	13s. 0d. $1\frac{8}{20}$(P)	6s. 3d. $1\frac{8}{20}$		1,784,499 / £2,025,983	10.46
Fustic (ton)		free		761 / £6,838	64.13
Logwood (cwt.)		free		44,790 / £26,583	117.75 [a]
Other dyewoods (ton)		free		780 / £7,665	46.03
ACT OF 1705					
Molasses (ton)	£7 10s.(P)	£2 11s. 4d.	6s. 4d.(D)	61 / £797	12.05
ACT OF 1764					
Pimento (lb.)		1d. $\frac{14\frac{29}{40}}{20}$	$\frac{2\frac{17}{20}(\text{D})}{20}$	2,282,071 / £57,434	103.42 [a]
Coffee (cwt.) [b]	£5 12s.(P)	£1 13s. 6d. $\frac{3}{20}$		44,741 / £311,980	109.14 [a]
Cocoa nuts (cwt.)		11s. 11d. $\frac{12\frac{1}{2}}{20}$		7,305 / £18,265	94.94

The statutes of enumeration are as follows: 1660—12 Car. II, c. 18; 1705—3 and 4 Anne, c. 3; 1764—4 Geo. III, c. 15. In calculating preferences granted for plantation commodities, comparisons were made with foreign goods carried in British ships and the discriminatory duties on French goods were disregarded. The percentages of goods exported are based upon quantity rather than value.

[a] Presumably the excess of exportations is accounted for by importations held over from previous years.

[b] The preference resulted from the assessment by 5 Geo. III, c. 45, of an "inland duty" on coffee used for domestic consumption.

TABLE 2. Goods Produced Chiefly in the Thirteen Colonies, Enumerated before the Reign of George III

ARTICLE AND UNIT OF MEASUREMENT	BOUNTY AND PREFERENCE	IMPORT DUTY	DUTY RETAINED, EXPORT TAX, AND BOUNTY REPAID	QUANTITY IMPORTED AND TOTAL ESTIMATED VALUE	PERCENTAGE REEXPORTED
ACT OF 1660					
Indigo (lb.)	4d.(B)	free		1,385,139 / £87,156	40.12
Tobacco (lb.) a	1s. 10d. $\frac{15\frac{16}{75}}{20}$(P)	6d. $\frac{19\frac{2}{3}}{20}$		100,482,007 / £1,006,530	96.27
ACT OF 1705					
Rice (cwt.)	6s. 4d. $1\frac{1}{20}$(P)	free	8d.(E)	468,915 / £347,245	79.30
Naval stores b					
Tar (last)	1s. 2d. $\frac{1\frac{1}{4}}{20}$(P); £3 6s.(B)	9s. 7d. $1\frac{1}{20}$	1s. 2d. $\frac{5}{20}$(D); £3 6s.(B)	7,691 / 68,847	4.79
Pitch (last)	1s. 2d. $\frac{1\frac{1}{4}}{20}$(P); £1 10s.(B)	9s. 7d. $1\frac{1}{20}$	1s. 2d. $\frac{5}{20}$(D); £1 10s.(B)	2,324 / £20,893	.57
Rosin (cwt.)	7d. $1\frac{1}{20}$(P)	1s. 3d. $\frac{8}{20}$	1d. $\frac{18}{20}$(D)	none	none c
Turpentine (cwt.)	1s. 6d. (ton)(B)	1s. 11d. $\frac{5}{20}$	2d. $\frac{17}{20}$(D); 1s. 6d.(B)	28,652 / £13,716	none c
Hemp (cwt.)	3s. 2d. $\frac{8}{20}$(P); 6s.(B)	free	6s.(B)	none	none c
Masts, yards, and bowsprits (ton) d	11d. $\frac{5}{20}$(P); £1 (B)	1s. 11d. $\frac{2}{20}$	2d. $1\frac{7}{20}$(D); £1(B)	4,442 / £13,866	none c

ARTICLE AND UNIT OF MEASUREMENT	BOUNTY AND PREFERENCE	IMPORT DUTY	DUTY RETAINED, EXPORT TAX, AND BOUNTY REPAID	QUANTITY IMPORTED AND TOTAL ESTIMATED VALUE	PERCENTAGE REEXPORTED
ACT OF 1722					
Beaver skins (ea.)		$1d.$	$1d.(D)$	6,170 pieces £509	57.81
Other furs (ea.)ᵉ		$1d. \frac{82\,9/40\ doz.}{20}$ to $£2\ 7s.\ 10d.\ 1\,1/20\ ea.\ \frac{7d.\ 3\,7/8}{20}$	$\frac{7d.(E)\ 2\,2/5\ doz.(D)}{20}$ to $4s.\ 9d.\ ea.(D)\ \frac{13\,7/8(D)}{20}$	133,153 pieces £7,447	95.56
Copper ore (cwt.)				382 £48	none

The statutes of enumeration are as follows: 1660—12 Car. II, c. 18; 1705—3 and 4 Anne, c. 3, c. 9; 1722—8 Geo. I, c. 15, c. 18. In calculating preferences granted for plantation commodities, comparisons were made with foreign goods carried in British ships and the discriminatory duties on French goods were disregarded. Although the import figures are for the thirteen colonies and West Indies only, the reëxport percentage has been computed from the total quantity imported from America and the total quantity reëxported from Britain, except in the case of beaver skins and other furs when imports from all areas were included.

ᵃ The duties listed are those for bonded tobacco, since 91.06 percent of the tobacco imported into England was this type.

ᵇ The figures given for tar are for common tar. Green tar, which received a bounty of £4 a ton in 1773, was seldom imported from the colonies. For ease in comparison, bounties have been converted from tons to units used in assessing duties. The enumeration of rosin lapsed in 1725, of hemp in 1741.

ᶜ Here (as elsewhere "none" is listed) most exports are shown not to be colonial products, the remainder being disregarded as negligible or obviously European.

ᵈ The duty given is that for middle masts. The duty varied for small and great masts. Yards and bowsprits are included as masts (Albion, *Forests and Sea Power*, p. xi).

ᵉ A duty of 8/20d. each was charged on the exportation of black fox skins. Import duties on furs ranged from a low for mole to a high for black fox.

TABLE 3. GOODS PRODUCED CHIEFLY IN THE THIRTEEN COLONIES, FIRST ENUMERATED IN THE REIGN OF GEORGE III

ARTICLE AND UNIT OF MEASUREMENT	BOUNTY AND PREFERENCE	IMPORT DUTY	DUTY RETAINED, EXPORT TAX, AND BOUNTY REPAID	QUANTITY IMPORTED AND TOTAL ESTIMATED VALUE	PERCENTAGE REEXPORTED
ACT OF 1764					
Whale fins (ton)	£81 14s. 6d. to £84 2s. (P) a	free to £2 7s. 6d.	none to £1 3s. 9d. (D)	10 / £1,641	1.20
Raw silk (lb.)	1s. 3d.(P) / 25% ad valorem(B)	free		1,317 / £1,119	none b
Hides and skins (ea.) c		$14\frac{2}{40}$ ea. to / 2s. 4d. $14\frac{1}{2}$ ea. / 20	$17\frac{3}{80}d.$ to $2d. 1\frac{7}{20}$(D) d / 20	387,472 / £45,129	25.75
Pot and pearl ashes (bbl.)	12s. 3d. $1\frac{5}{20}$(P)	free		27,407 / £68,576	12.84
Iron to Europe (ton)					
Bar	£2 8s. 6d. $\frac{3}{20}$(P)	free		847 / £8,567	2.36
Pig	4s. 9d. $\frac{9}{20}$(P)	free		3,153 / £4,595	none b
Lumber to Europe					
Staves (per 120)	6d. $1\frac{7}{3}$ to £1 2s. 10d. $\frac{9}{20}$(P) / 20 / from £6 per 2,400 to £6 per 1,200(B) e	free		52,080 / £34,010	14.61
Headings (per 120)	1s. 10d. $1\frac{8}{20}$(P) / £6 per 1,200(B)	free		392 / £184	none
Deals, planks, and boards (per 120)	1s. 5d. $3\frac{3}{4}$ to £4 5s. 10d. $1\frac{9}{20}$(P) / 20	free		varied quantities / £29,606	none
All other	10s. per 120(B) / various	free		varied quantities f / £25,404	none

ARTICLE AND UNIT OF MEASUREMENT	BOUNTY AND PREFERENCE	IMPORT DUTY	DUTY RETAINED, EXPORT TAX, AND BOUNTY REPAID	QUANTITY IMPORTED AND TOTAL ESTIMATED VALUE	PERCENTAGE REËXPORTED
ACT OF 1766					
All nonenumerated goods to Europe north of Cape Finisterre			various	various g £425,778	small

The statutes of enumeration are as follows: 1764—4 Geo. III, c. 15; 1766—6 Geo. III, c. 52.

In calculating preferences granted for plantation commodities, comparisons were made with foreign goods carried in British ships and the discriminatory duties on French goods were disregarded. Although the import figures are for articles from the thirteen colonies and the West Indies only, the reëxport percentage has been computed from the total quantity imported and the total quantity reëxported from Britain.

[a] In addition a bounty was allowed upon certain ships in the whaling trade, effective Dec. 25, 1771 (11 Geo. III, c. 38).

[b] The negligible reëxportations which occurred were attributed to European rather than to colonial importations because of the comparative unimportance of the latter.

[c] The range in duty is from that for sheep to that for moose. In distinguishing between hides, skins, and furs, deer, moose, elk, sheep, cow, ox, calf, and horsehide are listed as hides and skins; other skins, such as fox, bear, etc., are listed with beaver skins and furs. The statistics for deer skins have been reduced to a common denominator on the assumption that the average skin weighed 1½ lbs. *Infra*, p. 20n.

[d] There was also an export tax of 3s. 4d. per 100 on sheep pelts.

[e] The bounty was granted only to white-oak staves and headings. Entry figures do not give the composition of the staves and headings listed and all have been assumed to be of white oak.

[f] The value given here does not include that of foreign reëxports, such as mahogany, of which £14,434 was reëxported from the thirteen colonies and £40,130 shipped direct from the West Indies.

[g] Computed by subtracting enumerated goods from the total British imports from the thirteen colonies and West Indies.

continental colonies, we find a very different picture. Although there were bounties and preferential duties provided for by law, neither gave, in fact, the same advantage that the preferential rate on sugar accorded the West Indies. Moreover, as can readily be seen from the following chart, the price of many commodities was obviously determined by a world market, and great quantities passed through England merely en route to the Continent.

The requirement beginning in 1767 that all nonenumerated commodities shipped north of Cape Finisterre pass through England made surprisingly little difference to commerce. Such commodities exported from the continental colonies in 1770 amounted to only £117,771, which was 6.7 percent of their shipments to Britain that year, and only 3.4 percent of their entire exports. Moreover, since most of the newly restricted commodities consisted of wheat, flaxseed, or foreign lumber destined for consumption in Britain or Ireland, the regulation had little economic significance.[33] The purpose of the act was probably administrative—to minimize fraudulent shipments. It was easier to detect illicit cargoes by requiring all goods for northern Europe to be unladen in Britain than by an examination upon the high seas. Also the new method prevented the making of claims that shipments of indigo, dyewoods, sugar, and other commodities grown in both the British and foreign plantations were foreign products and therefore not covered by the enumeration when in fact they were of British growth and subject to the law.

Most of the continental products enumerated in 1764 do not appear to have been particularly affected by the new legislation. Despite the bounty, raw silk showed no greater tendency then than now to commercial cultivation in America.[34] The colonies themselves provided a growing market for American iron, and, except for that drawn to England by the preferential duties, there is no reason to expect that any quantity would have made its way to Europe.[35] Certainly little or none did after the Revolution. In the case of lumber, bounties drew a quantity of deals, planks,

[33] The nonenumerated commodities were allowed to go to Ireland, despite 6 Geo. III, c. 52 (1765), by 7 Geo. III, c. 2 (1766).

[34] In 1773 Georgia shipped 1,091 pounds of silk to England, Pennsylvania 216 pounds, and Carolina 10 pounds. The total exports in 1790 were 93 pounds to Britain and 84 pounds to France.

[35] *Supra*, p. 7.

boards, and white-oak staves to Britain, a few of which were re-exported. Other shipments went to southern Europe and to Ireland, since exportation there had again been made legal only one year after the enumeration.[36] In northern Europe the Baltic forests were too close for American products to attain much success, although they did surprisingly well after the Revolution. Their chief markets had been and were destined to be in the West Indies, with which trade was not restricted.[37] At all events, the enumeration does not seem to have adversely affected the price of staves in the Philadelphia market, which in general was higher after it than before, if we disregard the abnormally high prices during the closing years of the French and Indian War.[38] Although whale fins (whale bones) were enumerated and whale oil was not, both were drawn to Britain by the preferential treatment offered there. After the Revolution the American whaling industry was to find a market for its products in northern Europe. When it recovered from the losses incurred during wartime, it eventually attained much greater success than in the colonial period, but the reasons therefor are another story.[39]

The statistics for pot and pearl ashes and for hides and skins do not answer the question of how they were affected by the acts except to suggest that other factors were more potent. Although no preference was granted upon the importation of pot and pearl ashes, the duty retained upon reëxportation was not great. The quantity shipped from the thirteen colonies increased from 2,447 tons in 1773 to 8,599 tons in 1790, and was 7,164 tons in 1799, 8,553 tons in 1821, and 5,572 tons in 1840. The destinations varied markedly. In 1773 all, of course, was exported to Britain and com-

[36] 5 Geo. III, c. 45 (1765); 11 Geo. III, c. 50 (1770).

[37] In 1770 about 70 percent of all lumber exports, valued at £167,412, went to the West Indies; in 1790, 64.6 percent of total exports of $1,263,534; and in 1821, 84.4 percent out of $1,627,896. In 1790 Britain was the second largest purchaser of lumber, receiving 19 percent, valued at $240,174, and northern Europe was third with 9.3 percent or $117,127. In 1821, however, exports to Britain had fallen to $32,230 or 2.9 percent and those to northern Europe to $13,553 or only 1.2 percent.

[38] Anne Bezanson, R. D. Gray, and Miriam Hussey, *Prices in Colonial Pennsylvania* (Philadelphia, 1935), pp. 122–23.

[39] 91.7 percent of the 5,667 tons of whale oil exported from the continental colonies in 1770 went to Great Britain. Following the Revolution between 80 and 90 percent of both whale oil and whale fins went to north Europe, but the quantity declined to 1,971 tons of whale oil, 679 tons of sperm oil, and 54 tons of whale fins. These quantities rose markedly by 1840 to 17,940 tons of whale oil, 1,725 tons of sperm oil, and 845 tons of whale fins.

paratively little was reëxported. Britain took 89 percent or more in 1790 and in 1799 either directly or through Ireland and British North America. In 1821, 37.2 percent went to the British Isles and 43 percent to British North America, but in 1840 none went directly to Britain and only 7.2 percent to British North America.[40]

Hides and skins likewise were not materially affected by the customs duties. The chief difference between pre-Revolutionary and post-Revolutionary trade was the decrease in the quantity exported, which naturally resulted from the ruthless slaughter of deer in the colonial period.[41] Apparently England was the best market for about three-quarters of the United States' exports because, except for 1799 (when shipments to Britain dropped to 55.1 percent), she took approximately that percentage. Also it would seem to follow that it was cheaper to ship the remainder directly to its destination.[42]

Similarly, other factors appear to have played a greater part than the Navigation Acts in the production of copper ore and in the fur trade's development. The mine in New Jersey, news of which led to copper ore's enumeration in 1722,[43] produced 338 casks of ore for shipment to Britain and 110 casks for Holland in 1721, but production of that ore was not destined to be of great economic importance. Shipments from New York from 1720 to 1734 averaged slightly more than 400 casks and 200 barrels,[44] while

[40] In each of the years mentioned practically all of the remainder of the exports went to northern Europe.

[41] V. W. Crane, *The Southern Frontier, 1670–1732* (Philadelphia, 1929), pp. 111–12.

[42] In 1773, 25.75 percent of the skins Britain imported were reëxported; in 1790, she took 76.6 percent of the United States exports, in 1821 70.2 percent; and in 1840, although she received only 3.4 percent directly, 66.4 percent went to British North America, the remainder usually going to North Europe. Exact comparisons are rendered difficult because of changes in the base of compiling statistics, and consequently it is useful to know that the average skin weighed about one or two pounds (Leila Sellers, *Charleston Business on the Eve of the American Revolution* [Chapel Hill, 1934], p. 173; Crane, *The Southern Frontier*, p. 111). In 1773 the total imported to Britain from the thirteen colonies was given as 243,213 pieces and 208,576 pounds and was valued at £41,448. The total exports from the United States were valued at $33,494 in 1790 and amounted to 72,650 skins in 1799, 13,558 in 1821, and 112,500 in 1840. No segregation was made between domestic and foreign products in 1790 and 1799, but in 1821 and 1840 the value of foreign reëxports totaled $61,921 and $406,234 respectively, most of which went to northern Europe, less than 15 percent going to Britain directly or by way of her colonies.

[43] Andrews, *Colonial Period*, IV, 104–5.

[44] L. A. Harper and J. H. Cox, *A Commodity Analysis of the Imports and Exports*

the total quantity exported was only 19 tons in 1773, and none is listed in the post-Revolutionary years studied.

As for furs, their enumeration in 1722 does not appear to have had an immediately detrimental effect upon the volume of exports at New York, although 30 to 40 percent had been sent to Holland during the seven years preceding.[45] The fur trade of the thirteen colonies was destined to decline in comparative importance,[46] but the causes were other than legislative. Most of the furs from the thirteen colonies were of the cheaper sort, muskrat, martin, and raccoon, and the acquisition of Canada in 1763 provided a new source of supply for the more valuable otter, beaver, mink, fox, wolf, bear, and wolverine. Only 4.8 percent of the beaver skins shipped to Britain in 1773 came from the thirteen colonies, while their shipments formed 41.8 percent of the total of other furs. Most of the furs imported were reëxported, to the dismay of the London hatters, who had been losing their export trade to the French despite the fact that after 1763 the latter had to obtain their raw materials from Britain. Parliament attempted to help the hatters in 1764 when it repealed the old duty of 7d. on each beaver skin imported, all but 3d. of which had been repaid upon reëxportation, and substituted an import duty of 1d. without benefit of drawback, together with an export tax of 7d. per skin.[47] Except for beaver skins, however, the taxes not drawn back probably did not seriously affect trade. Unfortunately, statistics of post-Revolutionary trade show no consistent trend and consequently throw little light upon the routes that it might have followed if it had been unrestrained.[48]

of the Port of New York, 1716–1764 (a film book produced as a part of WPA Project No. 465–03–3–264 [Berkeley, 1938]).

45 *Idem.*

46 It is difficult to give comparative figures because the exportation of furs was not restricted in 1698, but an idea of the relative decline in the fur trade of the thirteen colonies can be gained by comparing the 104,755 skins valued at £7,605 which were exported by them to England in 1698 and the 140,319 skins valued at £7,912 which they sent to Britain in 1773. England's total importations in 1698 were 143,066 skins, valued at £14,933; in 1773, Britain imported 451,450 skins valued at £101,623.

47 4 Geo. III, c. 9. An export tax of 1s. 6d. was also placed upon every pound avoirdupois of beaver wool or wombs exported from Great Britain.

48 In 1790, 59.3 percent of a total exportation valued at $60,515 went to Britain; in 1799, 68.1 percent of $493,724; in 1821, 43.1 percent of $766,205; in 1840, 90.3 percent of $1,237,789. It should also be remembered that by virtue of the Louisiana Purchase and the opening of the West conditions differed greatly from those in colonial days.

The bounties granted for colonial naval stores had a greater effect than the restrictions placed upon their exportation.[49] By 1716, they at least permitted England to obtain most of her tar, pitch, rosin, and turpentine from her colonies rather than from the Baltic. When the bounties were discontinued from 1725 to 1729, shipments of turpentine continued to cross the Atlantic, but those of pitch and tar fell off markedly.[50] Exportations of tar and pitch diminished similarly after the Revolution, but those of rosin and turpentine increased.[51] If the Philadelphia quotations can be trusted, however, and if other circumstances were not exceptional, the prices of pitch and tar were determined by colonial conditions rather than by the bounty because from 1725 to 1729, contrary to what one would expect, they were higher rather than lower both before and after the five-year lapse in the bounty.[52] Hemp was offered a bounty also, but only 86 tons made its way to England in 1770, and none in 1773. The course of trade ran in the other direction, more than 1,000 tons being shipped from Britain to New England alone in 1773. Judging from the lack of any large

[49] Naval stores, including hemp and rosin, first received bounties but at different rates in 1705 (3 & 4 Anne, c. 9). Both enumeration and bounties except for hemp lapsed from 1725 to 1729 when they were renewed by 2 Geo. II, c. 35, which omitted rosin and added a bounty for turpentine. The bounty and enumeration on hemp lapsed in 1741 (8 Geo. I, c. 12). The bounty was renewed in 1764 but not the enumeration (4 Geo. III, c. 26). Flax, which was never enumerated, was placed on the free list in 1731 (4 Geo. II, c. 27) and its importation encouraged by a bounty of £8 per ton, which was lowered to £6 in 1771 (4 Geo. III, c. 26). But the colonists continued to prefer to export flaxseed rather than flax.

[50] E. L. Lord, *Industrial Experiments in the British Colonies of North America* (Baltimore, 1896), Appendix. The export from South Carolina of tar and pitch averaged 2,625 last per year from 1721 through 1724; there was no immediate drop following the lapse of the bounties, as the years 1725 and 1726 showed an exportation of 4,329 last and 3,153 last respectively, but the export for the years following fell sharply, being only 223 last in 1728 and 643 in 1729. There was a gradual rise from then on, from 1,025 last in 1730 to 2,760 in 1733, yet the quantities exported did not attain the pre-1725 average again until 1732 (Customs 3/23–3/33).

[51] Exports of rosin and turpentine were 17,237 barrels to Britain alone in 1773 and 2,063 more to the British West Indies. The total exports of such goods were 28,642 barrels in 1790, 56,778 barrels in 1799, 79,213 barrels in 1821, and 215,121 barrels in 1840. Exports of pitch and tar were 99,592 barrels in 1773, 93,942 barrels in 1790, 60,846 barrels in 1799, 71,196 barrels in 1821, and 44,655 in 1840. The percentage going to Great Britain was 95.4 percent in 1770, 83.1 percent in 1790, 50.3 percent in 1799, 59.8 percent in 1821, and 30.9 percent in 1840. In addition, sizeable shipments went to the British West Indies; others to British North America which probably eventually found their way to England constituted 6.4 percent of the total in 1799, 8.5 percent in 1821, and 27 percent in 1840.

[52] Bezanson, Gray, and Hussey, *Prices in Colonial Pennsylvania*, p. 424.

shipments after the Revolution,[53] the transportation of masts across the Atlantic, which totaled 3,043 tons valued at £16,616 in 1770, was the result of artificial stimulation. In all, the various bounties cost the British government £1,471,719, but whatever may have been the appreciation of the chief beneficiary, North Carolina, gratitude in New England was overwhelmed by hostility to the restrictions of the "Broad Arrow" policy which reserved the best trees for His Majesty's Navy.[54]

The extent of the burden placed upon rice does not appear at first glance. Permission was granted in 1730 to export rice south of Cape Finisterre and in 1764 to ship it to any part of America south of Georgia,[55] but other shipments, which formed about one-half of the total in 1770, were limited to the Empire. Until the British desire to develop a starch industry caused colonial rice to be made free, it normally paid the same duty on entering Britain as foreign rice, $6s.$ $41\frac{2}{20}d.$ a hundredweight, all of which could be drawn back upon reëxportation except $7d.$ and $1\frac{2}{20}$ per hundredweight. Although removal of import duties did not become a definite policy until 1773, a series of annual exemptions date it back to 1767. The gain, however, was primarily to the British consumer, because an export tax of $8d.$ per hundredweight was added when the import duty was removed.[56] The colonial producer was more interested in the world price, since 79 percent of the rice shipped to Britain was reëxported. After the Revolution, shipments to Britain dropped from 457,072 hundredweight in 1773 to 197,849 hundredweight in 1790 and even less thereafter.[57] The United States lost the southern European market but generally improved its position by gains in the West Indies and South America and by taking over the northern European market, especially in

[53] The exports of masts were not listed separately in 1790 or in 1799. They were valued at only $54,627 in 1821 when none went to Britain and 43.6 percent went to British North America. The value of the exports declined further to $29,049 in 1840, most of which went to the West Indies and South America, the figures for northern Europe being only $901, for British North America $1,260, and for the British Isles nothing at all.

[54] Albion, *Forests and Sea Power*, pp. 251–54, 418.

[55] 3 Geo. II, c. 28 (1730); 8 Geo. II, c. 19 (1735); 4 Geo. III, c. 27 (1764).

[56] 7 Geo. III, c. 47 (1767); 13 Geo. III, c. 7 (1773).

[57] Tierces were converted to hundredweight in accordance with the ratio of 600 pounds per tierce, following G. K. Holmes, *Rice Crop of the United States* (U.S. Dept. of Agriculture; Bureau of Statistics, Circular 34 [Washington, 1912]).

Germany, Holland, and France, which had previously been supplied by English merchants.[58]

The cultivation of indigo in Carolina and Georgia was undoubtedly stimulated by the bounty granted in Britain, which totaled £145,032 for the years 1749–73.[59] Strange to relate, indigo benefited most when the bounty was lowered in 1770 from 6d. to 4d. a pound, the explanation of the apparent paradox being that the 6d. had to be repaid upon reëxportation and the 4d. did not.[60] Consequently the reëxports, which had equaled 15.1 percent of the 647,960 pounds imported into Britain in 1767, rose to 40.12 percent of the 1,385,139 pounds imported in 1773.[61] Although large crops continued to be produced for a few years after the Revolution, the encouragement given by the British government to indigo's production in the British East Indies, together with the

[58] The following chart shows the distribution of rice exports before and after the Revolution:

Year	1770	1790	1799	1821	1840
Total quantity (in 1,000 lbs.)	76,511	74,136	67,234	52,253	60,970
Percent of total quantity to: Great Britain and Ireland	49.21	36.62	12.83	20.25	17.44
Northern Europe	none	34.75	19.94	37.20	40.43
Southern Europe	24.11	4.75	12.54	1.78	1.96
West Indies and South America	26.60	23.63	52.59	34.86	38.38
Other ports	.08	.43	2.10	5.91	1.79

The fact that the shipments in 1770 were exceptionally high causes the other figures to suggest that rice exports suffered after the Revolution. But figures in L. C. Gray (*History of Agriculture in the Southern United States* [Washington, 1933], II, 1030), which were used in the foregoing table to give the quantities exported but not the percentages to the several countries, show that the annual average of exports for the 25 years between 1744 and 1773 inclusive for which we have records was 45,606,000 lbs. and that it was 59,967,500 lbs. for the years 1790–1814, if one does not exclude 1807 and 1813, which were abnormally low because of the Embargo and the War of 1812, and 64,642,000 lbs. if one does. During the next quarter-century (1815–39) exports maintained an even higher average, 68,669,000 lbs.

[59] Edward Channing, *History of the United States* (New York, 1912), III, 35.

[60] The bounty was originally granted by 21 Geo. II, c. 30 (1748), and the rate was lowered by 3 Geo. III, c. 25 (1763).

[61] Customs 3/67, 3/73, 14/1B. For other statistics concerning indigo see Sellers, *Charleston Business on the Eve of the American Revolution,* p. 166; Gray, *History of Agriculture,* II, 1024. It is interesting to note that not only did the quantity exported increase but wholesale prices at Charleston rose. From 1765 to 1769 the average price was 22.84 shillings per pound; it rose to a peak of 41.2 shillings in 1772 and settled to an average of 31.93 shillings for 1773–75 (A. H. Cole, *Wholesale Commodity Prices in the United States, 1700–1861,* Statistical Supplement, Cambridge, 1938, pp. 54–70).

increased profitableness of cotton crops, caused the cultivation of indigo to be virtually abandoned.[62]

Tobacco ranked with sugar as the most important of the enumerated commodities but, unlike sugar, it proved a source of profit rather than an expense of mercantilism. Much emphasis has been laid upon the preferential duties granted American tobacco as against the products of Spain's and Portugal's colonies. They unquestionably were high, but there is reason to doubt whether colonial tobacco gained much from the preference. During the most difficult years of its early growth, in the first quarter of the seventeenth century, tobacco received more opposition than encouragement in England and turned to foreign markets, where it appeared able to hold its own in free competition.[63] Similarly, the prohibition of tobacco planting in England would appear to have had little effect upon American production. Although tobacco can be grown successfully in Great Britain, the colonial product had greater natural advantages. The reason for the English farmer's desire to grow tobacco and for the government's determination to stamp out its cultivation is to be found in the taxes assessed on it. They could be collected more easily at the waterside, and the difficulty which administrators had even there shows how impossible it would have been under seventeenth-century conditions to have assessed crops scattered throughout the English countryside.

The ultimate destination of most American tobacco was the continent of Europe. In 1773, Britain officially consumed only 3,747,979 pounds of the 100,482,007 pounds imported, the remainder being reëxported, mostly to Holland and Germany.[64] After the Revolution, the British government made a strenuous effort to retain her control of the trade, greatly simplifying the customs regulations governing tobacco passing through England, but without success. British importations of American tobacco steadily declined from 99.8 percent in 1773 to 62.2 percent in 1790,

[62] Gray, *op. cit.*, II, 610–11. In 1821 only $714 worth of the $417,682 of indigo exported had been produced in the United States, and in 1840 only $209 out of $179,419.

[63] Beer, *Origins*, pp. 78–94, 188–94.

[64] The actual consumption may have been greater because part of the exportations in 1773 may have been made from the previous year's crop. Also part of the tobacco exported may have been fraudulently relanded.

45.5 percent in 1799, 31.7 percent in 1821, and 22.7 percent in 1840. Tobacco went direct to its destination in Germany, Holland, France, and elsewhere.[65] It is true that the wars with France tended to disturb previous conditions, but if Britain had been a natural entrepôt, trade would once again have returned to the most favorable channel. It was not, and Bremen became the center for hogshead tobacco.[66]

The indirect routing required by the law had many detrimental effects on American economic interests. The import duty on tobacco was raised from time to time until it totaled $6d.\dfrac{19\frac{2}{3}}{20}$ per pound at the Revolution.[67] Although only $\frac{1}{2}d.$ a pound was retained upon exportation until 1723 and nothing thereafter,[68] the necessity of paying the entire amount or giving bond therefor upon entry placed control of the trade in the hands of the British. Few if any colonists had enough cash or sufficient security in England to meet the requirements.

So much of the pre-Revolutionary agitation centered around the taxes assessed in America that comparatively little attention is paid to the duties upon colonial trade which were actually collected in Britain. When examining the English Book of Rates and

[65] The following chart shows distribution of tobacco exports before and after the Revolution:

TOBACCO EXPORTS FROM THE UNITED STATES

Year	1770	1790	1799	1821	1840
Total quantity (hogsheads)		118,460	95,980	66,858	89,949
Total value	£906,637	$4,349,567		$5,648,962	$9,883,957
Percent of total quantity to:					
Great Britain and Ireland	99.8 [a]	61.41	45.56	30.8	30.17
North Europe					
Holland		19.79	1.79	19.76	28.52
France		9.18		4.76	14.91
Prussia		4.74	33.97	15.66	
Other countries		.68	3.76	2.68	4.45
South Europe		.47	5.79	7.26	9.47
West Indies	.17 [a]	3.16	6.85	6.65	4.89
Other ports	.03 [a]	.58	2.28	12.43	7.59

[a] Only percent of total value (not quantity) figures are given for 1770.

[66] J. R. Smith, "The World Entrepôt," *Jour. Pol. Econ.* XVIII (1910), 697–713, at p. 709.

[67] If paid in cash at entry the duty was only $6d.\frac{5}{20}$.   [68] 9 Geo. I, c. 21.

confronting charges of $5d. \frac{13\frac{5}{8}}{20}$ per skin for deerskins "in the hair" and $2d.$ $16\frac{13\frac{1}{16}}{20}$ a pound for the same article "Indian half-dressed" there is reason for hesitation, but fortunately the Inspector General's accounts give us contemporary figures which permit easy computations of the tax burden at the end of the seventeenth century.[69] They show that in 1698 the duties collected upon goods imported into England from the thirteen colonies amounted to £471,214 and upon those from the West Indies, £96,994. Of these duties, more than one-half were repaid when the commodities were reëxported to Europe. Ordinarily one would expect the duties on the goods sold in England to be paid by the English consumer, but the retail prices which we have are so fragmentary that we can draw no definite conclusion other than that the spread between the cost to the consumer and the price received by the producer was so great that the duties might well have been taken out of the wholesaler's profits.[70] Certainly all of the increases could not have been taken from the colonial planter's portion of the selling price because his entire share would have been insufficient. The duties, however, undoubtedly tended to hold down the amount which he might otherwise have received. But we cannot attempt to measure the extent at this point and shall have to pass on to those duties about which we can form more exact judgments. They fall into the following groups:

TAXES LEVIED IN 1698 ON COLONIAL TRADE IN ENGLAND

	THIRTEEN COLONIES	WEST INDIES
Duties retained on enumerated goods reëxported from England	£36,047	£12,425
Duties retained on foreign goods reëxported in time	2,493	2,786
Duties on foreign goods reëxported out of time	4,653	3,552
Duties on English manufactures exported to the colonies	5,394	3,032
TOTAL	£48,587	£21,795

[69] Customs 3/1 (1698).

[70] J. E. T. Rogers, *A History of Agricultural Prices in England* (Oxford, 1866–1902), V, 467–68; VII, pt. i, 372–78.

The duties retained on the enumerated goods reëxported from England, on foreign goods reëxported "in time," and on English exports to the colonies were undoubtedly passed on to the colonists, but it is more difficult to determine the incidence of taxation in the case of foreign goods shipped to the colonies "out of time," after the period allowed to receive the drawback had expired. Unlike their northern cousins who lived up to their Scottish traditions by collecting all but one-tenth of one percent of the drawback which the law allowed,[71] the English merchants were careless. The colonial planters were so far away and usually so deeply in debt that the English factors, instead of paying for their own carelessness, may have added the extra duty to their accounts—and collected a commission on it.

Unfortunately the customs system became too complex for the Inspector General's accounts to continue listing items about duties, and we must make our own estimate for 1773. Many changes had occurred between 1698 and the later date. In addition to allowing drawback of all the duties on tobacco beginning in 1723 and the change in the method of collecting the rice duties, which we have already noted, the most important were the removal of export duties on all British commodities, with a few exceptions like coal, and the abandonment in 1764 of the usual practice of repaying one-half of the Old Subsidy in so far as reëxports to the colonies in America were concerned. It would be a hopeless task to determine the exact amount of the duties, but we can come reasonably close by concentrating our efforts upon the most important. If, because of the impossibility of ascertaining what proportion was borne by the colonists, we again disregard the duties collected upon plantation goods imported into Britain, the amounts collected in 1773 can be divided into four groups:

TAXES LEVIED IN 1773 ON COLONIAL TRADE IN BRITAIN

Export duties paid on rice	£12,397
Duties retained on foreign goods reëxported to the colonies in time	19,625
Duties on foreign goods reëxported out of time	333
Duties on coal exported to the colonies	675
Total of duties borne by the thirteen colonies	£33,030

[71] Customs 14/1B (1773).

The elimination of the ½*d.* per pound on tobacco reëxported and of export duties on British manufactures accounts for the great decrease in these items. Scottish competition, which was absent in 1698, probably explains the decline in carelessness about exporting goods "out of time," while the natural growth of trade and the denial of drawback on one-half the Old Subsidy accounts for the increase in the amount retained on foreign goods reëxported to the colonies. Some adjustments in the figures should be made for the minor items necessarily omitted from our calculations, but even after making a liberal allowance for error, two points stand out clearly. The indirect taxes collected in Britain from the thirteen colonies each year exceeded the £31,000 raised annually in the colonies by measures such as the Sugar Acts, the Stamp Tax, and the Townshend Revenue Act [72] which caused so much excitement. Moreover, the burden of British mercantilism bore much more heavily upon the thirteen colonies in 1698 than in 1773, the per capita charge at the end of the seventeenth century being more than five times that of both the direct and indirect taxation of the Revolutionary era.[73]

The taxes collected by the government were, however, only a minor element in the burden which was placed upon the colonies. The normal uncertainties which attend trade and commerce were considerably increased by confusion in the laws. As Governor Glen of South Carolina said, "far from being so clear as he that runs may read them," the laws were "dark and difficult." [74] Even the authorities in England sometimes could not agree, as in the case of Canary wines, which could be legally imported if the Canary Islands were in Africa and could not if they formed part of Europe.[75] Also the rules and regulations necessary to keep the potential smuggler in line were a considerable nuisance burden which was borne by the fair trader as well as by the wrongdoer. In a frontier community of settlements scattered over a long coast line, the requirement that ships enter and clear at designated ports was a serious incon-

[72] Channing, *op. cit.*, III, 90.
[73] The population appears to have been between 200,000 and 250,000 in 1698 and between 2,000,000 and 2,500,000 in 1773 (E. B. Greene and V. D. Harrington, *American Population before the Federal Census of 1790* [New York, 1932], pp. 3–4, 6–7).
[74] Cited in L. W. Labaree, *Royal Instructions to British Colonial Governors, 1670–1776* (New York, 1935), II, 885–86.
[75] Andrews, *Colonial Period*, IV, 110–13.

venience to settlers. However well intentioned a merchant might have been, the complexities of commerce sometimes rendered it impossible to conform to regulations which administrative necessities required. Innocent mistakes might also occur. Such cases are ordinarily excused upon application or payment of a nominal fine. Yet under the Navigation Acts they led to forfeiture of the goods unless expensive petitions were sent across three thousand miles of ocean—and even then it was usually impossible to recover the third of the forfeiture which went to the officer who seized the goods. Honest and discreet officials might do much to mitigate administrative inconveniences, but on the other hand, as Laurens discovered in South Carolina, dishonest or malicious officials had many opportunities to harass those who had incurred their displeasure.[76]

Most important of all, the control of policy was in the hands of British mercantilists. It is difficult to support the concept of an impartial administrator carefully balancing the equities between the economic interests of colonies and those of mother country. All Englishmen did not state their views as bluntly as did Lord Cornbury, who declared in the early eighteenth century that "all these Colloneys which are but twigs belonging to the main Tree (England) ought to be kept entirely dependent upon and subservient to England, and that can never be, if they are suffered to goe on in the notions they have," or William Pitt, who recommended in 1766 that the sovereign authority of Britain over the colonies should be "made to extend to every part of legislation whatever, that we may bind their trade, confine their manufactures, and exercise every power whatsoever, except that of taking their money out of their pockets without their consent." [77] But all thought of the colonies in the terms of what England could gain from them. The statutes made it clear that England desired the colonies to be subservient to her. Sometimes Parliament clearly expressed its intention that the colonies be kept "in a firmer dependance" upon England and rendered "yet more beneficiall and advantagious unto it," as in the Act of 1663,[78] and sometimes the preferences ac-

---

[76] Harper, *The English Navigation Laws*, pp. 161–227; Sellers, *Charleston Business on the Eve of the American Revolution*, pp. 192–201.

[77] Bishop, *American Manufactures*, pp. 329, 370.

[78] 15 Car. II, c. 7.

corded British interests were so subtly provided that the Acts appear to be examples of British generosity. In mentioning the permission to ship sugar and rice south of Cape Finisterre, for example, notice is seldom taken of the administrative requirements which permitted the privilege to be enjoyed only by vessels which had sailed from Britain and eventually were to return there; thus control of the trade was retained for British merchants.[79]

The grant of bounties helped some of the colonies, but Parliament's purpose was not altruistic. It was to prevent the drain of coin from England and to provide the colonies with funds for the purchase of British manufactures.[80] Parliament declined to restrain colonial shipbuilding as the Thames shipbuilders wished, because by doing so it would increase freight costs and injure an even more important British group, the merchants. But it did try to restrain the manufacture of woolens, of hats, and of iron.

Certainly on fundamental issues there is no evidence of British self-sacrifice. In the enumeration clauses of 1660 and the Staple Act of 1663 the colonial producer and consumer gave way to the English merchant. In the Molasses Act of 1733 and the Sugar Act of 1764, the interests of the continental colonies which could only present arguments yielded to those of the absentee sugar planters who controlled votes in Parliament, but even the favored sugar colonies lost out after the American Revolution when the clash became one between the West Indian interest in cheap provisions and the British interest in more cargoes for British ships. These results were merely natural—not immoral—and we only blind ourselves to the nature of social processes if we endow imperialism with an altruism that it does not possess. Even assuming that those who determined policies were completely unbiased and were anxious to treat all parts of the Empire with perfect fairness, the colonies were at a disadvantage. It is human nature to yield to constant pressure, and the colonists resided across the Atlantic while their English competitors were always at hand to press their claims.

Although the full effect of economic dependence upon the colonies cannot be measured in dollars and cents, an estimate of its

[79] 3 Geo. II, c. 28 (1730); 12 Geo. II, c. 30 (1739).
[80] See, for example, 3 and 4 Anne, c. 9.

monetary cost should be of value. The requirement that goods pass through England imposed many obligations upon colonial trade in the guise of taxes, fees, cooperage, porterage, brokerage, warehouse rent, commissions, extra merchants' profits, and the like, which would never have been incurred in a direct trade with the ultimate markets. A Revolutionary pamphleteer claimed that the English mercantile system cost Virginia alone £5,987,500 currency, and William Pitt declared that colonial trade produced an annual profit of £2,000,000 sterling for British merchants.[81] Since it is probable that these claims, made in the heat of political controversy, are exaggerated and include costs of manufacture which the colonists would have had to pay wherever the goods were purchased, we must attempt to form our own estimate. Scattered bits of interesting information are readily available, such as that it cost £100,000 each year in commissions to send Chesapeake tobacco by way of England,[82] but they will not suffice. Our task is to determine how much less the colonists received for their products and how much more they had to pay for their purchases because of the Navigation Acts than would have been the case if their commerce had been unfettered.

Ideally, we should have lists of wholesale prices in America, Britain, and the principal markets of Europe. Some day the data may be more nearly complete, but meanwhile we must exercise our ingenuity in dealing with the data available and in devising methods to minimize the danger of error.

We can simplify our task by directing attention toward the principal drains upon the colonial economy: the restrictions placed upon the marketing of colonial tobacco and rice and the requirement that European manufactures be obtained in Britain. Some help can be had from the testimony of contemporaries about the elements of cost involved, but such testimony is often missing and usually fragmentary. Fortunately, recent studies of prices in the United States offer another point of departure.[83] They permit us

[81] A. M. Schlesinger, *The Colonial Merchants and the American Revolution, 1763–1776* (New York, 1918), p. 602; Channing, *op. cit.*, III, 34–35.

[82] Channing, *op. cit.*, III, 34.

[83] The colonial price quotations cited hereafter for Philadelphia are based upon the tables of Anne Bezanson, R. D. Gray, and Miriam Hussey, *Wholesale Prices in Philadelphia, 1784–1861* (2 vols., Philadelphia, 1936) and those in the volume by the same authors on *Prices in Colonial Pennsylvania*. The prices for Charleston and Bos-

to ascertain the average price of tobacco at Philadelphia and of rice at both Philadelphia and Charleston before and after the Revolution together with the prices of a few imported products. The chief objection to proceeding in this fashion is the chance that prices were influenced by other factors than freedom from English restraints. This objection can be met in part by increasing the prices for the colonial period by 78 percent to correspond with the increase in the general price level thereafter,[84] although there is always the danger that the commodities in which we are interested did not even approximately conform to the average.

Another method of procedure which avoids comparisons between different periods is to work from the Inspector General's accounts after making such corrections in the official values as seem necessary. A comparison of the value given tobacco, rice, and European products with the valuation set upon the same goods as they were exported to their ultimate destinations in Europe or America should represent the cost of their passing through Britain. The difficulty lies in the failure of subsequent officials to keep the estimates of 1696 up to date.[85] This unsatisfactory condition may be offset in part by the fact that our interest lies only in the difference between the import and reëxport values. Any tendency to overstatement may be guarded against by adjusting the official values on the basis of Moreau's "real values" for the twelve years 1763–74, which value imports as sold to the consumer, including the importer's profits and freight but excluding duties, and reexports according to "the average price current" exclusive of the freight outwards.[86]

---

ton are based upon the Statistical Supplement to Cole, *Wholesale Commodity Prices.* Percentages have been computed upon annual averages except in the case of Russian sail duck where they are based upon the average of separate monthly quotations. Colonial prices have been converted to dollars at the rates given in Cole, *op. cit.,* p. ix, but for the sake of convenience the pound sterling has been considered to be worth $5.

[84] Bezanson, Gray, and Hussey, *Wholesale Prices in Philadelphia, 1784–1861,* I, 301.

[85] G. N. Clark, *Guide to English Commercial Statistics* (London, 1938), pp. 33–42.

[86] Moreau, *Chronological Records of the British Navy,* pp. 17, 23, gives only the total value of England's trade with different countries, but such figures should be sufficient for our purposes because the commodities we are considering bulk so large in the trades which we have to study. The average error in the official valuation given upon importation of reëxports should correspond to the undervaluation of imports from northern Europe and Asia, since almost all of the goods reëxported to the thirteen colonies came from those regions. Similarly the undervaluation in the re-

There is a surprising unanimity of result in the various analyses of the effect of enumeration upon tobacco. The estimates of contemporary merchants placed the cost of sending tobacco through Britain at 2*d.* or 4 cents per pound.[87] A comparison of the prices at Philadelphia of unspecified qualities of tobacco during the years 1720–75 with those for James River tobacco from 1784 to 1861, adjusted to allow for a 78 percent rise in the general price level, indicates that the planters received 3.50 cents more per pound after they were freed from the restraints of the British legislation than before. Since the quality of pre-Revolutionary tobacco was unspecified, the comparison might involve an element of error for which allowance can be made by discounting the James River tobacco by 13.4 percent, which was the difference in price in 1770 between Virginia and Maryland tobacco.[88] On this basis the loss is 2.51 cents per pound instead of 3.50 cents. A comparison of the official valuations of imported and reëxported tobacco shows a spread of 2¼*d.* a pound. Deducting an allowance of £7 a ton or ¾*d.* a pound for freight from America to England, the estimated loss to the colonists is 1½*d.* or 3 cents a pound. Corrected to correspond with Moreau's tables, the loss is further reduced to only 1.14*d.* or 2¼ cents a pound.

In ascertaining the total cost of the enumeration, a question arises as to whether to calculate it against the total quantity shipped from the colonies or only against the amount reëxported from England. There should be no question as far as the Philadelphia prices are concerned, and in all probability the extra costs of shipping tobacco to Europe helped to beat down its price in Britain.

---

export price of tobacco and rice can be considered to be the same as that given for foreign or plantation goods reëxported to northern Europe, which was the great market for such products. On this basis a comparison of the official values with the "real values" given by Moreau shows an undervaluation in the official values for imports (of tobacco and rice) from the thirteen colonies of 58.14 percent; in the reexport price (of tobacco and rice) of 4.32 percent; in the imported value of goods later reëxported to the thirteen colonies of 40.34 percent; in the value given on reexportation of 11.60 percent.

[87] Gray, *op. cit.,* I, 223; C. P. Nettels, *The Roots of American Civilization* (New York, 1938), pp. 254–55.

[88] Gray, *op. cit.,* I, 274. The allowance probably was excessive because at least some of the tobacco in Philadelphia should have been Virginia tobacco. On the other hand, earlier differences in price between Maryland and Virginia tobacco may have been greater (*ibid.,* I, 270). A comparison of the post-Revolutionary prices for Kentucky tobacco instead of James River tobacco gives a figure of 2.76 cents per pound.

Yet for conservatism's sake it may be well to assume that it was borne only by reëxported tobacco. Calculating on that basis, the lowest estimate of the burden laid upon the thirteen colonies in 1773 by the enumeration of tobacco is $2,176,516 and the highest is $3,400,714.

The greater freedom which apparently was allowed in the exportation of rice might cause one to believe that unlike tobacco it did not feel the weight of the Navigation Acts, but such figures as we have do not support the assumption. Using the same procedure as followed in comparing the prices of tobacco, we find that an analysis of rice prices at Philadelphia assesses the cost of British mercantilism at $.62 per hundredweight of rice and of those at Charleston, $1.39 per hundredweight. The official British valuations did not provide as great a write-up in the value of reëxported rice as in the case of tobacco: 33 percent for rice as compared with 100 percent for tobacco, making the spread between import and reëxport values 5s. per hundredweight, from which we should probably deduct the freight rate, which ought not to have averaged more than £3 a ton or 3s. a hundredweight.[89] Calculations based upon Moreau make the import value higher than the reëxport value and obviously must be disregarded. Thus the burden arising from the enumeration of rice is between $185,925 and $516,-871.

The variety of European commodities imported by the colonies complicates the problem of ascertaining the extra expense involved in making shipments by way of England. A weighted average compiled from the official import and reëxport values in England for more than 75 percent of the foreign products sent to the thirteen colonies in 1773 shows that the average mark-up in prices was 53.1 percent of the import value or 34.8 percent of the reëxport value.[90] Recalculated to correspond with Moreau's ratio between official and real values, the percentages are lowered to 22.2 percent and 18.2 percent respectively. Although no sufficiently continuous

[89] Sellers, *op. cit.*, pp. 154–55.

[90] The total value of the reëxports from Britain to the thirteen colonies in 1773 was £572,845. The following are the most important examples of the mark-up between the import and reëxport prices: 37.5% on £17,711 of Russian broad linen; 100% on £148,316 of tea; 70% on £31,191 of Port; 47% on £38,775 of rough hemp; 37.5% on £38,154 of calico; 22.2% on £75,651 of German narrow linen; and 20% on £63,219 of Irish linen.

series of prices for imported goods in the colonies is available to corroborate the English figures, those which exist tend to confirm rather than to confute the theory that transshipment was costly. At Philadelphia the price of gunpowder fell markedly; that of pepper declined from an average of 41 cents a pound for the years 1766–75 to an average of 29 cents from 1784 to 1823; and at Boston the price of Russian duck, which had averaged 77.1 shillings per piece from 1753 to 1775, fell to 68.2 shillings from 1784 to 1795, all contrary to the trend of the general price level. Moreover, ample support is found in contemporary comments about the greater cheapness of Dutch products, especially in the seventeenth century when the English themselves acknowledged that the Dutch could undersell them by a third or a half.[91] Since the extra expense of importing competitive European products from England acted as a protective wall which permitted increases in English prices, the question arises as to whether in computing the cost of the Staple Act of 1663 to the colonies we should base our calculations only upon the value of the goods reëxported or upon the total value of both British and foreign goods sent to the colonies.[92] Depending upon the method employed, our estimates will range from $521,290 to $3,444,185.

Obviously, all the estimates cannot be correct, but the chances appear excellent that the truth lies somewhere between the extremes. Whenever two of the methods produce substantially the same result the probabilities would appear to be definitely in favor of its accuracy, and any estimate that is supported by three should be as certain as one can hope to obtain. There appears to be little likelihood that any except the highest estimate overstates the colonial losses, because our calculations omit so many items which might well be included in a list of charges against British mercantilism. We have excluded the expense to which smugglers were put in their efforts to evade the laws, which were none the less real because their activities were illicit. No allowance has been made for various legal trades forced to pass through Britain which, however minor in themselves, were not inconsiderable in the aggregate. Most important of all, no mention has been made

[91] *Supra,* note 5.

[92] In 1773 the total official value of British exports to the colonies, including reexports, was £1,980,412.

of the fact that, thanks to the hold which the Navigation Acts gave it on trade, British shipping managed to carry four-fifths of the trans-Atlantic commerce in the colonial period as contrasted with one-fifth in 1821 when competitive conditions were equal.[93] According to Champion, the carriage of tobacco and rice alone employed 80,000 tons of shipping,[94] which, at an average freightage of £4 a ton, represented no inconsiderable sum. Although many elements other than the Navigation Acts doubtless hindered participation of the colonial merchant marine in the trans-Atlantic trade until after independence, it would seem probable that some part of the $1,600,000 annual freight bill represents a profit which the colonists would have enjoyed except for their economic subservience under the Act.

Using only the estimates we have calculated and leaving the more intangible items as a margin of error, we can prepare a balance sheet of the cash burdens and advantages of British mercantilism in 1773. In arranging the figures it is interesting to note that the much-criticized values of the Inspector General's accounts appear to be the medium which is most probably in accord with the facts:

COST TO THE THIRTEEN COLONIES	LOWEST ESTIMATE	INTERMEDIATE ESTIMATE	HIGHEST ESTIMATE
On tobacco	$2,177,000	$2,428,000	$3,401,000
On rice	186,000	231,000	517,000
On European goods	521,000	997,000	3,444,000
	$2,884,000	$3,656,000	$7,362,000

CREDIT TO BOUNTIES PAID ON COLONIAL PRODUCTS				
On indigo [95]	£23,086			
On naval stores [96]	35,203			
On lumber [97]	6,557			
£64,846 or	324,000	324,000	324,000
	$2,560,000	$3,332,000	$7,038,000

[93] *Supra*, pp. 9, 10. [94] Champion, *Considerations*, p. 66.

[95] Calculated at 4*d*. per pound on total imports to Great Britain, see chart, *supra*, p. 24.

[96] Albion, *Forests and Sea Power*, p. 418.

[97] In 1769, the highest figure given in Beer, *British Colonial Policy*, p. 224.

At first glance the amounts do not appear particularly impressive, but the lowest estimate, which is made up of the figures from Moreau, is undoubtedly an understatement because the import values, which are necessarily used as a basis for ascertaining the price received by the colonial planter, include the British importer's profit which certainly never made its way to America. Yet, even so, the annual per capita burden it represented came within sixteen cents a person of meeting all the expenses of operating the national government during the last six years of Washington's administration, including the amortization costs of the Revolutionary War debt, the expenses of the Indian War of 1790 in the Northwest, the Whiskey Insurrection of 1794, and the tribute paid to Algiers in 1795. An annual per capita tax based upon the highest estimate would have raised an amount sufficient to pay all the costs of government and would have produced at the end of the ten-year period, 1791–1800, a fund sufficient to pay both the foreign and domestic Revolutionary War debt and still have left $7,000,000 with which to help meet the obligations incurred in assuming the state debts.[98]

Worst of all, the burdens under mercantilism were paid in Brittain. The tax burden after independence could have been much higher than before with much less detrimental effect because the money would have been spent for the most part within the United States. Conceding that frontier communities are usually in debt and that the colonies would probably have incurred obligations in any case, it seems reasonable to believe that the adverse balance of trade would have been smaller if the Navigation Acts had not been in force. The basic elements of the system—which did not originate with George III but date back to the reign of Charles II

98 The figures for United States expenditures beginning in 1791 are given in D. R. Dewey, *Financial History of the United States* (New York, 1934), pp. 89, 90, 93, 111. The annual average expenditure was $5,434,666 from 1791–96 and $6,633,100 from 1791–1800. Statistics for population growth furnish more difficulty but the population in 1775 was taken to be 2,507,180, as stated in S. H. Sutherland, *Population Distribution in Colonial America* (New York, 1936), p. 271, and the population during Washington's administration was assumed to be the mean between the 3,929,-625 of the 1790 census and the 5,308,483 of the 1800 census (W. J. Rossiter, *A Century of Population Growth, 1790–1900*, Dept. of Commerce and Labor, Bur. of the Census [Washington, 1909], p. 56). The calculations are not altogether accurate but should be sufficient for all practical purposes.

—tended to drain specie from America to Britain.[99] There is no need to quote colonial witnesses concerning the distress which results from a lack of ready cash. More than a century before the Revolution occurred, when England herself was pinched by lack of bullion, William Hodges called attention to "The Groans of the Poor, the Misery of Traders, and the Calamity of the Publick for the Spoiling of our Money, for the Want of our Money . . . ," and William Potter in his *Tradesman's Jewel* summarized the whole subject by quoting Ecclesiastes 10:19:

> They prepare bread for laughter
> and wine comforteth the living
> but money answereth to all.

Emphasis upon the burdens which were placed upon the thirteen colonies does not necessarily lead to a condemnation of British mercantilism nor to the conclusion that the Navigation Acts caused the Revolution. Other factors enter into the determination of those problems. Man can adjust himself to much, and the colonists had lived under the Acts for many years. During the Revolutionary period, public resentment was most actively directed against the taxes upon the West Indian trade, in which the colonists had sought a means of meeting their trans-Atlantic obligations. Moreover, the colonies received many advantages from the imperial tie, apart from the bounties and preferences of mercantilism, of which military and naval protection are merely the most conspicuous examples. Judged by contemporary standards, the colonies might have fared much worse. But the evaluation of all such considerations is another problem. The task undertaken here was merely to determine what price the colonists paid for what they received.

[99] For a good discussion of the early problems of the colonial money supply, see Nettels, *op. cit.*, pp. 266–75.

Writs of Assistance as a Cause
Of the Revolution ~~~ O. M. DICKERSON

AMERICAN histories without exception list writs of assistance as one of the active causes of the American Revolution. An examination of the treatment of this topic reveals that most of the material is drawn from Massachusetts experience and centers around the agitation in 1761 and especially the part taken by James Otis in that affair. Certain basic facts are agreed to by all writers. Such writs were issued by the superior court. They were first granted to Thomas Paxton, chief customs officer in the province in 1755; other writs similar in form were issued to other customs officers by the same court in 1758, 1759, and 1760. The writs were general in form and without limitation in time; all writs expired six months after the death of a monarch and to be valid had to be renewed. Following the death of George II, Thomas Lechmere, surveyor general of the customs in America, applied to the superior court of Massachusetts in 1761 for a renewal of his former writ and the writs of his officers. This application was opposed by Oxenbridge Thatcher and James Otis as attorneys for certain Boston merchants, and the application was supported by Jeremiah Gridley, the attorney general of the colony. The case was argued twice before a full bench, Thomas Hutchinson sitting as chief justice. Legal doubts were raised as a result of the opposition, and the court applied to England for instruction on the contested points of law. When these instructions arrived, they supported the legality of the issuing of the writs. The court unanimously approved the issuance of the writs on December 5, 1761, and the final form of such writs was drafted by Chief Justice Hutchinson. All the officers of the customs in Massachusetts had such writs from 1761 to the outbreak of the Revolution, and similar writs were issued by the superior court of New Hampshire, a colony that usually followed the governmental practices of Massachusetts. Agitation over writs of assistance largely died down in Massachusetts after 1761, and the topic almost disappears from the discussion of the causes of the Revolution after that time.[1]

Accepting the above statements as adequately established by historical evidence, the question still remains: How can that series of happenings, either singly or together, constitute a cause of the Revolution? Admittedly the incidents were confined mostly to Massachusetts, and there is little in the facts as established that involved the other colonies. If they were not concerned, was this a cause of irritation chiefly in Massachusetts? If the question of writs of assistance involved only Massachusetts—admittedly there was no agitation in New Hampshire—how did the other colonies come to make the cause their own and include it among the other acts of Great Britain that endangered their liberties? None of our secondary accounts supply adequate answers to these questions, yet all give prominent place to writs of assistance as one of the important causes of colonial unrest.

That this general opinion cannot be entirely wrong is evidenced by the fact that the Fourth Amendment to the Constitution deals with this question in such a way as to make general search warrants forever illegal in this country. Clearly no such precipitation of practice could have been written into the Bill of Rights of our Constitution unless there had been widespread public opinion on the matter that had to be satisfied. This amendment is no legal abstraction to deal with imaginary ills. Its contemporary importance is evidenced by the fact that it is made the subject matter of a completely separate amendment, while freedom of

---

[1] Richard Frothingham, *Rise of the Republic of the United States*, pp. 162, 168, treats writs as essentially a Massachusetts affair. Edward Channing, *History of the United States*, III, 5, says they were generally used from 1761 in Massachusetts and "in the other colonies as well." In his footnote he states that none was issued in Rhode Island, Connecticut, and Georgia. G. E. Howard, *Preliminaries of the Revolution*, pp. 73–83, confines his account to Massachusetts, but states (p. 82) that they were issued in no other colonies except New York and New Hampshire. J. T. Adams, *Revolutionary New England*, pp. 271, 272, 293, practically confines his discussion to the Otis period. The only adequate account is by Horace Gray, "Appendix 1," Josiah Quincy, *Reports of Cases Argued and Adjudged . . . Province of Massachusetts Bay, 1761–72*. For the writ issued by the Massachusetts Court, see Macdonald, *Select Charters*, pp. 259–61.

speech, press, and religion and trial by jury are all inserted as items in amendments dealing with several subjects.

For any policy to have contributed to the American Revolution, it must have been seriously irritating or have threatened rights and interests in such a way as to arouse grave concern in the minds both of influential members of society and of the general public. People cannot take sides on issues that they know nothing about; consequently, before a policy could become a cause of revolt, it must have become known to the public and the public must have taken sides actively on the issue. At the time of the Revolution there were more than 2,600,000 people in the British colonies, spread along the seaboard from Labrador to Mobile and from Bermuda to Belize.[2] Incidents happening in a single colony could not have been known in other colonies unless in some way they were re-ported in the common vehicles of public information. At that time travel was difficult and facilities for the spread of common information were limited. Newspapers and pamphlets were the only widespread means of dissemination for either important happenings or political agitation. Newspapers were local and had very limited circulation. Careful search of these discloses no general information about applications for writs of assistance nor much discussion of the question of issuing them, except that contained in the *Journal of the Times*.[3] So far, no contemporary pamphlet that has come to light has been devoted mainly to a discussion of writs of assistance. On the other hand, there are many such pamphlets dealing with practically every other issue connected with the British treatment of the American colonies.

Some writers have attempted to give the popular touch to the agitation over writs by playing up the speech of James Otis. The picture of the young patriot with tongue of flame rousing his countrymen to a realization of dangers threatening their liberty is one that is capable of interesting literary treatment.

But was there any such "rabble-rousing" speech? The hearing on the writs was before a bench of judges. There was no jury.

[2] See varying estimates for the thirteen colonies alone in E. B. Greene and V. Harrington, *American Population before the Federal Census of 1790* (New York, 1932), p. 7.

[3] Originally widely published in colonial newspapers. See Dickerson, *Boston under Military Rule, 1768–1769*, pp. 92–93.

The room was the council chamber of the Old State House. This is a small room, even according to standards of that day. It is doubtful if even one hundred persons could have crowded into the room. No one has suggested that there was any advance publicity that the hearing would be exciting. The legal arguments of attorneys were apparently as dull then as they are today. At that time Massachusetts had a population of about 200,000. The hearing was in Boston under conditions such that not one-tenth of one percent of the total population of the colony could have heard Otis's speech. The speech was not reported in the newspapers of the period and circulated to the 99.9 percent of the population that surely did not hear it. Of those present, apparently John Adams was the only one who was sufficiently impressed to take notes on what was said and he gave us the full account of it some fifty years after Otis delivered it.

Clearly the people living in Massachusetts in 1761 could not be expected to get excited about a speech in Boston that was to be given to the world in print for the first time in Tudor's *James Otis,* published in 1823. It is true that a partial account of Otis's speech was published by Adams in 1773 in the *Massachusetts Spy,* but that was twelve years after the event. Even admitting that Otis made the speech ascribed to him and that it was as eloquent as John Adams says it was, it cannot possibly be made out as arousing a popular animosity against writs of assistance, even in Massachusetts. Much less can that speech be described as rousing antagonisms against the writs on the part of the 1,500,000 inhabitants in other colonies that were not likely to have known that Otis made a speech on the subject.

Obviously there is something about writs of assistance that has never been brought to light. There was popular objection to them, not merely in Massachusetts but in practically all the colonies. The reaction was too widespread and too deep to be explained by local happenings in a single colony or by the single forensic effort of any local politician, however popular.

Writs of assistance were legalized by a series of acts of Parliament giving the customs officers authority to search for and seize uncustomed goods. These acts are regularly cited as 12 Car. II, c. 19; 13 and 14 Car. II, c. 11; 7 and 8 Wm. III, c. 22; and 7 Geo. III,

c. 46. They were supplemented by customary practices which became as much a part of the legal procedure as the law itself. The law alone was extended to America in 1767 when the colonial courts had before them no direct knowledge of the practices that had grown up in the British Court of Exchequer.

An examination of the law reveals grave obscurities as to what Parliament intended. By the first act of Charles II, the customs officer could search suspected houses in the daytime after going before a proper officer, making oath to the facts, receiving a warrant, and taking with him a sheriff or other suitable civil officer.[4] The requirement that oath had to be made before the warrant was granted is important.

The act of 1664 authorized any person with a writ of assistance under the seal of the Court of Exchequer to take a peace officer and, in the daytime, search any house or shop and seize uncustomed goods.[5] The law did not specify how the writ was to be secured. The act of 7 and 8 Wm. III, regulating the plantation trade, gave the customs officers in America the same right to search as the officers in England had and provided that they should have like assistance in the execution of their office. This clearly extended to the colonies the law regarding search by customs officers in England, whatever that law was.

[4] 12 Car. II, c. 19: "That then and in such case, upon oath thereof made before the Lord Treasurer or any of the barons of the Exchequer, a chief magistrate of the port or place where the offence shall be committed, or the place next adjoining thereunto, it shall be lawful to and for the Lord Treasurer, or any of the barons aforesaid, or chief magistrate of the port or place where the offence shall be committed, or the place next adjoining thereunto, to issue out a warrant to any person or persons, thereby enabling him or them, with the assistance of a sheriff, justice of the peace, or constable, to enter into any house in the daytime where such goods are suspected to be concealed, and in case of resistance to break open such houses and to seize and secure the same goods so concealed; and all officers and ministers of justice are hereby required to be aiding and assisting thereunto." Pickering, *Statutes at Large.*

[5] 13 and 14 Car. II, c. 11, cl. 5: "And it shall be lawful to or for any person or persons, authorized by writs of assistance under the seal of His Majesty's court of exchequer, to take a constable, headborough, or other public officer inhabiting near the place, and in the daytime to enter, and go into any house, shop, cellar, warehouse, room, or other place and in case of resistance to break open doors, chests, trunks, and other packages, there to seize, and from thence to bring, any kind of goods or merchandize, whatever, prohibited and uncustomed and to put and secure the same in His Majesty's storehouse, in the port next to the place where such seizure shall be made." A separate clause (32) requires all officers "to be aiding and assisting" all persons appointed to manage customs. *Ibid.*

It should be noted that the power to search came from the authority given to the customs officers, and in practice this power was expressly stated in their commissions.[6] The exercise of the power was directly limited in that it must be done in the presence of a court officer. The constables and other officers of the law were under the control of the judges and hence could act only when they had a legal direction from some judge to do so. The constable and other officers did not do the searching. The law specifically empowered the customs officers to do that. The writ, as its name implies, was a court order to the constables and other officers to assist the customs officers in the exercise of their duties; it was not an order for them to search personally. Consequently a writ of assistance was not a search warrant, as it did not authorize the search. It merely vouched for the identity of the customs officers who by their commissions were authorized to search. The local officers were directed to assist the customs officer, as they had the power to command the peace and maintain order which the customs officers did not have. Such writs were issued under the power

[6] The only commission that has come to light is a copy of one issued to George Roupell, Collector at Charleston, South Carolina. This is reproduced in full:

TO ALL PEOPLE TO WHOM THESE PRESENTS SHALL COME

We the Commissioners for managing and causing to be Levied His Majesty's Customs and other Duties in America Do hereby Depute and Impower GEORGE ROUPELL ESQR. to be Collector of the Customs at Charles Town South Carolina and to do and perform all things to the said Service or Office or Employment belonging. In virtue whereof He hath power to enter into any Ship Bottom, Boat or other Vessel and also in the daytime with a Writ of Assistance granted by his Majesty's Superior or Supreme Court of Justice and taking with him a Constable, Headborough or other Public Officer next inhabiting, to enter into any House, Shop, Cellar, Warehouse or other place whatsoever not only within the said Port but within any other Port or place within our Jurisdiction there to make diligent Search and in case of resistance to break open any Door, Trunk, Chest, Case, Pack, Truss or any other Parcel or package whatsoever for any Goods, Wares, or Merchandizes, prohibited to be exported out of or imported into the said Port, or whereof the Customs or other Duties have not been duly paid: And the same to Seize to His Majesty's use and to put and secure the same in the Warehouse in the Port next to the Place of Seizure. In all which Premises He is to proceed in such manner as the law directs. Hereby praying and requiring all and every His Majesty's Officers and Ministers and all others whom it may concern, to be aiding and assisting to Him in all things as becometh. Given under our hands and Seal at the Custom House, Boston this seventh day of April in the Twelfth Year of the Reign of our Sovereign Lord King George the Third and in the year of our Lord One Thousand Seven Hundred and Seventy Two. *Signed,* WM. BURCH HEN. HULTON CHAS. PAXTON.—Public Record Office, London, Treasury 1, Bundle 492.

of a judge to direct the officers of his court and to punish for contempt.

In practice, a writ of assistance recited the law and the authority given the customs officers as a preliminary to directing the local officers to assist. This recital of the provisions of the law and the officer's commission has been assumed to be an actual grant of power, which it was not.[7]

The law nowhere states that such writs of assistance should be general or standing writs, to be used any time a customs officer might need such help. All questions of length of time such writs were to run and the returns to be made under them were matters of legal practices in England that cannot be learned from any reading of the statute alone.

The act of 7 and 8 Wm. III specifically extended the operation of the act of 14 Car. II to the colonies in America, but did not name the courts that were authorized to issue such writs. No mention is made of extending the provisions of 12 Car. II. As the act of Charles II specifically provided that writs to the customs officers should be issued by the Court of Exchequer and there was no such court in the colonies, there was a legal doubt as to what court should or could act. This was the principal issue raised in the attempt to secure writs in Massachusetts in 1761. Was the superior court of Massachusetts a court of exchequer within the meaning of the law of 1662 as modified by the acts of 7 and 8 Wm. III? Legal advice from England answered this question in the affirmative, but it did not entirely dispose of the questions concerning the form the writ should take.

It is customary now for American legislatures, when they legalize court processes, to embody in the statute a specific form for such process. No such form is prescribed or even mentioned in the British acts covering this subject. Consequently the specific form of such writs was drawn by the attorneys for the Board of Customs Commissioners in England, submitted to the judges of the Court of Exchequer, and approved by them. There is no evidence that such forms were ever drawn by the courts, although they were approved by them. A century of practice in England preceded the

[7] Note that the powers recited by Hutchinson in the well-known Massachusetts writ of assistance are very similar to the commission of Roupell just quoted.

controversy in America. Charles Paxton and other customs officers in the colonies were acting under the orders and direct instructions of the Lords of the Treasury in England. When the first writ was issued in Massachusetts in 1755, it clearly followed a form transmitted to Paxton from the Board of Customs Commissioners in England, and the form that has come down to us is that drawn by Chief Justice Thomas Hutchinson, which is an adaptation of the form of the British writ. The main difference is apparently the insertion of the whereas clause reciting that the superior court of Massachusetts by act of the provincial legislature in 1700 was given the same jurisdiction as the courts of Kings Bench, Common Pleas, and Exchequer in England. The other changes were obviously to adapt the writ to the local governmental organization of the province. The writ was made perpetual by inserting in the third sentence from the end the words "from time to time." It was the form of the writ that was attacked by Otis, and it must be remembered that there is nothing in the law that specifies or warrants the particular form of writ that had grown up in practice in the Exchequer Court of England. If 12 Car. II, c. 19, were in force this form was clearly illegal.

There is another basic fact that confuses the discussion. The phrase "Writ of Assistance," or "Writ of Assistants" as it was regularly written by clerks in the Board of Customs Commissioners in Boston and by similar clerks in the Treasury Office in England, had two meanings. It was a generic term used to indicate any kind of a warrant supplied to a customs officer and it had also come to mean the specific form issued by the Exchequer to officers of the customs in England. The lawyers and judges in the American colonies knew only the practices of the courts of common law. Under such courts, search warrants were issued only on specific information, supported by oath or affirmation, and returnable to the court of issue. There was no other practice known to the law courts in America. All forms of such warrants complied with these common provisions. The term "Writ of Assistance" was regularly applied to writs commonly issued to customs officers. There is no phrase in the acts of Parliament already cited indicating that any form other than that employed in the ordinary courts was intended. American judges had no occasion to study the procedure of the Exchequer Court in England because the customs laws of England did not apply in the colonies. Consequently, when the American judges and lawyers were confronted with a form for a writ prepared by the customs officers, fundamentally different from the established practices of the courts of common law and apparently in direct conflict with 12 Car. II, c. 19, they could not avoid the conclusion that it was novel and entirely unsupported by law.

The controversy in Massachusetts terminated in 1761 and should be looked upon as an interesting episode in Massachusetts history. The Townshend Revenue Act of 1767 aroused in every other colony in America a similar controversy which continued down to the outbreak of hostilities. In this later controversy, writs of assistance became an issue throughout the colonies, involving nearly every judge and prominent lawyer in America outside of Massachusetts and New Hampshire.

As soon as the Board of Customs Commissioners at Boston had established itself and set up its customs office force at the various ports in America, it undertook to arm these officers with "writs of assistants" as authorized by the Revenue Act of 1767, section x. An opinion was obtained from the Attorney General in England that standing writs were regularly authorized by law; a copy of the form of the writ as issued by the Exchequer Court in England was also secured. These were then printed in Boston and sent out by the Solicitor of the Board of Customs Commissioners in a letter to the main officers of the customs in each colony, directing them to present the papers to the attorney general of their respective colonies and to request him to move the supreme or superior court of the colony to grant the writs. In some cases the communication took the form of an open circular letter to the attorney general. In no case was the communication directed personally to an individual attorney general, but to him through the customs officer.

The customs officers in Massachusetts and New Hampshire already had standing writs. In Nova Scotia there was some delay because the collector at Halifax reported in 1769 that he had no writs, as there was no attorney general to whom he could present the papers. Obviously, this request was soon remedied, because the Board reported to the Treasury officials in October, 1772, that the officers in Nova Scotia and the other colonies north of Connecticut had the writs.

That the courts in the outlying island ports also apparently received their writs on the first requests is shown by the same report. There is no evidence that writs were ever applied for in New Jersey, possibly due to the indiscretions of Hutton, who, as collector at Salem in that province, became involved in an acrimonious controversy with the courts and with the governor and council over an apparently illegal seizure which provoked a personal assault upon himself. There is also considerable doubt as to whether any application was made in North Carolina, because the customs officers there made no reports on the subject that have come to light.[8] Delaware followed the court practice of Pennsylvania as did New Hampshire that of Massachusetts. This left the controversy to develop in an acute form in Rhode Island, Connecticut, New York, Pennsylvania, Maryland, East Florida, Georgia, South Carolina, and Virginia. The issues raised and the action taken in each colony will be discussed in detail, with full quotations from reports made by the customs officers to their superiors in Boston.

Rhode Island

The first general instructions to apply for "Writs of Assistants" were sent out in 1768. Upon receipt of his orders, Charles Dudley, collector at the port of Providence, asked the attorney general to make regular application to the court. This was done at the March term, 1768, at Newport. Two of the justices were absent from court at the time; therefore, consideration of "said affair" was referred to the next term of court, and in the meantime "all persons in their several Stations are commanded to lend Due and lawful aid and Assistance to said Officers in the Execution of their

[8] The Board of Customs Commissioners reported to the Treasury in England on October 20, 1772, that writs of assistance has been issued as follows: Quebec; Nova Scotia; New Hampshire; Massachusetts at ports of Falmouth, Salem, Marblehead, and Boston; New York (a limited writ); Virginia (had a writ that was useless); East Florida (records do not support this); West Florida; Bahamas; and Bermuda. P.R.O., Treasury 1, Bundle 492.

several Offices." [9] This direction was not given out in the form of a special writ and therefore did not constitute a writ of assistance.

Apparently not fully trusting the industry of the attorney general, the customs officers at Newport prepared a regular memorial and presented it at the adjourned term of court at Newport, April 12, 1768.[10] To make sure that this was not pigeonholed, Dudley demanded and received a certificate from the clerk of the court that such application was regularly on file, and so reported to the Board of Customs Commissioners in Boston, supporting his statements with certified copies of the memorial and the certificate of the clerk of the court that their application was on file. No writs were received. Application was again made in 1769, with no better results. In November, 1771, the Customs Commissioners again directed all customs officers who did not have writs to renew their applications for them. Dudley at this time reported again the history of his efforts and asked the Commissioners to have their solicitor again make application to the attorney general of Rhode Island for action on the writs. About this time Dudley became involved in a serious difficulty over his attempted seizure of the *Polly* under very doubtful legal circumstances. In the course of this controversy, he charged definite lack of coöperation on the part of Governor Wanton and the courts and reiterated his charge

[9] Certified copy of the records of the court, enclosed in Charles Dudley's report to the Customs Commissioners. Treasury 1, Bundle 491. This record does not give the names of the judges who were present. The regular judges at that time were: James Helme, chief justice, and Job Bennett, Benoni Hall, Stephen Potter, and Samuel Nightingale, associate justices.

[10] This application was in the following form:

"To the Honorable Justices of the Superior Court of Judicature, Court of Assize and General Gaol Delivery now sitting at Newport in and for the County of Newport in said Colony by adjournment of the Twelfth day of April A.D. 1768.

"In consequence of and in conformity to an Act of Parliament made and passed in the seventh year of His present Majesty's Reign, entitled an Act for granting certain duties in the British Colonies and Plantations in America I Richard Beale Esqr Collector, John Nicoll Esqr Comptroller and Nicholas Lechmere Esqr Searcher of His Majesty's Customs for this Gov't Come into the Honorable Superior Court aforesaid, and pray the Honorable Justices of said Court to grant them respectively Writs of Assistants as in and by said recited Act of Parliament is directed."

Signed { RICHARD BEALE
         JOHN NICOLL
         NICHOL. LECHMERE

Certified copy enclosed by Dudley in his report to the Board of Customs Commissioners. Treasury 1, Bundle 491.

that the superior court had refused a proper request for "Writs of Assistance."

This controversy reached Secretary of State Hillsborough and produced a letter from Governor Wanton dated November 2, 1771, stating that the judges of the superior court individually appeared before the general assembly and testified, "upon their honor," that "no kind of application whatsoever had been made to them or any of them by any officers of the customs for any Writ of Assistance or other protection of any kind for several years last past." They added that when the customs officers should make any application to them for writs of assistance or other protection they would readily and cheerfully "give them every assistance in the execution of their duty which the law puts in the power of the Superior Court to give." [11]

Here is a direct conflict of evidence. There is the clearest documentary evidence that application had been made in 1768 and again in 1769 and that the applications were on file in the office of the clerk of the superior court.[12] Yet the judges appeared before the general assembly in 1771 and stated that no application had been made. It is not necessary to assume that the judges were not telling the truth. Under the procedure of the common law and the provisions of 12 Car. II, c. 19, they had never received a legal application for a writ of assistance. That procedure required that the applicant should state on oath that he had information that uncustomed goods were in a particular place. The application by the customs officers had not alleged any specific violation of the law nor named any specific place to be searched. Failing this, their applications were without legal standing and the judges ignored them. The last statement of the judges promising to give all assistance that "the law puts in their power to give" takes on special significance in the light of these facts. Evidently their understanding of the law differed from that of the customs officers.

[11] Treasury 1, Bundle 493. The judges in 1771 were Stephen Hopkins, chief justice, and James Helme, Benoni Hall, Metcalf Bowler, and Stephen Potter, associate justices. It is possible that none of these judges was present at the session of the court when the earlier applications for writs were made.

[12] Evidence of this application remains in the office of the clerk of the court, where is found a copy of the opinion of Attorney General De Grey referred to later—the only copy that has come to light. Horace Gray, "Writs of Assistance," Josiah Quincy, *Reports*, p. 454.

Apparently there was no further application for writs in that province. Dudley was fully occupied defending himself from the suits involved in his raid on the *Polly*. Then the *Gaspé* affair occurred and kept everyone busy. Writs of assistance had involved the attorney general, the judges of the superior court, the governor, every member of the general assembly, exciting court cases, and appeals to Secretary of State Hillsborough, as well as the Board of Customs Commissioners in Boston and their superiors in London. Clearly the writs were as live an issue in Rhode Island as in Massachusetts.

Connecticut

There were two ports of entry in Connecticut, one at New London, the other at New Haven. Each had two regular officers, a collector and a comptroller. These were Duncan Stewart and Thomas Moffatt at New London and Peter Harrison and George Mills at New Haven. All of these officers made application for writs when first directed to do so at the March term of the superior court, 1768. Stewart and Moffatt sent their application to Harrison at New Haven to present to the court, which he did together with his own. There are two independent reports as to what happened, one by Stewart and another by Harrison. As the court took no action, Stewart thought best to prepare a formal petition to the court, which he filed on March 28, 1768. Jared Ingersoll, recently appointed judge of the vice-admiralty court, was then appealed to by letter to ask for writs and to secure a reply to their application in writing, but the court broke up without action.[13] In a private conversation Harrison says that the chief justice and deputy governor (Jonathan Trumbull) told him the principal reason why the court did not grant the writs was that they were not clear that the writs were constitutional and "that they were strangers to every mode of application besides petition." Here again is the constitutional objection said to have been raised by Otis in 1761, and there is some evidence that the judges of Connecticut were familiar with the controversy in Massa-

---

[13] Letter of Peter Harrison to the Customs Commissioners, dated New Haven, March 2, 1768. Treasury 1, Bundle 491. The date indicates that the first application was made while the court was at New Haven, and the second while the court was at Norwich.

chusetts.[14] Judge Trumbull was not impressed when Harrison explained that the orders of the Customs Commissioners required him to proceed by general application and forbade him to use any other method.

Stewart reported that Ingersoll had made the regular application and had heard the judges discuss the matter in his presence.[15] Upon request, the clerk of the court supplied a copy of the court record certifying that the request for writs of assistance had been made, and "no information being made by said petition or otherways of any special reason for such writ," the court was of the opinion that it would be necessary to consider the purport of the act of 1767 and the manner and form of granting writs under it.[16]

The customs officers renewed their application for writs at the April term at Norwich in 1769 and a month later at Hartford. These applications were supported by De Grey's opinion and accompanied by copies of the law and the form of the writ used in England. Thomas Seymour, attorney for the customs officers, demanded a judicial determination of the motion for writs. Chief Justice Trumbull was unwilling to be rushed, as he believed the form of the writ that was demanded was not authorized by law. He entered into correspondence with judges in other colonies to find out how they proposed to rule on the question. Some of his letters indicate that this correspondence was intended to unite all the courts in America in uniform opposition. Only letters from the Rhode Island and Massachusetts judges have come to light. Both Trumbull and Judge Roger Sherman wrote to William S. Johnson,[17] the colonial agent in London, for definite information as to

14 See Gray, "Writs of Assistance," Quincy, *Reports*, pp. 504–7.

15 "This Petition was delivered yesterday to the Honorable Court at Norwich by the Comptroller—the Judges politely received it then read the Act of Parliament, and after mature deliberation amongst themselves in the recess of Court made answer— That it was unnecessary for the Comptroller to wait any longer at Norwich because the granting Writs of Assistance was a matter of so much importance that they would *not* determine upon it during their present sitting." Letter of Duncan Stewart and Thomas Moffatt to the Customs Commissioners, March 29, 1768. Treasury 1, Bundle 491.

16 Certified copy of the action of the court, signed by George Pitkin, clerk. *Ibid.* There is a copy of this in Gray, "Writs of Assistance," Quincy, *Reports*, p. 501, taken from Stuart, *Life of Trumbull*, p. 79, and a note that the petition is not in the permanent court records.

17 Later member of the Constitutional Convention at Philadelphia, author of the famous compromise on representation, and first president of Columbia University. G. C. Groce, *William Samuel Johnson* (New York, 1937).

the issuing of writs in England and the specific form of writ granted by the courts. Governor Pitkin did the same. The nature of this correspondence suggests the fear of the colonial officials that their refusal to grant writs might lead to a direct attack upon their charter. One of the judges, Eliphalet Dyer,[18] was reported as making a special point of consulting personally judges in the colonies "to the westward." Apparently the issue reached the general assembly,[19] where an attempt was made to unseat Trumbull as chief justice.[20]

Considering the prominence of the judges in Connecticut [21] and the agitation set on foot by the applications, it is not at all unlikely that the opposition aroused there was more important in influencing the later course of events than what had happened in Massachusetts.

New York

The supreme court of New York granted writs of assistance when first applied to by the customs officers in 1768. New York's seems to have been the only colonial court south of Massachusetts to comply so promptly with the act of 1767. The writ is dated April 28, 1768, is the only one secured by the Customs Commissioners that has come to light, and consequently is as important historically as the one drawn by Hutchinson in 1761. Because of this importance it is reproduced in full.

WRIT OF ASSISTANCE ISSUED IN NEW YORK, 1768

George the Third by the Grace of God of Great Britain, France, and Ireland, King, Defender of the Faith, etc. To our trusty Lambert Moore, Esquire, Comptroller of all the Rates and Duties and Impositions arising and growing due to us at New York in America, Greeting. WHEREAS we are given to understand that several Goods, Wares, and Manufactures have been and are daily imported into and Exported out of our Port of New York and are concealed from the person and persons appointed to manage our customs which ought not

---

18 For further details regarding Dyer's activities in the Revolutionary period, see *infra,* pp. 290–304.

19 Dickerson, *Boston under Military Rule, 1768–1769,* pp. 92–93.

20 There is a full treatment of writs of assistance in Connecticut in Gray, "Writs of Assistance," Quincy, *Reports,* pp. 504–7.

21 The judges of the superior court between 1768 and 1772 were: Jonathan Trumbull, Matthew Griswold, Eliphalet Dyer, Roger Sherman, William Pitkin, and William S. Johnson.

to be done, and for others the duties have not been paid or satisfied. AND WHEREAS some doubts have arisen whether the Officers for collecting and managing our Revenue and Inspecting the Plantation Trade in America are vested with the same powers and Authorities as the Officers of the Customs in England notwithstanding the Act of Parliament made in the seventh and eighth Years of King William the Third as no Authority is expressly given by the said Act to any particular Court to grant Writs of Assistants for the Officers of the Customs in the said Plantations, to obviate which doubts, by an Act of Parliament made and passed in the 7th year of our Reign it is Enacted that from and after the twentieth day of November one thousand seven hundred and sixty seven Writs of Assistants shall and may be granted by the Superior or Supreme Courts of Justice having jurisdiction within the Colonies or Plantations respectively. AND WHEREAS application hath been made to our Supreme Court of our Province of New York for Writs of Assistance to be granted to the several officers of our said customs within our said Province, And it hath thereupon been ordered by the said Court that Writs of Assistance should issue to the officers of our said customs within our said province severally according to the intention of said act, you are hereby authorized and impowered together with a Constable the Headborough or other Public Officer Inhabiting near unto the Place taking with you such Assistance as may be requisite and in the Day time to enter and go into any Ship Boat or other Vessell as also into any House, Warehouse, Shop, Cellar or other place in this colony and in Case of resistance to break open Doors, Chests, Trunks, and other Packages and to Seize and from thence to bring away any kind of Goods or Merchandizes whatsoever prohibited to be Imported or Exported or whereof the Customs or other Duties have not been and shall not be duly paid. And the same to Seize and from thence to bring away and to put and secure the same in our Store House next to the place where such seizure shall be made. Hereby requiring all and every our Officers and Ministers and all others whom it may concern to be aiding and assisting to you the said Lambert Moore in all things as becometh. In Testimony whereof we have caused the seal of our said Supreme Court to be herewith affixed. Witness Daniel Horsmanden, Esquire, our Chief Justice at our City of New York the twenty eighth day of April in the eighth year of our reign.

Signed CLARKE [22]

The like Writ was at the same time granted to Andrew Elliot, Esqr., Collector; Alex Colden, Esqr., Surveyor and Searcher; and James Parker, Land-waiter.[23]

---

[22] Obviously this was George Clarke, secretary of the province of New York and clerk of the court. Report of William Tryon, *Documents Relating to the Colonial History of New York*, VIII, 444–54.

[23] Treasury 1, Bundle 492.

There are some marked differences between this writ and that issued by Hutchinson. This authorizes searches in the daytime only, even of ships. It has no clause "from time to time" as did that issued by Hutchinson, which may have been a bar to its continued use; but so far as known that point was never challenged. It does not specifically authorize search upon suspicion and it is possible that officers using such a writ might be liable to heavy penalties for searching a place where no smuggled goods were actually found. The language, however, seems sweeping enough. So far as is known, this writ was used only once and on that occasion (1772) the officers reported it as very effective, "as on showing it to the Mayor, he immediately went with us attended by the Sheriff and other city officers." [24]

Although this writ had been issued in 1768, it was not in the specific form demanded by the Customs Commissioners; consequently the customs officers were instructed to apply for writs according to the prescribed form. The application forms in 1769 had included duplicates of the form of the writ desired and a copy of an opinion of the attorney general in England that the form was in accordance with British practice. These were placed in the hands of Attorney General John Tabor Kempe, who stated that he laid them before the judges when he moved for an issue of the writs. The forms were apparently mislaid by the judges, and Kempe asked for additional copies. In November, 1771, and again in 1772, the solicitor for the Commissioners in Boston had sent out other circular letters with the usual copies directing the attorneys general of the colonies to renew applications for writs. These were transmitted to Attorney General Kempe by the customs officers and finally, on February 1, 1773, Kempe returned a somewhat icily worded letter to the solicitor at Boston, in which he enclosed extracts of the records of the superior court to show the history of his applications. These extracts are so illuminating that they are repeated below:

At a Supreme Court of Judicature held for the Province of New York at the City Hall in the city of New York on Saturday, the 29th day of April, one thousand seven hundred and sixty nine in the ninth

---

[24] Letter from customs officers in New York to the Customs Commissioners at Boston, March 3, 1772. Treasury 1, Bundle 491.

year of our Sovereign Lord George the Third by the grace of God of
Great Britain, France, and Ireland, King, Defender of the Faith, and
so forth

Present

The Honorable Daniel Horsmanden, Esqr.⎫
The Honorable David Jones, Esqr. ⎬ Justices

The Attorney General having now and heretofore during this term
moved for Writs of Assistance for Mr. Elliott, Collector and Mr. Moore,
Comptroller and Mr. Colden, Surveyor and Searcher of the Port of
New York agreeable to a certain printed precedent received by him
from the Commissioners at Boston, and produced by him and filed in
this Court, the Court takes time to consider of this motion until next
term.

Friday the twenty-seventh day of October, one thousand seven hundred
and sixty nine.

Honorable David Jones ⎫
Honorable Robert R. Livingston ⎬ Justices

Mr. Attorney General moved the court for Writs of Assistance for
Mr. Elliott, Collector, Mr. Moore, Comptroller, and Mr. Colden, Surveyor and Searcher of the Port of New York agreeable to certain printed
precedents submitted by him from the Commissioners of Customs at
Boston, and formally produced by him and lodged in Court. The Court
asked time to consider further of this motion.

Saturday, the twenty-fifth day of January, one thousand seven hundred
and seventy-two.

Honorable Robert R. Livingston—Justice

Mr. Attorney General moved for Writs of Assistance to Mr. Elliott,
Collector, Mr. Moore, Comptroller, and Mr. Colden, Surveyor and
Searcher of the Port of New York. The Court takes time to consider
of this motion.

Tuesday, the twenty-fifth day of April, one thousand seven hundred
and seventy-two.

Honorable Daniel Horsmanden ⎫
Honorable Robert R. Livingston ⎬ Justices

Mr. Attorney General, having moved for Writs of Assistance to Mr.
Elliott, Collector, Mr. Moore, Comptroller, and Mr. Colden, Surveyor
and Searcher of the Port of New York, the court takes time to consider
of this motion.

Saturday, the second day of May, one thousand seven hundred and
seventy two.

Present

Honorable Robert R. Livingston ⎫
Honorable George Duncan Ludlow ⎬ Justices

The Attorney General again moved for Writs of Assistance to the several officers of the Customs of the Port of New York which the Court conceived themselves not authorized to grant by any statute and refused.

Saturday, the twenty-third of June, one thousand seven hundred and seventy three
        Present
    The Honorable Robert R. Livingston, Esqr. ⎱Justices
    The Honorable George Duncan Ludlow, Esqr. ⎰
    Mr. Attorney General moved for Writs of Assistance under the seal of this Court to Andrew Elliott, Esqr., Collector and Lambert Moore, Comptroller of His Majesty's Customs of the Port of New York agreeable to the form transmitted to him by the Secretary of the Board of Customs at Boston as the form in which such writs are issued by the Court of Exchequer in England, which form together with the opinion of His Majesty's Attorney General for that part of Great Britain called England, he laid before the Court—whereupon the Court observed that this matter, having been before moved and refused and no new arguments being now offered in support of the motion, it did not appear to them that such Writs according to the form now produced are warranted by law and therefore they could not grant the motion.[25]

Here the attempt to secure writs of assistance dragged through the courts of New York for five years, the motion repeated session after session only to be as regularly postponed and finally definitely refused by the court. A writ of assistance would not suffice—the customs officers already had one. It had to be a specific form of writ. During this effort to secure writs the issue must have become familiar to lawyers and merchants in New York. People could not avoid taking sides. Robert R. Livingston was presiding judge of the court when the final and decisive refusal to grant new writs was given. His action is in sharp contrast to that of Thomas Hutchinson of Massachusetts, and he had evidently taken ample time to examine the law on the subject.

Pennsylvania

John Swift was collector and Alexander Barclay was comptroller at the port of Philadelphia. Under their instructions the customs

[25] These transcripts are included in the letter of Attorney General Kempe, reporting his inability to secure copies of the writ as directed, February 1, 1773. Treasury 1, Bundle 501.

officers were directed to apply to a judge or judges of the superior court. They chose to apply to Chief Justice Allen, thus obliging him to decide the case on his own judgment. The application was made on April 12, 1768, and the answer was returned on May 10, the same year, in a personal letter to Swift, as follows:

PHILADELPHIA
May 10, 1768

SIR:

I have duly considered the application you made to grant you a Writ of Assistants. Though my duty and inclination would lead me to do everything in my power to promote the King's service, yet I conceive I am not Warranted by Law to issue any such Warrant. But not being willing to trust to my own judgment entirely, I have laid the matter before the Attorney General and another emminent lawyer who both concur with me in opinion that such a general writ as you have demanded is not agreeable to Law. I beg leave to assure you I am

Sir
Your Obedient Humble Servant
WILL ALLEN [26]

This letter of Chief Justice Allen's was transmitted to England with reports from some of the other colonies where the courts had either refused to issue writs of assistance or had postponed action. The customs officials prepared a statement of facts and submitted it to Attorney General William De Grey for an opinion on the legal questions involved. In the course of that opinion, De Grey refers specifically to the ruling of Chief Justice Allen, ascribes it to his lack of knowledge of the current practices in England, and advises that a copy of the form of the writ used in England be sent over to guide colonial judges.[27] This was done in the autumn of 1768 and this opinion of De Grey's and the specific form of the writ appear in all subsequent discussions.

Swift was directed to renew his application, this time accompanying it with a copy of De Grey's opinion, with its specific uncomplimentary reference to Chief Justice Allen's ruling, and the

---

[26] William Allen had received his legal education in London, had married a daughter of Andrew Hamilton, had been a member of the Pennsylvania Assembly, and mayor of Philadelphia, had assisted Franklin in the repeal of the Stamp Act, was author of the *American Crisis*, and was chief justice of Pennsylvania, 1750–74. He was a Tory and, like Hutchinson, fled to England. *Dictionary of American Biography*, I, 208. A copy of the above letter is in Treasury 1, Bundle 491.

[27] Gray, "Writs of Assistance," in Quincy, *Reports*, p. 454.

form used in England. The application, made this time to the supreme court, was again refused on the ground that there was no law authorizing the granting of standing writs. The court stated, however, that it would "grant particular writs whenever they are applied for upon oath" that the officer "either has an information or has reasons to believe that prohibited or uncustomed goods are lodged in any particular place." [28]

This answer was not sufficient, and in November, 1771, Swift was again directed to make application. It took him a very short time to find out what the answer would be. On November 30, 1771, he wrote his superiors that the court persisted in its refusal to grant writs according to the form submitted, the judges holding "that such writs are not warranted by law." He also reported a conference between the deputy collector and Chief Justice Allen over some seized goods that had been recently rescued from the customs officers. Allen was asked if he would issue a writ to search for such goods. His answer was: "Yes, if you will make oath that you have had an information that they are in any particular place. I will grant you a writ to search that particular place, but no general writ to search every house—I would not do that for any consideration." [29]

The customs officers at Philadelphia were changed, and the new officers, John Patterson and Zachariah Hood, received orders in 1773 to renew the applications. This time the attorney general applied to the entire bench of the superior court, supporting his application with the usual documents.

The Attorney General acquainted us that at the last sitting of the Supreme Court here, he moved that Writs of Assistance might be granted to the officers of the Customs in this port. That the Court were unanimously of opinion that they could not consistently, with their Ideas of Law, grant any such Writs, but upon an Information being made of a special occassion for them, and therefore rejected the motion. They said that upon a former application they carefully considered the Matter, and had taken into their assistance some of the most eminent Lawyers here, who perfectly coincided with them in sentiment that arming officers of the Customs with so extensive a power, to be exercised

---

[28] Letter to the Board of Customs Commissioners, May 5, 1769. Treasury 1, Bundle 491.

[29] Letter to the Board of Customs Commissioners. Treasury 1, Bundle 492.

totally at their own discretion would be of dangerous consequences and was not warranted by Law.[30]

In Pennsylvania the question was referred to the highest law officer of the British government as well as most of the local legal fraternity. Chief Justice Allen stated that he personally consulted the attorney general and another leading member of the Philadelphia bar when the applications were first made and that they were unanimous in holding that the form of writ asked for was not authorized by law; and the full court had consulted several of the best lawyers in the province. It was obvious that during the five years in which the issue was pressed Judge Allen and others had developed very positive opinions. On the other hand, it should be noted that the judges showed no disposition to hamper the customs officers. They showed great willingness to assist and offered to grant writs of assistance in special cases as often as they were asked to do so, and repeated this offer as applications were renewed and rejected by the court.

The most positive refusal of the Pennsylvania court came after it had been specifically overruled by an opinion of the attorney general of England. It took courage for a colonial chief justice, himself a Tory, to persist in his ruling when he had before him an opinion specifically referring to him and quoting adversely from his own decision.[31]

Maryland

There were two regular ports of entry in Maryland, one at Pocomoke on the eastern peninsula and the other at Patuxent near Annapolis. The collectors at these ports received copies of the first order regarding writs and applied for them independently. The collector at Patuxent, being nearer the court, applied first and stated that the judges neither granted him the writ nor took any

[30] Letter of the customs officers at Philadelphia to the Customs Commissioners, July 3, 1773. Treasury 1, Bundle 501.

[31] "I think it can only be because the Subject was entirely misunderstood, and the Practice in *England* unknown, that the Chief Justice in *Pennsylvania*, who is generally well spoken of, could imagine, that 'He was not Warranted by Law' to issue a Writ commanded by the Legislature; which Writ was founded upon the Common Law. And it appears accordingly that in *Boston* where a very able judge presides and some experience had been had on the Subject, no Difficulty was made in granting it." Opinion of De Grey, in Gray, "Writs of Assistance," Quincy, *Reports,* p. 454.

other notice of his application.[32] The collector at Pocomoke wrote
that he learned that the collector at Patuxent had made application but that his request would not be granted. Thinking that if
he waited until the next term the judges "might be in a better
humor," he withheld his application until that time. When his
letter, with the usual enclosure of forms of the desired writ, an
opinion of the attorney general in England as to its legality, and
copies of 7 Geo. III, c. 46, authorizing the writs and directing their
issue by the superior courts of each province, was presented in
court he received as an answer: "Let them apply for General Warrants (for so they called them) when they want them." [33]

As in the other colonies, this answer did not end the matter.
Pressure from the Commissioners in Boston continued, and as late
as April, 1773, the customs officers at Pocomoke renewed their demand upon the attorney general, again presenting the usual set of
papers. He was reported as being rather unwilling to act, although
he made assurances of coöperation. The collector waited eight
days for him to move the court for writs; and when he did so, there
was no answer. After some further delay the attorney general told
the customs officers to return to their offices, that at a suitable time
he would again move the court and would report his success by
letter. By July 28, following, there was still no letter.[34]

Here again the controversy over writs dragged through more
than five years. The decided attitude of the judges is important, as
is also the obviously unfriendly attitude of the attorney general.
The immediate characterization of the writs as "General Warrants" and their refusal to grant any writ except when some special
occasion necessitated it is in line with the general trend of opinion
in legal circles in the other colonies. The nature of the evidence
from this colony indicates that the whole matter of writs had been
thought through and discussed by all of those connected with the
courts and that at the time of the first application their minds were
fully made up on the issue.

There is a possibility that the Connecticut judges had consulted

[32] Letter from the collector at Patuxent to the Board of Customs Commissioners,
June 8, 1768. Treasury 1, Bundle 491.
[33] Letter from the collector at Pocomoke to the Board of Customs Commissioners,
June 12, 1769. Treasury 1, Bundle 491.
[34] Collector at Pocomoke to the Board, July 28, 1773. Treasury 1, Bundle 501.

the Maryland judges early in 1768. Jonathan Trumbull's letters show that he had undertaken to consult the judges of other colonies rather generally, with the object of bringing about concerted action by the courts.[35] One of his letters reveals that Judge Eliphalet Dyer of Connecticut "was bound on a Journey to the Westward, and that he intended to take the Opinion of the Judges there." [36] It is possible that Dyer visited and discussed the matter of writs with judges as far south as Maryland, as his business took him to Pennsylvania. It is also probable that the Maryland judges had been in consultation with the judges of Virginia. De Grey's opinion, with its uncomplimentary reference to Chief Justice Allen, was probably resented by the Maryland judges.

Florida

The Floridas were new provinces with a very small English population. The records contain only one report from West Florida which says that writs of assistance were issued in the prescribed form.[37] We have fuller reports from East Florida. There were two customs houses in that province, the more important of which was St. Augustine, where William Cummings was collector. A report by the Board of Customs Commissioners to the Treasury Office in 1772 states that the customs officers at both ports had writs according to the forms that had been sent out. There is a later report, however, that indicates that this account may not have been true. William Cummings had applied to William Drayton, chief justice, to execute a writ in accordance with instructions received from Boston on October 13, 1772. This, after "repeated applications," Drayton "absolutely and positively refused" to do,[38] stating his

[35] Gray, "Writs of Assistance," Quincy, *Reports*, pp. 501–7.

[36] Letter, J. A. Helme to Jonathan Trumbull, Aug. 7, 1769. Quoted by Gray, *ibid.*, p. 507.

[37] General summary of the status of applications for writs of assistance, prepared by the Board of Customs Commissioners, including reports through 1772. This states opposite East Florida: "The officers have been furnished with writs agreeable to the Form submitted." After West Florida is the notation "Ditto." The statement in regard to East Florida does not appear to be correct. There are no copies of letters from West Florida. Treasury 1, Bundle 501. There is an item in the *Boston Gazette*, Sept. 11, 1769, to the effect that both Georgia and Florida courts had refused to issue the writs. This is evidently based upon information leaking from the office of the Customs Commissioners.

[38] Collector at St. Augustine to the Board of Customs Commissioners, Nov. 18, 1772. *Ibid.*

reason for this refusal in a letter of November 17, 1772, as follows:

> In answer to your application to me for Writs of Assistance to be lodged in the hands of the Custom House Officers in this Province to search and seize prohibited or uncustomed goods within the same, I must inform you, That I am and always will be ready to issue such writs to search all places, which by oath made before me shall be suspected or known to contain goods of that kind.
>
> But I do not think myself justified by Law to issue general writs for that purpose to be lodged in the hands and to be used discretionally (perhaps without proper foundation) at the will of subordinate officers, to the injury of the rights of His Majesty's other loyal subjects.
>
> W. DRAYTON [39]

This letter throws some doubt upon the report of the Commissioners in Boston that the officers had writs at an earlier date. None of the earlier letters from Florida have come to light. It is possible that both records could be true. There may have been a change in officers at the port of St. Augustine, in which case there would be a new application for writs, as it was customary in the colonies issuing such writs to have new writs issued when any change of that kind occurred. It is also possible that the earlier writs referred to were in a different form and that it was not until 1772 that application was made for the standard form of writ. In the meantime Drayton may have been in correspondence with judges farther north and may have become acquainted with their action upon similar applications. Drayton's refusal is couched in language very similar to that of judges in other colonies and is as positive and clear as any on record.

Georgia

The attempts to secure writs of assistance in Georgia are similar to those in Florida. There is no record of the first applications or the dates when they were made. The first report, dated February 20, 1770, states that the customs officers did not have writs, that they had made application to a former judge and had been refused. A new judge had been appointed, but before application had been made the attorney general had resigned. It is probable that the collector at Savannah was negligent in pushing his application for

[39] Copy attached to letter from Cummings. *Ibid.*

writs. Pressure from his superiors in Boston continued. Late in 1771 he induced the attorney general of the province to make regular application, and secured a copy of the action of the court. This is so illuminating that it is reproduced in full:

IN THE GENERAL COURT OF GEORGIA

January, Friday 17, 1772

Mr. Attorney General, on the Behalf of the Commissioners of Customs in the British Colonies in America applied to the Court for Writs of Assistance and on reading the Acts of Parliament of the 12th & 14th of Charles the 2nd and also the Statute of 7th Geo. the 3rd respecting such writs of assistance, their honors the three assistant Judges were of opinion That notwithstanding they would at all times give their utmost assistance in discouraging Frauds on His Majesty's Customs, yet apprehending there was not an immediate occasion for such Writs which when there was they would be willing to grant them, therefore were of opinion no Writs of Assistance should be granted at present. And his honor the Chief Justice was of opinion that as such Writs were usually granted by the Court of Exchequer in England without affidavit being first made and as the Act of 7th George 3rd directs the Supreme Courts of America to grant such Writs on application to them for that purpose he therefore apprehended that the Court had no discretionary powers to refuse the same but were obliged to grant them. It is therefore ordered there being three judges against one that Mr. Attorney General do take nothing by his motion.

These are to certify that the above contains a true copy taken from the minutes of the court aforesaid. Examined by

PRESTON PRYCE C.G.C.[40]

Pleas Office

8th February, 1772 [41]

This action of the court was sent to the Lords of the Treasury in England, as were other refusals of colonial courts to grant writs. The failure of earlier applications did not deter the customs officers from having the attorney general renew their application on May 3, 1773. Again the attorney general secured a transcript of the action of the court, which shows how the court divided.

Their honors the Judges were of opinion as follows: Viz.

His Honor Mr. Justice Butler that as he apprehended there was not

---

[40] Clerk, General Court.

[41] Copy contained in a letter of James Hume, collector at Savannah to the Customs Commissioners, Feb. 8, 1772. Treasury 1, Bundle 491.

an occasion for them at present he was of opinion that the same should not be granted nor until there was a necessity for them. His Honor Mr. Justice Jones alleged as he has not come prepared on the matter, not being apprised of such intended application, he could not give any opinion thereupon. And His Honor the Chief Justice was of opinion that the Writs should be granted.[42]

Courts divided then as they do now. The chief justice [43] was in favor of granting the writs and believed the law made such action mandatory upon the part of the colonial courts. He could not, however, prevail upon the other judges to vote to issue them, as they stood rigidly for the established common law practice of issuing such warrants only upon affidavit that there was a specific occasion demanding such action by the court. It is obvious that the continued application for the writs, coupled with the recorded differences of opinion between the chief justice and his associates, must have been fully known to all of the legal fraternity and prominent citizens of the province. The failure of the *Georgia Gazette* to report the applications and their rejection does not by itself bespeak a lack of public interest in the issue.

South Carolina

South Carolina shows an important variant in the attempt to secure writs of assistance. In obedience to instructions, the customs officers applied to the assistant judges of the supreme court for such writs on April 15, 1768, but their application went unnoticed.[44] A renewal of the application was made early the next year, with no results.[45] These applications were repeated yearly without success until 1773. An application had been made in 1772, apparently to the chief justice, as the customs officers at Wynyaw reported that he told them personally that the matter was of such importance that he would have to consult the other judges. After some delay the attorney general reported that the writs had been issued and he enclosed copies for the officers at Charleston, Port Royal, and

---

[42] Certified copy of the court record included in letter of James Hume to Board of Customs Commissioners, May 19, 1773. Treasury 1, Bundle 501. The judges were Elisha Butler and Noble Jones.

[43] Anthony Stokes.

[44] Letter from customs officers at Charleston, S.C., to the Customs Commissioners, May 25, 1768. Treasury 1, Bundle 492.

[45] Letter of customs officers, Charleston, Feb. 8, 1769. *Ibid.*

Wynyaw.[46] There is no report of the arguments used or the tactics employed to bring about this change. George Roupell was collector at Charleston and Egerton Leigh was attorney general. These were the two gentlemen who were involved in the notorious attempts to rob Henry Laurens by the unfair seizure of his ships in 1768. The court had steadily refused to grant such writs for five years and finally, about April 8, 1773, it yielded. Apparently the writs were in the form demanded by the customs officers. It would be interesting to know whether the court yielded to political pressure or to legal argument. No minute of the court indicates the judges who approved the issue of the writ. It is strongly probable that the writs were issued by the chief justice alone, as that personage could hold sessions of the court without calling in assistant judges. A controversy of this type could not have been pending for nearly six years in a colony such as South Carolina without the full knowledge of the attorneys and other leading citizens of Charleston. There is reason to believe that the final issue of the writs was accomplished by patronage pressure on the court. It is known that Rawlins Lowndes had defied Chief Justice Thomas Knox Gordon on the bench in 1772 and was removed from the bench in 1773, and that four new assistant judges were installed between May 20, 1771, and April 23, 1772—a complete change in personnel.

Virginia

Our discussion of the writs in Virginia has been left to the last because the attempt to secure writs of assistance in that colony involved some of the most important issues in the entire controversy. Applications had been made for writs in this province as in all the others when directions were first received from the Commissioners of Customs. The supreme court took the matter under advisement and on April 29, 1769, directed that writs of assistance should be issued to the collectors and comptrollers of the customs districts of Accomac, South Potomac, Rappahannock River, York River, James River, lower district, and James River, upper district; and to the surveyor and searcher of Elizabeth and Nansemond River. Each officer is named in the court order and every port in

[46] Letter from Collector at Wynyaw, S.C., to the Customs Commissioners, April 15, 1773. Treasury 1, Bundle 501.

the colony is mentioned.[47] The order further states that these writs were "according to the Act of Parliament." John Randolph says that the writ as requested was strenuously opposed by the gentlemen of the bar but does not mention any names. Their objections were that the form of the writ did not conform to the provisions of the act of Parliament, that it was too general, that the law gave no authority to enter houses at night, and that such writs should be granted only upon oath. Randolph was directed to draft a proper writ, which he did.[48] No copy of this particular writ has come to light, but the customs officers apparently found it quite ineffectual and so reported it to their superiors at Boston. Evidently the Commissioners of Customs were far from satisfied with the form of the writ, for they transmitted a copy of it to the Lords of the Treasury in England with the comment that it appeared to them to be calculated "to impede and obstruct the execution of the Revenue Laws" in that province. Starke, advocate general for the vice-admiralty court in Virginia, characterized this writ as "no writ to the purpose of the Act of Parliament." [49]

The Treasury Board in England was evidently also much concerned by the action of the Virginia court in preparing its own writ instead of using the form supplied by the customs officers, and in stating that such writ was issued in accordance with the "Act of

[47] A copy of this, signed by Ben Walter, and attested by the customs officers, is included in the Commissioners of Customs correspondence. Treasury 1, Bundle 491.

[48] Letter from John Randolph to the Customs Commissioners, May 15, 1769: "Upon receipt of your favor of 21st March, inclosing the form of a Writ of Assistants, and the opinion of the Attorney General, shewing the legality of the same, I immediately laid them before our Supreme Court of Justice, which was then sitting; and moved that a similar Writ might be granted to those Officers of the Customs, whose names you mentioned in your Letter. The Gentlemen of our Bar very strenuously opposed the Motion, and insisted that the Writ sent was by no means conformable to the Act of Parliament; that its direction was too general, and ought to be regulated by the 32nd clause of the 14th Car. II; that the Act gave no authority to enter houses etc. in the night time; and that the Writ ought not to be a standing one, but granted from time to time, as the information of the Officer to the Supreme Court, on oath may render necessary. These observations at length prevailed, and the Court directed me to prepare a Writ agreeable to the words of the Act of Parliament, which was accordingly done, and approved of, a copy of which I thought proper to transmit to you." Gray, "Writs of Assistance," Quincy, *Reports,* p. 510. Gray states that he received a copy of this letter from Bancroft and that it was preserved in the State Paper Office in London. No such copy was found in Treasury 1. It is obviously genuine. A copy of this letter was sent to Lord Hillsborough by Governor Botetourt on May 16, 1769. The latter states that he was on the bench and concurred in the action of the court. *Ibid.*

[49] Letter to the Commissioners of Customs, May 17, 1772. Treasury 1, Bundle 491.

Parliament." Here was apparently a judicial defiance of a direction of the attorney general in England and a departure from the known practices of the Court of Exchequer. The Treasury Board transmitted the correspondence and a copy of the writ to the British attorney general for his opinion in the matter. It seems that the widespread legal objection to issuing the writs and the form proposed to be issued by the Virginia courts caused real alarm at the Treasury Office in London; hence it sought a solution of the whole question. The original letter to the attorney general and the opinion of the latter in the none-too-clear script of Edward Thurston is among the papers of the Customs Commissioners in the Treasury Bundles of the Public Record Office in London. It is so important in the entire controversy that the directly relevant sections are reproduced here.

BOARD OF CUSTOMS COMMISSIONERS

Boston

CASE submitted to the Attorney General in England.

Quotes Acts of Parliament

> 14 Charles II, ch. 11
> 7 and 8 William III, ch. 22
> 7 George III, ch. 46

Soon after this Act was passed into a law the officers of the customs in America applied to the Judges of the Superior Courts of Judicature in their respective provinces for general Writs of Assistants to be made use of as occassion should require, but most of the judges refused to grant such writs alledging that no information had been made to them of any special occassion for such writ, and unless such Information was made to them on oath they could not legally grant them, it being unconstitutional to lodge such a Writ in the hands of the officer which gave him unlimited power to act under it according to his own arbitrary Discretion.

The Refusal of the Judges being represented to the Lords of the Treasury, a case was laid before the late Attorney General De Grey, who was of opinion that the Superior Courts of Justice in America were bound by the 7th Geo. 3rd to issue such Writs of Assistants as the Court of Exchequer in England issues in similar Cases to the Officers of Customs.

The copy of Case and Opinion herewith, Icy'd marked No. 1. [This is the opinion of Attorney General De Grey.]

This Opinion being transmitted to the Commissioners of the Customs in America, together with the form of a Writ of Assistants as issued by the Court of Exchequer in England (a Copy of which is herewith Icy'd marked No. 2) the said Commissioners caused applications to be again made to the Superior Courts of Justice for similar Writs but some of them still refuse to grant a Writ of Assistants without an information on oath of some special occasion for such Writ. In a letter from the Attorney Genl in Virginia to the sollicitor of the Customs at Boston Marked No. 3. Also the form of a Writ of Assistants as prepared to be granted by the Superior Courts in Virginia (Marked No. 4) also an extract of a letter from the Collector and Comptroller of Pocomoke to the Commissioners of the Customs, Marked No. 5.

As the writ thus proposed to be granted appears to be rather calculated to impede and obstruct than to facilitate the Execution of the Revenue Laws a Copy thereof together with the Letters before mentioned were transmitted by the Said Commr's of Customs to the Lords of the Treasury who have been pleased to direct this letter to lay the said several papers before Mr. Attorney General for his Opinion of the following Querie.

Q——What measures are proper to be taken to oblige such of the Superior Courts of Justice in America as have refused so to do to grant Writs of Assistants according to the directions of the said Act of the 7th Geor. 3rd and agreeable to the Opinion of the Attorney General, and also whether it may be proper and what measures to oblige the Supreme Court of Justice in Virginia to grant the Writs agreeable to the Form used in His Majesty's Court of Exchequer in England in view of that which they have proposed to grant.

Answer [in the cramped style of the attorney general]

I know of no direct and effective means in the ordinary course of Law to compel the Judge of Chief Courts in the Colonies to award the Writ of Assistance according to the exigence of the Acts of 7 & 8 Wm 3 and 7 G 3. For tho in the form of their constitution they are not sovereign Courts yet as they are not within the body of the realm no mandamus will be to control them. It has been usual for the Privy Council to issue orders of this sort, but it is not obvious how that jurisdiction is founded; or what consequence would follow upon disobedience to such orders. Upon a case of obstinate and contumacious refusal to execute an English Act of Parliament, I apprehend the Judges might be impeached, But this is a measure of punishment out of controll.

The Supreme Court of Virginia seems to have proceeded upon a meer mistake of the law. They have issued an illegal warrant, proceeded on an obsolete law, the 12 C 2 c 19; at the same time refusing to issue a lawful one on 13th C 2 c 11 not observing as it would seem, that the first Act has a different object, and proceeds by different means. These were found useless and inconvenient, and to remedy the mischief, the second act was made on which the present Writ of Assistance in England is founded. This kind of authority has been in constant use above a century, has often been recognized and confirmed by judicial decisions; and it seems strange indeed, that any judge in the colonies should think the laws of the mother too harsh for the temper of American Liberty. I am therefore enclined to suppose that they proceed upon a meer mistake of the Law.

E. THURSTON
31 Aug. 1771 [50]

The attorney general in this case was charitable enough to assume that the Virginia judges had made a mistake in interpreting the law. He admitted that the British legal practice had no machinery by which courts in the colonies could be mandated by courts in England. Remedies lay only along lines of actual coercion if they chose to be recalcitrant, and, as the attorney general said, action in such cases was not a matter of the law.

On receipt of this reply, the Customs Commissioners directed the customs officers in Virginia to renew their application to the chief justice "for a proper Writ of Assistance instead of that already granted by him and acquaint us with the results of their application." [51] These applications were supported by copies of the acts of Parliament, the opinion of Attorney General De Grey, and the specific opinion of Attorney General Thurston on the Virginia form of writ. It was an even clearer attempt to overawe a colonial court than was the De Grey opinion in the Pennsylvania case.

The results are best stated in the letters of the customs officers to their Boston superiors. The collector at Accomac reported that:

Agreeable to your letter of November last we together with other officers made application for Writs of Assistants to the Supreme Court but were refused them for the same reasons as were given before (Viz.) that application must be made for them every time we have occassion for them and not for general Writs of Assistants.[52]

A year later the collector at James River, lower part, reported:

In obedience to your commands of the 20th November last we have again made application to our Superior Court for Writs of Assistants,

---

[50] Original in Treasury 1, Bundle 501.

[51] Letter of the Board of Customs Commissioners, Jan. 15, 1772. Treasury 1, Bundle 492.

[52] Letter to the Board, April 27, 1772. Treasury 1, Bundle 501.

(at the same time the Form of the Writ granted by the Court of Exchequer in England together with the Attorney General's opinion thereon being laid before them by the Attorney General here) but without success they inflexibly adhere to their former opinion, and desired we would not again trouble them on the subject.[53]

The collector at Rappahannock reported the affair in the following form:

At a General Court held at the Capital April 24, 1773 His Majesty's Attorney General in behalf of the collectors and Comptrollers of His Majesty's Customs in this colony again moved the Court to grant the said officers Writs of Assistants agreeable to the Form transmitted to him by the Commissioners of the Customs in America but the Court overruled the motion being of opinion that the Writs of Assistants by this court on the fifth of May 1769 is the proper Writ of Assistants warranted by the Statutes to be granted them.[54]

Attorney General John Randolph reported the failure in these words:

I have moved the Court for a Writ of Assistants, agreeable to the Desire of the Commissioners of the Customs, and according to the Form of the Writ said by the Attorney General of England to be practiced there, but they have positively refused it and declared that they can allow no other Writ, than such a one as was settled upon a former occassion agreeable to our Act of Assembly. I despair of even obtaining what is wished for.[55]

Of all the colonies, Virginia appears to be the one where the issue over writs of assistance was most stubbornly fought. It was the largest and most populous colony and had more ports of entry than any other. The appearance of all the customs officials at the capital at one time, accompanied by the attorney general, could not have failed to attract attention. The judges moved in the foremost social circle; the attorney general was a brother of Peyton Randolph and was related to the most prominent families; and the lawyers of the colony had taken an active part in forcing the first decision.

A session of a court in Virginia was always a matter of public interest. The issue was raised in 1769, 1772, and 1773. Randolph

---

[53] Letter to the Board, April 24, 1773. *Ibid.*

[54] Letter of Cary Nicoll to the Board, Nov. 17, 1773. *Ibid.*

[55] Letter to Cary Nicoll, included in the latter's letter to the Board, Nov. 17, 1773. *Ibid.*

knew that the decision of the court in 1769 had been transmitted to England and it is probable that it was known to others. The tone of the complaints of the customs officers and the judge advocate of the vice-admiralty court clearly indicates that they had discussed their unsatisfactory writs rather widely. The renewed demand, the special report of Attorney General Thurston, and the final very positive refusal to grant general writs, with the court admonition that it did not wish to be troubled further in the matter, all indicate that this colony had been made the crucial battleground on this issue. What happened in Massachusetts is tame compared with the struggle in Virginia. Here was an unyielding, unanimous court, convinced as to the soundness of its legal position and refusing to be moved from that position by argument, threats, or the most impressive array of legal opinion from England. In this struggle John Randolph played an unusual role. As attorney general he had to make the public motions in open court. In obedience to the directions of the court he had drafted the form of the writ authorized in 1769 and approved by the governor of the colony. It is difficult to believe that he favored the issue of writs in the form submitted to him, although he was a Tory and ultimately joined the émigrés in England. It is not unreasonable to infer that it must have been an unhappy experience for him to appear before the court repeatedly to move the judges to issue a writ different from the one which he himself had drawn and which the British attorney general had characterized as based upon ignorance of the law.

The issues thus raised were not easily allayed, and Virginia became the leader of the movement to prohibit forever the use of general warrants and unreasonable searches. These were first condemned by the Virginia Bill of Rights on June 12, 1776, and were reflected in the clauses of the Declaration of Independence denouncing the King because he had made judges dependent upon his will alone for their tenure and their salaries. The one practical result of this dependence was the effort to compel judges to grant writs of assistance in a prescribed form. The leadership of Virginia in outlawing general warrants and unreasonable searches was quickly followed by Pennsylvania on September 28, and by Maryland on November 11, 1776. North Carolina joined the procession on December 18 of the same year, while Massachusetts did not join the movement until 1780 and New Hampshire followed in 1784.[56]

It took courage for judges to refuse writs of assistance when demanded by the customs officers, since they held their commissions at the will of the Crown and were dependent for their salaries upon the revenues collected by the Customs Commissioners. Detailed reports were required of the customs officers as to the success of every application to a court or to a judge for writs. In no other case were courts watched so narrowly. Abstracts of court records were demanded and received. Private conversation was recorded at once in writing. Thus every attorney general and every judge knew that his rulings and opinions would be reported directly to the Customs Commissioners. They must also have known that any reported failure on their part to coöperate with the customs officers would be transmitted to England. They faced the possibility that they might at any time be deprived of their positions by royal order and have their pay reduced or stopped entirely. They must have also known that compliance on their part might be rewarded by preferment and possibly by increases in salary. It does not seem improbable that such possibilities were presented to them orally, although no written records verifying this assumption have come to light. In the face of such formidable pressure from official sources it is surprising that the judiciary from Connecticut to Florida, with one exception, stood firm in opposing the legality of the particular form of writ demanded of them and continued in their judicial obstinacy through six years of nearly constant efforts to force them to yield.

This unsung record of courage and fidelity to what they believed to be the law of the land must be considered in any appraisal of the colonial judiciary. The courts had nothing to gain and everything to lose by the course they pursued. A young lawyer in Boston, who was seeking to build up a practice, might acquire reputation and clients by appearing publicly in opposition to a motion before the court to grant general writs; but the judges in the colonies to the south could expect no such reward. Acting in private in most cases, they received no public plaudits. Their only reward was that of having decided a troublesome question of law in accordance with the best British practice.

[56] Poore, *Charters and Constitutions.*

The unanimity of the action of the courts south of Massachusetts is surprising, especially when one considers that there was no newspaper publicity and no reported public agitation. It was not a matter of politics. Tory judges were just as determined opponents of general writs as were their Whig associates. The evidence indicates that the outbreak of the Revolutionary War alone averted efforts to secure judicial changes that would have forced American judges to comply with the official British interpretation of law. The efforts to overrule the judges in Virginia have already been commented upon. The persistence and tenacity with which the Commissioners of Customs pursued their campaign for general writs indicate their determination to see the matter through, even though it required changes in the judicial system. In this they were not acting on their own initiative, but were under constant pressure from England. The American determination to keep the courts free from executive control grows in no small degree out of this experience.

Labor and Mercantilism in
The Revolutionary Era

RICHARD B. MORRIS

TO DISCOVER the reason for the introduction during the American Revolution of a system of controls for the regulation of commodities and labor services we must first ascertain the climate of economic practice and opinion in which the program evolved.[1] The labor problem was only one phase of the general problem of economic regulation under mercantilism, and a study of the labor codes apart from these general controls would serve to give to labor matters a false emphasis for that time and place. Mercantilism in England may be said to have rested upon two main pillars—the Acts of Trade and the Tudor labor statutes. The first provided for the external regulation and control of foreign trade and the subordination of colonial interests to those of the mother country.[2] The second comprised the industrial code and, as the chief of a goodly number of internal economic controls which characterized mercantilist policy, patterned colonial legislation and administrative practice.

The economic practices which prevailed in the American colonies in the seventeenth century combined medieval town regula-

[1] Grateful acknowledgment is due the Social Science Research Council for a grant-in-aid which made possible the completion of this study. The writer also wishes to express his indebtedness to Professor Eli F. Heckscher, of the University of Stockholm, for valued suggestions, and to three former students, Lester Jashnoff, of the New York bar, Jonathan Grossman, and Martin Kleinbard.

[2] For consideration of the effects of this program the reader is referred to pp. 2–39. Certain mercantilist legislation affecting colonial labor, such as the Hat Act, could be paralleled by internal English regulations such as the statute of 2 and 3 Philip and Mary, c. 11, providing that country weavers could keep only one loom and city weavers two, and by English guild regulations limiting the number of apprentices which a master might have. The courts tended to disregard such limitations. See Highamshire v. Baskin, 12 Mod. 46 (1693).

tions and centralizing mercantilist trends. Because of the absence of any effective colonial unification, mercantilism as a system of internal regulation for the strengthening of the national economy never attained in colonial life a fullness of vigor comparable with that in the mother country, where town regulatory activity was in the course of time subordinated to a broad national policy,[3] best exemplified in legislation such as the Statute of Artificers (1563) and the Tudor and Stuart Poor Laws. Typical urban regulations, such as those sustaining craft monopolies, were imported into some colonies for but a brief period, although by means of regulation of admission to the freemanship the colonial towns were long able to check competition in crafts and retail trades. While the local guild system was not successfully re-created at the time of settlement, regulations against forestalling, engrossing, and regrating, and local assizes of bread were vigorously enforced. In a number of the colonies, notably Massachusetts Bay, Connecticut, Pennsylvania, Maryland, Virginia, and Barbados, labor codes were adopted shortly after settlement. Maximum wage scales were in some instances laid down by enactment; in others, left to the discretion of local officials. These followed the general lines of the Tudor labor code. Except in New England, the labor codes seem to have been largely paper instruments that were soon abandoned. In the Bay colony the wage-fixing experiment extended well into the last quarter of the seventeenth century. The colonial poor laws, patterned closely upon the Tudor and Stuart models, on the other hand, enjoyed a longer life.

[3] Thus, it had been the aim of European mercantilists such as Colbert to abolish local tolls and tariffs impeding national trade. This could not be accomplished in the colonies, where towns as well as provinces could levy import duties (for example, Norfolk, Va., Common Council Minutes, f. 32 [1746] and colonies could prohibit the exportation of such staples as corn. See *South Carolina Gazette*, May 24, 1773; *Georgia Gazette*, Dec. 24, 1766; *Ga. Col. Rec.*, XII, 212 (1772). Typical Revolutionary legislation restricting exportation: act of 1776, authorizing the governor, with the advice of the council, to forbid by proclamation the exportation of articles deemed expedient to be kept within the state. *Session Laws of Connecticut, 1776*, p. 422; cf. also resolutions of 1777, *Journal of the Provincial Congress of New York*, I, 900, 975, 1077, 1084, 1089; *Delaware Council Minutes*, pp. 39, 40; MS, Archives of Maryland, Aug. 1, 1775; *Revolutionary Records of Georgia*, I, 310, 312, 325. Furthermore, the power over roads conferred on colonial county courts by statute might be used to impede traffic and trade, as it was used when a Virginia county court granted license to erect gates on a public highway; affirmed in King v. Harrison, Jefferson Reports 51 (1737).

In the eighteenth century one should not expect to find a repetition in practice or in theory of the same pattern, as that phase of mercantilism which dealt with internal centralizing regulation was in fairly general disrepute in the mother country by that time. In England the country justices seldom levied wage assessments, and a cumulative trend toward *laissez faire* was observable in the decisions of the central courts of common law, although there was no consistency in judicial practice. While this trend of the courts materially weakened the foundations, it did not topple the mercantilist labor structure, for through the enactment of maximum wage legislation in a number of industries and by means of the outlawry as criminal conspiracy of strikes in specific trades Parliament maintained effective controls over labor.

Turning to the more immediate background of economic practice, it is to be observed that by the eve of the Revolution the conflict in the colonies between *laissez faire* and mercantilism was becoming sharper, although in England *laissez faire* principles had by that time gained a much surer foothold. In the colonies both schools of economic thought had their adherents, and policy and practice in labor matters were marked by divided loyalties. Major evidence of *laissez faire* trends may be noted at this time. In the first place, the comprehensive wage codes had disappeared. In the second place, there was a reluctance on the part of the colonial authorities at that late date to maintain craft monopolies. This was apparent in the failure to protect local craftsmen against interlopers. Thus, in 1747 the New York authorities refused to intervene to prevent outside building-trades employees from working in New York.[4] They failed to act upon a similar request in 1769.[5] In the southern towns the problem was viewed from a different angle. There the authorities made vigorous efforts to protect white craftsmen and traders from Negro competition. The white artificers had their own monopolistic interests to main-

---

[4] "Burghers and Freemen of New York," in N. Y. Hist. Soc., *Collections* (1885), pp. 507–11; *N.Y. Calendar of Council Minutes*, p. 363.

[5] *Minutes of the Common Council*, VII, 177. In Massachusetts the law requiring strangers planning to start in trade in Boston to secure a license from the town clerk was renewed down through the Revolution (*Massachusetts Acts and Resolves*, V, 39, 88, 259, 460, 903, 1123), and during the first quarter of the century such permission was not infrequently withheld. *Boston Town Rec.*, XIII, 31, 33. But see *ibid.*, p. 202.

tain in the face of severe competition by Negro slaves farmed out at low wages as mechanics. In order to ensure a goodly supply of white workmen it was necessary for the authorities in the southern towns to maintain sufficient economic inducements.[6] But in this they were not successful. In Charleston the problem was critical. In 1744 a number of shipwrights of that town petitioned the legislature for relief on the ground that they were reduced to poverty owing to competition from Negroes in the shipbuilding industry. The master shipwrights opposed the workers, however. Apparently more affluent masters who employed slaves were the dissenters, as they retorted that

Industry and a more frugal way of life [would cure the ills complained of and] that many times they have refused to work at all, or if obliged to it by necessity only on Extravagant wages, That his Majesty's Ships have been repaired and refitted only by the assistance of Our slaves, And that without these Slaves the worst Consequences might Ensue, his Majesty's Ships may remain by the Walls at their discretion: Merchants who are bound by Charter party to load Vessels within a limitted time may be drawn into heavy demurrage, And no Merch[t] can have it in their power for the delivery of his rice, whilst such Men have it in their power to take or refuse work upon their own terms. That there is business enough for three times the number of Carpenters, That the Complaints were with no other View than to Engross the whole Trade into their own hands and thereby to have it in their power to make their own price.

A committee of the assembly reported it as their opinion "that the number of Negroes hired out, without a proportion of white men to do the business of ship-wrights or ship carpenters, is a discouragem[t] to white men of that business of ship-wrights." It further recommended that a bill be enacted for "the ascertaining of wages for Ship-wrights, as well white men as Negroes." Both recommendations for limitation of Negroes in the industry and for wage regulation were unanimously agreed to.[7] It is thus clear that while the assembly wished to control the craft for the benefit of the white

[6] In Virginia restrictions were placed on the entry of Negroes into retail trades. Elizabeth City County O.B., 1684–99, f. 11 (1693); Norfolk Common Council Mins., f. 96 (1764), f. 128 (1773), f. 161 (1783). As late as 1786 Norfolk had to consider regulating the hiring out of slaves in the town. *Ibid.*, fols. 189, 190. For North Carolina see New Bern Town Rec., 1797–1825, fols. 7, 46, 47, 151.

[7] South Carolina Assembly Journal, 1743–44, fols. 159, 160 (Jan. 25, 1744); S.C. Council Journal, 1744, fols. 6–9 (Jan. 18, 1744).

mechanics it had, at the same time, no desire to be faced with strikes and excessive wage demands, and in the latter point it yielded to the masters.[8] Despite a similar proposal later in the year, the interests of the employer class prevented passage of such a bill.[9] The failure of the legislature to act left the matter up to the town, which in 1751 declared in sweeping language "that no Inhabitant of Charleston shall be permitted to keep more than two male Slaves, to work out for Hire, as Porters, Labourers, Fishermen or Handicraftsmen." [10] The *Gazette* of October 29–November 5, 1763, reported that Negro chimney sweepers were competing with the whites and actually "had the insolence, by a combination amongst themselves, to raise the usual prices, and to refuse doing their work, unless their exorbitant demands are complied with. . . . Surely, these are evils that require some attention to suppress." The agreements of 1769 against the importation of Negro slaves were inspired apparently by a strong and unanimous stand of the mechanics, reinforced by some planters and merchants.[11] The manufacture of candles and soap was opposed on the ground that the business was handled entirely by Negroes working at night as well as by day.[12] In Georgia, legislation preventing the employment of Negroes and other slaves in the handicraft trades was enacted in 1758, and three years later a statute was passed prohibiting the inhabitants from hiring any Spaniards.[13] In West Florida, on the other hand, British army officers seemed to have been able in 1767 to bring down considerably the rate of wages of artificers en-

[8] A reading of the text indicates that a bill to determine wages was recommended—not, as Jernegan suggests, to make "an inquiry." *Laboring and Dependent Classes in Colonial America* (Chicago, 1931), p. 21. "Ascertain" was at that time used synonymously with "fix," as in *Conn. State Rec.*, I, 595 (Providence Convention).

[9] S.C. Assembly Journal, fols. 332–34.

[10] *S.C. Gazette*, May 6, 1751.

[11] *S.C. Gazette*, July 6, 27, Dec. 21, 28, 1769; Jan. 25, 1770.

[12] *S.C. Gazette*, Oct. 31, 1774. Time after time Charleston grand juries complained of Negroes being farmed out to do the work of artificers and of their irregularly selling produce and engaging in unfair trade practices. *S.C. Gazette*, March 23–30, 1734; Oct. 29–Nov. 4, 1737; Jan. 25, 1770; March 24, 1773; Oct. 31, 1774; May 31, 1777. In the post-Revolutionary period further drastic ordinances were adopted to no avail. *Gazette of the State of S.C.*, Dec. 11, 1783. Restrictions were placed on the number of Negro servants that one might keep (debated in *Columbian Herald,* July 31, and *Gazette of the State of S.C.*, Aug. 3, 1786). See also ordinances of 1796 and 1800, *Charleston Ordinances*, pp. 164, 193, 194.

[13] *Ga. Col. Rec.*, XIII, 276, 620.

gaged for the army by employing Negroes for certain tasks—a policy directly opposed to local sentiment as expressed in legislation, although not successfully carried out in practice.[14]

As restrictions against interlopers disappear, there is to be noted a corresponding trend toward the elimination of rigid craft differences. For example, in Massachusetts attempts were made in 1731 and 1732 to renew seventeenth-century regulations preventing butchers, curriers, and shoemakers from pursuing the "mystery" of tanners. This move was unsuccessful.[15] In the crafts, freedom of enterprise meant freedom for the domestic system of manufactures to develop despite the opposition of some workers and craftsmen. In 1772 "a Number of Weavers and Inhabitants" of Somerset County, New Jersey, petitioned the legislature for a law "to prohibit Farmers and others keeping Looms in their Houses, and following the Weaving Business." In defense of this practice, a large number of freeholders and others from Somerset, Morris, Hunterdon, and Cape May counties petitioned against the enactment of such a law or against a similar proposal to prevent private persons from tanning their own leather. Apparently in deference to the views of the farmers, the legislature took no action.[16]

Thirdly, further evidence of *laissez faire* trends, and closely connected with the failure to guard against interlopers, is the general relaxation of the rigid apprenticeship prerequisites. In some cities it would appear that, once a man had been admitted to the freedom of the city after having served an apprenticeship, he apparently could and did freely transfer to other crafts or trades if he wished.[17] Furthermore, the authorities at this time seem to have been reluctant to enforce the apprenticeship requirement. When, in December, 1771, five tanners petitioned the New Jersey assembly, praying for an act to regulate tanning of leather, "and causing all Persons who, in Future, shall follow that Business, to serve an

[14] C. E. Carter, ed., *Correspondence of General Thomas Gage* (New Haven, 1933), II, 405, 434.

[15] *Mass. Acts and Resolves*, I, 312, 313; *Journal of the House of Representatives*, X, 43; XI, 159.

[16] Notes of New Jersey assembly, Sept. 3, 1772; Nov. 1, 12, 17, 18, 23, 1772, New Jersey State Library. For the advocacy of home manufacture of linen see *The New American Magazine* (July, 1758).

[17] S. McKee, Jr., *Labor in Colonial New York 1664–1776* (New York, 1935), p. 44.

Apprenticeship thereto," a motion to introduce such a bill was tabled.[18] The relative ease with which the freemanship could be obtained in colonial towns on the eve of the Revolution testifies to the breakdown of restrictions on practicing the crafts or engaging in retail activities.[19]

In pursuing this program the colonial authorities were following English official practice. The English courts on the eve of the American Revolution encouraged the rise of a free labor market and large-scale industry, maintaining that "trade ought to be free and not restrained," [20] but even at that late date they did not hew to the line of logic and consistency in favoring freedom in the crafts or in curtailing the powers of craft and trade monopolies.[21]

[18] Notes of New Jersey assembly, Dec. 10, 1771.

[19] A Boston pamphlet of 1714 protested against proposed incorporation of the town, objecting to "paying for our Freedom, that was Free-born and in bondage to no man," and also to the possibility that shopkeepers and artisans who were undertaking several trades would have to give up the practice. N. Mathews, Jr., "Attempts to Incorporate Boston," Col. Soc. of Mass., *Publications*, X, 345–56. See also *Boston Town Rec., passim.*

New Haven admissions, in general, show a big increase beginning around 1742. Town Records, 1684–1765, e. g., fols. 461, 463, 469, 490, 497, *passim.* By an act of the common council of New York City of 1762 those unable to pay the fee for admission to the freedom were admitted without cost (*Mins. Com. Council*, V, 326)—a practice which had prevailed in the mayor's court of that city for many years before that date. See, e. g., admission of Potter (1721), *Select Cases of the Mayor's Court of New York City, 1674–1784*, ed. by R. B. Morris (Washington, D.C., 1935), p. 178, where a former servant was made a freeman "Gratis being a Poor Man." As a result, barriers to the freedom were virtually removed, and it is reported that in 1765, in one day alone, 216 inhabitants took up their freedom in the mayor's court. New York *Mercury*, Oct. 7, 1765. For Albany freedoms purchased in 1781 see Munsell, *Annals of Albany*, X, 153.

As early as 1677 one Thomas Hooten, remarking on monopolistic trends in Burlington, West Jersey, stated that "if it be not made free . . . as to the customs and government, then it will not be so well, and may hinder many that have desires to come." Samuel Smith, *History of the Colony of Nova-Caesaria* (Burlington, 1765; repr. Trenton, 1877), p. 105.

In Philadelphia the bars were let down early. Thus, between April 16 and May 27, 1717, 426 persons were admitted to the freedom, including laborers and a variety of artificers. *Mins. Com. Council of Philadelphia*, pp. 117–35. Shortly thereafter town craftsmen objected to nonqualified strangers coming into the town and exercising their trades. The council advised those trades seeking incorporation, including the tailors and cordwainers, to secure legal counsel with a view to preparing an ordinance for that purpose agreeable to the laws of both England and the province. *Ibid.*, pp. 145–47 (1718).

[20] See R. B. Morris, "Criminal Conspiracy and Early Labor Combinations in New York," *Pol. Science Quarterly*, LII, 69.

[21] As to the first matter, in Darcy v. Allin, Noy Rep. 173–85 (1603), the court endorsed the view that "to restrain men from any lawful trade whereunto they are inclined is unnatural and unmeet." Tolley's Case (1615) appears to establish the rule

More than a hint of *laissez faire* may be found in a speech of Governor Johnstone of West Florida in 1767 before the legislature sitting in Pensacola. He uged that trade be unrestrained and "that the prices of all things may ever continue free, at the option of the buyer and the seller without any of those unjust restraints which have ever defeated the purpose for which they have been enacted." [22]

Granted the rising tide of *laissez faire*, it is nonetheless true that on the eve of the Revolution economic regulation was a vital factor in colonial life and was evidenced in a number of widespread and deeply rooted practices. (1) The towns licensed certain quasi-public functionaries, such as porters, carmen, millers, smiths, chimney sweepers, gravediggers, and others, whose wages were customarily set by the licensing body. [23] (2) The prices of necessaries and public

---

that once a freeman of London had been lawfully apprenticed to certain trades for the required period, he might under the custom of London lawfully relinquish such trades and take up others. R. H. Tawney and E. Power, *Tudor Economic Documents* (London, 1924), III, 378–83. Much later Mansfield in Raynard v. Chase, 1 Burr. 2 (1756), indicated sympathy with the move to relax the requirements of the Statute of Artificers. But one should not conclude that the courts abandoned their control over crafts and trade. Even in the 18th century they respected corporation charters based upon immemorial custom and local rights while dealing cavalierly with those based on royal grant. In Hutchinson v. Player, 1 O. Bridgman 272 (1663), the court upheld the regulatory powers of the London city council over the wholesale trade in broadcloth, and by way of dictum Sir Orlando Bridgman insisted that prices of imported commodities must be regulated lest "every man turn adventurer." As late as 1790 Lord Loughborough, in Butchers Co. v. Morey, 1 Hen. Bl. 371, upheld the validity of craft by-laws regulating, not alone those exercising the trade who were members of the company, but also those who were not. On the other hand, after the Commonwealth period, such types of control as engrossing, forestalling, and regrating regulations were not the primary concern of the central courts until the revival under Lord Kenyon.

[22] *Georgia Gazette*, May 11, 1767.
[23] R. B. Morris and J. Grossman, "The Regulation of Wages in Early Massachusetts," *New England Quarterly*, XI, 498; *Mass. Acts and Resolves*, II, 487, 830, 831, 1067, 1068; IV, 606–8; V, 88, 460, 1121, 1123; *Boston Town Rec.*, VIII, 58, 63, 82, 83, 295, 296; XI, 196, 197; XIII, 51; XIV, 248, 311, 312, 321, 322. In 1717 a bill was proposed in the Massachusetts legislature to regulate the price of shoes. *Journal of the House of Representatives*, I, 225. For the regulation of the wages of carmen in New York City see R. B. Morris, "Criminal Conspiracy and Early Labor Combinations," *loc. cit.*, LII, 61, 62. In Philadelphia the rates of carters were customarily set. *Mins. Common Council of Philadelphia*, pp. 20, 147, 164. Virginia regulated smiths as early as 1660. Henings, *Statutes*, II, 11. As late as 1793 Norfolk, Va., regulated porters and laborers (Norfolk Common Council Mins., f. 293), and Charleston as late as 1801 established rates of wages for porters, for day laborers engaged in porterage, and for carting and loading, providing twenty lashes for any slave who demanded or received greater wages and a fine not exceeding five dollars from any freeman.

services were regulated, most consistently the assize of bread; the price of boards at the sawmill was set, as was the rate for grinding corn at gristmills and the legal fare which could be charged on ferries.[24] A South Carolina statute of 1749 advanced a good mercantilist argument for the assize of bread—the protection of the "poorer sort of people." [25] Furthermore, it was the general practice

---

The hours for labor were set "from sun rise to twilight in the evening, allowing one hour for breakfast, and one hour for dinner; except the months of June, July, August, and September, when two hours shall be allowed for dinner." *Charleston Ordinances*, pp. 217, 224. A Georgia act of 1774 empowered commissioners to regulate the hiring of slaves as porters and laborers in Savannah and set maximum allowances or wages to the slaveowners as follows: (1) for porter's work in Savannah, 1s. 6d. per diem, hours from daybreak until dark, allowing the slave a half-hour for breakfast and an hour for dinner; (2) for work on board ship, 2s. per diem, the owner to furnish provisions to his slave; (3) for porterage of bundles, casks, etc., 3d. per load; (4) "for all kind of work not herein particularly ascertained in proportion to the rates herein before mentioned." *Georgia Gazette*, March 30, 1774.

24 Assize of bread: see *Boston Town Rec.*, XI, XIII, XV, XVII, *passim*; Mass. Archives, CXX, f. 132. In Rhode Island the town councils were empowered to set the rate monthly. Act of 1707, Rider, *Laws of R.I.* (1719), p. 59; act of 1763, *Public Laws of R.I.* (revision of 1767), p. 23. For New York see R. B. Morris, "Criminal Conspiracy and Early Labor Combinations," *loc. cit.*, pp. 62–67; for Albany, Munsell, *Coll. Hist. of Albany*, I, 95, 99, 227, 298. The Pennsylvania practice of setting the price and weight of bread goes back very early. Scharf, *Hist. of Philadelphia*, III, 2297. A notable act of 1722, providing that the prices of beer and ale were to be set by the justices in the counties or by the mayor, recorder, and aldermen of Philadelphia, specifically authorized that "all the laws and statutes of that part of Great Britain, called England, shall be put in execution against all such combinations and evil practices, [as advancing prices of grain and provisions unduly] so that offenders shall be brought to the like punishments, and incur the same penalties, as those laws and statutes direct." Dallas, *Laws of Pennsylvania*, I, 170, 171. The act of 2 and 3 Edw. VI, c. 15, aimed primarily at combinations to keep up the prices charged consumers, would clearly be applicable under this statute.

In Wilmington, Del., the assize of bread was part of a general market code drawn up in 1740. Wilmington Mins. In Norfolk and other southern towns the assize was levied far beyond the Revolutionary period. Norfolk Common Council Mins., fols. 65–67 (1756), 73 (1758), 92 (1763), 217–19 (1788), 311 (1795).

Ferry rates set: Massachusetts: Hampshire Mins., 1728/9–35, fols. 53, 149 (1730, 1732); Rhode Island: *R.I. Col. Rec.*, IX, 171, 568; Pennsylvania: West Chester QS, 1733–42, f. 111 (1737); Virginia: Caroline O.B., 1777–80, f. 164 (1779); North Carolina County Courts: Brunswick, 1782–86 (1783); Chatham, 1774–91 (1776); Edgecomb, 1772–84 (1778, 1780, 1782, 1783); New Hanover, 1779–92 (1782, 1783); Richmond, 1779–85 (1779); Tryon, 1769–79 (1771); Tyrrell, 1783–88 (1783). For indictment of John T. Brock "for extortion in his ferriage," see Bucks, Pa., QS and CP, 1688–1730 (1690).

25 *Stat. of S.C.*, III, 715. Throughout the middle of the century the monthly assize of flour and bread was regularly set in Charleston—a practice which continued without apparent interruption during the Revolution. See files of *S.C. Gazette*, *passim*. In 1773 the Charleston District Grand Jury presented as a grievance the lack of enforcement of requirements for stamping of loaves with the names of the bakers and for the inspection of weights by the magistrates (*S.C. Gazette*, May 24,

to regulate the prices of liquors, foods, and lodging to be charged in taverns and ordinaries.[26] Even more comprehensive price scales

---

1773), and an enactment in 1774 made specific provisions to correct this breach (*ibid.*, Nov. 21, 1774). Ordinances regulating the price of bread and flour were enacted in Charleston as late as 1795. *Charleston Ordinances*, pp. 28, 40, 58, 125–28. See also *Columbian Herald*, Sept. 18, 1786.

For regulation in Savannah see *Georgia Gazette*, April 21, 1763; and for the assize of bread, *ibid.*, Sept. 27, 1764, 1768–69, *passim; Ga. Col. Rec.*, XVI, 310. West Florida under British rule also provided for the assize of bread. Act of Dec. 28, 1767.

However, by 1792 *laissez faire* arguments advanced by bakers in Boston and Philadelphia for discontinuance of such regulation were to prove effective. See Dunlap's *American Daily Advertiser*, April 4, 1793; R. C. Bull, "The Constitutional Significance of Early Pennsylvania Price-fixing Legislation," *Temple Law Quarterly*, XI, 318, 319.

26 In the southern colonies and Delaware this may be said to have been the most consistent phase of price regulation carried on by the county or sessions courts right through the Revolutionary period. In Revolutionary Delaware, for example, the court not only specified the legal rate for food, drink, and lodging, but specified that for "a good Bed with clean Sheets" the rate per night would be considerably higher than for common lodging. Breakfast, dinner, and supper rates also varied with the fare offered. Newcastle Gen. Sess. Mins., 1778–93, f. 33 (1778), 148 (1781), 168 (1782). See also *Council of Delaware Mins.*, pp. 116, 117, 122. In Maryland a dinner meant "A good hot Dyet with clean Table Linnen and a pint of small Beer or Syder," for which the sum of 1s.3d. was set, or "Victualls fresh and hath not eaten of before that is Roasted boyld or baked with wheat bread and small beer or Cyder." The rates rose sharply during Revolutionary times. See, e. g., Baltimore County Court, Lib.D., 1682–86 (1684); 1772–80 (1777, 1780); Ann Arundel County Court, 1720–21, f. 417 (1721); Charles County Court, 1696–98, f. 51 (1696); 1704–10, f. 7 (1704); 1734–38, f. 220 (1736), 366, 721 (1737); Prince George County Court, Lib. B., 1699–1705, f. 229 (1702); 1746–47, f. 17 (1746); Somerset County Court, 1722–24, f. 140 (1723); 1740–42, f. 144 (1741); Talbot County Court, Lib. AB, No. 8, f. 472 (1698); Queen Ann County Court, 1709–16 (1715); 1718–19 (1719); 1735–39 (1736, 1738); 1740–41 (1741); Cecil County Court, 1723–30 (1723).

Virginia: York O.B., 1706–10, f. 211 (1709); 1774–84, f. 260 (1780), 417 (1783); Yorktown Hustings Court Mins., 1787–93, f. 5 (1787); Accomac O.B., 1777–80, f. 40 (1777), 179 (1778); 1780–83 (1780); Henrico O.B., 1677–92, f. 32 (1678); Middlesex O.B., 1772–82, f. 61 (1773); f. 314 (1774), 402 (1775), 544 (1780), 573 (1781), 611 (1782); Fairfax O.B., 1772–74, f. 19 (1772); Spotsylvania O.B., 1730–38, f. 24 (1730), 379 (1735); Caroline O.B., 1777–80, f. 66 (1778); Cumberland O.B., 1749–51, fols. 49, 253 (1750, 1751); Fincastle O.B., 1773–77 (1774). The Botetourt County Court assessed a rate of 6d. for lodging in clean sheets, one in a bed; 3d. 3 farthings for two in a bed, and *nothing for more than two in a bed!* O.B., 1770–71, pt. I, f. 9 (1770).

North Carolina County Courts: Bertie, 1724–69 (1736, 1758, 1761); 1767–72 (1770); 1772–77 (1775); 1778–92 (1779, 1780); Bute, 1767–76, f. 130 (1770), 181 (1771), 230 (1772), 344 (1775), where rates were set for breakfast with or without coffee or chocolate and for lodging one in a bed or more than one; 1774–78, f. 37 (1775), 43 (1776); Carteret, 1723–47 (1741, 1747); 1747–64 (1755, 1761, 1764); 1764–77 (1766); Caswell, 1770–80 (1777); 1777–81 (1777, 1779), a marked increase; Chatham, 1774–79 (1774, 1778); 1781–85 (1782, 1783); Chowan, 1730–48, f. 20 (1741), 26 (1742), 70 (1746); 1741–45, f. 24 (1742); 1749–55, f. 53 (1753); 1755–61, f. 53 (1758); Craven, 1730–46, pt. I, f. 6 (1730); pt. II (1741, 1743, 1744, 1746); 1747–56 (1748, 1751, 1752); 1757–62 (1757, 1760); 1767–75 (1768); Cumberland, 1772–76 (1777, 1778); Edgecomb, 1772–84 (1783); Guilford, 1781–88, f. 43 (1782); Hyde, 1745–61 (1750, 1754, 1759); 1762–84 (1771, 1774); Johnston, 1759–83 (1759, 1764, 1768); Lincoln, 1779–82 (1769);

were proposed and in some cases actually adopted on the eve of the Revolution. Norfolk in 1754 appointed a committee "to make a Law regulating the price of Beef, Veal, Mutton, Lamb, Shoat, Geese, Turkeys, Fowles, Duck Eggs, Butter and Bread and Meal from time to time." [27] A few years later New York City, as a result of monopolistic price trends, adopted a comprehensive ordinance regulating the price of foodstuffs, including meats, and severely punished two violators of the assize.[28] As late as 1786 the Charleston commissioners of markets set prices which butchers might charge for meats.[29]

Nash, 1779–85 (1780, 1782); New Hanover, 1740–1814 (1741); Onslow, 1741–49, f. 15 (1742); 1749–65 (1751); 1765–78 (1767, 1778, 1783); Orange, 1762–66, f. 304 (1765); Pasquotank, 1758–60 (1759), 1761–62 (1761), 1768–77 (1777); Perquimans, 1759–61 (1759); Tryon, 1769–79 (1770, 1772, 1778); Tyrrell, 1759–61 (1760); 1761–70 (1764); 1770–82 (1771); 1783–88 (1783); Wilkes, 1778–85 (1778, 1781).

In 1774 the Camden, S.C., District Grand Jury presented "as a Grievance, that there is not a Law to ascertain the Prices of Entertainments at Public Houses, There being a great number of them in Camden District who frequently impose upon Strangers and Travelers, by making them pay exorbitantly for what they stand in need of." *S.C. Gazette*, Dec. 12, 1774.

"Proclamation" was made in the New Jersey courts of Oyer and Terminer for Hunterdon and Somerset in 1753, in the former "against Inhancing the price of Victuals," and in the latter "against Raising the Prices of Liquor and Provision for man and Horse." N.J. Court of Oyer and Terminer, 1749–62 (May, Oct., 1753). Most likely in both instances innkeepers' rates were involved rather than general commodity prices. See also Ackerman v. Cornelessen, a tavernkeeper who was fined £5 for taking 2s. for one night "for one horse with Hay." Bergen QS, 1756–72 (April 7, 1767). For other instances of regulation of tavern rates in New Jersey see: Essex QS and CP, 1734–39 (June, 1739); 1772–81 (April, 1772); Sussex QS and CP, 1753–64 (Nov., 1753; Feb., May, 1759; Aug., 1762; Nov., 1763—lodging: one in a bed, 5d.; two in a bed, 3d.; three in a bed, 2d.); 1764–69 (May, 1764; May, Nov., 1765; May, 1766); 1769–75 (May, 1772; May, Nov., 1773); 1778–82 (May, 1778) 1782–87 (May, 1783); Gloucester QS, 1738–61 (1742); Cape May QS and CP, 1774–90 (1783); Hunterdon QS and CP, 1721–28 (1722); 1737–50 (1748); Monmouth QS and CP, 1735–44 (1744). For Pennsylvania see Cumberland QS, 1777–89, f. 380 (1783).

Early in 1777 Connecticut passed an act to prevent taverners from demanding "unreasonable and extravagant prices for victuals, forage, liquors, and refreshments." *Session Laws of 1776*, p. 454. The New London town authorities set innkeepers' rates in 1777 and 1778, as did New Haven in the latter year. S. E. Baldwin, "The New Haven Convention of 1778," New Haven Hist. Soc., *Papers*, III, 43, 56.

[27] Norfolk Common Council Mins., f. 55 (1754).

[28] M.C.C., VI, 336, 337; Stokes, *Iconography*, IV, 737; Thomas F. De Voe, *The Market Book* (New York, 1862), I, 148, *et seq.* For regulation of meat prices in Albany, 1756–78, see Munsell, *Coll. Hist. of Albany*, I, 102, 108, 112, 115, 132, *passim.* For regulation of butchers' profits in Boston see *Boston Town Rec.*, XIV, 132, 135. See also the Barbados act of 1766 for ascertaining the rentals of houses, the wholesale prices of provisions, lumber, etc. *Pennsylvania Journal*, June 26, 1766.

[29] *State Gazette of S.C.*, May 18, 1786.

(3) The continuation of economic controls was buttressed by popular demand for a regulated market, manifest in the survival from the medieval urban economy of prohibitions on forestalling, engrossing, regrating, or monopolizing of necessaries—a policy which was to have enormous vitality in Revolutionary days.[30] Of all colonial towns, Charleston on the eve of the Revolution was perhaps most concerned with the enforcement of this policy. In 1763 the commissioners of markets reported that Negroes engaged in trade had combined "in the most impudent and notorious manner" to raise the prices of almost every necessary of life "beyond anything heretofore known, unless when some contagious disease has prevailed in this town," in order to satisfy the wages of their masters, and to the oppression of the poor. Strict regulation of such activities henceforth was decreed.[31] Arguing in behalf of incorporation of the town, a "Tradesman" in 1765 set forth mercantilist views which might very well have been voiced by Chatham or, later, Kenyon, and which definitely foreshadowed Revolutionary arguments:

CHARLES-TOWN, January 30, 1765.
MR. TIMOTHY,

If there is a Curse heavier than another, let it fall with fourfold vengeance upon the Head of a Forestaller, who is a Wretch, that Tyger-like, preys, with the same unrelenting Heart, on the Vitals of the Small and Great, and gluts his Avarice, that he may wallow for a Time, in ill-gotten Pelf.

The Character of a Highwayman is more respectable than an In-

---

[30] A demand for a regulated market was characteristic of every town by this time. Thus, inhabitants of Portsmouth, N.H., petitioned the General Court in 1765 against the practice of the market men of forestalling and selling provisions at an advance of twenty percent. "If these monopolizers were once prevented from purchasing other than necessary supplies, as may serve their own family Consumption every member of the Community would then have an equal Benefit of the Market. The consequences resulting from this Custom is at first View so manifest that your Petitioners think a further observation thereon would be insulting and reflected upon the Judgement of y^r Excellency and Honours." *New Hampshire State Papers*, XIII, 268. For a similar petition of 1772, see *ibid.*, p. 274. The Boston selectmen were urged in 1769 to prepare a bill to eliminate the "pernitious practice of forestalling the Market." *Boston Town Rec.*, XI, 301, 302; VII, 154.

[31] *S.C. Gazette*, Oct. 15–22, 1763. See also *S.C. Gazette*, Oct. 29–Nov. 5, 1763, for criticisms of market monopolies. In 1767 the grand jury presented as a grievance failure to stamp out forestalling. *S.C. Gazette*, Nov. 2–9, 1767.

grosser's; for a Man may stand on his Defence against the *former;* but neither Courage nor Prudence can shield him from the iniquitous Imposition of the *other;* who, as much in him lies, defeats the gracious Designs of Providence, in showering down its Blessings abundantly; but alas! the Multitude have not wherewithal to purchase them from the *Extortioner.*

He that forestalls the Necessaries of Life, *insults* his God, by making an artificial *scarcity,* though Plenty surrounds us; and in broad Day, he tramples upon the Bonds of Society, by plundering the Affluent, and *grinding* the Faces of the Poor with Impunity. He knows indeed that Loads of Imprecations are poured forth against him both in Public and in private; but his whole Soul is so engrossed by the Desire of Gain, that he is deaf to every Thing else, and a reasonable Profit will not content him.

When the Measure of some Men's Consciences will be full, no one can say? But it seems *Time,* and I am sure it is *necessary,* to set Bounds to them or we shall soon be obliged to build *more* Alms-Houses, to receive our poor distressed Inhabitants; for it is past a Doubt, that an industrious Man, who does not earn more than Thirty or Forty Shillings in the Day (and *few* do that) can possibly pay House-Rent, cloath and feed his Family, and pay Five Pounds out of his poor Pittance, to purchase a Cord of Firewood, that *ill-measured* too; an Article which he must have, either in small or greater Quantity: His Family therefore, must either be worse cloathed, worse fed, or both, if they will enjoy the Comfort of a Fire; so that one Way or the other, they must be pinched or half starved; and in Consequence Sickness and Distress must multiply.

Rouze then, Fellow-Citizens! and root out those Pests from the Community; for, be the Affluent ever so passive, under such barefaced Extortion, the Condition of the Many who are placed by Providence in lower Stations, surely deserves *some Consideration.*

Let us therefore directly *instruct* our Representatives; *petition* the General Assembly for a proper Law; apply for an Act to Incorporate the Town, or do any Thing else that becomes us, to extirpate this Evil of the blackest Dye. . . .

A Tradesman.[32]

---

[32] *S.C. Gazette,* Jan. 26–Feb. 2, 1765. Elsewhere, forestalling was restricted, as, for example, in Wilmington, Del., by its market code of 1741. Wilmington Mins. See also *Boston Town Rec.,* VIII, 206, 221, 224; XI, 67–72; *Mass. Acts and Resolves,* I, 237–39. Of all the colonies, Virginia had the most venerable body of enactments against forestalling, regrating, and engrossing, but these were principally prior to 1643 when price codes were still fashionable. An impressive body of legislation was enacted by that state on the subject during the Revolution. Hening, *Stat. of Va., passim.* As late as 1801 New Bern, N.C., in setting up its market code, declared that "it is of great

Writers in later Revolutionary years who scathingly denounced the engrosser, forestaller, and monopolizer as "locusts," "pests of society," and "bad men" were voicing sentiment deeply rooted by the eve of the conflict.[33] An integral part of this program of close market supervision was the regulation of public vendues with the object of preventing improper competition with established retail trades.[34]

(4) Further important evidence of the survival of a program of economic control is found in the enforcement of a poor-law policy which had been a cornerstone of Tudor mercantilism. This policy is notable, among other things, for its requirement that the children of persons who could not maintain themselves be taught a trade and set to work; that able-bodied vagrants or idle persons— those living "without a calling"—be compelled to work or else be punished by the criminal machinery; [35] and that the able-bodied unemployed be provided for by the establishment of workhouses— a conspicuous trend in American towns in the mid-eighteenth

---

importance to the prosperity of every town that the necessaries of life should be kept at as reasonable a rate as possible, and that all intermediate speculation between the Farmer Miller and Consumer . . . to raise such articles to an artificial Price should be cut off." New Bern Town Rec., 1792–1825, f. 46 (1801). The South Carolina acts of 1692 and 1739 against forestalling, regrating, and engrossing were patterned after English models, S.C. Assembly Journal, 1692, f. 15 (Sept. 30, 1692); *S.C. Gazette*, Dec. 8–15, 1729; cf. Pringle-Smith ("Government of the City of Charleston," *Charleston Year Book, 1881*, pp. 333 *et seq.*), who criticizes Lord Kenyon's eulogy of "these preposterous laws." In Charleston the enforcement of these acts was in the hands of the commissioner of markets. *S.C. Gazette*, April 16–23, 1737. Similar legislation was enacted also in colonial Georgia (*Ga. Col. Rec.*, XIII, 63, 277 [1755, 1758]) and in West Florida, despite opposition of the governor to trade restrictions. Act of May 18, 1767.

[33] See, e. g., *New York Journal*, Oct. 11, 1779.

[34] *M.C.C. of Phila.*, p. 410 (1742); *S. C. Gazette*, May 6–13, 1751.

[35] A New Haven quarter-session court in 1688 cited the statutes of Elizabeth and James I regarding vagabonds as being operative in the colony. New Haven County Court (QS Mins., Sept., 1688), f. 4. Typical laws against vagrancy: Massachusetts: *Acts and Resolves*, I, 67, 378–81, 538, 539, 654, 655; Journal of the House of Representatives, VIII, 232–34; XIV, 69, 76, 80, 83, 103; XV, 214, 220, 229, 231; Connecticut: *Conn. Col. Rec.*, VI, 82, VII, 127–30, VIII, 137–39, XIII, 237 (empowering the justice of the peace to send "all rogues, vagabonds, sturdy beggars, and other lewd, idle, dissolute, prophane and disorderly persons" to workhouses to be kept at hard labor; North Carolina (providing whipping and a maximum penalty of one year's service): Laws of 1755, c. 4; 1760, 4th sess., c. 13; 1766, c. 17; 1770, c. 29; Georgia: *Ga. Col. Rec.*, XIV, 93; West Florida: act of July 12, 1771. Vagrancy prosecutions are found in southern courts as well as northern. See Mackintosh's presentment, York, Va., O.B., 1706–10, f. 83 (1707).

century.[36] An acute suspicion of any distraction which might lead the working classes into the paths of immorality or idleness was not confined at this date to the Puritan towns but characterized southern regulation as well as northern.[37] This hostility to idle-

[36] The workhouse plan in the colonies actually antedates the 18th century. See, for example, *Plymouth Col. Rec.,* XI, 120; *Boston Town Rec.,* VII, 157. New Haven in 1767 provided for the establishment of a workhouse for the idle. New Haven Town Rec., 1684–1765, fols. 57, 573. See also *R.I. Col. Rec.,* V, 378, VI, 598; *Bristol Parish, Va., Vestry Book,* p. 160. As early as 1735 the Charleston, S.C., grand jury returned that, for want of a workhouse to punish the idle, the poor were flocking to the town. *S.C. Gazette,* March 23–30, 1734. See also presentment of 1768, *ibid.,* Jan. 25–Feb. 1, 1768; S.C. Council Journal, 1764–68, fols. 252, 255 (1768). See *S.C. Gazette, passim,* for regular lists of those committed to the workhouse.

The nonimportation agreements were a fillip not alone to domestic manufactures but also to plans for employment of the poor on such favored or subsidized projects as linen production. A cheap labor supply for the undertakers would thus be assured, as in Boston in 1768, although the undertakers of a duck and sailcloth venture disclaimed any profit motive and stated that their design was solely to employ "the many Poor we have in the Town and giving them a Livelihood." *Boston Town Rec.,* XVI, 226, 227, 230–32, 249. As unemployment increased, the responsibilities of the undertakers likewise were enhanced. It was reported that in April, 1769, over 200 unemployed in Boston were desirous of securing work at spinning and carding and that "their Numbers are dayly increasing," and funds were provided for setting up spinning schools to train children and for securing machinery, etc., to take care of the unemployed. This, it was reported by the committee, would not only reduce the numbers in the almshouses but would "habituate the People to Industry, and preserve their Morals who instead of their continuing a burden to society will become some of its most useful Members." *Ibid.,* pp. 273–76. For other projects to employ the poor on the eve of the Revolution, see *ibid.,* XVIII, 70, 71 (spinning wool, 1772; building of ships and wharves and paving streets as occupations for the unemployed sufferers from the Port Bill, 1774). Philadelphia as early as 1712 provided for the establishment of a workhouse to employ the idle poor. *M.C.C. of Phila.,* p. 80. A venture for the producers of coarse linen was established in that town in 1764 with the ostensible object of relieving unemployment. Buildings were erected and more than one hundred persons employed. The House of Employment eventually ran into financial difficulties. Scharf, *Hist. of Phila.,* III, 2309, 2310; *Pa. Col. Rec.,* IX, 567; *M.C.C. of Phila.,* p. 799. The United Company of Philadelphia for Promoting American Manufactures, the first joint-stock company for the manufacture of cotton, was set up in Philadelphia in 1775 and in its initial year employed 400 women in its factory. Scharf, *op. cit.,* III, 2314. Similarly, a company formed in the same year to encourage woolen manufactures was remarkably successful in its appeal to unemployed women spinners and appears to have had a like number of employees. *Ibid.,* p. 2301. Unemployed or surplus Negro artificers were required to the extent of 100 for the Aera Furnace erected in South Carolina during the Revolution. *Charleston Gazette,* Jan. 11, 1780.

[37] A report establishing "Idleness as the Parent of all Vices" was adopted by the town of Boston in 1769. *Boston Town Rec.,* XVI, 273, 274. It is also to be noted that a theatrical performance was suppressed by the common council in Philadelphia in 1750 on typically mercantilist grounds, i. e., "it was to be feared [that play-acting] would be attended with very mischievous Effects, such as the encouraging of Idleness and drawing great Sums of Money from weak and inconsiderate People, who are apt to be fond of such kinds of Entertainments tho' the Performance be ever so mean

ness, together with the general practice of regarding unemployment as prima facie evidence of a criminal status, is part and parcel of the advocacy by mercantilists of a large labor supply, low wages, and forced labor. The absence of centralized control over the unemployed in England after the Restoration makes the parallel between the English and colonial ways of dealing with this problem even more striking. As additional evidence of the survival of regulating tendencies one may cite the policy of compulsory labor on public works projects which prevailed throughout the colonies.[38]

and contemptible. Whereupon the Board unanimously requested the Magistrates to take the most effectual Measures for suppressing this Disorder, by sending for the Actors and binding them to their good Behaviour, or by such other Means as they should judge most proper." *M.C.C. of Phila.*, p. 523. As late as 1764 the Pennsylvania Assembly still concerned itself with the problem of idleness. *Pa. Col. Rec.*, IX, 166.

In 1738 the mayor of Norfolk reported that the selling of rum both to the idle and to Negroes caused them to become incorrigible, and the common council provided that henceforth liquor should not be retailed in amounts less than a gallon. This was class legislation aimed to keep the "Meaner sort of People" sober and industrious. Norfolk C.C. Mins., f. 11 (1738). In 1770 a Charleston grand jury presented Daniel Cane for keeping a "disorderly tippling and gaming house, where apprentices and other youth are entertained and debauched." The Charleston grand jury in 1774 found that the law reducing the number of dram shops had not been attended to, with resultant distraction to slaves and servants. *S.C. Gazette*, Oct. 31, 1774. The purport of ordinances passed in Charleston in 1783 and 1796, respectively, to restrict theatrical entertainments and prevent gambling, was that both encouraged idleness among young people, apprentices, and servants. *Charleston Ordinances*, pp. 15, 149.

[38] See Gowen's case, York Sess., VI, f. 402 (1715)—fine for refusal to labor on the highways. But cf. Rex v. Gay, Quincy Rep., pp. 91–93 (1763), which decided that a capias would not issue in Massachusetts for neglect in mending a highway, and was indicative of a trend away from impressment for public works. Massachusetts permitted the inhabitants to work off the road tax at a specified daily rate of pay. *Muddy River and Brookline Rec.*, pp. 90, 171; *Watertown Rec.*, III, 219; IV, 35, *passim; Lee Rec.*, pp. 20, 107. Prior to 1712 in Philadelphia the inhabitants were obliged to "Send Able Labourers" to work on road construction projects, but the common council, for reasons of economy, authorized the overseers to take 1s.6d. from those who were willing to pay to be excused from a day's labor. *M.C.C. of Phila.*, p. 80. For instances of forced labor on the roads in Pennsylvania, see West Chester QS, 1714–23 (1715); Bucks QS, 1715–45, f. 373 (1745); Lancaster Road and Sess. Docket, No. 3, 1760–68 (1761); in New Jersey, see *N.J. Gazette*, Oct. 28, 1778. For examples of impressment in the South see, e. g.: Virginia: Caroline O.B., 1777–80, f. 6 (1777); Charles City County O.B., 1655–65, f. 357 (1663); Fairfax O.B., 1768–70 (Lib. of Congress), f. 74 (1768); Fincastle O.B., 1773–77 (1773, 1776); North Carolina: Bertie, 1724–69 (1736, 1758); Bute, 1767–76, f. 79 (1769); Carteret, 1764–77 (1764, 1768); Caswell, 1770–80 (1777); 1777–81 (1777); Craven, 1767–75 (1768); Guilford, 1781–88 (1782, 1783); Rutherford, 1780–82 (July Term, 1782); Tyrrell, 1770–82 (1777). Occasionally motions of inhabitants for exemption from forced labor on the roads are considered (Onslow, 1741–49, f. 37 [1741]), and frequently overseers of the roads are indicted for not doing their duty (see, e. g., Rex v. Daniel, Halifax Reference or Prosecution Docket, 1759–70 [1770]). During the Revolution, South Carolina imposed a fine of $200 for failure to respond to a call for work on roads, bridges, etc. *S.C. Gazette*,

Local authorities set the wages to be paid for such work.[39] During the Revolution, Virginia took a strong stand on idleness, authorizing the seizure of those who would not betake themselves "to some lawful calling or honest labor" and sentence to a year's service on an armed vessel at the regular wages of volunteers. Those not sufficiently able-bodied for such active service were to be consigned for wages "to any person or persons approved of by" the nearest county court. Any able-bodied man without visible estate was accounted a vagabond under this statute.[40] During the war the county courts of North Carolina turned vagrants over to the continental army in accord with an act of assembly.[41] In the post-war period a South Carolina grand jury declared idleness to be "a great cause of many becoming, not only useless to themselves, but a nuisance to society." [42]

With the crisis of revolution and currency depreciation, a virtually national program of regulation, mercantilist in character, was launched the very first year of the war. The program was initiated by the northern states, acting together in regional conventions, but the Continental Congress lent encouragement. Here, as in the earlier controls, labor regulation was one phase of the larger program which had as its aim compulsory circulation of paper money by legal tender laws, buttressed by price and wage regulations and restraints against monopolistic practices. Therefore,

---

Feb. 24, 1779. Laborers could be conscripted for public works (*Gazette of the State of S.C.*, Feb. 9, 1780), and in the post-Revolutionary period masters might be required to send their slaves to work on canal and drainage projects (*ibid.*, March 16, 1786). In Georgia, slaves were included among the "hands" conscripted for road work. Chatham Mins., 1774–79 (1774); 1781–85 (1783, 1786). Impressment of seamen for the royal navy requires no elaboration here.

[39] For example, in New Castle, Del., wages and hours were fixed; in 1767 they were 3s. for a day's work from 7 A.M. until 6 P.M. The wages were raised to 4s. in 1770, and both wages and hours scales appear to have been retained until the Revolution. In 1778 the wages were raised to 18s. *Newcastle Town Rec.*, I, 26, 28, 30, 34, 42, 43, 45.

[40] Hening, *Stat. of Va.*, IX, 216, 217 (Oct., 1776).

[41] Act of 1778, c. 2, *N.C. State Rec.*, XXIV, 157. See, e. g., Guilford, 1781–88, f. 10 (1781), where James Critchton appealed to the Superior Court. In 1773 the grand jury at Long Bluff, Cheraws, presented the want of a vagrant act (*S.C. Gazette*, Dec. 2, 1773)—a demand which was taken up again by the Camden grand jury in 1785, which urged that every head of a family or householder without visible means of livelihood should be required to cultivate an acre of land for each person in his household, black and white. *Ibid.*, Dec. 12, 1785. See also ordinances of 1796, *Charleston Ordinances*, pp. 141, 143.

[42] *Gazette of the State of S.C.*, Dec. 12, 1785.

while due emphasis will be given the labor codes set up in regional conventions, enacted in state statutes, or adopted by county conventions and town meetings and carried through by local committees, the close relationship of such regulation to the larger program will be constantly borne in mind. In the light of these comprehensive proposals, it is purposed to evaluate and determine the role of mercantilist theory at this time of grave constitutional difficulties and military crisis when such theories were definitely on the wane among the nations of western Europe.

Although the states were to serve as the springboard for such regulation, the Continental Congress had, as a matter of fact, pointed the way in price control as early as 1774 by incorporating in the articles of association stipulations not to sell merchandise at rates in excess of those prevailing during the previous twelve months and to sell domestic manufactures "at reasonable prices, so that no undue advantage be taken of a future scarcity of goods." [43] Prices for tea, coffee, salt, pepper, sugar, and other imports were set both by Congress and by local committees in 1775 and 1776, violators of such orders being considered "enemies of the American cause" to be "treated accordingly." [44] In the course of 1776 Congress had occasion to rule that the military pay no higher prices for goods furnished the soldier "than the first cost of them, and five percent for charges," [45] and on October 31, 1776 that body recommended that "the assemblies, conventions, councils or committees of safety of the several states" take suitable measures for obtaining engrossed goods for the use of the army, allowing to the owners a reasonable price for them, and enact laws preventing monopolies.[46] Local committees enforced the congressional resolves and also set prices in some instances. In March, 1776, the Albany committee of correspondence asked Congress for an interpretation of its regulations as to whether they related "to the profits on such Goods or to the accustomed prices Goods were

[43] Ford, *Journals of the Continental Congress,* I, 78, 79. The nonconsumption agreements enforced by the towns frequently, as in Connecticut in September, 1774, embodied prohibitions against forestalling and engrossing. W. G. Sumner, *The Financier and Finances of the American Revolution* (New York, 1891), I, 53.

[44] Newport *Mercury,* March 25, 1775; May 13, June 13, 20, 1776; *N.Y. Gazette,* April 22, 1776.

[45] *Journals,* V, 591.

[46] *Ibid.,* VI, 915, 916.

sold at in 1774." [47] On a number of occasions during the year that body and its Schenectady counterpart set the price of tea, salt, pepper, sugar, and numerous other imported items.[48] In the spring of 1776 the committees of inspection of fifteen towns in Hartford County met at Hartford and fixed the prices for certain commodities.[49] In April the Philadelphia committee of inspection inquired whether they should continue to exercise the power of setting the price of goods in instances other than green tea. Congress replied that the association by its very nature was temporary, and, as supplies were now largely consumed and the risks of enterprise were to be encouraged, the power of such local committees to regulate prices in general ought, therefore, to terminate.[50] Nevertheless, within a month, on hearing that profiteers were monopolizing shoes, stockings, and other necessaries for the army, Congress recommended that the assembly of Pennsylvania adopt immediate measures adequate to remedy the evil.[51]

Of all areas, early New England had experimented most broadly with price and wage controls, so that it was in a way natural that the leadership in this movement should now be assumed by that section. At the outbreak of the Revolution, Connecticut passed a number of laws regulating wages and prices. At the May session of the General Assembly in 1776, an old statute concerning oppression in exacting high prices or wages was amended so as no longer to require the appraisers appointed by the authorities to be men of the same occupation or trade as the person complained of.[52] In October, penalties were prescribed against those who discriminated against continental bills in setting prices,[53] and in the following month a statute was enacted fixing the maximum price of farm labor in the summer season at 3s. per diem, "and so in the usual proportion at other seasons of the year; and other labor to be computed, and of mechanics and tradesmen according to the usages and customs that have heretofore been adopted and practised in the different parts of this state compared with farming labour and the prices hereafter set and established." Prices for numerous com-

[47] *Minutes of the Albany Committee of Correspondence*, I, 358.
[48] *Ibid.*, I, 385, 511, 512, 556; II, 1067.
[49] R. R. Hinman, *Historical Collection* (Hartford, 1842), p. 83.
[50] Ford, *Journals*, IV, 320; *Pa. Gazette*, May 6, 1776.   [51] *Journals*, VI, 980, 981.
[52] *Conn. Sessions Laws*, 1776, p. 422.   [53] *Ibid.*, p. 434.

modities were also fixed and violations of either the wages or price scales were to be punished by the state law against oppression.[54]

The first two conventions were called on the initiative of Massachusetts [55] in direct response to petitions for relief from high prices from some score of Massachusetts towns and four towns in New Hampshire.[56] The meeting at Providence at the close of 1776, comprising committees from New Hampshire, Massachusetts, Rhode Island, and Connecticut, was the first of these regional sessions. In addition to recommending military measures and taking steps to stabilize the credit of the paper bills in circulation, the Providence convention, under the presidency of William Bradford, adopted at its session of December 31, 1776, wage and price regulation as follows:

This Committee taking into Consideration the unbounded Avarice of many Persons, by daily adding to the now most intollerable exhorbitant Price of every necessary and convenient article of Life, and also *the most extravagant Price of Labour, in general,* which at this Time of Distress unless a speedy and effectual Stop be put thereto will be attended with the most Fatal and Pernicious consequences As it not only Disheartens and Disaffects the Soldiers who have Nobly enter'd into Service, for the best of Causes, by obliging them to give such unreasonable Prices for those things that are absolutely needful for their very existence that their Pay is not sufficient to Submit them, but is also very Detrimental to the Country in General.

Wherefore it is recommended by this Committee, that the Rates and Prices hereafter enumerated be affixed and settled within the respective States in New England, to wit:

Farming Labour in the Summer Season shall not exceed Three Shillings and Four Pence per Diem, and so in the usual Proportion at other Seasons of the Year, and the Labour of Mechanics and Tradesmen and other Labour to be computed according to the Usages and Customs that have heretofore been adopted and practised in different Parts of the several States compared with Farming Labour.[57]

---

[54] *Conn. State Rec.,* I, 62, 63 (Nov. 19, 1776).

[55] *Mass. Acts and Resolves,* V, 669. Connecticut first declined on the ground that Congress was considering the currency question and that state activity might foster jealousy and endanger the union. *Amer. Archives,* 5th ser., III, 1077. Rhode Island proposed broadening the scope of the convention to include (in addition to price measures) embargoes, regulation of public auctions, etc.—a view which prevailed.

[56] Journal of the House of Representatives, March 14, 20, 1776, *Acts and Resolves,* V, 669–73.

[57] MS, Journals of the Convention of the New England States with Accompanying Resolutions, 1776–80, Rhode Island State Archives; Force Transcripts, Vol. XIII, Library of Congress, also in modernized form in *Conn. State Rec.,* I, 592–96.

The committee also set the prices for some twenty-seven domestic commodities, including wheat, corn, and wool, and recommended that, "notwithstanding the great risque of a voyage to and from Europe, the high rate of insurance, the difficulty of procuring articles suitable for that market, the loss upon those exported, the increased expence and length of the voyage, and the real necessity of importing many commodities" from Europe, the wholesale price of imported goods should not exceed by from 250 to 275 percent the original cost, and the retail price should be no more than 20 percent greater than the wholesale. In addition to this comprehensive schedule, the committee further recommended that the respective state legislatures fix the price of wood, hay, pine boards, plank, joist, hoops, shingle, charcoal, tanned leather, cotton and linen cloths, mutton, veal, and flour, "and also the Rates of carting, which can be much better done in the several States than by this Committee." Severe penalties for violations were also proposed.

The states represented at the meeting acted with commendable speed. Connecticut immediately set up a wage and price scale, raising the maximum for farm labor to accord with the new schedule to 3s.4d. from the 3s. set the previous month, in fact repealing the previous act.[58] New Hampshire, Massachusetts, and Rhode Island likewise fell into line at once.[59] Under the Massachusetts statute, rates of labor were only 3s. per diem as compared with the 3s.4d. in the Providence recommendation. But the merchants gained what the laborers lost, as they were to be allowed the maximum convention rate of 275 percent of the cost of goods in European ports. The prices set in this law applied to Boston; in other towns the selectmen were authorized to regulate prices in accordance with this scale, making the necessary allowance for differences in the cost of transportation. Rhode Island, in addition to setting the established scale for farm labor, specified wages as follows:

[58] *Conn. State Rec.*, I, 98–100; Harlow, *Amer. Hist. Rev.*, XXXV, 57. The wages of farm labor appear to have been accepted as a standard of value, commodity prices being ascertained with reference thereto.

[59] *Laws of New Hampshire*, IV, 78–82; *Prov. Papers of New Hampshire*, VIII, 455–56, 471; *Mass. Acts and Resolves*, V, 583–89. The Massachusetts act as originally passed had no time limit, but later a time limit of three years was set. *Ibid.*, V, 647; MS, *R.I. Col. Rec.*, 1772–77, f. 548 *et seq.; R.I. Col. Rec.*, VIII, 85.

per diem

Teaming work, the teamster finding himself and cattle,
for one Hand with Cart or Waggon, one Yoke of Oxen,
and a good draught-Horse, or two Yoke of Oxen .   .   13/

Teaming to and from Sea Port Markets and for the army
per Ton per Mile, if not more than one mile 4/. For every
Mile after the first mile out 1/6.

Horse-keeping, at Sea Port Towns per Night or 24 Hours, 2/6.

Horse-shoeing all round, with steel Corks, Heel and Toe, 6/.

Ox-Shoeing and other Blacksmith's Work in the same Proportion.

Ships Iron-work—weight-work at 3d. per lb. and all light
work in the same Proportion, excepting cast Iron.

House-Carpenters, finding themselves   5/
Ship-Carpenters,   "   "   6/
Caulkers   "   "   7/
Masons   "   "   6/6

Taylors making a plain suit of best Broadcloth Cloths,
24/ and their daily wage, the employer finding them, at   3/

Trucking, 1/6 per Hogshead, and other things in Proportion

Best Beaver Hats, at 42/. Best Felt Hats at 8/.

Coopers, find themselves 5/
setting and finding Hogshead Hoops, 3d. each
setting and finding Barrel hoops, 2d. each

Barbers for shaving. 3d.[60]

By March of the following year Rhode Island found it necessary to raise maximum wages in some categories and at the
same time to ascertain more precisely the seasonal wages of farm
labor, as follows:

The Price of Farming Labour, viz. for Mowing and Reaping in their
Season, shall not exceed three Shillings and six Pence per Day, and in
the three Winter Months one shilling and six pence per Day, and at all
other Times of the Year two Shillings per Day: That for the Three
Summer Months the Price of Labour by the Month shall not exceed
forty-eight shillings when found, and at all other Seasons in the same
Proportion compared with Day Labour: That Common Labour in
the Town of Providence shall not exceed four shillings and six Pence
per Day, they finding themselves, and three shillings when found . . .[61]

---

[60] Prosecutions for violation could be brought in any court of record.
[61] MS, R.I. Col. Rec., 1772–77, f. 641 *et seq.*; *R.I. Col. Rec.*, VIII, 183.

The proceedings of the convention were laid before Congress on January 28, 1777, and evoked a spirited debate. William Ellery wrote Governor Cooke of Rhode Island that he had no doubt that they would be approved.[62] As to their reception, the partisan Samuel Adams reported that they were "much applauded as being wise and salutary." [63] Nonetheless, over the course of the next few weeks the issue was warmly debated on at least three occasions. As the arguments formulated were fairly representative of the division of opinion on the wisdom of regulation, it seems desirable to consider them in some detail. On February 4, a resolution of the Committee of the Whole was debated setting forth the opinion of the committee "that the peculiar Situation of the New England States, whose Communication with Congress was in a great Measure cut off, and who were invaded or threatened with an immediate Invasion by the Enemy, rendered the Appointment and Meeting of the Committee proper and necessary, and consequently worthy of the Approbation of Congress." [64] For the affirmative, Sam Adams defended as the privilege of freemen the right of assembly "upon all occasions to consult measures for promoting liberty and happiness," and Richard Henry Lee maintained that, as the states were not yet confederated, no law of the union was infringed. As the New England program of price regulation was very popular with Congress, according to the admission made on February 7 by John Adams, who himself felt that no permanent good could come of it,[65] it was necessary for the opposition to muster an impressive array of talent. Those arguing in the negative were in general to prove opponents of mercantilist controls, although favoring a stronger political union—a point of view which ultimately prevailed in 1787. Thus, Wilson maintained that, as the business transacted was "continental" in scope, it required the approval of Congress. John Adams, while defending the convention as "founded in necessity," conceded "that the four New England States bore the same relation to the Congress that four

[62] Burnett, *Letters of Members of the Continental Congress,* II, 227.
[63] *Ibid.,* II, 233.
[64] Ford, *Journals,* VII, 80, 81. Benjamin Rush reported the motion as: "Whether it did not stand in need of the Approbation of Congress to make it *valid,*" thus raising a nice constitutional question. Burnett, *Letters,* II, 234.
[65] *Familiar Letters of John Adams and His Wife Abigail Adams during the Revolution* (New York, 1876), p. 239.

counties bore to a single State. These four counties have a right to meet to regulate roads, and affairs that relate to the poor, but they have no right to tax or execute any other branch of legislation." Since the convention had dealt with continental as distinguished from local matters it stood in need of approbation. Dr. Benjamin Rush regarded the Providence meeting as "full of great and interesting consequences, which should be regarded with a serious and jealous eye." He charged that body with usurping the power of Congress, just as four counties would usurp the power of the state legislature if they attempted to tax themselves. He also accused the convention of contravening an express resolution of Congress by regulating the price of goods.

The motion was decided in the affirmative on February 4, but, when reconsidered, was defeated a few days later by one vote, only to be reopened on February 14.[66] At that time the opponents of the motion were reinforced by additional men of eminence in Congress. James Smith maintained that a recommendation to the other states would be an interference with their "domestic police," a subject of "too delicate a nature to be touched by Congress." Benjamin Rush left off constitutional grounds and turned to economic theory, stating emphatically:

I am against the whole of this resolution. It is founded in the contrary of justice, policy and necessity as has been declared in the resolution. The wisdom and power of government have been employed in all ages to regulate the price of necessaries to no purpose. It was attempted in Eng^d in the reign of Edward II by the English parliament but without effect. The laws for limiting the price of every thing were repealed, and Mr. Hume who mentions this fact records even the very attempt as a monument to human folly. The congress with all its authority have failed in a former instance of regulating the price of goods. You have limited Bohea tea to ¾ of a dollar, and yet it is daily

---

[66] Ford, *Journals*, VII, 87; Burnett, *Letters*, II, 234, 235; Benjamin Rush, Diary, Library Co. of Philadelphia, Ridgway Branch. According to Thomas Burke, some of the states, including North Carolina, voted against approbation for fear that further disputes might arise. Burnett, *Letters*, II, 249; *N.C. State Rec.*, XI, 389. After a favorable vote by the committee of the whole on February 5, the proceedings of the Providence convention were referred to a committee of five: Richard Henry Lee, James Wilson, Samuel Chase, John Adams, and Roger Sherman. Its report of the following day was tabled for the time being. Ford, *Journals*, VII, 93, 97. The report of James Wilson is in Papers of the Continental Congress, No. 24, f. 375, Lib. of Congress.

sold before your eyes for 30/. The Committee of Philada. limited the price of West India goods about a year ago. But what was the consequence? The merchants it is true sold their rum, sugar and molasses at the price limited by the committee, but they charged a heavy profit upon the barrel, or the paper which contained the rum or the sugar. Consider Sir the danger of failing in this experiment. The Salvation of this continent depends upon the Authority of this Congress being held as sacred as the cause of liberty itself. Suppose we should fail of producing the effects we wish for by the resolution before you. Have we any character to spare? Have we committed no mistakes in the management of the public Affairs of America? We have Sir. It becomes us therefore to be careful of the remains of our Authority and character. It is a common thing to cry aloud of the rapacity and extortion in every branch of business etc. among every class of men. This has led some people to decry the *public Virtue* of this country. True Sir there is not so much of it as we could wish, but there is much more than is sometimes allowed on this floor. We estimate our Virtue by a false barometer when we measure it by the price of goods. The extortion we complain of arises only from the excessive quantity of our money. Now Sir a failure in this Attempt to regulate the price of goods will encrease the clamors against the rapacity of dealers, and thus depreciate our public virtue. Consider Sir the consequence of measuring our virtue by this false standard. You will add weight to the Arguments used at St. James's to explode patriotism altogether, and by denying its existence in this country destroy it forever. Persuade a Woman that there is no such thing as chastity, and if there is that She does not possess it, and She may be easily seduced if She was as chaste as Diana. Sir, The price of goods may be compared to a number of light substances in a bason of water. The hand may keep them down for a while, but nothing can detain them on the bottom of the bason but an Abstraction of the Water. The continent labours under a universal malady. From the crown of her head to the Soal of her feet She is full of disorders. She requires the most powerful tonic medicines. The resolution before you is Nothing but an *Opiate*. It may compose the continent for a night, but She will soon awaken again to a fresh sense of her pain and misery.

Richard Henry Lee promptly replied that the continent labored under a spasm, "and Spasms . . . require *palliative* medicines." Samuel Chase took up the defense at this point, arguing from utter necessity, and urging that the "mines of Peru would not support a war at the present high price of the necessaries of life," and that unless the prices of clothing and other articles were limited the pay of soldiers would have to be raised. Sergeant, Wilson, and Witherspoon denied the practicability of the measure.

Sergeant insisted that "the price of goods cannot be regulated while the quantity of our money and the articles of life are allowed to fluctuate." James Wilson stated dramatically:

There are certain things Sir which Absolute power cannot do. The whole power of the Roman Emperors could not add a single letter to the Alphabet. Augustus could not compel old batchelors to marry. He found out his error, and wisely repealed his edict least they should bring his authority into contempt. Let us recommend the resolution to the *consideration* of the States only without giving our Opinion on it, that they may discuss it with unbiassed minds.

Witherspoon's argument was perhaps the most forceful:

Sir, it is a wise maxim to avoid those things which our enemies wish us to practise. Now I find that our enemies have published the Act of the Assembly of Connecticut for regulating the price of necessaries in the New York papers in order to shew our distress from that Quarter. I believe the regulations would be just, if the quantity of money and the scarcity of goods bore an exact proportion to each other. But the price of goods is by no means proportioned to the quantity of money in every thing. The encrease of price began 1st upon the *Luxuries* 2ly Necessaries, 3rd Manufactories and 4ly grain, and Other produce of the earth. Now the reason why it has reached the grain etc last, is owing to their quantity being plentiful and to an overproportion of money. Remember laws are not almighty. It is beyond the power of despotic princes to regulate the price of goods. Tea and Salt are higher in proportion than any Other Articles of trade owing entirely to their price being limited. In Pennsylvania salt was limited to 15/ but was sold for 60. per bushel, while at the same time it was sold in Virginia where there was no limitation for 10/ a bushel. I fear if we fail in this measure we shall weaken the Authority of Congress. We shall do mischief by teaching the continent to *rest* upon it. If we limit *one* article, we must limit *every* thing, and this is impossible.

John Adams doubted "the justice, policy and necessity of the resolution," and pointed out that the experiment "was tried in vain even in the absolute government of France. The high price of many Articles arises from their scarcity. If we regulate the price of imports we shall immediately put a stop to them for ever." [67]

[67] Shortly thereafter Adams referred to the wage and price codes as "mere temporary Expedients" and palliatives, and advised a radical cure—ceasing to emit paper currency and redemption in gold and silver through importation of the precious metals. John Adams to Joseph Palmer, Feb. 20, 1777. Myers Coll., N.Y. Public Library.

Rush, in closing for the negative, supported Adams in the view that the rise in prices in Philadelphia was not due to Tory monopolizers and speculators, but rather to the constant emissions of currency which led to speculation. The Philadelphia committee supported by the "country people" had attempted unsuccessfully to sustain prices. Then, retorting to Lee, he diagnosed the malady of the continent as "not a spasm, but a dropsy," for which he wrote the following prescription:

(1) Raising the interest of the money we borrow to 6 per cent. This like a cold Bath will give an immediate Spring to our affairs; and (2) *taxation*. This like *tapping*, will diminish the Quantity of our Money, and give a proper value to what remains.[68]

As a result of this debate, the resolution was amended. The Providence plan, in so far as it related to wages and prices, was not specifically endorsed as historians have insisted,[69] but "the propriety of adopting similar Measures" was "referred" to the "serious Consideration" of the other states.[70] Congress then proceeded to call a meeting for March, 1777, to be held at York, Pa., of commissioners from New York, New Jersey, Pennsylvania, Delaware, Maryland, and Virginia; and at Charleston, S.C., for commissioners from North and South Carolina and Georgia, in both cases to adopt "such a System of Regulation as may be most suitable to those States."

At the York meeting a report was brought in establishing a maximum price tariff for goods needed for the military services and recommending that the respective legislatures fix the prices of other articles so that these prices would be in the same proportion as those enumerated were to the prices that obtained before the war. Likewise, in order to make certain that "the price of labor and of manufacture" would be "proportionate to each other," it was proposed that manufactures bear the same proportion to wages as they did before the conflict. The delegates from Pennsylvania, Delaware, and Maryland voted to reject the report, and New York, New Jersey, and Virginia voted for adoption. The opponents of

---

[68] Burnett, *Letters*, II, 250 *et seq.*; Rush, Diary, Feb. 14, 1777.

[69] W. G. Sumner, *op. cit.*, I, 56; A. S. Bolles, *The Financial History of the United States* (New York, 1879), p. 159; Burnett, *Letters*, II, xii, xiii.

[70] Ford, *Journals*, VII, 124, 125; Papers of the Continental Congress, No. 24, f. 393. See also Burnett, *Letters*, II, 266; *N.C. State Rec.*, XI, 39.

regulation argued that it would be "productive of the most fatal consequences." The convention, hopelessly divided, contented itself, therefore, with sending copies of the proceedings to Congress and the states represented.[71] The failure of the middle states to agree on a price and wage schedule deterred action by local committees in that area at this time. For example, in May, 1777, the Albany committee of correspondence resolved that "as the necessaries of Life and other Merchandize are not ascertained this Committee do decline to undertake the Task of Regulating and ascertaining the Prices or Wages to be allowed for Sloops in the public service." [72]

Despite criticism in high places, these early conventions were clearly representative of a substantial body of public opinion which favored curbs on all sorts of profiteering; and the immediate reaction to the New England legislation incorporating the Providence proposals was distinctly cordial. The acts were praised for "rightly considering the several classes of men, allotting to the farmer, to the manufacturer, to the day laborer, and to the trader, the allowance respectively proper for them." [73] They were endorsed at public meetings held in various towns, notably New Haven and Boston, which set up special committees to enforce the law, in the latter town a committee of thirty-six persons not in trade to aid the selectmen and the committee of correspondence by furnishing information and legal assistance.[74] In Boston the act was not deemed sufficiently comprehensive, and on April 14 prices were laid down for at least fifty additional commodities and such services as carting and trucking not enumerated in the state law.[75]

Nevertheless the precipitate decline in the value of money soon created deep dissatisfaction with these measures in New England. The Massachusetts farmers refused to bring produce to the markets and the townsmen charged them with bad faith; whereas the country people regarded the Bostonians as speculators and profit-

---

[71] *N.J. Exec. Corr.*, pp. 34–35; Burnett, *Letters*, II, 340; Ford, *Journals*, VII, 267.

[72] *Mins. Albany Comm. of Corr.*, I, 772.

[73] *Continental Journal*, Feb. 6, 1777. See also appeal to farmers and laborers for support of the acts in *ibid.*, Feb. 13, 1777.

[74] New Haven Town Rec., Jan. 30, 1777; *Independent Ledger*, April 24, 1777; *Boston Rec.*, XVIII, 260, 261; *Mass. Acts and Resolves*, V, 262–64. See also F. W. Caulkins, *History of Norwich* (Hartford, 1866), p. 243.

[75] *Continental Journal*, April 17; *Boston Gazette*, April 28, 1777.

eers.[76] As early as January the Massachusetts House of Representatives found it necessary to revise some prices, and further modifications were proposed by a committee of the council on March 17, including an increase in horsekeeping per night from 2s. to 2s.8d., and of teaming per ton per mile from 1s.6d. to 2s. The proposal was rejected, but a new committee on April 4 favored repeal of as much of the law as related to flour, a general revision of the price code, and the calling of a new intercolonial convention to meet that month.[77] On May 10 the act was revised. The new statute established maximum prices on some thirty enumerated articles and services, including teaming, and conferred broad powers upon the selectmen to fix prices of nonenumerated articles and to seize the goods of engrossers and place them on the market. Under authority of the act the towns were to choose committees annually to aid in its enforcement. Certain labor services and prices generally were revised upwards. Thus, teaming per ton per mile was raised from 1s.6d. in the act of January 28 to 2s. in the act of May 10.[78] This gave rise to dissatisfaction in neighboring states which had been parties to the Providence convention. The governor of Rhode Island protested that he could not enforce his own wage and price codes if the larger states did not live up to their part of the bargain.[79] In some Massachusetts towns the response to the revised code was sympathetic. A convention of committees of correspondence in Plymouth, meeting on May 21, urged support and strict enforcement,[80] and the following week Watertown chose a committee of five to put the act into effect.[81] To criticisms made at the Plymouth sessions that the wages of labor were too high, a writer in the *Independent Chronicle* replied that the increased cost of provisions and depreciation of the currency justified the prevailing wages.[82] Another writer admitted that the workers were endeavoring to secure wages which would bear the same proportion

---

[76] R. V. Harlow, "Economic Conditions in Massachusetts during the American Revolution," Colonial Society of Massachusetts, *Publications*, XX, 167–71, and authorities cited.

[77] *Mass. Acts and Resolves*, V, 674, 723, 724; *Boston Gazette*, March 17, 1777; *Continental Journal*, March 20, 1777.

[78] *Mass. Acts and Resolves*, V, 642–47; *Boston Gazette*, June 23, 1777.

[79] *Mass. Acts and Resolves*, V, 724; Mass. Archives, Vol. 137, f. 50.

[80] *Boston Gazette*, June 16, 1777.   [81] *Watertown Rec.*, IV, pt. vi, 161.

[82] [Boston] *Independent Chronicle*, Aug. 29, 1777.

to the price of imported articles and necessaries as they formerly did.[83] No sooner was the act passed, therefore, than revisions were considered by the General Court.[84]

Elsewhere the effects of the regulating acts set up under the Providence convention were denounced. The other New England states found it necessary in the spring of 1777 to authorize higher price levels.[85] Thus, the town of Providence specifically instructed her representatives in the legislature that the act was

so intricate, variable, and complicated, that it cannot remain any time equitable . . . It was made to cheapen the articles of life, but it has in fact raised their prices, by producing an artificial and in some articles a real scarcity. It was made to unite us in good agreement respecting prices; but hath produced animosity, and ill will between town and country, and between buyers and sellers in general. It was made to bring us up to some equitable standard of honesty . . . but hath produced a sharping set of mushroom peddlars, who adulterate their commodities, and take every advantage to evade the . . . act, by . . . quibbles and lies. It was done to give credit to our currency; . . . but it tends to introduce bartering and make a currency of almost everything but money.[86]

Those were days when official bodies did not hesitate to call a spade by its name. As the Massachusetts towns were in complete sympathy with these sentiments, on June 27 a joint committee of the Massachusetts Council and House of Representatives reported a motion for the calling of an interstate convention, including delegates from New Hampshire, Massachusetts, Rhode Island, Connecticut, and New York, to meet at Springfield on July 30 to consider such interstate problems as currency depreciation and monopoly.[87] The Springfield convention resolved on August 4 that the acts against monopoly and oppression, being "attended with inconveniences," be repealed "so far as they relate to affixing the prices at which the articles therein enumerated shall be sold, and creating penalties for not observing the same." Severe penalties were urged for engrossers and profiteers.[88] As a matter of fact the states

83 *Ibid.*, Sept. 11, 1777.
84 *Mass. Acts and Resolves*, V, 810–13; Mass. Archives, Vol. 137, f. 133.
85 April 10, 1777, *Laws of New Hampshire*, IV, 88–92; March, 1777, *R.I. Col. Rec.*, VIII, 183–85; May, 1777, *Conn. State Rec.*, I, 230–31.
86 *Providence Gazette*, June 21, 1777.   87 *Mass. Acts and Resolves*, V, 812, 813.
88 *Conn. State Rec.*, I, 599–606.

outdid the Springfield proposals and repealed the entire act, including, generally, restrictions upon engrossers and public auctions as well as price and wage controls.[89] This ended direct regulation of prices and wages by the central government in Massachusetts, although further legislation regulating engrossing and monopolizing, establishing embargoes, and restricting public auctions was passed from time to time during the Revolution. One of the methods of dealing with engrossers and profiteers adopted in Connecticut was to empower the town selectmen acting as assessors to increase their assessment by an additional £50 minimum—a crude form of war profits tax.[90]

At this stage the Continental Congress, which had, in the face of widespread popular support of such measures at the beginning of the war, refused by a close vote to endorse the original Providence plan, came out in November, 1777, after the New Englanders had found it expedient to scuttle the price and wage codes, with a recommendation for a broad scheme of price and wage regulation. A call was issued for three interstate conventions: (1) for South Carolina and Georgia to meet at Charleston on February 15; (2) for North Carolina, Virginia, and Maryland to meet at Fredericksburg, Va., on January 15; and (3) for the remaining eight northern states to meet on the latter date at New Haven "to regulate and ascertain the price of labour, manufacturing, internal produce" and imported commodities, and also to determine innkeepers' tariffs.[91] Despite the demonstrated futility of such legislation in the face of unsound fiscal policies, some prominent members of Congress, notably Richard Henry Lee, were optimistic about regulation and were not easily swayed by economic theories or theorists. Thus, Lee wrote Sam Adams, another warm advocate of regulation, on November 23:

I know my friend Mr. John Adams will say the regulation of prices wont do. I agree it will not singly answer, and I know that Taxation

---

[89] *Mass. Acts and Resolves,* V, 733–34; *Laws of New Hampshire,* IV, 126; *Conn. State Rec.,* I, 366. Shortly after repeal the inhabitants of Coventry memorialized the Connecticut legislature to revive the regulatory measures (Oct., 1777). Conn. State Archives, Revolutionary War, VIII, f. 66.

[90] "And others in like proportion according to their gains." *Conn. State Rec.,* I, 365, 366.

[91] Ford, *Journals,* IX, 956; *Mass. Acts and Resolves,* V, 1012; Papers of the Continental Congress, No. 19, III, fols. 155–63.

with Oeconomy are the radical cures. But I also know that the best Physicians sometimes attend to Symptoms, apply palliatives and under favor of the Truce thus obtained, introduce cause removing medicines. Let us for a moment check the enormity of the evil by this method, whilst the other more sure, but more slow methods secure us against a return of the mischief. The middle and southern States (particularly the insatiable avarice of Pennsylvania) having refused to join in the plan formerly, rendered the experiment on your part inconclusive and partial; therefore I do not think Mr. Adams's argument drawn from that trial quite decisive against the Measure. I incline to think that the necessity of the case will now procure its adoption universally, and then we shall see what great things may be effected by common consent. The American conduct has already shattered and overset the conclusions of the best Theorists, and I hope this will be another instance.[92]

The New Haven meeting, the only one of the three actually held, resulted in the addition of a group of the middle states to the numbers enacting wage and price codes. The New Haven convention went on record excoriating engrossers as enemies of the cause and not unlike "the man who, zealously professing Christianity, lives in continued practice of the breach of its precepts." Conceding that in the long run the reduction of the circulating medium and the meeting of expenditures through adequate taxation and loans were the essential remedies, it vigorously defended price regulation as founded in necessity, rhetorically asking:

Why do we complain of a partial infringement of liberty manifestly tending to the preservation of the whole? Must the lunatick run uncontrouled to the destruction of himself and neighbours merely because he is under the operation of medicines which may in time work his cure? and indeed without the use of those medicines will the confinement cure him? Must we be suffered to continue the exaction of such high prices to the destruction of the common cause, and of ourselves with it, merely because the reduction of the quantity of our currency may in time redress the evil; and because any other method may be complained of as an infringement of liberty?

The commissioners observed that their wage and price schedules were "much higher than anyone will suppose they ought to be." As to labor, the New Haven meeting set up the following schedule: (1) labor of farmers, mechanics "and others" at rates not exceed-

[92] Samuel Adams Papers, N.Y. Public Library; *Letters of Richard Henry Lee,* I, 353.

ing seventy-five percent advance over those obtaining in the several states in 1774; (2) teaming and all land transportation not to exceed the rate of five-twelfths of a continental dollar for the carriage of 2,000 "neat weight per mile, including all expences attending the same." Manufactures and domestic produce were likewise allowed a seventy-five percent advance over 1774; trades were allowed twenty-five percent increases, with additions for cost of transportation; and innholders were not allowed more than fifty percent advance on liquors, and for other articles of entertainment, refreshment, or forage not more than seventy-five percent over the 1774 prices. In setting prices for the enumerated commodities, variations were made on the basis of three zones: (1) New Hampshire; (2) Massachusetts and Rhode Island; (3) Connecticut, New York, New Jersey, and Pennsylvania, although throughout the constituent states one price was to obtain for manufactured products such as tanned leather, shoes, iron, steel, and a few other products. The idea of price and wage differentials thus clearly antedates the New Deal program. As Delaware did not send a delegate, the convention at its closing session on January 31, 1778, transmitted a copy of the proceedings and noted in a covering communication that, while they had "omitted to regulate the prices of labour, etc. for your State," they did not doubt but that from her "zealous attachment to the common cause similar measures would be immediately adopted by her." [93]

The resolves of the New Haven convention met a mingled reception. New Hampshire, Massachusetts, and Rhode Island took no action. In Massachusetts it was claimed that the public was sharply divided on the program,[94] and her two neighbors deferred to her leadership.[95] Governor Trumbull of Connecticut cautioned the legislature that "if we affix a low price to provisions and articles of importation, we shall find that the Farmer will cease to till the ground for more than is necessary for his own subsistence, and the

[93] Library of Congress transcript of the journal of the New Haven convention; *Conn. State Rec.,* I, 607–20; S. E. Baldwin, "The New Haven Convention of 1778," New Haven Hist. Soc., *Papers,* III, 33–62.

[94] *Mass. Acts and Resolves,* V, 1016, 1017.

[95] Henry Phillips, Jr., *Historical Sketches of the Paper Currency of the American Colonies* (Roxbury, Mass., 1865–66), II, 243; Sumner, *op. cit.,* I, 66. For Rhode Island's failure to comply see Conn. State Archives, Revolutionary War, X, f. 222; *R.I. Col. Rec.,* VIII, 423–25.

merchant to risque his fortune on a small and precarious prospect of gain." [96] Nonetheless the Connecticut General Assembly incorporated the New Haven recommendations in its enactments, specifically authorizing the selectmen to determine such wages of labor, prices of commodities, and charges of innholders as were not particularly enumerated. The act further provided that no resident of the state could sue in law or equity before taking oath that he had not willingly "received or contracted to receive for any labour done or article sold" more than the rate fixed by this law. Statutes were also passed in New York, New Jersey, and Pennsylvania establishing rates of wages and prices in close conformity to the New Haven proposals.[97]

Opponents of regulation in Congress had seen nothing in the recent course of events to shake them in their opposition. John Witherspoon, writing at the end of January, expressed the view that the New Haven scheme was "impracticable and absurd," as "fixing prices by Law never had nor ever will have any Effect but stopping Commerce and making Things scarce and dear." [98] The regulating act was the Achan, troubler of Israel, Oliver Wolcott wrote his wife, and stated that "no Regard is paid to any Act of this Kind in this State [Pennsylvania]. No such Act to the Southward of it Exists nor ever will." [99] On the other hand, Eliphalet Dyer, in justifying the calling of the New Haven convention, attributed the price rise not to the large emissions of bills or the scarcity of goods but to "that corrupt, avaricious, unnatural, infectious Disease, which was spread'g thro every State, and which Nothing but extraordinary Remedies could check and Controul." [100]

When Thomas Cushing, president of the New Haven convention, under date of January 30, sent a report of the proceedings to

[96] Conn. State Archives, Revolutionary War, X, f. 90.

[97] *Conn. State Rec.*, I, 524–28; *Connecticut Journal*, March 4, 1778. Copies of this act were ordered to be sent to the legislature of the constituent states. *Ibid.*, p. 536. 1 *Laws of New York*, 1st sess., c. 34; *New Jersey Laws* (Wilson ed.), p. 34; *N.J. Archives*, 2d ser., I, 519; *Pa. Statutes at Large*, IX, 236–38, 283–84. Reports of proceedings of the Poughkeepsie convention of Jan. 11, 1778, and of the General Assembly of Pennsylvania of Jan. 30, 1778, enacting this program, are in the Rhode Island State Archives. See also *Minutes of the Delaware Council*, pp. 194, *passim*.

[98] Burnett, *Letters*, III, 57.

[99] *Ibid.*, III, 167, 168; Oliver Wolcott MSS, II, 51, Connecticut Historical Society.

[100] *Ibid.*, III, 125, 126.

Congress, that body referred the matter to a committee. Witherspoon, leading opponent of regulation, was a member for a time
but was later replaced. On April 8, the committee recommended
that the proceedings be transmitted to the states from Maryland
to Georgia inclusive, "with the Propriety of adopting similar Measures to be referred to their serious Consideration, and that it be
recommended to Delaware, Pennsylvania and the States eastward
thereof to suspend the Execution of the Plan of the Convention,
for regulating Prices, until Congress shall inform them of the Proceedings of the Southern States on the same subject." [101] Action
was delayed until June, when Congress decided to follow the second recommendation of the committee and to ignore the first on
the ground that "it hath been found by Experience that Limitation upon the Prices of Commodities are not only ineffectual for
the Purposes proposed, but likewise productive of very evil Consequences to the great Detriment of the public Service and griev-
ous Oppression of Individuals." It thus reversed its action of the
previous January and recommended that the states repeal such
laws "limiting, regulating, or restraining the Price of any Article,
Manufacture or Commodity." [102] Wages of labor were not specifically singled out, but were understood by the states to be included
in the repeal recommendation. Those states that had enacted the
New Haven schedule promptly repealed their statutes. [103]

For the better part of a year no broad wage or price regulations
were enacted by any state legislature. From this it might be inferred that the disapproval expressed by Congress of the sad experience with earlier measures had brought regulation into disrepute. However, as a matter of fact, through the instrumentality of
town meetings and county and regional conventions, wage and
price regulation was revived within the year with considerable

[101] Ford, *Journals*, X, 172, 260, 322–24. The report, in the writing of Elbridge
Gerry, is in the Papers of the Continental Congress, No. 24, f. 393.

[102] *Ibid.*, XI, 472, 569. The report, in the writing of Gouverneur Morris, is in the
Papers of the Continental Congress, No. 19, VI, f. 123.

[103] Conn. State Archives, Revolutionary War, X, f. 248a, XIII, f. 126; *Session Laws,
1778*, p. 499; Pa. Mins. House of Rep., I, 211, which suspended the act in May. The
northern states were convinced that those to the south would never adopt these regulations. See letter of Connecticut delegates to Governor Trumbull, York, April 29,
1778, in Burnett, *Letters*, III, 202.

éclat.[104] The catastrophic decline of paper currency was mainly responsible for the renewed activity. Notable in adopting such measures were the towns of Massachusetts, which state actually passed for the remainder of the war no more legislation fixing wage or price levels.[105] On May 25, 1779, the town of Boston adopted the report of a committee enumerating the prices of some fifteen articles on a month-to-month basis.[106] A few weeks later a group of Boston merchants agreed at a public meeting to a scale of prices to be in force among themselves and to a further limitation of prices, after July 1 next ensuing, to levels which had prevailed on the first of May, provided other Massachusetts towns coöperated.[107] These resolves were promptly endorsed at a Watertown meeting, where a pledge was given that if the Boston prices remained constant both the farmers and the mechanics of Watertown would lower their prices in accord with the decline in foreign commodity rates. A committee was appointed to fix prices, and the meeting declared that persons selling their goods at excessive rates would be deemed "enemies of their country and cried as such by the town clerk for six months after every public meeting of the town." [108] Pursuant to a general endorsement, on the part of the town of Boston, of the merchants' price agreement, with specific instructions to seek the advice of other local committees as to the best measures to be adopted in the emergency, the Boston committee of correspondence called a convention to be held at Concord on July 14 to consider the regulation of the wages of labor and the prices of produce and manufactured articles. This call was widely endorsed.[109] At the July Convention at Concord some 140

---

[104] One writer in the *Connecticut Journal,* under date of Oct. 14, 1778, maintained that prices ought to be fixed at what they were before the war and kept so until the conflict was over. See also Phillips, *Continental Paper Money,* p. 84.

[105] A number of towns, including Rehoboth, petitioned the legislature at this time for a new price regulation law, but, although the committee considering the matter reported favorably, the legislature remained adamant. *Mass. Acts and Resolves,* V, 1243.

[106] *Independent Chronicle,* June 10, 1779. A few weeks later Mendon set prices. *Continental Journal,* July 1, 1779.

[107] *Independent Chronicle,* June 24; *Boston Gazette,* June 21; *Massachusetts Spy,* July 1, 1779.

[108] *Watertown Rec.,* IV, pt. vi, 203–4.

[109] *Continental Journal,* July 15, 1779 (Roxbury); *Plymouth Town Rec.,* III, 375; *Watertown Rec.,* IV, pt. vi, 206.

Massachusetts towns from eight counties were present. By general agreement the convention set maximum prices for certain enumerated commodities, violators to have their names published in the newspapers as enemies of the country, and directed the towns to fix the wages of labor, the prices of innholders, teaming, manufactures, and goods "in Proportion to the rates of the Necessaries of Life, as stated in the above Regulations," cautioning them "to keep a watchful Eye over each other, that no Evasion or infringement of these Resolutions may escape Nature." [110] The convention's resolves were endorsed enthusiastically by town after town, which proceeded to set prices on nonenumerated articles and appointed committees to enforce price regulations.[111] At least seventy-five towns ratified the convention.[112] To avoid great disparities in labor and price scales, counties also held regulating conventions. As regards wages, there were some differences in the prevailing scales, especially in the skilled crafts. Common labor generally received £3 per day, and skilled workers £4 in Falmouth, £3/18 in Boston, and £3/8 in Plymouth. Variations were noted also in wages for such enumerated trades as barbers, hatters, tanners, curriers, butchers, and tailors, and in certain labor services, such as carting [113] and horseshoeing.[114] These conventions sought to stabilize wages and prices within the counties and to iron out discrepancies wherever possible. Thus, the Worcester county convention of August 11, in which thirty-eight towns participated, set maximum wages for common labor at £2 4s. per diem during the best season; female labor was to receive a mere £2 a week, and mechanics and skilled workers were to be paid proportionately. At a convention on August 31 of Middlesex and Suffolk county towns, in addition to seeking wage and price uniformity, recommendations were made to fix prices even for such articles as drugs and medicines.[115]

110 *Boston Gazette*, Aug. 2, 1779.
111 *Boston Gazette*, Aug. 9, 1779; Col. Soc. of Mass., *Publications*, Vol. X (Hengham).
112 See *Boston Gazette*, Aug. 16, 30, Sept. 6, 1779; *Watertown Rec.*, IV, pt. vi, 206–10; *Massachusetts Spy*, Aug. 16, 1779; *Independent Chronicle*, Aug. 19, Sept. 16, 1779; *Boston Rec.*, XXVI, 80, 81; *Plymouth Town Rec.*, III, 379–81.
113 Watertown, 18s.; Plymouth, 13s.
114 Watertown, 5s.; Plymouth, 4s.; Boston, 6s.
115 *Massachusetts Spy,* Aug. 19, 26, 1779; *Independent Chronicle*, Sept. 6, 9, 23, Oct. 14, 1779; *Boston Gazette,* Sept. 6, 1779; Lovell, *Worcester in the Revolution,* pp. 96–98.

In the face of the express disapproval of the Continental Congress and repeal by the state legislatures, wage and price fixing conventions were held not alone in Massachusetts but also in New Hampshire, Rhode Island, New York, and Pennsylvania in order to check the rapid descent of the currency. The Providence action, taken on August 31, was in response to a resolve adopted at a convention of Rhode Island towns held at East Greenwich on August 10, parallel to the Concord convention in Massachusetts.[116] The wage code adopted is typical of New England at this time, but its sweeping enumerations and careful gradations are worthy of separate examination:

	per diem
Common laborers, "finding themselves"	48s.
Ship-carpenters, caulkers, masons	73s.
House-carpenters, ship-joiners, riggers	72s.

Blacksmiths, 10s. per lb. "For shoeing a horse all round, 41/10. For steeling and corking all round, 6l. For new setting all round 1l. 7s. For a good ax well steeled, 6l. and other work in proportion.

Tanners, 18s. per pound for good sole leather and other leather in proportion.

Shoemakers. For best customers shoes 6l. 6s. per pair, and other work in proportion. Best boots 25l. per pair.

Printers, Physicians, Apothecaries, Blockmakers, Cabinet-makers, Pewterers, Rope-makers, Boat-builders, Tin-men, and Painters, shall reduce their prices Twenty per cent.

Leather-Dressers. For the best Deer's leather breeches, 33l. and other work in proportion.

Hatters. For the best Beaver hats, 35l.; best castor ditto, 21l. Best Felt ditto, 4l.

Taylors. For making a plain suit of broadcloth cloaths, 17l. and other cloaths in proportion.

Card makers. For best wool-cards, made in this State, 39l. 12l. per doz. pair, and 72s. per single pair.

Glaziers. For setting glass and finding puttey not more than 4s. per square.

Innholders and Victuallers, shall reduce their prices for victualling and horse-keeping Twenty per cent.

Goldsmiths shall not take more than the weight of the plate they

---

[116] *Pennsylvania Packet,* Sept. 2, 1779.

work, and sixteen times what they had for their labour in
the year 1774.
Saddlers. For a good man's saddle, with a housing or saddle
cloth, £43.
For a good man's bridle, 4*l*. 10*s*. and all other work in proportion.
Sail-makers. For working new duck 5*l*. 8*s*. per bolt. . . .
All other tradesmen and mechanics not before mentioned
shall reduce their work and manufactures in average proportion with the above.[117]

While the scale for common labor was considerably lower than
that adopted in Massachusetts as a result of the Concord convention, both common and skilled labor were allowed a wage level
some fifteen times higher than that which had obtained in the
beginning of 1777—eloquent testimony to the extent of currency
depreciation.

Philadelphia had acted in the meantime. Mass meetings, parades,
and handbills during May of 1779 announced the determination
of the inhabitants to regulate prices. The action of a meeting held
in the State House yard, at which a committee was appointed to
fix a scale of prices, was referred to by Daniel of St. Thomas Jenifer
as that of a "Mob . . . assembled to regulate prices." Members of
Congress were alarmed. "What will be the issue God knows," said
one at this time.[118] The committee published its scale on June 29,
along with a refutation of the view that "trade will regulate itself."
To do so, ran the argument, trade must not be "clogged with a
disease." It favored action by similar committees in every state
and county to the end that the prices obtaining in 1774 might be
multiplied by some certain number to be agreed upon by all in
order to ascertain the regulated price.[119] The artillery company of
Philadelphia promptly passed resolutions offering, if necessary, to
support the committee with their arms.[120] In June, 1779, a price
schedule was adopted at a town meeting in Lancaster and the same
month a committee in New Castle County, Delaware, took similar

117 *American Journal and General Advertiser,* Sept. 2, 1779.
118 *Ibid.,* IV, 232; *Maryland Archives,* XXI, 417. See also *Pennsylvania Packet,*
June 22, 26, 1779.
119 *Pennsylvania Packet,* June 29, 1779. For the pro-regulation arguments of
"Philodemus" at this time see *ibid.,* June 19, 1779.
120 *Ibid.,* May 27, June 29, July 1, 1779; A. McF. Davis, "Limitation of Prices in
Massachusetts, 1776–79," Col. Soc. of Mass., *Publications,* X, 12, 13; Sumner, *op. cit.,*
I, 72, 73; Bolles, *op. cit.,* pp. 162, 163.

measures and adopted a resolution regarding wages couched in the following language:

Resolved also, That it be recommended to the good people of this county, not to give a higher price to labourers the ensuing harvest, than one bushel of wheat, or the value thereof as above stipulated, for two days reaping or mowing, or one day's cradling; nor to give the mechanicks higher prices than were current the first day of May last.[121]

One Albany correspondent, writing in June, 1779, reported that "all our districts have chosen Committees, and are regulating the prices of country produce." [122] During the summer, meetings were held in upstate New York, notably in Albany, Orange, and Dutchess counties, to consider the problem of depreciation, profiteering, and hoarding; and specific measures were adopted by the Schenectady committee of correspondence.[123] The Dutchess County committees, meeting at Poughkeepsie on August 14, restricted the increase of prices of imported articles as follows: "dry goods at 12½% retale, to be added to the first cost on the original invoice, and the cost of transportation." It was further resolved "that it be recommended to the mechanicks, labourers and others, to regulate their prices according to the above price." [124] During the summer also the Essex County, New Jersey, committee fixed rates for transportation and wholesale and retail prices for numerous commodities and, in accordance with instructions from the county, ruled that "not more than fifteen for one from the price of 1774, ought to be demanded or given" for labor, produce, and manufactures, "which it is expected will very soon be reduced." [125]

This spontaneous convention activity was viewed with apprehension by opponents of regulation in Congress, among them William Ellery, who expressed opposition at this time to "unnatural restraints" which "eventually do no good," at the same time conceding that only through universal adoption of regulation could its efficacy be fairly tested.[126] Meriwether Smith, writing to Thomas Jefferson in the summer of 1779, expressed alarm at the growth of

---

121 *Pennsylvania Packet,* July 3, 1779.   122 *Ibid.,* June 29, 1779.

123 *N.Y. Journal,* July 19, 26, Aug. 2, 16, 1779; *Mins. of the Schenectady Committee of Correspondence,* II, 1146–48, 1157, 1158; *Pa. Packet,* June 20, 1779. For arguments at this time urging limitation and trade regulation, see *N.Y. Journal,* April 26, Oct. 11, 1779.

124 *N.Y. Journal,* Aug. 16, 1779.   125 *N.J. Journal,* July 20, 1779.

126 To John Langdon, York, March 2, 1778. Burnett, *Letters,* III, 105.

the activities of local committees: "The most pernicious Effect will flow from the establishment of those Bodies." He quoted Gerard as charging that they were in fact "instruments in the Hands of designing Men." [127]

The Concord convention had voted to resume sessions in October, at which time was adopted a new schedule of wages and prices reflecting further the steady rise in the premium of gold and silver and also the trend toward increasing by many times the number of enumerated commodities.[128] The towns were authorized to fix the wages of common labor and mechanics and the rates of innkeepers. Immediate response to the second convention program was cordial,[129] but considered reflection led to the abandonment of serious attempts to enforce the code. A Boston committee reported to its town meeting that they had found it impracticable to fix the prices of goods which they had been requested to do.[130] Shortly thereafter the publishers of the five Boston newspapers announced that they were forced to raise the price of their papers, as regulation had been "of no effect for them to stem the tide of avarice alone." [131] A published observation commented on "the various evasions by which the resolves of the late Convention . . . which with apparent cheerfulness and unanimity were adopted by their constituents, have in many instances failed of their desired effect." [132] In New Jersey, voluntary associations were proposed as a substitute for penal laws which, one proponent conceded, had failed to restrain "exorbitant prices." [133]

But the cause of regulation was not permitted to die. "Crito," writing in the *New Jersey Gazette,* June 16, 1779, urged joint action on the part of New York, New Jersey, and Pennsylvania to regulate wages and prices. In October, 1779, New Jersey and New York strongly urged upon Congress a renewed program of regulation. New Jersey had never repealed her regulatory act, but merely suspended it until other states adopted similar programs, for, in the words of Woodbury Langdon, it was deemed "very impolitic for any particular state to regulate Prices unless it becomes general

---

127 *Ibid.,* IV, 348 (July 26, 1779).   128 *Massachusetts Spy,* Nov. 5, 1779.
129 *Boston Gazette,* Oct. 25; *Independent Chronicle,* Oct. 21, 1779; *Boston Town Rec.,* XXVI, 98, 99.
130 *Boston Town Rec.,* XXVI, 100, 101.   131 *Independent Chronicle,* Nov. 25, 1779.
132 *Boston Gazette,* Oct. 25, 1779.   133 *N.J. Journal,* June 20, 1779.

throughout the United States." [134] On the twentieth of October
commissioners from the New England states and New York met
at Hartford and defended the necessity of regulation,

especially when it is considered that the engrosser, monopolizer, opulent
farmer and trader, will be induced, and it will be in their power (unless
restricted) to encrease the price of the articles they have on hand in
proportion to the encrease of their taxes, which will not only defeat
the end and the purpose of taxation, oblige Congress to make further
emissions, or the army be left destitute, but too great a burden of the
taxes will be cast on the poor and middling farmer, and will produce
a further depreciation of our currency, which if not prevented may
soon end in very unhappy effects.

It was the sense of the meeting that price limitation would have
a tendency to prevent further depreciation of the currency, and
that "to render such limitation permanent and salutary" all the
states, or at least "as far westward as Virginia," should accede to
the program. To this end it urged that a convention of the northern and middle states and Maryland and Virginia be held in Philadelphia in January, 1780. In the light of price-fixing action taken
by conventions in New Hampshire, Massachusetts, and Rhode Island, the remaining constituent states—Connecticut and New York
—were urged to adopt similar measures.[135] If additional prompt-
ing were needed, it was provided by Congress, which considered
the report of the Hartford meeting, transmitted by its president,
Stephen Hopkins, and promptly resolved that a general limitation
be enacted throughout the states, whereby wages and prices for
farming and common labor, tradesmen and mechanics, water and
land carriage, and domestic produce were "not to exceed twentyfold of the prices current through the various seasons of the year
1774." [136] The Hartford proceedings were specifically endorsed
and recommended to the nonparticipant states.[137] In justification
of this recommendation, Congress maintained that the advance of

[134] *N.J. Exec. Corr.*, pp. 195–97; Burnett, *Letters*, IV, 485, 495; MS, R.I. Archives,
Letters to the Governors, 1779–80, f. 19; W. R. Staples, *Rhode Island in the Continental Congress* (Providence, 1870), pp. 253, 254.

[135] *Conn. State Rec.*, II, 566–69. "There is not a doubt but the proposition will be
cheerfully acceded to by this state." *N.Y. Journal*, Nov. 30, 1779.

[136] *Mass. Acts and Resolves*, V, 1261, 1262; *Conn. State Rec.*, II, 562, 563; *N.C.
State Rec.*, XIV, 214; Burnett, *Letters*, IV, 514, 519, 522; Ford, *Journals*, XV, 1289.

[137] Burnett, *Letters*, IV, 542.

prices was due to "unprincipled and disaffected people"—a view not unlike that of President Hoover, who held that the stock market debacle after 1929 was due to bear raids rather than to fundamental economic causes. The argument *ad hominem* is always good politics, if unsound economic thinking. This view was held by Congress as late as January, 1780.[138] As to the value of this latest resolve, some members of Congress reserved judgment. Samuel Huntington felt that only time and experience would "bring all men to agree in Judgment" as to the wisdom of this plan.[139] Allen Jones, who entered Congress a few weeks later, was unenthusiastic and convinced that the plan would not be generally adopted.[140]

In response to the joint urgings of the Hartford convention and Congress, Connecticut and New York took prompt action. At the January session, 1780, Connecticut passed "An act for a general limitation of prices, to prevent the withholding from sale the necessaries of life." [141] This was endorsed: "To lie unpublished till further order from the Governor," who was to so order on receiving word that the other New England states and New York had passed similar acts of limitation agreeable to the Congressional resolves. But this statute was neither printed nor recorded. New York, on February 26, 1780, passed "An act for a general limitation of prices, and to prevent engrossing and withholding within this State." [142] Under this act a penalty of treble the value or price of the services or commodities could be exacted, but actually the "wages of tradesmen and mechanics," though mentioned, were not ascertained in the statute, which dealt primarily with commodities. This act was not to be effective until twenty days after proclamation by the governor stating that information had come to him that Massachusetts, Connecticut, and Pennsylvania had passed laws for the like purpose. New Jersey likewise fell into line, and in Maryland a bill limiting prices was proposed, but never enacted.[143]

The drama of futility was drawing to a close. In their instructions to their delegates to the final price-fixing convention the

---

138 Ford, *Journals*, XVI, 57–59. See also *Boston Gazette*, April 6, 1778, for a similar view, charging depreciation of the currency to avarice.

139 Burnett, *Letters*, IV, 527; V, 1.   140 *Ibid.*, IV, 548.

141 Conn. State Archives, Revolutionary War, XVIII, f. 71; *N.Y. Journal*, April 10, 1780.

142 *Laws of N.Y.*, 3d sess., c. 43.   143 Burnett, *Letters*, IV, 550; V, 4, 6.

Massachusetts General Court advised them to consider the advantages of such a plan and to give "equal attention" to the question of "the practicability of its being carried into execution," being careful to point out that previous efforts had "Shut up our Granaries, discouraged Husbandry and Commerce and starved our Sea Ports," creating "such a stagnation of Business and such a withholding of articles as has obliged the People to give up its measure or submit to starving." [144] James Lovell, in a letter to Sam Adams, dated January 28, 1780, prophesied just what would take place. "I do not know," he wrote, "but the regulating Convention may again get effectively together, but if they do, I suspect the Consequences will not only be to let *us* and *themselves* down easily." [145]

At the final Philadelphia session in February, 1780, New York and Virginia did not attend, although the former gave pledges that she would carry into effect a general plan for regulating prices. Both states were requested to appoint commissioners, a committee was set up to propose a general plan for price limitation and to report, and the convention adjourned to the fourth day of April, but never appears to have reassembled.[146] On February 15 the Connecticut delegates wrote Governor Trumbull: "We hope that some Measures will be soon adopted for introducing a stable Medium of Trade that will render a limitation of prices unnecessary." [147] Such measures were soon taken by Congress, which apparently did not subscribe to the optimistic view of the North Carolina delegates that, even among the affluent, prices would "find limits beyond which they cannot go, and Commerce will so regulate itself that even paper money will find a certain fixed value as a general representative of Industry." [148] The action of Congress on March 18 fixing the value of continental bills in circulation at not more than one-fortieth of their denominational value and requesting the states to call in and destroy their bills in circulation did not end the price crisis at once. For some time thereafter continental bills still in circulation continued to depreciate, and the view of Davis that "prices would now take care

---

[144] *Mass. Acts and Resolves*, V, 1263.
[145] Samuel Adams Papers, N.Y. Public Library.
[146] Mass. Hist. Soc., *Collections*, 7th ser., III, 15; *Conn. State Rec.*, II, 577–79; Staples, *Rhode Island in the Continental Congress*, p. 272; Burnett, *Letters*, V, 16, 23, 27.
[147] Burnett, *Letters*, V, 36.   [148] Burnett, *Letters*, V, 57 (Feb. 29, 1780).

of themselves and be governed by natural laws" [149] is by no means borne out by the facts.

Throughout the price crisis in the winter of 1780 one member of Congress, John Armstrong, stubbornly maintained his advocacy of regulation in the face of increasing opposition. The issue to him was "whether we shall proceed in this same natural or rather slothful and timid way, leaving our internal commerce to regulate itself, and take chance for the event, or attempt the plain highway of Law and publick authority, in the regulation of Prices generally." For him this question had no "alternative that can promise success." Regulation, he urged, was founded in critical necessity. "The Hacknied Maxim, that Trade must always Regulate itself, Is in our situation as impolitick as it is arrogant and absurd, and patience but scarcely restrains from bestowing upon it the severer epithets due to a possession so very ill-timed." The blockade, speculation, and hoarding forced this exception to the "Mercantile rule." Opposition was due in good part, according to Armstrong, to "an idle refinement of civil rights and lethargic timidity." [150]

There is no doubt that Armstrong's views were still popular, as regional meetings subsequent to the Philadelphia fiasco demonstrate; but students of finance were distinctly hostile. Pelatiah Webster, whose first *Essay on Free Trade and Finance,* published in July, 1779, had wide influence, clearly understood the relation between paper money and the price structure and likened the "utmost effect" of these laws to "that of water sprinkled on a blacksmith's forge, which indeed deadens the flame for a moment, but never fails to increase the heat and force of the internal fire." [151] "Honestus," writing in the *New Jersey Gazette,* offered to prove his charge that regulation and depreciation were in reality taxes, "but of the most unequal and oppressive kind," with "three

[149] Col. Soc. of Mass., *Publications,* X, 20; Harlow, *American Historical Review,* XXXV, 60.

[150] Letters of Armstrong to George Washington, Joseph Reed, and Horatio Gates, Oct.–March, 1780, in Burnett, *Letters,* IV, 490; V, 8, 13, 14, 38, 76–78; Reed MSS, Vol. VI, and Gates MSS, Vol. XVI, N.Y. Historical Society.

[151] *Political Essays on the Nature and Operation of Money, Public Finances, and Other Subjects* (Philadelphia, 1791), pp. 11–18, 128n, 129, 132; Bradford, *History of Massachusetts,* II, 172. See also W. B. Reed, *Life and Correspondence of Joseph Reed* (Philadelphia, 1847), II, 140.

words." To him regulation was "a solecism in politics," for, he observed:

Let A stand for the quantity of trade, that is the quantity of goods bought and sold; let B stand for the quantity of money, or circulating medium, necessary to carry on that trade; then consequently $A = B$; but regulation would make $A = 2B = 3B$, etc., etc., than which what can be a greater absurdity? [152]

Replying, a "True Patriot" denied the validity of the equation on the ground that the artificial factors of monopoly, engrossing, and forestalling produced an artificial scarcity in "A." Regulation of prices was justifiable to him on the same grounds as the usury and forestalling laws:

The stale saying, Trade must regulate itself, holds good where the requisite circumstances correspond; but ours manifestly indicate an exception to this rule.
But say some, a general regulation is not possible.—Why not? Is not interest regulated? Is there not a standard of profits in trade which custom has settled in all nations? Whence can this impossibility arise? [153]

"Eumenes," in the *New York Journal,* made his contribution to the confusion, pointing out that periodic revisions of the regulatory schedules with the idea of gradual price reductions would actually curb trade and manufactures and deter the farmer from producing more than his immediate needs.[154]

Such arguments were rooted in *laissez faire* reasoning. Occasionally, however, resort was had to constitutional principles. For example, one writer as early as May, 1777, maintained that the regulating of price by penal statute "always has and ever will be impracticable in a free country, because no law can be framed to limit a man in the purchase or disposal of property, but what must infringe those principles of liberty for which we are gloriously fighting." [155] Again in August, 1779, a group of Philadelphians memorialized the city for repeal of regulation, emphasizing the argument that limitation violated property rights by compelling a person to accept less in exchange for his goods than he could obtain in an uncontrolled market and therefore operated as a class tax. In reply, a committee of thirteen defended limitation upon his-

152 *N.J. Gazette,* Dec. 8, 1779.   153 *Ibid.,* March 29, 1780.
154 *N.Y. Journal,* Dec. 21, 1779.   155 *Connecticut Courant,* May 12, 1777.

torical grounds, citing instances in the past, such as usury laws and limitations of porters' and carriers' charges and of ferry rates, among other examples, and urging the parallel to general trade prices on the ground that restraints must be imposed to prevent a favored group from taking unjust advantage of the public's necessity. In conclusion, the committee asserted: "We have had the experience of four years without limitation or regulations; the consequence of which had very nearly been the total ruin of the currency and resting it here, we prefer this single case to all the arguments that can be produced against it." In 1783 the Pennsylvania Council of Censors declared that such regulations constituted "invasions of the right of property." [156]

The very same men who viewed wage and price controls as an invasion of property rights also expressed concern over the tendency of states to act in combination. Later New England conventions in 1780 and 1781, while not attempting to enforce further price codes, did make important recommendations of an economic nature and favored stronger Federal government.[157] The Articles of Confederation contained a prohibition of such combinations between states, and Hamilton and Madison were clearly opposed.[158] Nevertheless, the convention idea survived within the states, even though the original objectives were no longer determining. Local conventions within the counties continued to deal with economic and social grievances in such states as Massachusetts, and Shays's Rebellion can trace its lineage to a long line of county meetings starting in Revolutionary times. At the same time, the road for the Constitutional Convention of 1787 was actually paved by the interstate conventions on economic affairs, most notable being the last at Annapolis. From the failure of these experiments with economic controls, two consequences followed: (1) the creation of a strong Federal government; and (2) the crystallization of senti-

[156] *Pa. Packet*, Aug. 10, 1779; *Proceedings of the Constitutional Conventions of 1776 and 1790* (Harrisburg, 1825), pp. 86, 87; Bull, *op. cit.*, pp. 327–29. Historical arguments supporting regulation and their repudiation on common law grounds also advanced in the 19th century in Munn v. Illinois, 94 U.S. 113 (1876).

[157] "Doings of the Committee of the States of New Hampshire, Massachusetts, and Connecticut, assembled at Boston, August, 1780, to consider the Affairs relating to the War," Force transcripts, Vol. XIV, Library of Congress; *R.I. Col. Rec.*, IX, 153, 161. For the Hartford meeting of Nov., 1780, see Conn. State Archives, Revolutionary War, Vol. XIX, fols. 13, 250, 282, 285.

[158] *Madison Papers*, I, 429; Sumner, *op. cit.*, I, 93.

ment among members of the Convention in favor of *laissez faire* policies in the internal economic life of the nation.

Before considering the extent to which the wages and price schedules were actually enforced by the courts or other agencies, it should be borne in mind that, along with the regulatory code, there was enacted during the Revolution in virtually every state extensive legislation against forestalling, engrossing, and regrating, against selling for a lower price in specie than in paper money, against refusing to accept paper currency, imposing restrictions upon public auctions, and establishing embargoes on exports.[159] Such measures, though instigated at the time of the nonimportation agreements,[160] were in harmony with the general course of colonial legislation. In some communities these "violators" were still subject to prosecution considerably after the close of the war.[161] Some of these war measures actually specified the rate of profit considered legitimate for a licensed trader.[162] Monopolizers and forestallers were universally reprobated as creating "artificial scarcities and taking advantage of people's necessities." In the north in the early years of the war this legislation was largely inspired by resentment on the part of urban groups against profiteering by farmers and middlemen. In the south hostility was manifest early in the struggle against merchant profiteers, many of whom were felt to be loyalist in sympathy. "A Carolina Planter" communicated his views to the *North Carolina Gazette* on December 12, 1777, urging that monopoly and extortion by the merchants was a

---

[159] See, for example, act of Nov. 27, 1777, *Laws of N.H.*, IV, 115 (repealed May 23, 1778); act of Jan. 2, 1778, *ibid.*, IV, 139; act of April 3, 1779, *ibid.*, IV, 209; act of June 23, 1779, *ibid.*, IV, 211; *Mass. Acts and Resolves*, V, 483 (1775–76, c. 18, sec. 5), 924, 1073, 1114 (1779, repealed 1780, p. 1395); *R.I. Col. Rec.*, IX, 92 (June, 1780); act of Dec. 11, 1777, Wilson, *Acts of N.J. Ass.*, p. 34; act of June 22, 1778, *ibid.*, p. 54; act of Oct. 7, 1778, *ibid.*, p. 58; act of Dec. 3, 1778, *ibid.*, p. 62; act of Dec. 21, 1779, *ibid.*, p. 104; act of Jan. 2, 1778, Mitchell and Flanders, *Stat. at Large of Pa.*, XII, 177; act of April 1, 1778, *ibid.*, IX, 245–47; act of April 5, 1779, *ibid.*, IX, 387; act of Oct. 8, 1779 (repealed March 22, 1780), *ibid.*, IX, 421; act of March 22, 1780, *ibid.*, X, 175; act of Oct., 1777, carefully defining forestallers, regrators, and engrossers, Hening, *Va. Stat.*, IX, 382–84; act of Oct., 1778, *ibid.*, pp. 581, 584; act of Oct., 1779, *ibid.*, X, 157; act of May, 1781, *ibid.*, X, 425; proclamation of Sept. 5, 1777, *N.C. Gazette*, Sept. 5, 1777; of Feb. 1, 1778, *ibid.*, Feb. 6, 1778; acts of 1777, *Gazette of the State of S.C.*, April 28, Sept. 15, Nov. 12, Dec. 15, 1777; act of 1780, S.C. Journal of the House of Representatives, Vol. CV, f. 160; *Gazette of the State of S.C.*, Feb. 9, 1780. Such activities were branded as "distressing and ruinous to the industrious poor, and most heinously criminal." *Pa. Col. Rec.*, XI, 671.

[160] *S.C. Gazette*, Oct. 3, 1774.   [161] *Columbian Herald* (S.C.), Sept. 21, 1786.

[162] See, e. g., act of 1780, *N.C. State Rec.*, XXIV, 318; repealed, p. 354.

matter properly within "the province of the legislature and in their power alone." His concluding observations are indicative of this hostility to trade:

The Carthaginians provided different residences for Merchants and would not suffer them to live in Common with their other Citizens. The Grecians did not receive them within their walls; more similar instances I could mention. There was an ancient law among many commonwealths, that no merchant should be a magistrate, or admitted into senate or council. And merchandizing has been condemned by canonical decrees, and utterly forbid by many of the antient fathers, I could mention but St. Chrysostroms [sic] words are to the following effect. Let no Christian be a merchant, and he will be, so let him be cast out of the church.

On December 26 a "Merchant" replied, defending his associates from the charge of keeping up prices, while at the same time reprobating the practice of monopolizing and forestalling as creating "artificial scarcities and taking advantage of people's necessities." The merchants who remained in the state were acquitted by this writer of Tory bias, and the nature of their employment defended as of value to society.

The price regulation and antimonopolizing statutes were closely related. Both often specifically empowered courts of record and local justices to punish violators. But instances of enforcement by the courts are rare. In the record of the June session of the Philadelphia quarter sessions we find the following item, which is so unusual that it is reproduced in full:

Pursuant to the Directions of an Act of the General Assembly of the Commonwealth of Pennsylvania, passed at Philadelphia the twentieth Day of March last past, entitled "An Act for the Regulation of the Militia of the Commonwealth of Pennsylvania," We the Subscribers, being a Majority of the Justices attending at the Court of General Quarter Sessions of the Peace now held at Philadelphia for the County aforesaid, have this Day ascertained and do hereby fix and determine the Average Price of Common Labour at this Time by the Day to be Twenty Dollars within the said County. Witness our Hand and Seal at Philadelphia this sixth Day of June, Anno Domini 1780.

Isaac Howell (LS)	John Ord (LS)
William Rush (LS)	Andw Knox (LS)
Seth Quec (LS)	Willm McMullan (LS)
Benjamin Paschall (LS)	David Kennedy (LS) [163]

163 Philadelphia QS, 1773–80 (June, 1780).

During the same month the Northampton, Pa., quarter sessions set the average daily wage of common labor at seventeen dollars,[164] and the Bucks County justices set wages at twenty-four dollars.[165] In August the Lancaster quarter sessions, under authority of the same act, fixed the "price of common labor" at "ten pounds per day to the end of next Sessions." [166] In September the Philadelphia quarter sessions levied the wages of labor at the June rate.[167] Instances of penalties being imposed by the courts for violation of wage assessments in these four Pennsylvania counties have not been found in the court records. In other Pennsylvania quarter sessions courts no such wage assessments appear to have been levied.[168] However, in a number of jurisdictions, prosecutions are found for this period under statutes imposing penalties for "selling for hard money," [169] for forestalling,[170] and for regrating.[171] When in the April term, 1778 George Mitchell and three others entered an appeal in the Essex County, N.J., quarter sessions court "from Judgments given against them on the regulating Law, "the court, doubtful of the propriety of such appeals, referred the matter to the consideration of a later sitting, but no further action in the matter appears in the record.[172]

In New York in April, 1779, the first judges of the courts of common pleas of Albany, Dutchess, and Orange levied an assize, ascer-

164 Northampton QS (June session, 1780).   165 Bucks QS, 1754–82, f. 627.

166 Lancaster Road and Sessions Docket, No. 5, 1776–82 (Aug. session, 1780).

167 Philadelphia QS, 1773–80 (Sept. session, 1780).

168 Dockets at West Chester, York, Reading, and Carlisle for this period give no hint of such activity.

169 Comm. v. Stapler, April, 1780, verdict: not guilty; Same v. Elizabeth Felfard, Philadelphia QS, 1773–80. For prosecutions for attempting to depreciate state or Federal bills of credit see Hanks's case, Windham, Conn., County Court Rec., 1777–82, f. 15 (1777); Fitch's case, Conn. Superior Court Rec., XIX (1778).

170 State v. Nitingale, Gloucester County, N.J., QS and C.P., 1771–82 (Dec., 1780), verdict: guilty, fined £3 hard money; Comm. v. Williams, Philadelphia QS, 1779–82 (July, 1780), verdict: not guilty. The peak of such prosecutions occurred in the Morris County, N.J., quarter sessions. For the year 1780 the docket reveals eighteen indictments for forestalling. In two cases the juries returned not guilty verdicts; in one the prisoner was convicted and fined £50. In the remainder the accused were apparently never brought to trial. There were two indictments returned in 1781, both of which were quashed. Morris QS and C.P., 1778–82, fols. 78, 79, 81, 91, 93, 101, 130, 144, 145.

171 State v. McCable, Same v. Barnes, Queen Ann, Md., County Court Records, 1771–80 (June, 1779), both fined 7s.6d current money of Maryland; Same v. McCallister, *ibid.* (March, 1780); Philadelphia QS, 1779–82: Comm. v. Williams and McKitterick (April, 1780); Comm. v. Burt (Oct., 1780); Comm. v. Burt (Jan., 1781), verdict: not guilty.

172 Essex QS and C.P., 1772–81 (April, 1778).

taining the pay and wages for teams, carriages, horses, and drivers impressed for the public service pursuant to an act of the state legislature. Rations to the amount of 8s. per day were to be deducted from the drivers' pay and "in Case of extraordinary services, or in very bad Weather, such Quantity of Liquor to be allowed to the respective Drivers, as has been heretofore customary in such Cases." [173] In April of the following year, at a time when the state regulatory legislation had been suspended, the first and second judges of common pleas in Dutchess and the Orange County third judge of pleas similarly fixed the pay for such services at a rate some five or six times higher than the schedule of '79. In addition, they ascertained the price of hay at $248 per ton, of rye at $32 per bushel, of Indian corn at $27 per bushel, and of oats and buckwheat at $16 per bushel. [174]

In May, 1780, Thomas Younghusband, a country justice, was indicted in the Edenton, N.C., district court for saying publicly: "Damn the Congress!" and "Damn the Currency!" and for refusing to take paper money for liquor purchased at his inn. [175] In Connecticut and Delaware, hoarding was criminally prosecuted, [176] and in the latter state a ferryman was presented for demanding a fare in excess of the legal rate for transporting passengers. [177] Considering the comprehensive set of economic controls in operation during this period, the relative infrequency of prosecutions, however, is conclusive that the common law courts functioned only in a minor way in enforcing these regulations.

State legislatures and local officials, such as committees of correspondence and of safety, selectmen, or town committees devoted more attention than did the courts to enforcing this system of economic control. Typical of countless instances was the action of the

---

[173] *N.Y. Journal,* April 12, 1779.   [174] *Ibid.,* April 10, 1780.
[175] Edenton, N.C., District Court Papers, 1751–87.
[176] Hayward's case, Windham, Conn., County Court Rec., 1777–82, f. 47 (1778); Chandle's case, *ibid.,* f. 202 (1780); Mervin's case, New Haven County Court Rec., 1774–83, f. 400 (1779); Delaware v. Moses Cochran, Newcastle General Sessions Mins., 1778–93, f. 125 (Nov., 1780).
[177] Delaware v. Haines, Newcastle General Sessions Mins., 1780–81 (May, Aug., 1781). For other prosecutions for profiteering or "oppression" see Prescott's case, New Haven County Court Rec., 1774–83 (1777), fined £125/9 and costs; Flint's case, Windham, Conn., County Court Rec., 1777–82, f. 41 (1778); Smith's petition for relief from a sentence for profiteering, Conn. State Archives, Revolutionary War, X, f. 319a (1778).

Providence town meeting which set up its price and wage code in August, 1779, and authorized its committee of inspection to receive complaints against offenders and report the same to the committee of correspondence, who were "empowered either to proceed to inflict a proper punishment, by advertising them as enemies to their country, or in cases of any peculiar difficulty to lay the whole before the town to be finally determined." [178] Expulsion, corporal punishment, or fines were not customarily meted out. Instead, publication of breaches of the schedules was normally the sole punishment. At a time when speculators and hoarders were linked in the public mind with loyalists, when the opprobrium "Monopolizer," was one to be dreaded as suitable only for canker worms, "vermin," "rats," and "worse enemies to the country than Burgoyne," [179] this form of social ostracism might well have been effective. Actually, publication of profiteers went back to the regulations that were in force following the First Continental Congress.[180]

Numerous cases are on record where such bodies punished either by fine or public denunciation for charging higher than the regulated price for goods or for refusing to sell at such a price,[181] for

[178] *American Journal and General Advertiser* (Providence, R.I.), Sept. 2, 1779.
[179] *Boston Gazette,* Jan. 8, 1777.
[180] See *Newport Mercury,* Nov. 28, 1774; Dec. 18, 1775.
[181] Massachusetts: Moses Fessenden (*Boston Gazette,* April 21; *Continental Journal,* April 24, May 2, 1777); Stephen Hall (*Boston Gazette,* Aug. 30, Sept. 6, 1779; *Independent Chronicle,* Sept. 2, 1779; *Continental Journal,* Sept. 9, 1779); Thomas Fessenden (*Independent Chronicle,* Sept. 23, Nov. 5, 1779); Gideon Putnam of Danvers—defense: price in accord with the Ipswich Convention (*Ind. Chron.,* Oct. 14, 1779); Josiah Draper's case, in which the Attleborough committee of correspondence was divided, some members maintaining that Draper's salt was of high quality (*Cont. Journal,* Oct. 28, 1779).
New York: case of Robinson and Price, Nov. 3, 1775 (*Journal of the Provincial Congress, Provincial Convention, Committee of Safety and Council of Safety of the State of N.Y., 1775–77,* I, 193, 349); Mrs. Jonathan Lawrence, complained of by the committee of New Windsor, June 14, 1776 (*ibid.,* pp. 494, 495); *Minutes of the Albany Committee of Correspondence:* case of Volkert P. Douw and six other merchants, March, 1776 (I, 351); Robert McClallen, April 24, 1776 (I, 387); John Boyd, Sr., John Boyd, Jr., and Absalom Woodworth, May 8, 1776 (I, 400, 428); James Williams, July 26, 1776 (I, 502); Joseph R. Hubbard, Sept. 5, 1776 (I, 540); *Minutes of the Committee for Detecting Conspiracies in New York:* information against Lewis Vincent, David Heusted, and Joseph Emory, Jan. 13, 1777 (I, 96, 97); *Minutes of the Schenectady Committee of Correspondence:* David Frank, July 2, 1779 (II, 1147); Hugh Mitchell, July 8, 1779—acquitted (II, 1148); complaint against Mrs. Morton, Mrs. Robbison, and Caleb Beck, July 3, 1779 (II, 1155); John Van Antwerp, Aug. 3, 1779 (II, 1156).
New Jersey: *Minutes of the Council of Safety:* David Layton, Jan. 24, 1778 (p. 196);

refusing to accept specie in payment of debts or in exchange for commodities; [182] for valuing specie higher than paper currency,[183] and for attempting to corner or monopolize commodities.[184] In addition to publication, the offenders might be cried through the city, have the money in excess of the regulated price returned, or suffer a fine, and in Albany further humiliating punishment might be exacted, such as being forced to stand on a scaffold erected in the market place and publicly swear obedience to the committee.[185] In New York and New Jersey the violator might also be imprisoned until he could post bond for his good behavior or "till farther orders." [186] On rare occasions the vendee in the illegal transaction might be fined along with the seller,[187] and the purchaser for hard money prosecuted as well as the taker.[188] Occasionally the jurisdiction of such committees was challenged, as by Nathaniel Pearce of Stoughton, who, denounced for profiteering, retorted that "he would be damned if he went across the town to hear or be heard by the Committee," and that nobody could stop him from selling at any price he could obtain.[189]

Few cases have been recorded involving violations of the labor

---

John Smyth, Jan. 26, 1778 (p. 196); Samuel Titus, Woolingston Redman, March 10, 1778 (pp. 212, 213); Samuel Smith, innkeeper—fines particularized, May 4, 1778 (p. 232); *Morris County Committee:* cases of Curtis and Norris (*N.J. Journal*, Sept. 7, 1779).

[182] Capt. Thomas Harnot, May 28, 1775 (*Journal of the N.Y. Prov. Congress*, I, 465); William Newton, May 25, 1776, Andrew Gautier's case appealed from the general committee of New York to the Provincial Congress, June 4, 1776 (*ibid.*, pp. 461, 473); Cornelius Glen, June 4, 1776 (*Minutes of the Albany Committee of Correspondence*, I, 430); Abraham Jacob Lansingh, Feb. 18, 1777 (*ibid.*, p. 680); cases of Samuel Car and Charles Barclay, June 16, 1778 (*Minutes of the New Jersey Council of Safety*, p. 255).

[183] Boston Committee of Public Safety: Abraham Salomon (*Ind. Chron.*, March 12, 1777); Bowle's case (*Cont. Journal*, Jan. 8, 1778); William Pemberton, June 5, 1776 (*Minutes of the Albany Comm. of Corr.*, I, 432); Marmaduke Abbot, Oct. 16, 1777 (*Minutes of the N.J. Council of Safety*, p. 147).

[184] John Nazro, Martin Becker, and Enoch Brown felt impelled to deny publicly such accusations. *Cont. Journal*, Jan. 23, Oct. 2, 9, 1777; *Boston Gazette*, April 21, 28, 1777; *Ind. Chron.*, May 2, Oct. 9, 1777; *Boston Town Rec.*, XXVI, *passim*.

[185] *Pa. Packet*, June 29, 1777.

[186] Van Vranken's case, *Albany Comm. of Corr. Mins.*, I, 944 (March 18, 1778).

[187] William Sloan, fined £6 "for paying more for sugar than the law allows." A similar fine and a huge forfeiture were exacted of the sugar merchant (June 19, 1778), *Mins. of the N.J. Council of Safety*, p. 257.

[188] See Glifford's case (July 20, 1779), *Schenectady Comm. of Corr. Mins.*, II, 1152.

[189] *Ind. Chron.*, Oct. 14, 1779.

and service codes, and such cases as there are generally involve prices exacted by master workers for finished products or wages for piece work rather than per diem. As early as January 7, 1776, the Philadelphia committee censured a hatter, among others, for refusal on grounds of conscience to accept continental money.[190] For a similar offense, a cordwainer was declared an enemy of his country and committed to jail by the Pennsylvania Council of Safety.[191] In July, 1779, John Van Epps was cited to appear before the committee of correspondence of Schenectady for charging three dollars an ell for weaving striped coarse linen and twelve shillings an ell for very coarse plain linen. Two outside weavers were given the cloth to examine and estimate "how much they used to weave such cloth for." According to the record:

Hall said that He wove for grain and did not weave much for money. Wesselse said the one sort he wove for six shillings an Ell and the other for nine shillings an Ell. Thereupon Resolved that said John B[t] Van Epps Jun[r] do return the sum of twenty three pounds twelve shillings which in the opinion of this board was *extorted* from said De Graaf by said V. Eps Jun[r] which we hope will prevent all extortioners from pursuing the same evil practices by which said V. Eps is become an object of public resentment.

Epps was published for this "extortion." [192] Offering "hard specie for work" was as serious an offense as offering specie for commodities, as the result would be the cornering of the labor market. During the same month just such a charge was brought against Elias Rosa before the Schenectady committee.[193]

Perhaps the most notable case in this category was that of Sarson Belcher of Boston, denounced in 1779 as an "enemy of his country" for selling a beaver hat for £48, £13 above the regulated price. Belcher, in a published refutation, claimed that the price of £35 set by the committee was ridiculously low as he had formerly received as much as £60 for beaver hats. The price he had charged, he claimed, amounted to a twenty percent reduction from the former price and corresponded exactly to the amount by which other trades were forced to reduce their prices. Such a scale was needed to support his family and purchase necessaries, and in this

[190] See also *Amer. Archives*, 4th ser., III, 1388; IV, 564 (Dover, Del., committee).
[191] *Pa. Col. Rec.*, X, 774. See also *ibid.*, XI, 70; *Journal of Congress*, II, 475.
[192] *Schenectady Comm. of Corr. Mins.*, II, 1150.   [193] *Ibid.*, p. 1152.

contention, he had the solid support of the hatters' industry.
Twenty hatters signed a statement justifying Belcher's action.
Nevertheless the Boston town meeting voted to let the publication
stand, denounced him for his attack upon the committee, and
warned the other hatters that unless they retracted they would
earn a similar public denunciation. Only four hatters retracted
under pressure; the other sixteen, when denounced, defended
Belcher's prices and countered that, as most hatters were withholding their products instead of placing them on sale at the stipulated price, Belcher was really doing a service by relieving the hat
shortage. County hatters, they insisted, were selling no better hats
for £50, and no hand was turned against them. Belcher himself
appealed publicly to the town, claiming that actually only fifteen
persons at an unusually small town meeting had voted against
him.[194]

More drastic extralegal measures, such as expulsion and tarring
and feathering, were occasionally taken. Such penalties were generally the result of vigilantist activity fostered by mounting popular indignation against profiteers. In Boston the activities of Joyce
Junior and his cohorts in enforcing the state acts against monopoly
enjoyed considerable publicity. In April, 1777, under his leadership five "Tory Villains"—four Bostonians and one resident of
Cape Ann—were carted over the Boston line for profiteering;
warnings were issued to shopkeepers who had refused to sell dry
goods and West Indian produce, had adulterated products, or had
turned down paper money. Orders went out to all who had "left
Butchering, Droving, Horse jockeying, Shoemaking, sand-driving,
and assum'd selling by Wholesale or Retail West India Goods, and
all others in the same Business, and of Huxtering, that they forth-
with open their Stores and Shops," and sell commodities openly
at the prices set by law.[195] Describing these carting incidents, Abigail Adams wrote that about 500 people followed "Joice Junior,
who was mounted on horseback, with a red coat, a white wig, and
a drawn sword, with drum and fife following." [196] Urging that

[194] *Boston Gazette,* Sept. 27, 1779; *Continental Journal,* Sept. 23, Oct. 2, 7, 1779.
[195] *Boston Gazette,* March 17, April 21, 24, 1777.
[196] *Familiar Letters,* pp. 262, 263; Mathews, Col. Soc. of Mass., *Publications,*
VIII, 94.

"Connecticut take the Alarm!" and proudly claiming that opposition to the Stamp Act also had originated in Boston, "Vox Populi" warned that "an unabating vengeance" would descend "on the heads of monopolizers, as it did on the odious stamp masters." [197] Elsewhere riots against profiteers broke out. Peter Messier of New York charged, in May, 1777, that a party consisting of two continental soldiers and twenty-two women had descended upon his house, refused his wife the price that she had asked for tea, and seized as much tea as they wanted, leaving an amount that they judged fair, and that several other parties had visited him subsequently, searching the premises in the name of the committee for detecting conspiracies, beating the complainant and his servants, and committing acts of vandalism. These incidents were apparently not unusual.[198]

Civilian regulation was actually only one phase of the Revolutionary system of price and wage controls; for in addition to the courts, local officials and committees, and extralegal bodies, the armies, both continental and British, were forced to set prices for articles required in the conduct of the war, to fix wage schedules for their artisans, and to seize hoarded goods needed in the military service. Yet when all known prosecutions, both civil and military, are taken into consideration, there is no justification for Pelatiah Webster's charge that these regulations were "executed with a relentless severity." [199]

In Massachusetts as early as 1777 it was necessary to defend labor against the charge of demanding excessive wages. Such defense rested on the cost of provisions and the depreciation of the circulating medium. A large part of the population, one writer admitted, was only striving to boost its wages to a level which would bear the same proportion to imported articles and necessaries as it formerly did.[200] In March, 1778, the town of Boston memorialized the general court against the rise in farm prices, pointing out

[197] *Pa. Packet,* June 22, 1779.

[198] *Mins. of the N.Y. Committee for Detecting Conspiracies,* I, 301–3.

[199] *Political Essays,* p. 129n. Evidence supports the view that violators who were prosecuted "were invariably of little importance in the business community; the great merchants were seldom interfered with." R. A. East, *Business Enterprise in the American Revolutionary Era* (New York, 1938), p. 204.

[200] *Independent Chronicle,* Aug. 27, Sept. 11, 1777.

that labor had not shared in that price rise; customarily farm labor had received the equivalent of one bushel of corn for a day's work, but at that time the daily wage was equivalent to merely three pecks of corn.[201] Conditions were similar as to wages of town mechanics. According to one informer, the price scale prevailing in Boston in 1779 was reducing many to beggary.[202] "Mobility," in the *Boston Gazette,* warned hoarders that "Hunger will break through stone walls, and the resentment excited by it may end in your destruction." [203] John Eliot wrote: "Did the country farmers *feel* like the Bostonian mechanics, I don't know what would be the consequence." [204]

The gap between wages and prices was patent at the time of the New Haven convention. There were so many exceptions to the rule limiting advances in produce to seventy-five percent over 1774 that the wage restriction to that level operated to the disadvantage of labor. As a matter of fact, wages of skilled artisans were about three times as high in 1778 as in 1774. Boston newspapers were in the later year advertising carpenter's wages at nine shillings a day with board as against between three and four shillings in 1774.[205] Under the Concord scale of 1779, common labor received from three to four pounds a day, but in Watertown the authorities fixed a rate of pay for road work of only forty shillings. On the other hand, the recommendation of Congress that common labor for 1780 should not exceed by twentyfold the scale of 1774 was not regarded in that town, where road wages rose from three shillings before the war to nine pounds in 1780.[206] However, before any definitive conclusion could be drawn as to the effect of regulation on real wages, it would be necessary to compare wages and prices in all communities where regulation was in effect. From the very limited evidence at hand, admittedly conflicting, it may be tentatively inferred, though, that the regulatory program in Massa-

201 *Mass. Acts and Resolves,* V, 1016n.

202 Harlow, Col. Soc. of Mass., *Publications,* XX, 178, quoting from Pickering MSS, XVII, fols. 242–43 (Feb. 28, 1779).

203 *Boston Gazette,* April 26, 1779; see also *ibid.,* June 24, 1779.

204 Mass. Hist. Soc., *Collections,* 6th ser., IV, 176–83 (March 29, 1780).

205 *Boston Gazette,* March 9, 1778. For wages in Salem in 1775 see Essex Institute, *Hist. Coll.,* II, 259.

206 *Watertown Rec.,* IV, 72, 194, 221.

chusetts actually checked real wages, which suffered a decline during this period.[207]

In New York, as early as 1776, one prosecution witness in an action for profiteering in tea brought on appeal to the Provincial Congress testified that he replied to a demand for hard money for tea in this manner: "Mr. Sickles, I thought you was joking; where should cartmen get hard money; we work for the Continent and get Continental money," and further that it was hard "not to be able to purchase" with that currency "the necessaries for his family." [208] The Albany committee of correspondence attempted to meet "exorbitant Prices" in setting service and labor schedules.[209] That delicate balance between prices and wages was carefully analyzed by "Rationalis" in a contribution to the *New Jersey Gazette*. Although maintaining that "trade can best regulate it's own prices," that writer conceded that on extraordinary occasions legislative intervention was justifiable. Such schedules, he urged, should bear equitably on all groups in the community and should favor the production of necessaries. His calculations, however, bear so directly on this general question of the disparity between wage and price levels that they are worthy of inclusion *in extenso:*

. . . in order to find out how to proportion the limitations duly, it may be necessary to have recourse to calculation.

By the law lately passed for regulating prices, the legislature seem to have aimed at fixing most of the articles of internal produce at double the former prices. This may perhaps be a proper standard for some articles; but when the matter is fairly considered, it will be found that the same reasons which require the prices of some things to be doubled, will call for a similar advance on some others, and on others again a much greater. Of the latter kind are such articles as derive their value chiefly from labour, and require the use of some commodity, either imported from abroad, or which, from it's scarcity, cannot be obtained but at a very high price. To explain my meaning I shall subjoin a few calculations.

I. As to farmers. Let us suppose a farm, the annual produce of which is for sale, exclusive of what was necessary for the

---

[207] However, for the view that "things in general were raised fifty per cent" by the Connecticut regulating act of 1777 see *Conn. Courant*, May 12, 1777.

[208] *Journal of the Provincial Congress of N.Y.*, I, 473.

[209] *Albany Comm. of Corr. Mins.*, I, 915 (Jan. 31, 1778).

consumption of such parts of the family as do not labour, would sell in former time for £300.0.0

It is said to be a large allowance, to admit that one half of this value is paid for labour, supposing the whole to be done on hire 150.0.0

Annual profit remaining 150.0.0

Supposing the price of labour to be doubled, the labour on the same farm will be worth 300.0.0

The consumption of the family will be the same, and allow the same annual profit as formerly 150.0.0

The extraordinary price of salt may be 15.0.0

Allow, moreover, the use of as much rum, tea, sugar, and other luxuries that will cost extra 35.0.0

500.0.0

The farmer ought therefore to have for his produce on an average now 5s. for what he would formerly have sold for 3s. or 1s.8 now for 1s. formerly.

II. As to labourers. Let us suppose a labourer, finding his own provisions and cloathing, formerly earned per annum .. 45.0.0

That his provisions cost him 20.0.0

And his cloathing 10.0.0

Profit toward maintenance of his family ... 15.0.0

45.0.0

Provisions at double price will be 40.0.0

Cloathing will cost at least three times the old price 30.0.0

His profit for the use of his family ought to be at least double as they must purchase all they consume 30.0.0

100.0.0

His wages therefore ought to be increased to 10s. for every 4s.6 he would formerly have received; or 1s.8 now for 9d. formerly.

The same proportion will be requisite for mechanicks, handicraftsmen, lawyers, clerks, etc. so far as their several productions derive their value from labour; making the proper additions or deductions for what the prices of their respective materials may exceed or fall short of that proportion.

It will be observed that I have stated the price of labour at double the former price to the farmer, though I have shewn it must cost more to others; and that I have stated provisions at double to labourers, etc. though I have said the farmer ought to sell them at a lower rate. A little reflection will justify these diversities. As to the first, the farmer having the advantage of feeding; and, in a great measure, clothing and paying his labourers from his own produce without purchase, (to say nothing of the advantage he may derive from the labour of his children and servants) can always procure at a much cheaper rate than a person of any other class. And as to the second,—Suppose the price of the common articles of provisions should be fixed at the rate of 5s. now, for 3s. formerly, as above stated, if we move but a small allowance for the extraordinary prices of salt, sugar, tea, rum, etc.—and some of these must and will use as their neighbours,—we shall find the average price of provisions to labourers, mechanicks, &c. will not be less than doubled. I have heard it remarked that a great majority of the members of the legislature being farmers, their limitations are calculated greatly in favour of that class of men. If there is any truth in the remark, I am persuaded it must arise from their want of proper information, as I cannot suppose they would designedly oppress others for their own emolument. As faithful representatives of the people, I should suppose they would be particularly watchful that no just ground should be given for a suspicion of this kind. . . .[210]

Workers themselves were moved to express dissatisfaction with the price schedules ascertained for various manufactured products. These protestants were usually master artificers or piece workers, but they regarded their interests as identical with the journeymen's. For example, in July, 1779, ten Philadelphia cordwainers publicly declared that they had subscribed to the town regulations of May 25 as regards the prices of shoes in the expectation that others would deal likewise with them for articles needed in their trade or for their families. They were joined a few days later by the tanners and curriers in their open opposition to the price schedules on the ground that they were detrimental to the labor interests:

Our business requires a considerable number of journeymen, who after labouring the whole week, with unabated diligence, have usually found themselves where they began, not being able to lay up any thing out of their scanty wages; this useful body of men will be immediately thrown out of employ, if the regulations take place; they must seek bread elsewhere, and will leave their employers in a state of poverty, and want, and the citizens barefooted; this is by no means exaggeration or ill grounded surmise, but may be fairly deduced as a necessary consequence from the following prices.

---

[210] *N.J. Gazette,* March 11, 1778.

They then proceeded to point out that, in general, commodities, according to the schedule, were increased in price by twenty times, whereas the prices for their products were held down to fourteenfold. While it is not usual for labor groups in this period to advance *laissez faire* arguments, these remonstrants urged:

It is absurd and contrary to every principle of trade, where no man will purchase if he knows the market is falling. It will destroy every spring of industry, and will make it the interest of every one to decline all business. . . . Trade should be free as air, uninterrupted as the tide, and though it will necessarily like this be sometimes high at one place and low at another, yet it will ever return of itself, sufficiently near to a proper level, if the banks and dams, or, in other words, injudicious attempts to regulate it, are not interposed; this maxim, we apprehend, admits of no exception but in the case of a besieged city.

To the "Whig Shoemaker" who charged them with Toryism, they retorted that they were acting in defense of their families. In championing their chairman, who had been accused by "Justice" of selling his shoes in excess of the regulated price, they pointed out that others had not obeyed the schedules, and that therefore in raising his prices he was acting out of necessity.[211]

As for commodities, the rare instances when merchants made a point of stipulating in their advertisements that produce was for sale at the regulated price is indicative that these were unusual bargains to be parceled out in small quantities—as, in the case of tea, one pound to a family.[212] On one occasion the governor of Rhode Island protested to Massachusetts that he could not enforce his own wage and price law if the larger states did not keep to their schedules.[213] In addition to withholding produce from the market, many persons endeavored to evade the price and wage schedules by resorting to barter.[214] Whether or not these price schedules were effective in braking the price rise, it is clear that within a very short time after their promulgation they were obsolete. Thus, prices obtaining in Boston within three months after

211 *Pa. Packet*, July 15, 20, 1779.
212 *Pa. Packet*, April 22, 1776; *Continental Journal*, Feb. 27, March 6, 1777; *Boston Gazette*, April 28, 1777; *Independent Chronicle*, May 2, 1777; *Continental Journal*, Aug. 12, 19, 1779.
213 *Mass. Acts and Resolves*, V, 724; Mass. Arch., Vol. 194, f. 50.
214 See, e. g., *Continental Journal*, Aug. 12, 1779; *Massachusetts Spy*, July 29, Aug. 5, 12, 1779.

the passage of the Massachusetts regulating act of 1777 were from twenty to 140 percent higher than the legal schedule.[215]

Economic historians have been harsh in their judgment of these wage and price controls. "All such methods," declares Bullock, "were as idle as attempts to violate the natural laws of money have always proved to be." [216] Even if one were to concede the theoretical soundness of their position, it is nonetheless clear that it is unrelated to reality. In the stress of war, nations cannot be guided exclusively by theoretical considerations; for, apart from budgetary abnormalities, such crises bring about an unhealthy stimulation of industry which in turn is reflected in greater purchasing power and a sharp upward surge in prices and wages. At other times and in other places, in like military emergencies, similar regulatory measures were tried. The maximum price legislation adopted by the Committee of Public Safety in France in 1793 ran parallel to the earlier American program, and the spontaneous rise of anti-hoarding sentiments in French municipalities at that time is indicative of the popular support behind the program.[217] During the World War it was necessary to regulate profiteering and hoarding and to fix prices for many commodities and manufactured products.[218] Through labor boards, Great Britain established maximum wages.[219] "Perhaps the greatest economic lesson the war has taught," wrote one authority, "is how inadequate and inequitable the fixing of prices by the law of supply and demand becomes when one party is under pressure of absolute necessity, and either supply or demand is limited." [220] Another writer finds in the regu-

[215] For other instances, see table of prices in Harlow, Col. Soc. of Mass., *Publications*, XX, 168.

[216] C. J. Bullock, *Essays on the Monetary History of the United States* (New York, 1900), p. 66. See also J. Backman, *Government Price Fixing* (New York, 1939).

[217] See Bourne, "Maximum Prices in France," *American Historical Review* (Oct., 1917), pp. 110, 112, 133; "Food Control and Price Fixing in Revolutionary France," *Journal of Political Economy* (Feb., March, 1919).

[218] F. W. Taussig, "Price Fixing as Seen by a Price Fixer," *Quarterly Journal of Economics* (Feb., 1919), p. 238; S. Litman, *Prices and Price Control in Great Britain and the United States during the World War* (N.Y., 1920), p. 318; E. M. H. Lloyd, *Experiments in State Control at the War Office and the Ministry of Food* (Oxford, 1924), pp. 50–64.

[219] M. B. Hammond, *British Labor Conditions and Legislation during the War* (N.Y., 1919), pp. 100, 188, *et seq.*

[220] C. W. Baker, *Government Control and Operation of Industry in Great Britain and the United States during the World War* (N.Y., 1921), p. 126.

latory practices of the World War a curious commentary on the "eternal" truths of economics that the heretical doctrine of regulation enjoyed "a greater vogue and more important practical consequences than many of the abstract generalizations which are supposed to be true for all time but are never strictly applicable except in a hypothetical world." [221] Then, as in Revolutionary times, it was clearly recognized that the principal factor in price appreciation was currency inflation.[222] As a matter of fact, the failure to check inflationary trends in industry and finance during and after the World War brought on a major depression. Again, with the commencement of European hostilities in the fall of 1939 price and wage controls were immediately imposed in the belligerent countries. Current proposals to finance future wars entirely through levies of excess-profits taxes on industry and labor are in reality attempts to control the price and wage structure during military emergencies.[223] Few will argue today that the *laissez faire* doctrine presents a satisfactory program for capitalism in crises. One should be generous, therefore, in evaluating a comprehensive experiment in regulation during the greatest military crisis in American history when any program along truly national lines was virtually impossible to effectuate.

Those who have opposed controls have at times been forced to concede that at certain periods in American history regulation was very much in evidence. Chief Justice Chapman of Massachusetts, commenting on a much later occasion on the practice of fixing wages by the towns during the Revolution, said: "Experience and increasing intelligence led to the abolition of all such restrictions, and to the establishment of freedom for all branches of labor and business. . . . Freedom is the policy of this country." [224] Those who demand a free market have also postulated a "natural rate of wages." Needless to say, some reflection on the sources of wages

[221] Lloyd, *op. cit.*, p. 283.

[222] *Parl. Debates, House of Lords*, XXVI, 1077 (Nov. 20, 1917).

[223] Even in the Revolution the idea of taxing excess profits to underwrite the war was considered. William Whipple wrote James Bartlett, May 21, 1779: "If the whole sum could be drawn from those speculating miscreants, who have been sucking the Blood of their country, it would be a most happy circumstance." Burnett, *Letters*, IV, 223. In Connecticut, special taxes on profiteers were levied. *Conn. State Rec.*, I, 365, 366.

[224] Carew v. Rutherford *et al.*, 106 Mass. 1, 14, 15 (1870).

and the degree to which determining factors are subject to control should lead to the conclusion that any dichotomy into "natural" and "artificial" wage categories is clearly unreal, and, in the words of two close students of the problem, " 'the natural rate of wages,' like the 'normal' world to which it belongs, exists only in books and in the minds of men." [225]

[225] Walton Hamilton and Stacy May, *The Control of Wages* (New York, 1928), p. 112.

The American Balance
Of Power and European Diplomacy,
1713-78 ~~~ MAX SAVELLE

ALTHOUGH the concept of a continental balance of power was old in Europe by the beginning of the eighteenth century, the idea of a balance of colonial power was relatively new.[1] For this new principle in international relations had come into being only with the flourishing of the British and French colonial empires in America to rival those of the Spaniards and the Portuguese. The concept fitted nicely into the mercantilist philosophy of the State; since the relative power of a State depended, in the last analysis, upon its colonial and controlled overseas commerce, the balance of power in Europe depended upon the maintenance of an equilibrium of maritime commercial strength—a term that is used to include especially colonial trade.

The existence of a colonial balance of power was already recognized as early as the "partition treaties" of 1698 and 1700, and the idea received clearer enunciation and greater emphasis by diplomats and publicists as the eighteenth century wore on. Notable among the many who commented upon this international phase of mercantilism were Fénelon in France,[2] Uztaritz and Ulloa in Spain,[3] and Vattel, who published his *Droit des gens* in England

[1] The research necessary for the preparation of this study was made possible by a grant-in-aid from the Social Science Research Council, which the writer gratefully acknowledges.

[2] François de Salignac de la Mothe, Marquis de Fénelon, Archbishop of Cambrai, *Œuvres choisis de Fénelon* (Paris, 1872), IV, 360–64.

[3] Geronimo de Uztaritz, *Theorica y practica de comercio y de marina, en diferentes discursos y calificados exemplares, que, con especificas providencias, se procuran adaptar a la monarchia Española, para su prompta restauración, beneficio universal, y mayor fortaleza contra los emulos de la real corona, y enemigos de la fe catolica . . .* (Madrid, 1724), pp. 2, 17–18, 141, 234, 324, *passim;* Bernardo de Ulloa, *Rétablissement des manufactures et du commerce d'Espagne* ("Traduit de l'espagnol . . ." Amsterdam, 1753; originally published at Madrid in 1740), Pt. I, pp. 2–7; Pt. II, pp. 24–32.

in 1758.[4]

At the beginning of the century France seemed to be threatening the international equilibrium, both in Europe and in America, and Great Britain and Holland assumed the role of its champions. Their fear of the enormous power that had accrued to France by reason of the accession of the Duc d'Anjou to the throne of Spain, expressed by King William III before the British Parliament,[5] was stated in the treaty of The Hague (September 7, 1701) as the chief reason for the Second Grand Alliance. By this statement the principle of a colonial balance of power, as a corollary of the continental balance, achieved the status of international law.[6] The Second Grand Alliance was formed against France, "especially in order that the French shall never come into possession of the Spanish Indies nor be permitted, directly or indirectly . . . to navigate there for the purpose of carrying on trade." [7] The enmity of Holland and England toward France had been aroused by the acquisition of the Assiento by the French and was essentially commercial and colonial in nature. The two powers were determined to prevent a union of the French and Spanish crowns; but they were especially determined to prevent France from getting into a position to block their own commercial and territorial ambitions in the New World. Fearful for their own designs, they resorted to the doctrine of the balance of power as a means of forestalling those of their great rival.[8]

The Peace of Utrecht was a great triumph for the defenders of the maritime and colonial balance of power, and, particularly, for Great Britain. So great was their triumph, indeed, that the scales of colonial power were tipped over now almost as rakishly in favor of Great Britain as they had threatened to be by the union of France and Spain. The treaties that collectively made up the peace

[4] Emmerich de Vattel, *Le Droit des gens: ou Principes de la loi naturelle, appliqués à la conduite & aux affaires des nations et des souverains* (2 vols., London, 1758), I, 81–92; II, 39 *et seq.*

[5] *Cobbett's Parliamentary History of England* (36 vols., London, 1806–20), V, 1329–30.

[6] Frances G. Davenport, ed., *European Treaties Bearing on the History of the United States and Its Dependencies* (3 vols., Washington, 1917–34; Vol. IV, Washington, 1937, was edited by C. O. Paullin), III, 84–85.

[7] *Ibid.*, III, 86.

[8] A. Legrelle, *La Diplomatie française et la succession d'Espagne* (4 vols., Paris, 1888–92), IV, 124–25.

were based upon the principle of international equilibrium, in the New World as in the Old. In the first place, the balance of political power in Europe was as firmly fixed upon the European states system as it was possible for treaties to fix it. The crowns of France and Spain were forever separated, and this principle applied to the American empires of the two monarchies as well as to their European holdings.[9] But the territorial settlement that gave to the British Empire Hudson Bay, Newfoundland, Acadia, and St. Christopher's reduced by that much France's possessions in America and because of the supplies of fish, furs, and sugar thus added to the potential British resources, tipped the scales of the colonial balance toward Britain even more heavily than might be indicated by the mere area or population of the ceded territories. England, always in the name of the balance of power, induced Spain to promise never to alienate any of her American possessions and, lest France by some means defeat this promise, herself undertook, along with France, to guarantee the territorial status quo in the Spanish American empire.[10] Similarly, France was forced to renounce any claim it might have upon the territory and trade along the river Amazon and elsewhere in the Portuguese possessions in America and to prohibit its subjects from going to those places for trade. This arrangement was also "guaranteed" by Great Britain.[11]

But it was in the realm of commerce that the British made the most sweeping advances at Utrecht. France and Spain were prevailed upon to make liberal commercial treaties with Great Britain. The British South Sea Company was given the great trading privileges represented by the Assiento for the Negro traffic in the Spanish colonies.[12] France was deliberately excluded from the Assiento and from the favored position she had occupied in Spanish colonial commerce since the beginning of the century.[13]

Thus the treaties of Utrecht established a threefold equilibrium. First, the political balance in the affairs of Europe was thought to have been established by the eternal separation of the crowns of

[9] Jean Dumont, ed., *Corps universel diplomatique du droit des gens* (8 vols., Amsterdam, 1726–31), Vol. VIII, Pt. I, pp. 340, 370, 395; Archives du ministère des affaires étrangères: correspondence politique, Espagne, Vol. 227, fols. 2–5, 12. Charles Giraud, *Le Traité d'Utrecht* (Paris, 1847), pp. 126–27; D. J. Hill, *A History of European Diplomacy* (3 vols., New York, 1914), III, 338.

[10] Dumont, *op. cit.*, Vol. VIII, Pt. I, pp. 394–95.   [11] *Ibid.*, pp. 353–55.
[12] *Ibid.*, pp. 394–95; Davenport, *op. cit.*, III, 167–85.   [13] *Ibid.*, pp. 340, 371.

France and Spain and by the renunciations that accompanied it. Second, the territorial balance, which was readjusted in Europe, was fixed in America, with the exception of the cessions made to Great Britain, in the condition it had been in at the time of Charles II of Spain, and the continuance of that status was guaranteed by Great Britain—a guarantee that constituted a sort of British Monroe Doctrine. Finally, the commercial equilibrium, especially with regard to Spain and its Indies, was equally asserted in the treaties of peace and the treaties of commerce, and this principle was directed chiefly against the rising commercial power of France.

The "joker" in the whole arrangement was the treaty of the Assiento, which not only gave the British South Sea Company the right to introduce Negroes into the Spanish colonies and establish stations there but also, by the admission of the "annual ship," opened the door to an almost unlimited contraband trade. Yet despite the fact that France had renounced its commercial ambitions in the Spanish colonies, the fact that a French king ruled Spain made for commercial favor there. And it was no accident that French merchants henceforth occupied the most favored position in the colonial trade of Cádiz—a position that balanced somewhat the predominant position that had been acquired by British traders in the Spanish colonies themselves.[14]

The twenty years following the Peace of Utrecht constituted one of the most confused periods in the history of European diplomacy. In general, the chief preoccupation of the maritime powers was the maintenance of the commercial and colonial equilibrium established by that peace; but there were numerous exceptions. The almost constant threat of a general European war resulting from the ambitions of the continental powers diverted the attention of all the major states and left the consideration of colonial questions in a position of distinctly secondary importance. Surprisingly enough, France and Great Britain, the two great "natural enemies," found it to their advantage to work together for the maintenance of the Utrecht settlement until French policy began to take a more "natural" turn in the Franco-Spanish *pacte de famille*

[14] Cf. Richard Pares, *War and Trade in the West Indies, 1739–1763* (Oxford, 1936), pp. 12, 13.

in 1733. Thus it came about that in 1717 the Triple Alliance of Great Britain, France, and Holland was formed to preserve the system of Utrecht, and that, as a result of the blundering attack of Spain on Italy in 1717, it became by the admission of Austria a Quadruple Alliance, strengthened in 1718 by the admission of Savoy, and, two years later, by the admission of Spain herself.[15]

The colonies were not forgotten, however. The tergiversations of Spain led, in 1717, to open warfare with Austria, France, and England, in the course of which some fighting took place in the New World and France took Pensacola from the Spaniards. In this war Spain was the disturber of the equilibrium of Utrecht, and the combination of Austria, France, and England was formed in defense of that equilibrium. The treaty of peace, signed at Madrid in 1721, provided for a restoration of the status quo and reaffirmed the arrangements of colonial commerce and territories made at Utrecht. The three signatories, England, France, and Spain mutually guaranteed their respective territories "in whatever part of the world they may be situated," whether those recognized by the Peace of Utrecht or those to be arranged by an international congress, provided for in the treaty, that was presently to meet at Cambrai. The privileges accorded the French and British merchants in Spain and the Indies were specifically reaffirmed, and the British and French guarantees of the Spanish territorial possessions in America were renewed in separate Anglo-Spanish and Franco-Spanish treaties.[16]

Thus was Spain disposed of as a disturber of the equilibrium. The congress of Cambrai, called for by the Treaty of Madrid, was delayed by the Emperor, for reasons of his own, until 1724.[17] In the meantime, Austria became the second disturber of the colonial balance, for the treaties of Utrecht had given the former Spanish Low Countries to Charles VI, who, desirous of promoting the economic welfare of his subjects there and of freeing them from their commercial bondage to England and Holland, created (December,

---

[15] Cf. Pares, *op. cit.*, p. 13; Hill, *op. cit.*, III, 432–39; *The Cambridge History of the British Empire*, Vol. I (New York, 1929), chap. xii.

[16] AE. Cor. Pol. Espagne, 310: 98–108, 187–91; Paullin, *op. cit.*, IV, 20–28.

[17] *Recueil des instructions données aux ambassadeurs et ministres de France depuis les traités de Westphalie jusqu'à la Révolution Française, Espagne*, III, 58–65; *Cambridge History of the British Empire*, I, 364; Hill, *op. cit.*, III, 400.

1722) the Ostend Company for the expansion of Belgium commerce overseas and the development of an "Imperial" colonial empire.[18] But this was much too much for the maritime powers, Great Britain and Holland. Both governments quickly protested, and demanded, in the name of the maritime settlement made at Utrecht, the immediate destruction of the Ostend Company, the creation of which they considered a violation of the treaties of Utrecht and Münster.[19] They did not hesitate to add threat to protest, and the Emperor, on the defensive, began to listen to the overtures of the adventurer Ripperdá for a *rapprochement* between Austria and Spain, a *rapprochement* that resulted in the somewhat fantastic treaties of Vienna (1725).[20] By the terms of these treaties Spain and the Emperor made peace between themselves and a defensive alliance against their enemies. The Emperor finally recognized Philip V as king of Spain and the Indies; Spain promised to give the ships of the Emperor's subjects "most favored nation" treatment; and permission was given them, specifically to the Ostend Company, to bring the commodities of the East Indies to "any of the dominions" of the king of Spain. Otherwise, the Emperor's subjects were accorded with regard to the Spanish Indies all the privileges conceded to the Dutch in the Treaty of Münster.[21] All these provisions were protested by Holland and England as constituting a disturbance of the status quo set up at Utrecht and a violation of the treaties of both Münster and Utrecht.[22]

The key to the situation was held by Fleury, who, taking charge of French affairs in 1726, proposed to the Emperor a compromise in the form of recognition of the Pragmatic Sanction, upon which the Emperor had set his heart, in return for the suppression of the offending Ostend Company. This compromise the Emperor was inclined to accept, and after some negotiation a preliminary

---

[18] Michel Huisman, *La Belgique Commerciale sous l'empereur Charles VI. La Compagnie d'Ostende* (Bruxelles, 1902), pp. viii, ix, 156, *passim*.

[19] *Ibid.*, p. 382; AE. Cor. Pol. Espagne, 342: 180–86vo, 398–400.

[20] Abbreviated texts of these treaties are in Paullin, *op. cit.*, IV, 31–32, 33–36, 38–39; they are printed in full in Alejandro del Cantillo, *Tratados, convenios y declaraciones de paz y de comercio que han hecho con las potencias extranjeras los monarcas españoles de la casa de Bourbon. Desde el año de 1700 hasta el dia* (Madrid, 1843), pp. 202–12, 216–28.

[21] Cantillo, *op. cit.*, pp. 216–28. [22] AE. Cor. Pol. Espagne, 342: 180–86vo, 398–400.

convention was signed on May 31, 1727, that embodied these general principles and provided for a new international congress to meet at Soissons to iron out the obstacles in the way of a general peace. The congress met in June, 1728, but made little progress. The new war that had broken out between Great Britain and Spain demonstrated the hollowness of the Austro-Spanish alliance, and when Spain was induced to sign the Treaty of Seville with Britain and France in November, 1729, the separation of Spain from Austria became complete; for by this treaty Elizabeth Farnese won Anglo-French approval for her schemes in Italy, British and French trading privileges withdrawn after the treaties of Vienna were restored, and a specific agreement was included to the effect that the Ostend Company must be destroyed.[23] The Emperor, deserted by Spain and threatened by France, Holland, and England, finally gave way and traded off the existence of the Ostend Company for the recognition of the Pragmatic Sanction. The Treaty of Vienna (March 16, 1731) embodying the terms of this deal was agreed to by Spain in July of the same year, and Holland, after long and bitter haggling over the terms of the demise of the Ostend Company, finally concurred in 1732.[24]

In 1733 the question of the Polish succession arose to disturb the European balance. This question and the war that was fought to settle it had little connection with the colonial situation. Yet certain diplomatic events that grew out of this war had important effects upon the principle of colonial balance and set the stage for still more important events later on. For the growing colonial power of England was bringing home to France and Spain a realization of their common interests in the New World and the desirability of a united front in the face of their common rival. The two events that seem to have been most responsible for the turn of the trend of French and Spanish policy were the one-sided Anglo-Spanish declaration of February 8, 1732, and the settlement of the colony of Georgia in 1733. Evidently Great Britain was becoming the great disturber of the colonial equilibrium; the Family Com-

[23] AE. Cor. Pol. Espagne, 364: 158–64; Paullin, *op. cit.,* IV, 35, 36; Hill, *op. cit.,* III, 432; Huisman, *op. cit.,* p. 454.

[24] C. von Höfler, ed., *Der Congress von Soissons* (2 vols., Wein, 1871–76), II, v, vi, 1, *passim;* Huisman, *op. cit.,* p. 475.

pact of 1733 was, in part at least, a Franco-Spanish answer to the threatened British preponderance.

Both Frenchmen and Spaniards had long realized the desirability of curbing British expansion in America; only the exigencies of the continental situation had preserved the Anglo-French entente. The existence of the entente, however, did not prevent the regency and Fleury from taking active steps to block the British advance. As early as 1716 the Council of Regency was alive to the problem. In a memorandum considered by the council in that year the colony of Louisiana was described as "a sort of advance guard against the English colonies." The growing power of the British empire was described as a threat at French security, both at home and in America: and "it is not difficult to guess that their purpose is to drive us entirely out of the continent of North America." If the British took Canada, France would lose the cod fishery, one of the most important branches of French commerce; and after Canada the British would take Louisiana. After Louisiana, they would go on to take the mines of New Mexico; they would snatch from France the best part of its commerce, in the isles and in Brazil; they would seize the best parts of the Indies and would draw from them immense wealth. "But what would be for Europe the consequences and the shock of [such] a revolution, which it is easy to see might take place so easily in America?" Evidently, a disturbance of the economic, and therefore the political, equilibrium of the Old World. It would therefore be highly desirable for France and Spain to come to an understanding, even though the latter country were at the moment highly distrustful of France, and for France to encourage for obvious strategic reasons the growth of Louisiana as well as the other French colonies.[25]

This memorandum expresses the three major ideas that underlay French diplomacy with regard to the colonies throughout the century. Great Britain was rapidly expanding its colonial power, and that expansion must be blocked, whether in Hudson Bay, Acadia, the Great Lakes, Georgia, or the West Indies. Repeatedly the French colonial experts attributed to Britain the actual design of driving France out of North America and of attacking the Span-

[25] Archives nationales [series] "Colonies," Vol. C13A/4, fols. 49–80.

ish empire with a view to adding Spain's colonial wealth to its own. Repeatedly, also, they pointed to the necessity for building up the power and the stability of the French colonies themselves, both because of their potential or actual economic value to the mother country and because only thus could they be put into a condition to resist the onslaughts of the British.[26]

The natural line for both French and Spanish policy to take was the one that tended to bring them together in the face of the British threat. The consummation of this policy was delayed for twenty years or more by the exigencies of the continental situation and by the difficulties France encountered in its efforts to stabilize the position of French merchants engaged in the colonial trade of Cádiz—a position that was repeatedly jeopardized by the penchant of the Spanish monarchs arbitrarily to raise the indulto on foreign goods transported to Spain in the *azogues*.[27] Yet it was easy to find points in the colonial situation where the interests of France and Spain met: in the prosperity of the Cádiz trade as against the contraband trade with the Spanish colonies carried on by British merchants; in the territorial expansion of Great Britain on the continent of North America, particularly along the Carolina frontier, and in the West Indies; and in the abuses of the British merchants under the treaty of the Assiento, which France never ceased to attack as an unfair discrimination in favor of Great Britain against the interests of all the other maritime nations.[28] Generally, also, the argument for the rectification of the commercial equilibrium of Utrecht was linked with the guarantee of the territorial status quo; needless to say, the territorial argument received a great fillip with the establishment of Georgia.[29]

[26] One of the most eloquent advocates of this policy was the Marquis de la Galissonière. See his memorandum on the colonial situation of 1749 in E. B. O'Callaghan, ed., *Documents Relative to the Colonial History of New York* (15 vols., Albany, 1853–87), X, 220–32. See also various memoranda in AN. Colonies C11A; C11E, *passim;* C13A, B, C, *passim;* and, notably, C10C/1: "Mémoire concernant la propriété de la France sur l'Isle de Ste Lucie ou Ste Alouzie en Amerique, pour servir à M. le Cardinal de Fleury, et à Mrs le Marquis de Fenelon et le Comte de Brancas Cerest Plenipotentiaires du Roy au Congress de Soissons" [1727].

[27] AN. Colonies C13A/6: 99–110; AE. Cor. Pol. Espagne, 344: 160–67; 365: 211–21vo; Alfred Baudrillart, *Philippe V et la cour de France* (4 vols., Paris, 1890–1901), IV, 538–47.

[28] AE. Cor. Pol. Espagne, 343: 511–14, 534–41; 344: 160–67; 365: 211–21vo; 366: 7–30.

[29] AE. Cor. Pol. Espagne, 346: 556–61vo; cf. John T. Lanning, *The Diplomatic History of Georgia* (Chapel Hill, 1936), pp. 7–33, 55–84.

As for Spain, no less interested than France in the colonial equilibrium, diplomacy with regard to the colonies turned upon four major considerations: (1) the regulation of the colonial trade of Cádiz; (2) the suppression of contraband in the colonies, especially the contraband trade of the British and the Dutch, and the abuses under the Assiento; (3) the exclusion of interlopers on Spanish territory in Honduras, Campeche, and, later, Georgia; and (4) the general fear, fanned by France, that Great Britain might, sooner or later, seize all the Spanish colonies, with a consequent reduction of Spanish power in Europe. In general, all but the first of these considerations pointed toward a *rapprochement* with France. During the negotiations preceding the Treaty of Seville, Spain might easily have taken advantage of France's jealousy of British colonial power to force a reduction of the British demands for the renewal of privileges in the colonial sphere. But in the midst of the negotiations the Queen announced an extraordinary indulto, and this single act threw France into the arms of England against Spain.[30]

The Treaty of Seville, therefore, while it gave Spain what the Queen wanted in Italy, represented a real sacrifice of Spanish interest in the colonies. For, in addition to the provisions already noted, this treaty provided for a restoration of the commerce of the Spanish Indies to the status quo preceding 1725—a provision that marked the surrender of a gain that might have been retained. The Assiento was renewed and provision was made for joint commissions to examine the claims of the three countries against each other with regard to contraband, seizures of ships, and territories.[31] Despite the treaty, however, conditions in America continued much as they had been before, and while the Anglo-Spanish commission wrangled, British merchants continued their contraband trade and Spanish *garda-costas* continued to seize British ships. Benjamin Keene, British minister at Madrid, succeeded in getting the Spanish government to sign a joint Anglo-Spanish declaration in February, 1732, which, ostensibly made to bring these disorders

[30] Basil Williams, "The Foreign Policy of England under Walpole," *English Historical Review*, XVI, 308–27.

[31] Paullin, *op. cit.*, IV, 46–48. The Anglo-Spanish commission met but accomplished nothing. Apparently the Franco-Spanish commission provided for was never appointed.

to an end, only gave a freer hand to the British disturbers of the American peace. For in it the Spanish king promised to order his governors and officers in America not to molest "legitimate" shipping, and made the *garda-costas* responsible for damages they might cause British merchants by the unjust seizure of their ships. King George II, on his side, merely promised that British ships of war should not give protection to merchant ships engaged in illicit trade.[32]

Thus matters stood between Great Britain and Spain when the outbreak of the War of the Polish Succession gave a new impetus to the *rapprochement* of Spain with France. Their common enmity to the Emperor drew the two countries together in the first *pacte de famille* (1733). But while the major emphasis of this alliance was upon the continental situation, the emphasis given the colonial and commercial situation, as dominated by Great Britain, showed the determination of the two countries to present a common front in that part of the world. Thus, aside from its provisions pertaining to the continent, the *pacte de famille* provided for a mutual guarantee of territories, whether in Europe or elsewhere; should Britain attack Spain, whether in Europe or in the colonies, France agreed to come to Spain's aid. Further, the two crowns agreed to coöperate for the reduction of the exaggerated commercial privileges enjoyed by the British in both Europe and America.[33]

The *pacte de famille* marked a turning point in French and Spanish diplomacy vis-à-vis Great Britain and the colonies, for it finally brought them into a coöperative effort in the face of their common enemy. From this event onward, the two countries were generally to be found working together to prevent the too great accumulation of British power in America. Their more immediate efforts were directed toward stopping British efforts to expand in the colonies at the expense of Spain.

The long-brewing colonial disputes between Great Britain and Spain came to a head in 1739. There were several issues at stake. The question of illicit trade with the Spanish colonies was probably most important; linked with that was the question of the

[32] *Ibid.*, pp. 52–53.
[33] Cantillo, *op. cit.*, pp. 277–81; AE. Cor. Pol. Espagne, 403: 207–18.

right of the Spanish *garda-costas,* in their attempt to stamp out illicit commerce, to search or seize merchant ships on the high seas. Spain was also disturbed over the British wood-cutter settlements on the coasts of Honduras and Campeche, and was infuriated by the settlement of Georgia in flagrant violation, according to the Spanish view, of the treaties of Madrid (1670) and Utrecht.

Spain had long complained of the contraband trade of the British shippers. But the British were not alone in their smuggling; Dutch and French interlopers also engaged in a profitable trade with the Spanish colonies. Curaçao was to the Dutch what Jamaica was to the British. French contraband was less important, for the French merchants interested in colonial commerce occupied a favored position in the trade of Cádiz. Yet all three powers were interested in the business, and especially in the issue of the freedom of the seas championed by Great Britain. Spain had regretted the privileges granted the British merchants in the Indies, and one of the chief aims of Spanish diplomacy, especially during the ministry of José Patiño (1726–36), was the reduction of British privilege and abuse and, eventually, the complete suppression of the Assiento in favor of Spanish merchants. France naturally encouraged this policy, for a reduction of the illicit British trade with the Indies would result in an increase of the Cádiz trade to the benefit of the French merchants there.[34]

The settlement of Georgia was not merely a violation of existing treaties: it was a threat at both the French colony of Louisiana and the Spanish colony of Florida. Moreover, the location of another strong British base on the Florida channel would place the British in a position in time of war to capture or destroy the homeward-bound treasure ships at will. Such an event, it was thought, would severely cripple Spain and would have a disastrous effect upon the economic life of France as well.[35] To Spain's protests against British smuggling, therefore, was added the bitter complaint against the establishment of Georgia in lands that Spain regarded as incontestably its own. Naturally the fear of Georgia

[34] AE. Cor. Pol. Espagne, 448: 226–30vo, 243–54; 456: 48–54.
[35] AE. Méms. et docs. Angleterre, 9: 104–10; AE. Cor. Pol. Espagne, 448: 226–30, 243–54; 456: 193–94.

was shared by France as well as Spain, and the appearance of the colony gave a new impetus to the tendency of the two nations to draw together.[36]

Various proposals made for the settlement of the Anglo-Spanish disputes between 1732 and 1736 failed. A new negotiation resulted, finally, in the convention of the Pardo, signed in January, 1739. Under the terms of this convention, commissioners were immediately to be appointed to consider the matters in dispute, specifically the questions arising out of the British contraband trade and the seizure of British ships on the high seas in America, the limits of Florida and Carolina, and the Assiento. The mutual claims for damages against each other were to be considered as settled, and Spain agreed to pay to Great Britain the sum of £95,000 sterling, representing the balance due British subjects after all Spanish claims should be paid. This did not apply, however, to claims arising under the Assiento.[37]

Ostensibly the just claims of Great Britain were satisfied, and an instrument provided for the decision of questions of rights on the high seas and of territorial boundaries. But the British parliamentary opposition was not satisfied. Walpole's power was failing, and the opposition made the convention the occasion for testing his strength and, if possible, for driving him from office. They raised the cry of "freedom of the seas," and pointed to the convention as an ignominious surrender of British maritime rights. The debate, calling forth the arguments on both sides of the British position, elicited some extremely interesting comments on the American balance of power.

The Walpole government was frankly loath to disturb the commercial and colonial equilibrium established at Utrecht. Even the founding of Georgia had been accomplished largely by the efforts of members of the opposition and against the best judgment of Walpole and Newcastle.[38] Now, in the debates on the quarrel with Spain, the ministry was apprehensive lest further demands upon Spain excite the fears of other nations interested in America and call down upon England the combined forces of at least Spain and France. Should England precipitately enter a war with Spain, said

[36] AE. Cor. Pol. Espagne, 448: 226–30vo; 456: 193–94, 195–96.
[37] Paullin, *op. cit.,* IV, 57–60.   [38] Lanning, *op. cit.,* pp. 34, 69, 74.

Newcastle, without giving Spain an opportunity to make repara-
tion, the other powers of Europe would take alarm:

they might look on our proceedings as the effect of a design, . . . to
seize upon some part of the Spanish dominions in America, and to
annex it to our crown. . . . Did any of our European neighbours, my
Lords, suspect that we had formed a design to dismember any part of
the Spanish monarchy from that crown, there is not the least doubt
but they would look upon us with a very jealous eye; because, as your
lordships know, the further alienation of any part of that monarchy is
strictly guarded against in a separate article of the treaty of Utrecht,
and for the observance of this article both we and the French are
guarantees. If if were suspected, that we designed to force the Spaniards
to allow us a free trade in all its branches to their settlements in America,
the French would not fail to oppose us in such a design, the king of
Spain, in the same treaty, having laid himself under an engagement, not
to grant it to the subjects of any nation of Europe except his own:
and the French monarch, by the same treaty, was obliged to give up all
claim to the exercise of any commerce to the Spanish settlements there.
This, my Lords, has always been looked upon as a necessary step towards
preventing any one nation from becoming too rich and too powerful
for the rest.

Doubtless, if there should be a war and the differences should
come to be settled by treaty, it would again be found, to Newcastle's way of thinking, that the best way to preserve the general
peace was to leave the Spanish settlements in their present situation.[39]

   To Newcastle's argument Walpole added his own, given in
similar vein.[40] Even the opposition, far from denying the existence
of the American balance of power, readily admitted it; they simply
advocated defiance of it. Said Lord Chesterfield:

I am entirely of his grace's opinion, that the preservation of the Spanish
dominions in America in that crown has been a point much regarded
by the powers of Europe; but why should they be less jealous of an
exhorbitant growth of the strength of Spain, than the just privileges
of British commerce?

In any case, he thought, Holland was busy elsewhere, and France
had more to gain by neutrality than by participation in the dispute on the side of Spain.[41] Lord Carteret added that Britain's
hesitancy to give alarm to the other powers interested in America

[39] *Parliamentary History*, X, 771–72.   [40] *Ibid.*, X, 1313.   [41] *Ibid.*, X, 780.

was no less than a manifestation of timidity that would give the other nations an excuse for attack. But the only nation capable of attacking Great Britain was France, and Fleury was so old that he could be counted upon to maintain peace. No, said Carteret, instead of being afraid of a combination of the other powers interested in America, let Britain deliberately take as much Spanish colonial territory and as many cities as might contribute to the expansion of British navigation and commerce and assure British liberty upon the high seas.[42]

Thus Great Britain was divided on the question of respecting the American balance of power. The government was opposed to precipitate war and favored the maintenance of the territorial and economic status quo laid down by the Treaty of Utrecht and by subsequent agreements. The opposition favored war, and aggressive war at that. And the opposition won. For Britain, the War of Jenkins's Ear was frankly an imperialistic war, undertaken, in part at least, with a view to extending British colonial and commercial power in the New World. Failing annexation of territory, there was a strong body of British opinion that favored and actually promoted a policy of encouraging the Spanish-American colonies to declare their independence of Spain and to establish themselves as sovereign states under British protection.[43]

The position of France in the presence of this outright threat to the balance of power in America was a difficult one. Fleury was old, as Carteret said, but he was still no fool. Fundamentally, the natural impulse of France was to align herself with Spain, and negotiations for the formation of a new Family Alliance were begun with the mission of the Comte de la Marck to Madrid in the fall of 1738.[44] But France's chief interest in Spain was a commercial one, and Fleury was not willing to sign any alliance without first making sure that the position of French merchants in Spain, particularly those at Cádiz, still regulated under the antiquated Treaty of the Pyrenees, should be revised for the benefit of France. Of special interest was the long-mooted question of the indulto. Second to this came France's desire to reduce the commercial privileges of England, and, particularly, to bring about a final sup-

---

[42] *Ibid.*, XI, 17, 835.   [43] Pares, *op. cit.*, pp. 65–77.
[44] *Recueil des instructions, Espagne*, III, 201, 219.

pression of the Assiento.[45] With regard to territorial questions, and particularly with regard to Georgia, France stood shoulder to shoulder with Spain. Georgia impinged upon Louisiana as well as upon Florida; and it was easy to believe that the British actually intended to drive the Spaniards out of Florida, use it as a base of operations for preying upon Spanish trade along the Florida channel, and then turn and drive the French out of Louisiana.[46] It seemed advisable for France, therefore, to support in every possible way the Spanish resistance to British territorial aggrandizement.[47]

On the problem of the freedom of the seas, on the other hand, France had to recognize that the old Spanish pretension to ownership of the open sea in the Gulf of Mexico and the Caribbean was as inimical to French interests as it was to those of the British. For it was easy to see that French merchants might find themselves in precisely the same position as the innocent British ships trading back and forth between the British colonies that were being seized and condemned by the *garda-costas*. Thus, while recognizing that it was to French interest to side with Spain on questions of commerce and territory, French policy was made cautious by the obvious community of interest with Holland and England on the question of the freedom of the seas.[48] This reason, coupled with the continental situation, explains the reluctance of France to hasten to Spain's aid in the War of Jenkins's Ear without having in hand a recognizable and considerable *quid pro quo*. France refused to sign an alliance without a treaty of commerce;[49] Spain, extremely anxious for French aid, gave in, and all but one of the articles of each of the two treaties were ready when news of the death of the Emperor diverted the attention of both France and Spain once again from America to the continent of Europe and the problem of the Austrian succession.[50]

In the meantime, old Cardinal Fleury, "lover of peace," had already taken two steps of considerable importance. He had de-

[45] AE. Cor. Pol. Espagne, 448: 243–54; 456: 193–94, 412–14.
[46] AE. Cor. Pol. Espagne, 448: 226–30vo; AE. Méms. et docs. Angleterre, IX, 104–10.
[47] AE. Méms. et docs. Angleterre, IX, 111–20.
[48] AE. Méms. et docs. Angleterre, IX, 104–10vo.
[49] AE. Cor. Pol. Espagne, 456: 412–14; 457: 62–63.
[50] *Recueil des instructions, Espagne*, III, 216–22.

cided to send a fleet to America to protect Spanish territories, and he had seriously considered proposing a French mediation of the Anglo-Spanish contest. Fleury had often warned Waldegrave, the British ambassador at Paris, that if Great Britain seized Spanish territory in America France would come to Spain's aid,[51] but he had not been taken seriously.[52] In 1740 he actually dispatched a squadron, without, however, expecting that step to be considered a *casus foederis* by Great Britain—as it was not. The idea of French mediation never took more definite form than Fleury's informal suggestion that Admiral Haddock be ordered out of the Mediterranean and that Spain pay England the £95,000 agreed upon in the convention of the Pardo, and it is doubtful whether, even had it been made formal, it would have been accepted by British public opinion.[53]

The turn of events following upon the death of the Emperor in 1740 quickly involved Europe in a general war over the Pragmatic Sanction and the Austrian succession and relegated the Anglo-Spanish war to a position of distinctly secondary importance. Yet the added strain on Anglo-French relations made it almost certain that France and Spain would soon be fighting side by side in America as well as in Europe. France hoped to make an alliance with Sardinia against Austria, to which Spain would accede; this effort seemed to be at the point of success when Amelot, now French foreign minister, learned that Sardinia, fearful of Spain's Italian ambitions, had formed a defensive alliance with Austria (September 13, 1743). This event threw France into the arms of Spain, and Amelot, overlooking the treaty of commerce, put through the Spanish alliance project, nearly completed by La Marck.[54]

This treaty, the second *pacte de famille,* brought America again into the sphere of immediate consideration. For it renewed the mutual guarantees of territory contained in the first *pacte de famille,* and engaged France specifically to aid Spain in the destruction of the British colony of Georgia and in the restoration of all Spanish territory seized by the British during the war. Spain,

[51] AE. Cor. Pol. Espagne, 461: 274–78; Pares, *op. cit.,* p. 160.
[52] BM. Add. MSS 32692: 152–53; P.R.O., SP. 78/221: 276–79; 78/223: 385–87.
[53] Pares, *op. cit.,* pp. 145–46.   [54] *Recueil des instructions, Espagne,* III, 243.

on its side, promised not to renew the Assiento to Great Britain after the war, but to grant it only to Spaniards—a project long the object of French negotiation at the Spanish court.[55] France had finally, without having received the commercial favors it had been demanding as a *quid pro quo,* come to the aid of Spain in America in the name of the equilibrium established at Utrecht. She did so, however, only when compelled by the exigencies of a war fought in the name of the continental equilibrium over the possessions of the Empress-Queen.

It remains to be noted only that the position of Holland in 1739 was as ambiguous as that of France. Fundamentally, Holland was almost as interested in the freedom of the seas as England; but the Dutch had a continental frontier to protect, and they could not forget the invasion of their country by Louis XIV. As it was to France's interest to keep the Dutch neutral in the Anglo-Spanish quarrel, Holland could rely upon France to plead its cause at Madrid, which it did with considerable success. France prevailed upon Spain to make an amicable declaration to the authorities at The Hague, relative to the Dutch ships seized by the *garda-costas* and to the general question of the freedom of the seas in America. But before this negotiation could come to a fruitful conclusion, the death of the Emperor and the consequent debacle caused its suspension, and Holland took a halfhearted part in the War of the Austrian Succession.[56]

The Peace of Aix-la-Chapelle did little more than restore the status quo ante bellum. The European balance was reëstablished; so was the balance in America: the British attempt to modify or upset the American equilibrium had failed.

The idea was abroad, however, that Britain was definitely planning to expand its American empire at the expense of France and Spain, and this idea received ample confirmation in the Anglo-French quarrels over their possessions in North America that came to a head immediately after the peace. As early as 1746 the bishop of Rennes, French ambassador at Madrid, had warned his court that France must cultivate a close union with Spain in order to

[55] Paullin, *op. cit.,* IV, 65–67; Cantillo, *op. cit.,* pp. 367–71; AE. Cor. Pol. Espagne, 448: 243–54, 255–60vo.

[56] *Recueil des instructions, Espagne,* III, 231–34; cf. Pares, *op. cit.,* pp. 128–30, 149–56.

maintain the economic equilibrium.[57] One of the arguments advanced for the restoration of Cap Breton to France was that the island was essential to the defense of Canada; without it, Canada would be lost, and after Canada, Louisiana. From Louisiana the British would go on to absorb Florida and New Mexico and would become masters of the commerce of the New World by reason of their control of Spanish shipping passing through the Florida channel.[58] These usurpations, if successful, would soon place the British in a position of dominance in America that must surely result in an exaggerated and dangerous British superiority in Europe.[59]

This was another repetition of an old argument; but by 1750 responsible statesmen had gone so far as to believe that the balance of power in Europe rested ultimately upon the balance of power in the colonial world; that the success and security of the maritime European states depended upon their possession of large colonial empires; and that no one of them should be allowed to become predominantly powerful in the New World at the expense of the others. This was of course the flowering of the general idea written into the colonial and commercial settlement of Utrecht, the difference being that, whereas in 1713 the system was established as a defensive measure against the expansion of France, in 1750 it was Great Britain that was at once the dangerous disturber of the equilibrium and the perfect example of the wealth and power to be derived from empire.[60]

It was for reasons such as these that Spain was determined, once and for all, to end the Assiento and place the Negro trade of the colonies in the hands of Spaniards. It was for reasons such as these, also, that France attempted to regain Spain's confidence despite the coolness at Madrid resulting from France's desertion of Spain's interests at Aix-la-Chapelle.[61] Great Britain, on the other hand, sought to separate France and Spain, and by reason of the uncanny influence of Benjamin Keene, enjoyed an increasing measure of success up to the disgrace of Enseñada in 1754. The Assiento, de-

[57] AE. Cor. Pol. Espagne, 492: 3–15vo.
[58] AE. Cor. Pol. Espagne, 494: 210–14vo; 503: 45–46vo.
[59] AN. Colonies C11A/96: 248–70.
[60] AE. Méms. et docs. Espagne, 82: 100–100verso; cf. Vattel, *loc. cit.*
[61] AE. Cor. Pol. Espagne, 504: 228–33vo; AN. Colonies C13A/33: 64–66vo.

spite Spain's promises to France, was renewed by the Treaty of Aix-la-Chapelle and confirmed in the Anglo-Spanish treaty of 1750. It had long since ceased to have anything but a theoretical value anyway, and was surrendered by Great Britain in return for a payment by Spain of £100,000 sterling.[62]

The conflict between the British establishment in America, augmenting its bounds with expansive energy, and the relatively static French colonies, now definitely on the defensive, developed, in the seven years following the Peace of Aix-la-Chapelle, steadily toward war. Repeated efforts of a more or less halfhearted nature were made to arrive at a peaceful compromise, but with the Washington expedition into the Ohio valley in 1754, war became practically inevitable. France was convinced that Britain was deliberately expanding at the expense of France and Spain and was simply using the "mediocre" issue of the Ohio valley as a blind for its vast designs on the whole of America. Britain's refusal to restore the American situation to the status quo of Utrecht seemed to Rouillé, French foreign minister, to be proof enough that "the English, in order to satisfy their unjust views of ambition and conquest, wish to destroy in the New World the balance of power that it is essential to maintain there for the security and the interests of all the commercial nations."[63]

Meanwhile, both sides were looking around for allies. France, realizing that the old struggle with Austria had lost its *raison d'être*, began the *rapprochement* with the Empress-Queen that eventuated in the Alliance of Versailles (May 1, 1756).[64] The French objective in this alliance was to separate the pending American struggle from any possible European conflict; but unfortunately for that objective, the treaties of Versailles created a situation too favorable to Maria Theresa's desire for revenge upon Frederick II for the rape of Silesia to be resisted; and, far from isolating the American struggle, they tied it to the Seven Years' War on the continent. If Pitt could afterwards say that Great Britain was "conquering America in Germany," it was certainly true that France gambled —and lost—America in Austria.[65]

[62] Paullin, *op. cit.*, IV, 79–80.   [63] AE. Cor. Pol. Angleterre, 438: 280–83.
[64] Paullin, *op. cit.*, IV, 81, 82.
[65] *Recueil des instructions, Autriche*, pp. 23–25, 356; Hill, *op. cit.*, III, 548.

However, it was to Spain that both England and France most anxiously turned for aid. France played up to Spain the apparent threat at French and Spanish possessions in America in an effort to win Spain to a new *pacte de famille*.[66] But Spain's susceptibilities had been hurt by France at Aix-la-Chapelle, and Spain was decidedly cool toward the idea of a new family compact. On the other hand, Great Britain was hardly more successful, and even Pitt's hysterical offer of a generous settlement of all the points between them in return for Spain's aid failed to move Ricardo Wall from his position of neutrality.[67] Holland, as ever, was interested in the situation in America; but, as ever, Holland's continental interests dictated a policy of neutrality. In the last analysis, Holland was faced with a choice between a land war with France and the destruction of its neutral shipping by Great Britain, and it chose the latter. The famous "Rule of 1756" was laid down by Britain partly in retaliation for Dutch neutrality and partly to prevent the Dutch from aiding the French to supply their colonies with food, men, and munitions.[68]

The Duc de Choiseul, who took charge of French foreign affairs in 1758, was devoted to the idea of a union between France and Spain.[69] He realized the error that had been made in the Austrian alliance, but he also knew that it was now too late to rectify that error. On the other hand, he believed that a union of the forces of France and Spain against Britain in the colonial war would be able to stop the British advance and rectify the disturbed American balance. Shortly after assuming office, therefore, he communicated his ideas to King Charles of Naples, heir apparent to the Spanish throne. His plea for Spanish aid on this occasion is one of the classic expressions of the idea of an American balance of power:

The King [of France] believes, Monsieur, that it is possessions in America that will in the future form the balance of power in Europe, and that, if the English invade that part of the world, as it appears they

---

[66] AE. Cor. Pol. Espagne, 511: 244–53vo.

[67] P.R.O., Chatham MSS, Vol. XCII, *passim.*

[68] *Recueil des instructions, Hollande,* I, lxvi; P. Coquelle, *L'Alliance franco-hollandaise contre l'Angleterre* (Paris, 1902), pp. 55–58, 65–67.

[69] Alfred Bourguet, *Le Duc de Choiseul et l'alliance espagnole* (Paris, 1906), pp. 1, *passim.*

have the intention of doing, it will result therefrom that England will usurp the commerce of the nations, and that she alone will remain rich in Europe. The Spanish possessions in America are of as great interest to the King as his own, and should the English attack those possessions, aside from the friendship and the union that would not permit the King to suffer the English to encroach on the dominions of the King his cousin, the interest of France and all the nations is sufficient to cause the nations to unite for the purpose of limiting English ambition in the region of America. But if it should unhappily happen that the events of this war force the King to make the English any cessions in that region, the weakness of France that would result from those cessions would no longer permit it to make any considerable efforts to arrest the ambitious views of the court of London. Then, should that court attack Spain, . . . and should it become Spain's portion to experience reverses in that future war that one must foresee, . . . France and Spain would become second-rate powers vis-à-vis England.[70]

The negotiations thus begun while "Don Carlos" was still in Naples continued with increasing success after he became Charles III of Spain in 1759. Charles was entirely convinced by Choiseul's argument of the importance of the balance of power in America, and he expressed himself as ready to come to France's aid as soon as his forces might be ready.[71] Even Ricardo Wall, disillusioned by the haughtiness of William Pitt with regard to the Spanish complaints and increasingly nervous over the continued British triumphs in America, began to look with favor upon an alliance with France.

Early in 1761, when Choiseul undertook to negotiate a peace with Pitt, this favorable turn of Spanish feeling became Choiseul's strongest trump; and the possible Spanish alliance became the club with which he hoped to beat the intractable Pitt into making a reasonable settlement of the war. But he was doomed to disappointment, for Pitt refused to be awed by the threat of a Franco-Spanish alliance. When Choiseul finally made the alliance in August, 1761, and called Spain in to aid him in 1762, the French minister found that the combination of forces upon which he had counted was too feeble, and that his ally had entered the war too late to do any good. The Treaty of Paris, February 10, 1763, was in

[70] AE. Cor. Pol. Naples, 78: 44–54; printed in *Recueil des instructions, Espagne,* III, 349–50.
[71] AE. Cor. Pol. Espagne, 526: 144–49, 181–88.

large measure the result of Choiseul's conviction that he must now make peace at any price and build up the Franco-Spanish alliance to the point where it would be more successful in the subsequent struggle for redress of the balance of power in America that he regarded as inevitable. The price he paid for peace was high, for it practically eliminated France as a colonial power in America; but for him it was only a temporary peace.[72]

The Peace of Paris ended the old tripartite balance of power in America and established a new balance in which the two great counterweights were Great Britain and Spain. It did not end the conviction of Choiseul and his disciple Vergennes, however, that the balance of power in America must be made to serve their purpose for the rectification of the balance in Europe, and that the best mechanism for that rectification was the Family Alliance. This persistent idea, which dates with increasing importance from the beginning of the eighteenth century, became one of the determining motives—probably the most important—in the formulation of the French attitude toward the American Revolution.

As early as 1764 Choiseul had foreseen a revolt of the British continental colonies and had sent agents to America to watch developments. He had laid his plans to take advantage of the anticipated revolt, whenever it might come, in order to bring about a reduction of the colonial power of Britain and a rectification of the European balance by the restoration of France to the position of power and prestige it had occupied before the Seven Years' War.[73]

Even while he was negotiating the peace in the spring of 1762, Choiseul received a memorandum from one Buchet Dupavillon that in considerable measure reflected his own convictions regard-

[72] For the Third Family Compact and the Treaty of Paris, see Paullin, *op. cit.*, IV, 83, 92–98. For the diplomatic exchanges leading up to the Treaty of Paris, see Max Savelle, "The Diplomatic History of the Canadian Boundary, 1749–63," (in preparation).

[73] Charles Giraud, ed., "Mémoire de Monsieur de Choiseul remis au Roi en 1765," *Journal des Savants* (1881), pp. 171–84, 250–57; Henri Doniol, *Histoire de la participation de la France à l'établissement des États-Unis d'Amérique* (6 vols., Paris, 1886–99), I, 2–4; cf. Louis Blart, *Les Rapports de la France et de l'Espagne après le Pacte de Famille, jusqu'à la fin du Ministère du duc de Choiseul* (Paris, 1915), p. 74, *passim;* and Samuel F. Bemis, *The Diplomacy of the American Revolution* (New York, 1935), pp. 4–12.

ing America: "The discovery of America changed the interests of Europe; that part of the world today places such a preponderant weight in the balance of political powers that it seems that Europe will soon be such only as an accessory to this new world." Dupavillon predicted that America would throw off the yoke of Europe; but the time for that event had not come, and in the meantime superiority in Europe would reside with the nation controlling the greatest part of America. "The possession of America," he said, "is today the most abundant and the most dependable source of political power; it is only by reason of the riches that commerce bears thence that the nations may be compared with each other." It was up to France, he thought, to force Great Britain by an invasion of England or Holland to give up the colonies taken from France during the war, or, failing that, to call for a redistribution of colonies all round—a sort of new deal in the colonial world—to rectify the American balance so violently disturbed by British success in the war.[74] Choiseul was not impressed by Dupavillon's call for a new deal; that, he said, "is much easier to imagine than to do." But he was impressed by the other "good ideas" in the memorandum and sent it on to his cousin, the Comte de Choiseul, who had relieved him of the duties of the foreign ministry with the exception of French relations with Spain, which the Duc considered the "axle" of French foreign policy.[75]

The Duc de Choiseul was convinced that, now that France had lost its American empire and much of its European prestige, the only way to recover the old French position would be to diminish the inflated power of Great Britain. But, he said, "it is only the revolution of [British] America, which will take place, but which we probably shall not see, that will reduce England to the state of feebleness in which she will no longer be feared in Europe." While waiting for that moment to come, France, he felt, must prepare the way, not so much by inciting Britain's enemies as by causing Britain the greatest possible economic losses, especially, if and when possible, the loss of her American colonies.[76] Following this line of thought, Choiseul intently observed the resistance of the colonies

---

[74] AE. Méms. et docs. Angleterre, 56: 14–19vo.
[75] AE. Méms. et docs. Angleterre, 56: 20.   [76] Giraud, *op. cit.*, p. 178.

to the mother country in the hope that the long-awaited opportunity might have arrived.[77]

The Duc de Choiseul retired from office in 1770, but there remains in the archives a memorandum which probably represents his thinking at that date. Its title is suggestive: "Means for France to employ in order to reduce England to the position it ought to occupy in the Balance of Europe." Repeating the mercantilist argument, the memorandum held that the state in the preëminent place among colonial and maritime nations not only had the greatest power itself but could even dictate the amount of power its neighbors might have. Great Britain was that state at the moment, and Europe should fear and avoid—if, indeed, there still were time— the coup that Great Britain would be prepared to deliver if allowed to maintain her overwhelming maritime power. But the power of Britain need be only temporary; France, for her part, was under the moral obligation to recover its place among the nations.

The means suggested were four: France should, for the present, avoid a war; second, Spain and Holland should ally themselves with France "to achieve the great object of the rectification of the equilibrium"; third, every effort should be made to weaken British financial credit, since it was by her financial strength that England maintained her international preëminence; finally, since the commerce of Great Britain drew its principal existence from (1) the British colonies and (2) the treasures of the Spaniards and Portuguese colonies, and since the British colonies were threatening to become independent, France should (a) promote in every possible way the independence of the British American colonies and (b) take every possible means to cut off or reduce the commerce between Britain on the one side and Spain and Portugal and their colonies on the other.

The British American colonies, the memorandum continued, had already indicated their disposition sooner or later to separate from their mother country. If this tendency were retarded, it could only be by the indulgence of the mother country, as a result of which England would have to renounce its monopolistic posi-

<hr />

[77] Duc de Choiseul to Comte de Guerchy, May 14, 1767, in Cornelius de Witt, *Thomas Jefferson* (3d. ed., Paris, 1861), pp. 418–19; Choiseul to Durand, Aug. 24, 1767, *ibid.*, pp. 425–26.

tion with regard to colonial commerce; this in itself would partially accomplish France's purpose. At the same time, France could hasten matters by "solidly" establishing the contraband trade between the French islands and British America, by attracting the direct Anglo-Spanish trade to France, and by diminishing the enormous quantities of British-caught fish consumed in Spain—this last by the subsidizing of a French fishing company or by an appeal to the Pope for an indulgence in Spain's favor! [78]

Parts of this remarkable memorandum seem fantastic; yet it bears a striking analogy to the policies actually followed by the Comte de Vergennes. For the moment, to be sure, France ceased to take a very active part in European diplomacy: America was delivered to the ambitions of Great Britain, and Poland was abandoned to her devourers in the North. But upon the accession of Vergennes to power in 1774, the theories and policies of Choiseul were revived; and the lines of French policy with regard to the crisis now rapidly developing in the British empire were those laid down by him in the period just following the Peace of Paris of 1763.

The Comte de Vergennes was a man of orderly mind and habits. Soon after taking office he outlined the policies he was to follow. To begin with, the nadir of French humiliation, it seemed to him, had been reached with the partition of Poland. France could not tolerate the humble position to which she had been reduced, but must seek every means of accomplishing a *revanche*. France must not permit the continental balance of power to be further upset; but it was England that was France's deadliest enemy. The power of England, now in the ascendant in the world, must be reduced. The trouble brewing in the British colonies seemed to offer the opportunity, foreseen by Choiseul, for France to strike a blow at the British hegemony, and the most promising instrument for striking that blow was the alliance with Spain. Thus the Family Compact must be the cornerstone of French policy.[79]

The quarrel between the British colonies and their mother country seemed to Vergennes to be of the utmost importance to France and Spain. It appeared that the colonies were moving toward independence; should they have to face England alone,

[78] AE. Méms. et docs. Angleterre, 56: 32–39.   [79] Doniol, *op. cit.*, I, 2–4, 13–22.

they must inevitably be subjected, albeit at great expense to England. But by their subjugation, England

will conserve at least the mercantile benefits that her commerce with America has procured for her up to the present and she will consequently be able to sustain her manufactures and her marine. She will above all prevent the colonies from placing, as they would do, if independent, a considerable weight in the balance in favor of some other power. Further, one may say that, whatever be the method by which England maintain her supremacy in America, there must always redound to her from that condition very considerable advantages, whereas by losing it she would suffer an incalculable loss.

France must seize upon the opportunity to weaken England, he argued, by the loss of her colonies; for by their loss Britain's military power would be reduced, her commerce would suffer an "irreparable loss" to the benefit of French commerce, and France would recover a part, perhaps, of her former possessions in America.[80]

It was for these reasons that Vergennes adopted a policy of encouraging the revolting colonies. Turning to Spain for coöperation in this effort, he revived the old French argument that His Catholic Majesty was interested equally with France in the rectification of the American balance, and urged the necessity for a united Franco-Spanish front against the aggressive designs of the British. Chatham was the same old Pitt, he said, now proposing an amicable settlement of the difficulties with the colonies in order to launch a destructive offensive against the colonies of France and Spain; those two countries must be prepared to defend themselves.[81]

From this argument Vergennes went on to a more aggressive one. Great Britain offered to guarantee the existing status quo in America if France and Spain would stay out of the colonial conflict, but these proposals Vergennes rejected.[82] He was determined that Britain's power must be reduced; that the balance of power in America and in Europe, so heavily disturbed by the Peace of 1763, must be rectified. He emphasized the aggressive nature of the schemes of Chatham and argued that the failure of France and Spain to aid the revolting colonies would be equivalent to forcing

[80] *Ibid.*, I, 243–44.   [81] *Ibid.*, I, 42–43; II, 449, 773–75.
[82] *Ibid.*, II, 147–49; J. F. Yela y Utrillo, *España ante la independencia de los Estados Unidos* (2 vols., Lerida, 1925), I, 55–56.

them to make peace with England, after which they would be compelled to become the allies of Great Britain in a war upon the American possessions of France and Spain.[83] Spain remained unconvinced, being influenced by the fear that the example of encouraging the British colonies to revolt might have an unfortunate effect upon her own colonies; but finally, in April, 1779, she entered into a military convention with France and joined in the war more to reduce British might than to aid American independence.

Meanwhile, Vergennes had prevailed upon the Dutch to remain neutral, which they did until Great Britain, irritated by Holland's refusal to make war upon France and Spain and by Dutch aid to the colonies, declared war in 1780.[84]

The culmination of Vergennes's policy of encouragement toward the American Revolution was the recognition of the independence of the United States in the two treaties signed on February 6, 1778. These treaties had the double objective of reducing Britain's commercial monopoly of the trade with her former colonies and of subtracting their potential military power from the military power of the British Empire. The Franco-American alliance provided for a mutual guarantee of territories, France undertaking to guarantee to the United States the possession of whatever territories they might gain in North America during the war and the United States undertaking a similar guarantee to France with regard to the West Indies.[85]

Thus France took the final step in the culmination of the policies of Choiseul and Vergennes for the rectification of the American balance of power disturbed by the Treaty of Paris in 1763. The successful conclusion of the American Revolution, while it had no appreciable effect upon French territorial holdings in the New World, did greatly reduce the possessions of Great Britain. It might even be said that a new tripartite balance had been established, with the United States of America occupying the position of the third, or balancing, power between Britain and Spain, the

[83] *Ibid.,* II, 449, 563, 774-75.

[84] *Recueil des instructions, Espagne,* III, 361; *Hollande,* I, lviii; Bemis, *op. cit., passim.*

[85] David Hunter Miller, ed., *Treaties and Other International Acts of the United States of America* (6 vols., Washington, 1931–   ), II, 3-34, 35-44, 45-46.

position formerly occupied by France. In any case, Vergennes might then have said, as George Canning did say nearly fifty years later, "I called the New World into existence to redress the balance of the Old." [86]

Practically every colonial war fought in America in the course of the eighteenth century, including the American Revolution, was fought over the maintenance or the disturbance of the American balance of power. Yet it is probable that European diplomats, in using the argument of the balance of power, whether in America or in Europe, were never entirely without their tongues in their cheeks. This cynical evaluation of the doctrine was often expressed, even by the very men who used it; but never more succinctly than in the instructions to the Marquis d'Hautefort, French ambassador to Austria, in 1750:

The equilibrium of power in Europe is the rallying cry that unites in one concert of measures, although for very different motives, the courts of Vienna and London, the Estates-General of the United Provinces and the majority of the princes of Germany. Although this equilibrium be, to speak the truth, a thing of pure opinion which everyone interprets according to his own views and his private interests, it has nevertheless served as a pretext and a motive for the leagues which for nearly eighty years have been formed and renewed against France. England and Holland, who believe themselves specially interested in the maintenance of this equilibrium of power, regard the court of Vienna as the sole power which, aided by their help, is in a position to counterbalance the forces of the House of Bourbon; and it is for that reason . . . that they have for long been the constant allies of the House of Austria.[87]

So far as America was concerned, certain general conclusions seem to be justified. First, the idea of an equilibrium of commercial and territorial power in America was a genuine and important consideration in the minds of European diplomats from about 1700 to 1778 and a more significant determinant of both American and European history than is generally recognized. Second, it appears that with the growth of emphasis upon the economic and political value of colonies, the equilibrium of colonial power became more and more important as the century wore on, until, in the epoch of

[86] *The Speeches of the Right Honourable George Canning* (6 vols., London, 1828), VI, 111.
[87] *Recueil des instructions, Autriche,* p. 310.

the American Revolution, the balance of European power was thought actually to rest upon the balance in the colonial world in general and in America in particular. Finally, it seems clear that the success of the American Revolution, due as it was to French, Spanish, and Dutch aid, became a reality because France was moved by the century-old idea of an equilibrium of empires and by the burning desire to bring about a reëstablishment of its own international weight and importance by the reduction of that of Great Britain. The idea of a colonial balance of power may have been merely the rationalization of more selfish motives; nevertheless, as a determinant in the international affairs of the eighteenth century it is nonetheless real, for all that, and nonetheless important in the achievement of American independence.

The Office of Commander in Chief: A Phase of Imperial Unity on the Eve of The Revolution ∽ CLARENCE E. CARTER

IN RECENT years the investigation of the causes of the American war for independence has been pursued along novel lines. It has notably been the vogue to attribute the Revolution to such movements and interests, among others, as the so-called conflict between social classes, involving a supposed democratic upheaval; sectional divisions within the colonies; and even western land problems. Contributions to knowledge respecting these phases of the early Revolutionary era have, admittedly, supplied an abundance of authentic and useful information; but the very multiplicity of the new theories renders it most unlikely that any one of them involves a fundamental or even a principal cause of the Revolution. Although such approaches to an interpretation are, to be sure, not wholly irrelevant in that they have drawn attention to interesting and possibly significant contributory factors, they are nevertheless pervaded by a common weakness.

It is, of course, indubitable that the causes of the Revolution were complex, that no single explanation will suffice. Yet in the exploration of the field to discover new attributions of causes there has been an evident tendency, as is true of many microscopic studies, to overlook obvious elements which a realistic view of that epoch must necessarily envisage if a balanced historical perspective is to be restored and maintained. As an instance, the general failure to give adequate place to the distinctive and growing fear in America of an ultimate consolidation of the colonies under a regime that might become wholly military has not, since Bancroft's day, received the emphasis which it not only deserves but demands. We hasten to advise, however, that the present chapter is not a synthesis of the causes of the Revolution. It is rather a brief exposition of a phase of colonial history which is viewed as essentially relevant to an appreciation of the raising of a wall of resistance to the evident consolidating tendencies of British policy —a policy which seemed to Americans to be incompatible with the provincialism to which they were long accustomed.

Instances of the contemporary fear mentioned are not difficult to discover. Governor Pitkin of Connecticut asserted in 1768 that "maintaining troops in the Colonies now, in this time of profound peace, would be an unnecessary expense, and have an unhappy tendency to produce uneasiness among the people, hurt their morals and hinder their industry." [1] Benjamin Franklin was suggesting in 1770 that the keeping of a standing army in America without the consent of the assemblies "is not agreeable to the Constitution," [2] and in the same year Thomas Pownall evinced the fear not only that the policy of taxation was inimical to the best interests of the British colonies in North America, but that the people were becoming increasingly apprehensive of the presence of armed forces in their midst. Pownall then declared:

Whilst their minds are oppressed with these doubts [taxation], they apprehend and think they feel a military power established among them independent of, and paramount to, their civil jurisdiction, by which (if they had no apprehension of any design to alter their civil constitutions) they do think it is meant to throw a kind of military net over them. And have they not foundation, Sir, for these fears? . . . When they see a military power established within the jurisdiction of their government—neither depending for its establishment on the will of the community nor exercising its power by command derived from the supreme authority of that jurisdiction, they think this military body foreign to their community, and brought upon them by force of external power. [3]

In 1774 the first Continental Congress placed conspicuous emphasis as a grievance on the maintenance of a standing army "without the consent of our assemblies," and asserted that "this army, with a considerable naval armament, has been employed to enforce the collection of taxes." It was further alleged by the con-

[1] Massachusetts Historical Society, *Collections*, 5th ser., IX, 288.
[2] A. H. Smyth, ed., *Writings of Benjamin Franklin* (New York, 1905–7), V, 259.
[3] *Parliamentary History*, XVI, 987.

gress that "the Authority of the commander in chief, and under him, of the brigadier's general, has in time of peace been rendered supreme in all the civil governments in America." The same charge finds place in the Declaration of Independence in the passage which asserts that the King "has affected to render the Military independent of and superior to the Civil Power."

Such expressions of opinion respecting the significance of the unwonted military arm in the colonies are representative of the views of those who thought they perceived a new system of constitutional (or unconstitutional) government superimposed upon the old order in America. Whether right or wrong, such was the position taken by an influential section of the population, as also by certain minds in England. The truth of the matter cannot be found, however, by merely quoting critical expressions either by opponents of the alleged military encroachment or by apologists of that regime, if it may be so termed. Any appraisal of the situation necessarily involves a reconstruction of the relevant conditions and circumstances on which the views in question were predicated.

In all ages, the possession of distant posts of trade and colonization has raised difficulties for the owner, centrifugal forces generally being stronger than efforts toward the creation of cohesive ties. A solution of the always baffling problem of unification by devising and enforcing general imperial laws and by creating agencies of defense was affected by the intervention of domestic politics, by economic theories and practices, by the character of dependent populations, and by distance and difficulties of communication. These factors were particularly relevant in the experience of England in her colonial ventures of the seventeenth and eighteenth centuries. The establishment of a commercial system designed to bring the colonies within the orbit of the mother country has already been sufficiently emphasized.[4] But more than the establishment of a commercial system was necessary. The long effort of the home government to establish some form of political and military union between the scattered colonies and the struggles of the whole dominion and the mother country to provide insurance against invasion by a hostile power and to attain a more complete realization of their economic benefits are also well known

4 See *supra*, pp. 3–39.

though usually less emphasized. An interpretation of the fateful years from 1763 to 1775 cannot be made wholly understandable, therefore, without a preliminary glimpse of the earlier development.

At the opening of the eighteenth century, English authorities were confronted with a twofold problem in the planning of an effective system of administration for the American colonies. The strong particularistic tendencies of the colonies obstructed an efficient administration of the commercial laws and at the same time reduced the effectiveness of colonial defense. From 1690 to 1754 the government explored various plans in the hope of finding some mode of cementing the different fragments of its American dominions in order to bring better order and discipline into the administration of the trade laws and the Indian trade, and to present a united front against the common enemy. This would doubtless have been early accomplished had William III been willing to continue, even in modified form, the Dominion of New England, which had been created for the purpose of overcoming these deficiencies. On account of William's reluctance to continue that experiment, however, the opportunity to create a permanent consolidation on the earlier basis disappeared.[5] Yet the problem did not vanish; as particularism grew and as the danger from external enemies became more menacing, it was plain that some form of centralized administration must be devised. Attempts to unite the militia of several colonies under the rule of one governor, and similar projects undertaken from time to time, were temporary makeshifts and consequently failed to meet the realities of the problem.

The whole question was taken under consideration by the Board of Trade in 1721 in an effort to find a solution. In its well-known report of that year the board pointed out certain weaknesses in the colonial establishment, with reference especially to the paramount questions of defense, the management of Indian affairs, and the commercial system. It was recommended that the several provinces be placed under a lord lieutenant or captain general, from whom the governors of particular colonies should receive

[5] Viola F. Barnes, *The Dominion of New England* (New Haven, 1923), pp. 212–30, 262–72.

their orders for the King's service. Such a plan, it was urged, would render the colonies mutually subservient to each other's support, and the problem of raising men and money for military purposes would thus be solved.[6]

These recommendations were laid aside, however, and it was not until 1754 that the problem was again approached from a similar angle.[7] Confronted in that year by the impending conflict with France and the continued disunity of the colonies, the board proposed to bring about a general concert of the provincial governments for their mutual and common defense.[8] In its outline we observe a statement of the same general issues as heretofore: the fixing of a certain and permanent system of maintaining frontier forts, the determination of a method of raising troops within the colonies, and a plan for the management of Indian affairs. And the board recurs again to the former idea of the appointment by the Crown of a commander in chief, with command over forts and garrisons and all troops raised for emergencies, together with complete direction over Indian affairs. The colonies themselves were to reach an agreement to be confirmed by the Crown; failing this, the interposition of Parliament was the only alternative. It will be noted that the plan thus projected by the board contemplated only a military union, differing radically, therefore, from the Albany plan of 1754, which involved also a political union. The rejection of the latter proposal by the colonies themselves revealed the improbability of gaining the desired end through a concert voluntarily entered into by the provinces. There remained no

---

[6] Sept. 8, 1721, *Documents Relating to the Colonial History of New York*, V, 629–30.

[7] There were other proposals designed to facilitate colonial defense which were to contribute precedents: from time to time when the exigencies of defense demanded, schemes were advanced for the enlistment of colonials in British regiments under American officers; and in 1748 Governor Shirley of Massachusetts broached the proposition of a permanent British garrison in New York, with a parliamentary tax for its maintenance. The theme throughout is the devising of a plan of unifying defense at colonial expense. For a lucid account of the various proposals, see Stanley Pargellis, *Lord Loudoun in North America* (New Haven, 1933), pp. 1–21.

[8] Representation of the Board of Trade, Aug. 9, 1754, *Docs. Rel. Col. Hist. N.Y.*, VI, 901–2; "Plan for a General Coöperation of the North American Colonies," Aug. 9, 1754, *ibid.*, pp. 903–6; Secretary Robinson to Governor Sharpe, Oct. 26, 1754, *Maryland Archives*, VI, 108; Robinson to Board of Trade, Nov. 24, 1754, *Docs. Rel. Col. Hist. N.Y.*, VI, 844; Sharpe to Lord Baltimore, Jan. 17, 1755, *Md. Archives*, VI, 160.

doubt on the part of the Board of Trade, however, concerning the power of the Crown to appoint a supreme commander in chief. The Crown "may legally and by virtue of its authority, invest any person with such powers." [9]

The sudden outbreak of war in 1754 rendered precipitate action imperative, and General Braddock was appointed as the first of a line of supreme commanders of the forces in North America. The appointment in question included, along with the usual instructions to take command at once of all forts and of all men in arms, power to assume control of Indian relations. He was likewise instructed to seek the coöperation of the colonial governments in everything that pertained to the raising of men and supplies and to questions of transportation.[10] At the same time Sir Thomas Robinson, Secretary of State, urged the colonial governors to enlist the aid of the assemblies for these purposes.[11]

For the first time, then, there was one supreme official in America who could and did act in concert with the provinces, and a regular correspondence was conducted by the successive commanders in chief directly with the colonial governors. The latter were called into conference and urged to work in harmony with each other and with the military officials; [12] the different colonies were dealt with on the same basis. But Pitt's reluctance to arouse colonial opposition led by 1758 to a decided curtailment of the activities of the imperial military officials. Otherwise the exigencies of the war might have led to a much greater degree of union and to the paving of the way for ultimate consolidation.

Thus matters stood at the close of the war. The military or-

[9] *Docs. Rel. Col. Hist. N.Y.*, VI, 901–2.

[10] General Braddock's instructions, 1754, *Pennsylvania Archives*, II, 203–7. His private instructions are printed in Stanley Pargellis, ed., *Military Affairs in North America, 1748–1765* (New York, 1936), pp. 53–54.

[11] Robinson to Governor Sharpe, Oct. 26, 1754, *Md. Archives*, VI, 108.

[12] In a circular letter to the governors of New Hampshire, Massachusetts, Connecticut, Rhode Island, New York, and New Jersey, March 13, 1756, Secretary Fox announced the appointment of Loudoun as commander in chief of all forces in North America "whatsoever . . . for the Public Service," and included the following instruction: "The Governors of the above named provinces should be ready to give His Lordship, and the Troops from England, all the assistance in your power on their arrival in America agreable to the orders sent you in Sir Thomas Robinson's letter of October 26, 1754, and you will correspond with, and apply to the Earl of Loudoun, on all occasions, in the same manner as you were directed to do, with the late General Braddock and Major General Shirley." *Docs. Rel. Col. Hist. N.Y.*, VII, 75.

ganization perfected during that struggle, although shorn of some of its powers acquired up to 1758, was not demobilized at the conclusion of peace in 1763. The protection of the now greatly enlarged empire against savage subjects and possible external enemies, still the essential problem, was made more difficult by the disunited state of the colonies and particularly by their loss of interest in military matters after 1760. The situation, therefore, gave a vital aspect and definite proportions to the Grenville proposals in 1763 to maintain a standing army of ten thousand troops in America and to find a means for their partial support in the colonies. Linked with these propositions, of course, was the plan for a more unified administration of the trade laws.

The formula thus announced by the ministry in 1763 was primarily designed to contribute to the unification of the empire on a prerogative basis in a time of nominal peace. Yet it recommended as a policy nothing unique, since it was in line with various earlier proposals in its object of providing for imperial defense, partly at colonial expense, and for a reconstruction of the trade laws. In the execution of the plan, however, developments appeared which were little short of revolutionary in character. This military edifice, long anticipated by English officials, which was erected through the urgent circumstances of the late war, assumed tasks in the era of peace that gave it a place of exceptional importance in the administration of American affairs. The status quo ante bellum no longer prevailed; an army, with a commander in chief resident in New York, was now a fixed peacetime institution in America; this institution turned out to be the most cohesive element that had yet appeared in the American colonies. At the height of the French and Indian war it was inevitable that a supreme commander should have attained a wide-reaching prestige. His central position and his authority and responsibilities made his office tangent to numerous interests and objects, many of which were not of a purely military character. As during the war, so now, it was around the authority and prestige of the office of the commander in chief that the administration of imperial affairs tended to be organized.

In this regard, the chief personality throughout the period subsequent to 1763 was Major General Thomas Gage. While acting as lieutenant governor of the district of Montreal he had been instructed to assume the temporary command of the troops in North America during the absence of General Sir Jeffrey Amherst,[13] whose application for leave of absence to return to England had just been granted.[14] Gage left Montreal as soon as his command of that district had been transferred to his successor; he arrived in New York November 16, 1763, and on the following day received orders and instructions from Amherst. He assumed command immediately.[15] Among the documents transmitted by Amherst in the transfer of the office were copies of his commissions, special orders, and instructions; correspondence with home officials and with the governors; contracts for provisions and supplies; plans for the suppression of the Indian revolt then in progress; abstracts of present and future dispositions of the troops; and proposals for the abandonment of certain of the smaller forts.[16] This budget of papers was covered by a letter embodying a summary of the entire situation, the administration of which now devolved upon General Gage.[17] Gage was given a permanent status as commander in chief one year later when he received a commission under the Great Seal [18] and instructions for the government of the forces.[19]

The symbols of authority thus given conveyed merely the ordinary powers of governing troops, such as the punishing of deserters and other offenders, summoning courts-martial, and appointing a provost marshal and a judge advocate. We look vainly in the documents in question for clues to the sources of other powers and functions which were actually wielded; the latter were derived in large part from precedents, orders, and instructions left behind by his predecessors in the office [20] and from subsequent commands from home authorities. The exercise of general administrative authority over Indian affairs, for example, stemmed from Braddock's instructions in 1754. Such official documents thus

[13] Egremont to Gage, Aug. 13, 1763, in C. E. Carter, ed., *Correspondence of General Thomas Gage* (2 vols., New Haven, 1931, 1933), I, 1, hereafter referred to as *Gage Corr.*
[14] Egremont to Amherst, Aug. 13, 1763, *ibid.*, II, 207.   [15] *Ibid.*, I, 1–2.
[16] These papers are found among the Gage MSS, W. L. Clements Library.
[17] Nov. 17, 1763, *Gage Corr.*, II, 209–14.
[18] Dated Nov. 13, 1764.   [19] Dated Nov. 16, 1764.
[20] A systematic account of such precedents during the command of Lord Loudoun is found in Pargellis, *Lord Loudoun, passim.*

formed the general bases of the extensive powers of the office. By and large, however, historical mutations do not stem entirely from formal documents, the fact being that commissions, orders, proclamations, and legislative enactments by no means illumine the whole process of history. A host of minor happenings and the not infrequent intervention of purely fortuitous events have more often than otherwise supplied the bases of new lines of development. In the present instance the authority of General Gage's office was not completely implemented, and since it had to cope with many unpredictable contingencies the necessity of acting on occasion without specific orders or instructions was plain.

Let us first glimpse some characteristics of the new commander in chief, who has not fared too well at the hands of historians. The ability and personality of the man have been largely obscured by his ill-fated experience in Boston in 1774 and 1775. That he was not a great soldier is demonstrable; had he possessed the qualities of effective leadership in times of acute crises, as in the period of his governorship of Massachusetts, the American Revolution might have been averted. He was not, of course, devoid of field experience as an officer, though in the main undistinguished; he had served on the continent of Europe and had fought, perhaps as gloriously as Braddock and Washington, at the Monongahela. He had been progressively rewarded with advances in rank until by 1761 he was a major general and was entrusted with the military governorship of the district of Montreal, where we find him at the date of his appointment to the highest position in America. In the course of his service he had become well acquainted with the country, and he was associated with it more intimately by a marriage alliance with a prominent New Jersey family.[21]

A careful perusal of his military papers discloses a phase of the career of Thomas Gage which has not heretofore been emphasized. His job in peacetime was of course mainly administrative in character; in that connection the fact is indisputable that he received without exception the strongest commendations from his superiors in England. His official correspondence clearly reveals that he

21 He married, on Dec. 8, 1758, Margaret Kemble, daughter of Peter Kemble, a member of the New Jersey Council. His eldest son, Henry, succeeded his uncle as the third Viscount Gage, of Firle, Sussex, England. *Dictionary of American Biography*, VII, 87–88.

ran the military organization, spread as it was from Newfoundland to Florida and from Bermuda to the Great Lakes and the Mississippi River and comprising more than fifty stations and garrisons, with a minimum of friction during the dozen years of his command. The supreme military command involved, however, much more than the giving of routine marching orders, the filing of regimental returns, and the authorizing of courts-martial. It was also a huge business, and to some extent political, enterprise, involving the service of supply, the opening of roads, and the administration of Indian affairs, to mention only a few items. The necessity of promptly forwarding provisions, clothing, ammunition, and money to such remote outposts on the periphery of the Empire as those in Newfoundland, Nova Scotia, Quebec, Detroit, the Illinois country, the Floridas, and New Providence, as well as to many less remote garrisons, was continuous; the service never broke down despite seasonal conditions, poor avenues of communication, and other obstacles. Foresight, patience, energy, and coöperation with others enabled the business to be executed with comparative success at all times.

There was a regular and frequent correspondence with such officials in America as the mustermaster general, wagon master general, barrack master general, apothecary general, deputy quartermaster general, deputy commissary general, chief engineer, storekeeper of ordnance, deputy judge advocate, Indian superintendents and agents, brigadiers general, commandants of posts, forts, and detachments, local commissaries, paymasters, postmasters, surveyors, chaplains, contractors and their agents, customs commissioners, admirals of the fleet, masters of transports, superintendents of the navy on the lakes, and colonial governors. Back of all this was a stream of communications passing between General Gage and the Secretaries of State, Secretaries at War, the Treasury Board, and the Ordnance Board.

Of course a multiplicity of purely technical questions connected with the service was discussed in the course of the vast correspondence in question: promotions, reductions, resignations, half pay, purchase and sale of commissions, construction of engineering projects, garrison returns, estimates for supplies, review reports, marching and embarkation orders, stoppages, fire and candle, bat and forage, desertion, recruiting, invalids, militia, carriages, quartering, and the like. Not all of these subjects, to be sure, were touched with a public interest, though such issues as desertion, recruiting, militia, carriages, quartering, and supplies were so affected.

It is evident that Gage possessed extraordinary patience on most occasions, so long as that quality could remain a virtue, despite the almost infinite variety of bewildering and perplexing issues which dogged his path. The constant admonition to his subordinates to use discretion and good sense in their relations with each other and with the civil powers, toward Indians, and with dependent populations reflected his own practice in that regard. Even desertion was not viewed as a serious crime; his orders were usually to receive such persons back without penalty.[22] But disobedience to orders, indignities conferred upon his own office, and stupid errors aroused his indignation and in such instances he did not hesitate to pen stinging reprimands or to take appropriate action. On one occasion a provincial governor dared to cast aspersions on the military service in a manner which called forth the following curt reply:

As the Answer I may be tempted to give to your letter . . . can't certainly be of use to the King's service, or indeed promote any good purpose, You will excuse me that I do not more than merely acknowledge the receipt of that letter, and to add only that it is my humble request to You, that you write to Me no more in that stile, or that you wou'd not take it amiss if, for the future, Epistles of that Sort, should be immediately returned to You.[23]

The feelings of a subordinate who made a mistake in judgment were not spared. When Captain Hugh Lord imprisoned a drunken Chickasaw Indian at Kaskaskia, an action which had serious repercussions, Gage admonished that officer thus:

If you had known Indians better I presume that the quarrell you relate with the Chickasaws would never have happened. You have dealt with rioutous Indians as if they had been a Dublin mob, and the making one of them a prisoner appears to have been the cause of the Tragedy that followed. . . . You must get out of a bad scrape as well as you can.[24]

22 Gage to Pomeroy, March 6, 1769, Gage MSS.
23 To Governor Johnston, Nov. 18, 1765, *loc. cit.*   24 Aug. 30, 1772, *loc. cit.*

Lieutenant Colonel John Wilkins, Lord's predecessor in command
of the Illinois posts, became involved in sundry scandalous proceedings and to him was addressed the tart message: "That you
have many Enemies is certain, how they became so, you may devise
better than me. . . . I must have been more than weak to make
myself longer answerable for your Conduct." [25]

Colonel Bradstreet's stupidity in concluding a treaty with the
western Indians in 1764, when his distinct instructions had been
merely to offer peace under certain conditions, brought a reply
which Bradstreet probably never forgot:

The peace you have thought proper to conclude with the Shawnese and
Delawares, you had no Power to conclude, nor do I approve or will I
ratify, or confirm any Peace so derogatory to the Honor and Credit of
His Majesty's Arms amongst the Indian Nations. . . .[26]

On the other hand, Gage's obliging disposition toward officers
in whom he had confidence and his capacity for close understanding, even warm friendship, with his associates are characteristics clearly illustrated in his relations with such men as Sir William Johnson, Brigadier General Frederick Haldimand, Brigadier
General Burton, and Sir Guy Carleton. And fortunate it was, since
these worthies occupied key positions in the edifice, and mutual
confidence was therefore essential. A touch of human quality is
found also in his relations with General Monckton, whose Greenwich mansion Gage occupied for a time.

Necessity has induced me to take a Liberty with you, which I should
not have ventured to take with many others; but your Goodness and
obliging Disposition assure me already that you will easily pardon it.
The Case is, that according to New York Custom, I shall be turned
out of my House on the first of May; and have no other immediately
prepared, into which I can get, till the Month of June. In this Dilemma
I have made free of your Country House, which Freedom I hope you
will excuse, as I can very soon remove out of it, If I hear of your Return
to this Part of the World. I wish I had a House in England to offer
you in exchange for yours, but we younger Brothers don't abound much
in Houses or Lands; whatever else is in my power to do for your Service,
you will be pleased always to Command.[27]

[25] Aug. 5, 1772, *loc. cit.*
[26] Sept. 2, 1764. General Gage's Letters, Harvard College Library.
[27] April 14, 1764, *Gage Corr.*, II, 226.

Recurring to the main theme, we are here concerned, as has already been indicated, only with the military phase of the broad general policy of unification, which also included the creation of a new customs board and the new vice admiralty court, new financial measures, and the establishment of a department of state for the colonies. And it cannot be assumed that the developments hereinafter described were unconnected with the more distinctly political measures. It now, therefore, remains to enumerate some of the functions exercised by this central imperial power which definitely contributed to the unification of the American dominions in the years of comparative peace following the settlement of 1763. There were three chief functions performed by the commander in chief: (1) the exercise of supreme authority in spheres beyond the competence of the colonies to perform; (2) coöperation with the local governments in the suppression of civil disorder; and (3) the assembling of information for various ministerial offices.

One of the principal and clearly imperial duties performed by the army was the policing and administering of a large portion of the new territory ceded to Great Britain in 1763. Three new provinces, Quebec, East Florida, and West Florida, had been carved out of these cessions by royal proclamation.[28] But an extensive domain, comprehending substantially the region lying between the Alleghenies and the Mississippi, had been reserved, by clauses of the same document, for the Indians, and new settlements were prohibited in the reservation without the consent of the Crown. In the present connection, we need not be concerned with the mixed motives which induced the framing of the relevant clauses in the proclamation in question.[29] It is sufficient to note that one of the immediate objectives in mind was the appeasement of the Indians and that the plan thus incorporated in the document was in no sense deemed a permanent disposal of the region, which was thus left for the time being without any provision for

[28] Oct. 7, 1763. Adam Shortt and A. G. Doughty, eds., *Documents Relating to the Constitutional History of Canada, 1759–1791* (2d ed., Ottawa, 1918), pp. 163–68.

[29] This problem was brilliantly analyzed by the late Professor Clarence W. Alvord in his "Genesis of the Proclamation of 1763," in Michigan Historical Society, *Collections*, XXXVI, 20–52, and in his *The Mississippi Valley in British Politics* (2 vols., Cleveland, 1917), I, 183–210.

its civil organization and government. Nor with respect to any form of administration is there the slightest hint in the text of the proclamation, though it was known that there were white settlements located within its boundaries which, previous to the cession of 1763, had been governed by France from New Orleans and Quebec as centers.

It is significant, however, that during the formulation of the policy thus outlined there was a suggestion by Secretary of State Egremont that it might be well to attach the reservation in question to one of the colonies in order that criminals and fugitives from justice might be retaken.[30] At the same time Lord Shelburne, president of the Board of Trade, while opposing Egremont's suggestion, definitely proposed that the commanding general of the forces be given jurisdiction over the unorganized territory for the express purpose of protecting the Indians and the fur trade, and that the commander in chief be instructed to return fugitives from justice.[31] This view received the approval also of Lord Halifax, who was Secretary of State when General Gage was promoted to the high command of the army in America.[32] No formal action was taken, however, and no instructions were prepared to that end; the question of administration was consequently left unsettled.

Similarly, English law was not extended to the old French settlements, as was done in the newly created provinces to the north and south of the reservation. By virtue, however, of accepted principles of international law the old settlers would continue to live, so far as local regulations were concerned, under their ancient laws and customs.[33]

There were not, to be sure, very many resident inhabitants within the boundaries of the reservation, the more or less permanent settlers, mainly of French extraction, probably numbering less than three thousand persons, exclusive of an undetermined number of black slaves and wandering traders. But the problem of their government was no less acute because of their comparatively small number. A natural attachment of these people to their

---

[30] *Docs. Rel. Const. Hist. Can.*, p. 148. [31] *Ibid.*, pp. 151–52. [32] *Ibid.*, p. 154.
[33] Campbell v. Hall (1774), *ibid.*, pp. 522–31; William Blackstone, *Commentaries on the Laws of England* (T. M. Cooley, ed., Chicago, 1884), introd., sec. 4, p. 107; R. B. Morris, *Studies in the History of American Law* (New York, 1930), pp. 13, 83, 84, 117.

former French rulers, their close relations with the Indians and with French and Spanish traders, and the possibility of a state of anarchy if no restraining hand were placed over them presented a problem of more than local importance. It involved their loyalty to the new regime and the destruction of such connections with the old order as might endanger British security.

Hence General Gage was faced at once with more than a mere technical command over men and posts; by virtue of the new and unanticipated circumstances mentioned he was to become in effect, though not in name, a governor general. In this regard he was already seasoned by his previous rather long experience (1760–63) as military governor of a dependent population in Montreal.[34] He had also supervised the affairs of East Florida and West Florida from the date of his appointment as commander in chief in 1763 until the arrival of the civil governors late in 1764,[35] and was consequently acquainted with some of the difficulties involved, such as the administration of justice and the relations of the military commandants to the local inhabitants. But in these instances, and particularly with respect to Montreal, General Gage had been under specific instructions respecting his procedure with the civil population. In the present situation, with no formal machinery for the administration of justice and no relevant instructions, he was compelled to rely upon his own resources, especially at the outset.

In civil disputes between the inhabitants in the western settlements the customary practice was not only to permit but to encourage them to apply their old laws and customs in their adjudications, and commanders of posts were accordingly instructed.

You do right in refering all Disputes to Arbitration, and I don't know any other manner to decide them, unless they go to the King and Council, and that you will say is an Expence and Delay too great for People to think of. . . .[36] I have given my Opinion before on this head, as far as to Advise you, to meddle as little as possible with the Affairs of Justice, and to let the People settle their Disputes as well as they could; and to

---

[34] His instructions from Amherst, Sept. 22, 1760, are printed in *Docs. Rel. Const. Hist. Can.* (2d ed.), pp. 91–96.

[35] C. E. Carter, "The Beginnings of British West Florida," *Mississippi Valley Historical Review*, IV (Dec., 1917), 314–28.

[36] To Major Bruce (Detroit), Aug. 6, 1770, Gage MSS.

Avoid doing any thing, that would entail Litigious Suits upon you, on your comeing into any of the Provinces.[37]

In brief, except for occasional minor vexations which irritated the commandants, the course of civil justice flowed on without the necessity of much interference by the military power. But there were other elements of western society which tried the patience of the local commanding officers. It was not unusual for individuals of that day, as of other days, to depart for the frontier to escape debts and other difficulties at home. The general in chief undertook to facilitate the collection of debts when appeals were made to his office by creditors in the old colonies.

I enclose you a Letter from a Merchant of this Town [New York] concerning Money that is owing to him by People at the Detroit. . . . I can only desire you to do all you can to make People pay their just Debts, for the Indian country is become not only an Asylum for Fugitive Debtors, but for People guilty of all Crimes.[38]

The judicial control of traders presented a problem which was never wholly solved, though it was the subject of almost continuous discussion by General Gage and the Indian superintendents. When the western trade was opened in 1764, traders were given passes by the governors of the respective provinces, and their operation up to 1768 was confined to the different posts where it was under the scrutiny of the military commandants and the Indian commissaries. But the traders were a difficult group; they paid little attention either to the trade regulations or to the civil and criminal laws of the provinces whence they came. Gage possessed a sensitive awareness when any mishap occurred in the Indian country because of its probable repercussions on the peaceful relations with the Indians. He therefore urged the governors, unsuccessfully, to grant commissions of the peace to Indian agents and commissaries.[39] In the open country a state of virtual anarchy prevailed which was due largely to the failure of the governors to cooperate in the control of their own traders, a situation that doubt-

[37] To Lt. Col. Wilkins (Fort de Chartres), Aug. 27, 1770, *loc. cit.*
[38] To Major Bassett (Detroit), Sept. 10, 1772, *loc. cit.* See, similarly, letter to Captain Campbell, also of Detroit, March 7, 1765, *loc. cit.*
[39] To Stuart, April 30 and June 21, 1766, and to Johnson, Dec. 1, 1766 and July 28, 1772, *loc. cit.*

less contributed to the decision of the British government in 1768 to wash its hands of the Indian trade.

The practice respecting the trial of persons accused of capital crimes in the unorganized territory was predicated entirely upon orders emanating from the commanding general during the years prior to the passage of the Mutiny Act of 1765. In the earlier period instructions were issued by the commander in chief to his subordinates to try cases involving murder and espionage by courts-martial,[40] though, wherever practicable, rebels in arms were to be brought within the jurisdiction of civil courts for trial. A significant instance was the apprehension by Colonel Henry Bouquet of one Hicks, which occurred beyond the frontier line of Pennsylvania. The instructions were to try Hicks by court-martial as a spy and, if he were found guilty, to order him to be hanged.[41] But a few months later, after the record of Hicks's condemnation had been reviewed by Gage, the following comment was embodied in another letter of instructions:

I wish the Evidence against Hicks was a little more plain, there is nothing to prove him a Spy but his own Confession extorted from him by Threats of Death. I can't therefore, confirm the Sentence. Both He and his Brother have been in Arms. And you will endeavour to get what Proofs you can of this that they may be tried as Traitors to their Country. But these trials must be in the Country below by the Civil Magistrates, to whom they should be given up. The Military may hang a Spy in Time of War, but Rebels in Arms are tried by the Civil Courts.[42]

This rather fine distinction, however, was disregarded with respect to the more remote posts, when the instructions were to try civilian offenders by the sole authority of the commanding officer.

The Delinquents shou'd be tried and punished on the Spot. I had no other powers at Montreal . . . and they are sufficient, more particularly in a Country without any Civil Court of Judicature, and in a State of actual War. If it were necessary, you might by the law of arms, on a person being proved a Spy, order him for Execution, by your own authority.[43]

Pending the adoption of a more definite and regular procedure, therefore, Gage administered such criminal justice as there was by

[40] To Bouquet, Dec. 22, 1763, British Museum, Add. MSS, 21,638.
[41] To Bouquet, May 14, 1764, *loc. cit.*   [42] Oct. 15, 1764, *loc. cit.*
[43] To Gladwin, April 25, 1764, *loc. cit.*

purely military courts. Meanwhile, he was making urgent recommendations to home authorities for a general revision of the Mutiny Act with reference, among other items to be mentioned later, to the addition of a clause investing the military authorities at the posts with commissions of the peace. He submitted a draft of such changes which he inclosed in a letter to the Secretary at War, January 22, 1765.[44] The Mutiny Act of 1765, which was designed particularly for North America, contained a clause which provided that when persons other than soldiers committed crimes not punishable by courts-martial it would be lawful for any person to apprehend such offenders and bring them before the military commander, who was empowered to take testimony in writing, under oath, and to send the persons to the nearest civil court to stand trial.[45] This provision was in harmony with the ideas of Lord Shelburne and Lord Halifax, as already mentioned, but it was not viewed by General Gage as a proper solution of the problem. "I have once Represented the Necessity of having Courts of Justice in the Uninhabited Country, but all I could get was the clause in the Mutiny Act." [46]

The clause in question outlined a cumbersome procedure, and the disclosure of its successful operation in a number of cases is therefore of more than passing interest. The prosecution of Michael Dué for the murder of one Isenhart at Detroit is a clear-cut illustration of the process in question. Dué was duly arrested and brought before Captain Stevenson, the commandant, before whom depositions of witnesses were made and sworn, and General Gage was notified.[47] Upon receipt of this information, the latter instructed Stevenson to send the accused to Montreal [48] and requested acting Governor Cramahé, of the province of Quebec, to cause Captain Stevenson to be notified of the date of the trial in order that the witnesses might be sent on to testify against Dué.[49] In this connection Gage expressed his approval of the action of the commandant: "Captain Stevenson has proceeded in this Business, in the Manner directed by a Clause in the Mutiny Act. . . ." On October 2, 1771, the general wrote to Stevenson:

[44] *Gage Corr.*, II, pp. 263, 266.   [45] 5 Geo. III, c. 33, cl. 25.
[46] To Sir William Johnson, July 17, 1766, Gage MSS.
[47] Stevenson to Gage, July 1, 1771, *loc. cit.*   [48] Aug. 14, 1771, *loc. cit.*
[49] Aug. 14, 1771, *loc. cit.* Answered Sept. 5, 1771, *loc. cit.*

I find by a Letter from Chief Justice Hey,[50] that the Prisoner Dué, accused of the Murder of Isenhart, is arrived, and delivered into safe Custody at Montreal; But his Tryal could not be brought on, thro' the Want of Witnesses. In my Answer to your letter upon the Subject, I desired you to send the Witnesses, which I hope you have found means to do. But should they not be sent forward, it will be too late after this reaches you, for them to go to Montreal this fall, and you can forward them in the Spring. I need not point out to you the bad Consequences that must attend this Villain's escaping Punishment by any means whatever, and am therefore to direct you, that you send them down, tho' forceably, as early as possible in the Spring. I transmit a Letter to you from Chief Justice Hey, wherein I imagine he has pointed out to you the proper means to pursue, to convict the Prisoner, And I transmit also a List of the Witnesses required at his Tryal. I doubt not with your own Authority and that of the Chief Justice of Canada, that you will be able to effect the Business required of you.[51]

The trial, conviction, and execution of Dué occurred the following summer,[52] news of which prompted the commander in chief to express the "hope the punishment of that infamous wretch will be a terror to those Lawless vagabonds who infest the upper Country." [53]

Other aspects of the administration of the reservation will be quickly passed in review. It was the duty of the commander in chief to cause the old inhabitants either to take the oath of allegiance to Great Britain within a stipulated time of nine months or to remove from the country, an action which had been enforced elsewhere,[54] though in the case of the residents of the Illinois country the date was computed from the time of occupation.[55] There was also the problem of the collection of quitrents, fines of alienation, and the maintenance of the town's pickets, all of which had been exacted by the French government. General Gage recom-

---

[50] Sept. 15, 1771, *loc. cit.*   [51] *Loc. cit.*   [52] Cramahé to Gage, Aug. 13, 1772, *loc. cit.*
[53] To Cramahé, Sept. 8, 1772, *loc. cit.* The law was understood to apply to persons accused of offenses against Indians as well as white people. See an account of proceedings against one Ramsay for the murder of certain Indians, in Gage to Johnson, Sept. 7 and Nov. 30, 1772, and to Cramahé, March 24 and May 26, 1773, *loc. cit.* Some Indians were murdered at Fort de Chartres in 1769, and one of the murderers was sent to Fort Pitt for safekeeping until he could be sent to Philadelphia for trial. Edmonstone to Gage, Sept. 10 and 20, 1769, *loc. cit.* Gage to Hillsborough, Oct. 7, 1769, *Gage Corr.,* I, 239.
[54] For example in West Florida, where eighteen months were given. Carter, "Beginnings of Brit. West Fla.," *Miss. Valley Hist. Rev.,* IV, 328.
[55] To Captain Sterling, Dec. 30, 1765, Gage MSS.

mended to the Secretary of State that in view of the then straitened circumstances of the inhabitants of Detroit the customary rents and fines should be remitted.[56] Instead of collecting the taxes and fines of alienation, therefore, Gage instructed the commanders to insist, in lieu thereof, upon the furnishing of firewood and pickets.[57] "You will please to Acquaint the Inhabitants, that the Conditions of their Grants must be Complied with; that if they continue Obstinate, and will not, their lands will be taken from them and granted to Others that will Comply with them." [58]

Travel across the country between Louisiana and the province of Quebec was prohibited by military order; the governors were authorized to issue passes only in exceptional circumstances. Such instructions were, of course, issued as a measure of preventing a possible interference in the relations between the Indians and the British.[59] Rum sale in the West was also under the jurisdiction of the commander in chief's office, and strenuous, though in general ineffectual, efforts were made to prevent illicit commerce in that article.[60] It was only with the approval of the military power that additional Catholic priests were assigned by the Church to the French inhabitants,[61] and its approval of the designs of sending Protestant missionaries among the Indians was likewise deemed necessary.[62]

Instructions to form the inhabitants into militia companies under their own officers were carried out.[63] The appointment of justices of the peace by the local commandants, usually though not always confined to officers of the militia, was approved by the commander in chief.[64]

Another phase of supreme authority exercised by the military office was the administration of Indian affairs, which had been

[56] To Shelburne, Oct. 10, 1766, *Gage Corr.*, I, 110–11.
[57] To Turnbull, Nov. 17, 1766, and June 1, 1767, and other letters of similar import. Gage MSS. The injunction against the collection of taxes applied also to the Illinois country. See Gage to Farmer, March 14, 1766, and to Reed, Aug. 10, 1767, *loc. cit.*
[58] To Turnbull, May 2, 1767, *loc. cit.*
[59] To Carleton, May 2, 1767, and to Glazier (Michillimackinac), Sept. 3, 1768, *loc. cit.*
[60] To Stuart, May 13, 1765; to Massey (Montreal), Aug. 23, 1766; to Grant (Lancaster, Pa.), Oct. 15, 1766; and to Johnson, Jan. 14, 1768, *loc. cit.*
[61] To Sterling, Dec. 30, 1765, and to Carleton, April 4, 1768, *loc. cit.*
[62] To Williams, Sept. 20, 1765, *loc. cit.*
[63] To Wilkins, Aug. 8, 1768, and to Turnbull, June 21, 1768, *loc. cit.*
[64] To Turnbull, June 27, 1767, *loc. cit.*

designated by the Crown in 1755 to the commander in chief in America; it continued to be so directed. The immediate first step in this new policy had been taken for purely administrative purposes in connection with defensive measures. In the year mentioned above, General Braddock handed a commission, with instructions, to Major General William Johnson as superintendent of the affairs of the Six Nations and their allies. This developed into the superintendency of the northern district, and a corresponding southern department was created at about the same time. The commissions to the respective superintendents were renewed by the Crown, thus continuing the departments, with certain additions and subtractions, until the Revolution. Johnson's commission in 1761 contained a provision respecting the payment of salaries within his jurisdiction by the commander in chief, whose "commands and directions" Johnson was "punctually to observe in all matters" respecting Indian affairs.[65] It is not without significance that the areas included in the northern and southern superintendencies corresponded in general with the two military districts created in 1764, each under a brigadier general.

The superintendents believed that their functions were such as to give them a separate status; and though they were surely aware of the source of their powers they stoutly opposed the complete subordination of their departments.[66] Sir William Johnson, for example, lodged a series of complaints, but he appears to have become reconciled to the relationship by the time General Gage became his superior. John Stuart, the southern superintendent, continued to chafe under the restriction for some time, however. In 1766, eleven years after the beginning of the system, Lord Shelburne found it necessary to remind him, and the superintendents in general, of their proper position:

As to what you propose of Instructions to be given to the Government to correspond with the Superintendents, His Majesty thinks it will answer sufficiently that your regular and fixed correspondence be with the Commander in Chief of His Majesty's Forces, the System of Indian Affairs as managed by the Superintendants must ultimately be under his Direction. The different Governors can scarcely be supposed to coin-

---

[65] *Docs. Rel. Col. Hist. N.Y.*, VII, 458–59.

[66] C. E. Carter, "The Significance of the Military Office in America," *American Historical Review*, XXVIII (April, 1923), 480.

cide in opinion, nor is it possible for so many to act in Concert. You are therefore to take the Orders of the Commander in Chief on all interesting Occasions, who being settled in the Center of the Colonies will carry on the Correspondence with the Governors on all such Points . . . and as he will be very particularly instructed by Administration, you are to look upon him as a proper Medium of material Intelligence either to or from England or the Colonies.[67]

Such instructions were sufficiently explicit as to admit of no reservations and seem definitely to have settled the relationship. Conversely, the military officers in the southern district were instructed to correspond regularly with Stuart and to inform him of all transactions with the Indians, their disposition, and so on.[68]

As already suggested, the payment of salaries of Indian officials was lodged in the office of the commander in chief.[69] The same practice was followed respecting the payment of expenses connected with Indian congresses, when such assemblies had the prior approval of the home office, and of expenses incurred in drawing the Indian boundary lines unless the latter were initiated by the separate colonies.[70] Extraordinary charges incurred in the Indian service Gage was not authorized to pay; such accounts the superintendents were instructed to forward to the Treasury. He also viewed the establishment of boundary lines back of individual colonies as a provincial affair, even though participated in by the Indian superintendents, and he therefore refused to be answerable for the expenses of such transactions.[71]

A careful division was worked out between the duties and functions of the civil and military phases of Indian administration. To the superintendents and their agents went the business of nego-

[67] Dec. 11, 1766. Illinois Historical Library, *Collections,* XL, 453. Similar instructions were sent to Johnson on the same date. *Ibid.,* p. 450.

[68] Feb. 8, 1764, Gage MSS.

[69] "Sir William Johnson's Pay, with that of his assistants, Interpreters, Smiths, etc., are all put together and particular warrants made for it, and all their Receipts are tacked to the warrant or lodged in the office. I am really tired with Accts., which you will believe I have not much time to inspect; and yet it is expected, with many other Things, which it can't reasonably be thought that I have Time to do, or sufficient Knowledge to transact properly." Gage to Bouquet, July 5, 1764, B.M., Add. MSS, 21, 638.

[70] Johnson to Gage, April 8, 1768, General Gage's Letters, Harvard College Library; Gage to Johnson, April 18, 1768, Gage MSS; Helen L. Shaw, *British Administration of the Southern Indians* (Lancaster, Pa., 1929), pp. 21–22, 58, 173–74.

[71] To Blair (Virginia), July 15, 1768, and to Stuart, Oct. 11, 1768, and Sept. 30, 1772, Gage MSS.

tiations with the Indians, subject always, of course, to the final approval of the commander in chief. And during the years of imperial management of the Indian trade (1764–68), which devolved upon the army and the superintendents to administer, detailed instructions were given to the commandants at the various interior posts to refrain from interfering with the work of the trade commissaries appointed by the superintendents to treat with the Indians and to manage the trade. On the other hand, the military officers in charge were to aid and assist the commissaries in the discharge of their duties, to certify their accounts, and to afford them lodgment in the garrisons.[72] The officers in question were forbidden to carry on negotiations without fully acquainting the superintendents,[73] while the commissaries had no authority to give passes for traders to travel from post to post—that was the function of the commanders, who must give such passes over their own authority.[74] The military officers were also deputed to enforce the conditions of the passes issued to traders by the governors, in so far as enforcement was possible.[75]

Indian politics, comprising such phases as trade, alliances, incipient wars, boundaries, relations between the various tribes, alien influences among the Indians, and relations between British traders and military officials and between these and the Indians, required a large amount of patience, judgment, and imagination. It is not insignificant that General Gage was able to maintain the peace in this part of the Empire at critical moments, which was doubtless due in a measure to his willingness to depend upon the wisdom of his subordinates in both the military and Indian branches of the service, especially the latter.

He was not reluctant on occasion, however, to assume responsibility in the shaping of policies which he believed would enhance the prospect of peaceful relationship with the Indians. He refused, for example, to approve of the withdrawal of traders from the interior merely because a few of them had been killed, on the

[72] General orders, July 22, 1766; Gage to Stuart, Jan. 7, 1765, *loc. cit.*
[73] To Stuart, Dec. 31, 1764, *loc. cit.*   [74] To Turnbull, May 2, 1768, *loc. cit.*
[75] General orders, June 17, 1765, *loc. cit.* This arrangement sometimes resulted in altercations between the respective branches of the service, which are discussed in Gage to Bayard, June 29, 1767, and to Haldimand, March 20, 1767, *loc. cit.*

ground that such action would be tantamount in Indian eyes to a declaration of war.[76] He advised the encouragement of intertribal wars, notably in the case of the Creek-Choctaw war, even though he was aware that such a policy was generally opposed at home.[77] The Creek nation was particularly troublesome on the southern frontier, and it was his considered opinion that it was better for the Indians to "cut each others throats" than to cut the throats of the British.[78] Conversely, he opposed alliances between the southern and northern and between the western and southern nations.[79] In order to eliminate the influence of alien agents and traders, the diversion of the Indian trade wholly into British hands was recommended and attempted.[80] Finally, his condemnation of a provincial governor for unauthorized interference in Indian relations led to the latter's recall.[81]

It will be noted that thus far concurrent authority is nowhere to be found. Power was shared with no civil department whatever, though it was the connecting link between the civil governments and the Indian service. In this connection, a further step was taken to tie up the plans and policies of the individual colonies with the imperial control through the appointment by the Crown of the Indian superintendents to seats in the governors' councils.

An important aspect of the evolution of a unified control in America is observed in the authority exercised by the commander in chief over western expansion. The King's proclamation of 1763 not only interdicted the acquirement of land by settlement or purchase in the Indian reservation, but also prohibited the settlement of vacant Indian lands within the borders of the colonies; such lands must first be purchased in public transactions with the Indians. The enforcement of the latter provision did entail the exercise of concurrent authority; it was entrusted equally to the

[76] To Tayler, acting brigadier general, southern district, Dec. 18, 1766, B.M., Add. MSS, 21, 662.
[77] Shelburne to Gage, Dec. 11, 1766, *Gage Corr.*, II, 51.
[78] To Stuart, Aug. 30, 1766, and June 26, 1768, and to Haldimand, April 26, 1767, Gage MSS.
[79] To Hillsborough, Sept. 9, 1769, *Gage Corr.*, I, 236.
[80] To Conway, July 15, 1766, *Gage Corr.*, I, 99.
[81] To Tayler, Dec. 18, 1766, B.M., Add. MSS, 21, 662.

commander in chief and the governors.[82] In point of fact the task of controlling such expansion, in so far as it could be controlled, devolved almost exclusively upon the commander in chief, who found himself, however, legally incompetent to rout the intruders without first receiving a request from the governor or governors.[83] His hands were therefore in general effectively tied.

Space forbids the relation of the painful efforts by General Gage to secure the active coöperation of the governments of the colonies most directly concerned. He was chagrined and perturbed by the continued and stubborn refusal of the provinces in question to place a voluntary check on their expansionist forces. His success in extracting proclamations from Governors Fauquier and Penn ordering settlers to remove from the prohibited area [84] and in securing a law from the Pennsylvania assembly [85] attaching penalties to encroachments on unpurchased lands was tempered by the fact that these public acts were not implemented and therefore impotent and by the further knowledge that in most instances militiamen and justices of the peace were themselves either concerned in or sympathetic with the movement onto vacant lands. The governors were consequently powerless to give effect to their laws and proclamation. "The Disorder lyes in the Weakness of the Governments to enforce obedience to the Laws . . . every Villain finds some powerful Protector." [86] Never sanguine concerning the possibility of preventing the spread of illegal settlements, Gage's enthusiasm was chilled by the juncture of affairs which thus presented itself. Nevertheless, when he did receive authority from

[82] "His Majesty's Commander in Chief has received express orders to coöperate with the civil government, for the enforcing a due obedience to that proclamation, and His Majesty requires and expects every measure to be taken, which prudence can dictate, for the removing such settlers, preventing in future any such settlements as are contrary to the intention of the proclamation, and for apprehending such offenders whose daring crimes have so direct a tendency to involve the whole of His Majesty's provinces in America, in an Indian war." A circular letter to all the governors, Sept. 13, 1766, Connecticut Historical Society, *Collections,* XIX, 30. Instructions of the same tenor were embodied in Shelburne to Gage, Sept. 13, 1766, *Gage Corr.,* II, 45.

[83] To Shelburne, June 13, 1767, *Gage Corr.,* I, 142–43, and to Murray, March 8, 1767, Gage MSS.

[84] Fauquier's proclamation, July 13, 1766, *Pennsylvania Archives,* 1st ser., IV, 255. See Gage to Murray, Oct. 6, 1766, relative to Penn's proclamation, Gage MSS. For a fuller account of Gage's relations with Fauquier, see *infra,* pp. 235–36.

[85] Feb. 3, 1768, *Pa. Archives,* 1st ser., IV, 283–85.

[86] To Johnson, May 5, 1766, Gage MSS.

Governor Penn the military detachment at Fort Pitt succeeded in quickly extirpating the settlement at Redstone.[87] But this process had to be repeated again and again, for the settlers were incorrigible in their determination to hold their ground. Whether the application of force would have succeeded ultimately cannot be told, since the withdrawal of troops from the frontier posts in the early 1770s epitomizes a new departure in British policy.

The exercise of concurrent power was thus demonstrated in the above instance to have fallen short of success. Over against it must be offered the experience of the military authority in suppressing any attempt at new settlements in the interior, where its power was supreme. Here the old French settlements supplied an easy excuse for expansion. But the commander in chief issued direct and positive instructions to the commanders of posts not only to refrain from making individual grants of land but to forbid any person to settle on new lands under any pretense.[88] Indian lands were held by him to be free from occupation without the consent of the Indians, and such a step must await the approval of the Crown.[89] The claims of Canadians to land by virtue of Indian deeds were summarily rejected,[90] though no question was raised concerning the validity of titles already properly recorded at Quebec.

In the settled provinces, old as well as new, general headquarters in New York came into frequent and sometimes disconcerting relations with the civil powers, for an army close at hand in peacetime was a new experience in America. Be it remembered, however, that the commanding general and his forces were charged first of all with the defense of North America. Such was the avowed purpose of the continuance of the establishment, which formed one part of Grenville's threefold plan as announced in 1763. But Governor Shirley had called attention to other purposes of an army as early as 1755, and in 1762 a plan was drawn by an un-

---

[87] The whole question of protecting the frontier line against encroachments has been gone into fully by Paul O. Carr, "The Defense of the Frontier, 1760–75," an unpublished monograph (State University of Iowa). A situation similar to the one described above was taking place at the same time in the southern provinces of South Carolina and Georgia. Halifax to Amherst, Oct. 19, 1763, *Docs. Rel. Col. Hist. N.Y.*, VII, 571; Gage to Cochrane (S.C.), Aug. 10, 1764, to Governor Grant (E. Fla.), Oct. 5, 1767, and to Stuart, Sept. 30, 1772, Gage MSS.

[88] To Stephenson (Detroit), Sept. 28, 1770, and April 8, 1771, Gage MSS.

[89] To Turnbull, Jan. 26, 1767, *loc. cit.*   [90] To Turnbull, May 6, 1767, *loc. cit.*

named British official which contained the definite statement that the "constitutional dependence of the colonies upon Great Britain" should be one objective in retaining a standing army.[91] Disregarding the question of motive in the present connection, however, the presence of the forces would inevitably accumulate both liabilities and assets with respect to imperial relations. The inconvenience to the colonies resulting from the necessity of providing quarters and carriages (to say nothing of the ways in which the troops might be, and were, employed from time to time) and, as already suggested, the current issues of taxation and a closer supervision of the customs were vital accompaniments of the policy in question.

It is necessary first to examine briefly the Mutiny Act as extended to America in 1765, which embodied specially relevant provisions.[92] Although the sequential mutiny acts prior to the one mentioned had contained clauses applicable to British soldiers in the colonies, American conditions differed greatly from conditions in England. Besides, there was a general inclination to ignore the law after 1763, and General Gage was therefore impelled to urge strongly the passage of clarifying amendments to the end that the service might be more effectively carried on. "It is declared generaly," he wrote the Secretary at War, "that the Mutiny Act does not extend to America, but in Such clauses only, wherein it is particularly mentioned. . . ." He went on to assert that soldiers were induced to desert, and were then secreted and finally indented as servants. Officers had been fined for returning deserters to the service; they had been sent to jail for occupying quarters assigned to them and prosecuted for impressing carriages. "It will soon become difficult in the present Situation, to keep soldiers in the Service, or provide to quarter or March them . . . without Numberless Prosecutions, or perhaps worse Consequences." [93] At the same time Gage enclosed a draft of amendments deemed essential for the service.[94]

[91] George L. Beer, *British Colonial Policy, 1754–1765* (New York, 1907), p. 266.
[92] 5 Geo. III, c. 33.
[93] Jan. 22, 1765, *Gage Corr.*, II, 262–63. The same statement was made to the Secretary of State, Jan. 23, 1765, *ibid.*, I, 49. Justices of the peace were threatened with prosecution by Mayor Ten Eyck of Albany. Gage to Colden, Jan. 30, 1764, Emmet Collection, New York Public Library.
[94] *Gage Corr.*, II, 265–66.

The preamble of the act referred to announced the purpose of correcting the situation due to an insufficient number of barracks and public houses available in America for the quartering of soldiers, and of strengthening the provisions of previous acts as to the furnishing of carriages for the extensive marches so frequently necessary. In the text of the act it was provided that the expense of quartering troops and procuring carriages and drivers was to be defrayed by the respective colonies. Constables and other local officials were required, on notice from a commanding officer, to house the soldiers in barracks provided by the colonies, and in the event of a deficiency of barracks for that purpose, the residue of the troops were to be established in public houses and livery stables. If these places were still insufficient to take care of the men, the governor and council of the province concerned, or the justices of the peace in the default of the former, were required to see to it that uninhabited houses, barns, and so on were hired and repaired to meet the requirements of the law. It was, on the other hand, the duty of the commanding officers to give notice to the appropriate officials announcing the marching of troops and their exact number in season for the providing of quarters. In this connection, military officers were forbidden, under penalty of being cashiered, to exercise any form of intimidation on local officials, and persons aggrieved by the billeting of more than a proportionate share of soldiers were given the right to complain to the justice of the peace for relief. On due notice from a commanding officer, justices of the peace were required to issue warrants to local officers to requisition carriages and drivers, the rates therefore being stipulated in the act.

Particularly important was the clause respecting desertion. The duty was expressly laid on local officials to apprehend persons suspected of desertion and to bring the suspects before a justice of the peace. If found guilty, the accused was to be remanded to jail and his commanding officer notified. There was also a penalty for harboring deserters, as well as for an officer who broke into a house without a warrant in search of deserters. Finally, the prosecution of suits arising from the application of the law was to be in civil courts of record.

The responsibility for the execution of the law was laid mainly at the door of the civil power in each of the provinces. But actually it was divided between the executive, the assembly, local civil officials, and the courts of law. The duties of military officers under the act were largely supplementary, and in some instances their participation in its administration was so closely defined and hedged with exceptions that legal action for alleged infractions could be brought against them more easily than against civil officials. Penalties assessable against military officers were severe. On the other hand, penalty clauses attaching to civil officials who refused to comply were virtually unenforceable, since military measures to compel compliance were excluded and civil action was entirely in the hands of the law officers and the courts. Even conviction would entail so small a monetary loss as to fail to deter individuals from refusal to take steps to quarter the troops. "To Prosecute the Magistrates according to the Tenor of the Act will avail very little" was General Gage's comment in this connection.[95] The commander in chief therefore possessed no power of direct coercion in the enforcement of the law thus described, his chief role consisting, in addition to timely notification of the need for quarters, of using the influence of his office with the governors and assemblies to facilitate the enactment of the necessary appropriation laws to compensate persons on whom soldiers would be billeted.

Copies of the act in question were received by General Gage on August 1, 1765, and were immediately transmitted to all the governors in North America and to the commanding officers of various detachments.[96] Although the law had been framed without exceptions or reservations with respect to particular colonies, plainly such new provinces as Nova Scotia, Quebec, and East and West Florida would be unable to fulfill its terms because of the impossibility of raising money; troops were consequently quartered in these colonies in barracks erected and supported entirely at the expense of the Crown.[97] In the old colonies, the provinces of Massachusetts, Connecticut, New York, New Jersey, Pennsylvania, and South Carolina were principally affected. New York, New Jersey,

95 To Barrington, Feb. 21, 1766, *Gage Corr.*, II, 339.   96 Gage MSS.
97 Gage to Murray, March 2, 1766, *loc. cit.*; Robertson (Barrack Master General) to Barrington, March 28, 1766, P.R.O., War Office, I, 7.

and Pennsylvania were involved not so much by reason of the large number of troops stationed within their borders at any one time as by the fact that they were directly in the path of the movement of detachments passing to and from the northern, western, and southern parts of the dominions. The demand for quarters and carriages was therefore fairly continuous throughout the period. And so it was in connection with these colonies, and with Massachusetts from 1768, that the act derives its chief significance in the developing antagonism to one of the principal policies of the British government.

The issue may be still further narrowed by the categorical statement that so far as the province of Pennsylvania was concerned there was never, at any time, any challenge or attempted evasion of the act. There the demands of the military authorities for quarters and carriages were invariably met, the assembly answering all requests for the appropriation of funds for that purpose.[98] In New Jersey the same general situation prevailed, except for one brief occasion when the assembly disclosed a spirit of opposition.[99]

But in New York conditions were not invariably harmonious. Here, and in Massachusetts, the issue was contested from the beginning to the end. The test came early: on December 1, 1765, General Gage notified the governor to take immediate steps for the quartering of such troops as were then in the province and to see to it that a general provision was made for quarters and carriages for such forces as might in the future be located in the colony or have occasion to march through it.[100] Since action by the assembly was required to enable the magistrates to perform their duties under the law, the military had to await the deliberations of that body. Meanwhile the situation at Albany with respect to quarters for the officers was pressing for solution,[101] and the commander in chief asserted in that connection that no quarters could in any circumstances be provided except in public houses and barracks and that the governor "could not do much even in this till the Assembly should meet, and the Act be laid before them, to make proper

[98] Gage to Conway, June 24, 1766; to Shelburne, Oct. 10, 1766; and to Hillsborough, July 2, 1771, *Gage Corr.*, I, 95, 110, 302.

[99] Gage to Conway, June 24, 1766; to Richmond, Sept. 13, 1766; to Hillsborough, Dec. 16, 1769, July 2, 1771, and Jan. 8, 1772, *ibid.*, pp. 95, 108, 243, 302, 303, 315.

[100] Gage MSS.   [101] Bradstreet to Gage, Nov. 25, 1765, *loc. cit.*

provisions for putting it in Execution." [102] In this first instance the assembly evaded meeting the issue directly by declaring that the barracks in New York and Albany were King's barracks, that until they were proven inadequate no action was necessary, and that, in any case, there was time enough to provide for expenses when they were incurred. No assurance was offered that the magistrates would be reimbursed, even though the commander in chief spoke individually to members of the assembly, to whom he explained the act.[103] Gage then informed Bradstreet at Albany that the only alternatives were to make formal demands of the magistrates and to institute proceedings against them through the attorney general of the province.[104]

Succeeding assemblies, however, through the strong intercession of General Gage and the governor, did make financial provisions to defray partially the cost of quartering, though such action was taken by omitting entirely any reference to the Mutiny Act and by disregarding certain of its clauses.[105] The parliamentary act of 1767, which forbade the governor of New York to pass any legislation until full compliance with the Mutiny Act was offered by the colony,[106] was enacted after the assembly had already voted the essential supplies. It was nevertheless a further indication of the determination of the government to continue to maintain the troops at colonial expense. The total effect of the act mentioned, however, was the increase of the fear in America regarding the permanency of the military establishment.[107] A similar, or worse, situation obtained in Massachusetts where the combined efforts of the commander in chief and the governor were powerless to effect a satisfactory settlement of the issue. Downright refusal to comply with the act forced the army to rely entirely upon support by the Crown for whatever quarters were secured.[108]

Although General Gage was determined to push the execution

---

102 To Bradstreet, Dec. 2, 1765, *loc. cit.*
103 To Conway, Dec. 25, 1765, *Gage Corr.*, I, 77.   104 Dec. 24, 1765, Gage MSS.
105 *Gage Corr.*, I, 89, 95, 99, 118, 127, 150, 243, 248, 262, 302; *ibid.*, II, 406, 446-47; *Docs. Rel. Col. Hist. N.Y.*, VII, 831-32, 848, 948-49.
106 7 Geo. III, c. 59.
107 William Samuel Johnson to Pitkin, May 16, 1767, Massachusetts Historical Society, *Collections*, 5th ser., IX, 229-31.
108 *Gage Corr.*, I, 201-4, 225, 229, 232-33, 259, 262; Edward Channing, ed., *The Barrington-Bernard Correspondence* (Cambridge, 1912), pp. 186, 195, 207.

of the Mutiny Act as far as he was able, at the same time he expressed the view that it was unenforceable as it stood.

Upon the whole it appears, that unless the Act is altered, and that the Quartering of the Troops shall rest upon some more certain foundation, it will never answer the general purposes intended. . . . It depends too much upon the temper and whim of an Assembly, One may perhaps grant, the Next, not, one province consents, Another refuses, So that it can never be certain Whether the troops can obtain Quarters or not.[109]

In a private letter to the Secretary at War, Gage further averred in the same connection that "the Colonists are taking great strides towards Independency; and that it concerns Great Britain by a speedy and spirited Conduct to shew them that these provinces are British Colonies dependent on her, and that they are not independent States." [110] Acting upon his belief as to the central weakness of the law, he recommended to the Secretary of State that the act be extended to cover the quartering of soldiers on butchers, bakers, and others who profited by the troops, as was done in Scotland, "except where for the Ease and Contentment of the Inhabitants the Provinces shall make provision" for the quartering of troops in accordance with the other clauses of the act. In other words, it was suggested that troops be quartered in private houses. It was likewise proposed that governors be made directly responsible for compliance and that heavy fines be imposed on magistrates who neglected to do their duty.[111]

The result of the general's representations was the resolution of the cabinet to prepare certain alterations and amendments to the Mutiny Act. The proposals in question followed closely Gage's suggestions, with the additional resolve that the governors be authorized to appoint commissaries to billet the troops, and another that the act should not apply to those colonies in which the assemblies had already passed laws, subject to the Crown's approval, for quartering and billeting the troops.[112] The act as passed in 1769, however, did not embody clauses in harmony with all these recommendations. Only the last one mentioned above was passed, to-

---

[109] To Conway, May 6, 1766, *Gage Corr.*, I, 89–90.
[110] To Barrington, Jan. 17, 1767, *ibid.*, II, 406.   [111] April 3, 1766, *ibid.*, I, 127.
[112] Sir John Fortescue, ed., *The Correspondence of George III* (6 vols., London, 1927), II, 84.

gether with another article which opened the way for local magistrates and military officials to enter into signed agreements for billeting "in a manner most convenient to them and the country. . . ." [113] The inner history of the changes made in the bill before its introduction and in the course of its passage is significant. The colonial agents, aware of the original proposal, immediately began their intercession for a milder measure and they found an ally in Thomas Pownall, and even in Lord North, whose veto of the stronger terms of the proposed bill, particularly with respect to quartering troops in private houses, was decisive. [114] The new law was a distinct compromise, therefore, though still carrying the implication that any action by a colonial assembly regarding quartering must be in recognition of an obligation under the Mutiny Act of 1765.

No colony, however, took advantage of the clause which provided for voluntary laws such as the new act made possible. [115] And the commanding general was by no means sanguine concerning the future possibility of securing uniform acquiescence in the law. He expressed the view that there was little use in passing further legislation unless there was a determination at home to see to its enforcement.

Things are not as they were, the precipitate and hasty repeal of the Stamp Act, the support Americans received in that, and every opposition they have since made to the Authority of the Mother Country . . . amongst you, with the flat refusal of the Massachusetts Bay to obey your edicts, have near annihilated all the Authority of the British Legislature over the Colonies. [116]

The enforcement of the desertion clause of the Mutiny Act also brought the military into frequent collision with the civil power. Desertion, which was rampant in the army in America, was one of the chief difficulties with which the commander in chief had to contend. [117] It extended to every part of the dominions where troops were stationed or through which they marched. In the southwest

[113] 9 Geo. III, c. 18.
[114] William Samuel Johnson to Pitkin, March 23, 1769, Massachusetts Historical Society, *Collections*, 5th ser., IX, 326–29.
[115] To Hillsborough, July 2, 1771, *Gage Corr.*, I, 302.
[116] To Barrington, Nov. 6, 1771, *ibid.*, II, 592.
[117] To Hillsborough, Aug. 18, 1768, *ibid.*, I, 188.

men fled to Louisiana;[118] in South Carolina and Georgia they escaped to the Indian country.[119] But these were instances which, in the main, fell outside the application of the law under consideration. In New York and New England it was not unusual for deserters to receive aid and comfort from the local population—indeed, concealment of such fugitives was a common practice. But it went further than concealment: a deserter, in return for this favor, was often legally bound out as an indentured servant. It was at the instance of the commander in chief, therefore, that when the act was passed some attention was paid to the issue of desertion.[120]

Thus as a routine matter the commanding general requested that the governors give the necessary orders to the justices of the peace and other magistrates to assist the commanders of detachments in apprehending deserters.[121] Although this application of the law met with a partial success in some provinces, as for example in Connecticut and New Hampshire,[122] so many subterfuges were adopted to defeat its purpose that it was necessary to adopt other measures to effect the return of deserters, which accounts for the advice of the commander in chief to his subordinates that they publish proclamations announcing that if deserters returned to their detachments there would be no prosecution.[123] But sometimes such fugitives were apprehended independently by civil authorities, were tried for alleged burglary or other crimes, and were sentenced either to be cropped and branded or sold as servants.[124] To meet this policy of the magistrates, commanding officers were instructed to secure copies of the records of trials of soldiers in order to determine how far the government should go in supporting them.[125] On the whole, it is plain that the question of detection and return of deserters, combined with the ill-treatment of soldiers generally, had its repercussions in the increasing tension between the army and the public. This ill-feeling was further accentuated by the use

---

[118] To Shelburne, April 24, 1768, *ibid.*, p. 168.

[119] To Governor Wright, Sept. 19, 1767, Gage MSS.

[120] To Halifax, Jan. 23, 1765, *Gage Corr.*, I, 49; to Shelburne, May 27, 1767, *ibid.*, p. 140; to Colonel Mackay, July 2, 1769, Gage MSS.

[121] To the governor of Connecticut, May 14, 1767, Gage MSS.

[122] To Colonel Pomeroy (Boston), April 23, 1769, *loc. cit.*

[123] To Colonel Pomeroy, March 6, 1769, *loc. cit.*

[124] To Mackay, June 28, 1769, and to Thaddeus Burr, sheriff of Fairfield County, Conn., April 30, 1773, *loc. cit.*

[125] To Mackay, July 2, 1769, *loc. cit.*

of the soldiers in the suppression of civil disorders within the provinces.

Imperial forces had been used prior to 1764 in establishing law and order, when Lord Loudoun ordered a detachment of troops in 1756 to protect the property of Robert Livingston against squatters from the Massachusetts border.[126] An initial step along the same line of policy was taken by General Gage in 1764 when he instructed the commanding officer at Carlisle to use troops under his command to support the civil authority, and in that regard to pay due obedience to such orders as Governor Penn should judge necessary to transmit.[127]

And if matters should come to an Extremity, you will take Care that it shall appear, that any Mischief which shall happen has been thro' the Management and Orders of the *Civil Authority,* and that the Military are in no way concerned, but in obeying the *Civil Magistrates,* and in supporting them in the due Execution of the Laws.

The governor's orders alone were not sufficient: troops were not to fire without the order of a civil magistrate on the spot.[128] In 1765 the general approved the action of the commanding officer in South Carolina in acceding to the request of the governor not to send troops away from Charleston.

Till the Inhabitants in the lower part of the Country are made sensible of their Duty, the Frontiers must take their Chance, and should these Disturbances continue, the Out Posts must not be held in Competition with the assistance Lieut. Governor Bull may have occasion for to keep the lower part of the Country in due Obedience to Government.[129]

In response to requests from the governors of Maryland and New Jersey for troops to quell riots due to the attempted enforcement of the Stamp Act, a detachment of one hundred men was promised for each province,[130] and instructions were at once transmitted to the commandant at Fort Pitt to dispatch a force to Annapolis.[131] But notwithstanding the general practice already estab-

[126] *Docs. Rel. Col. Hist. N.Y.,* VII, 207.   [127] Jan. 6, 1764, *Pa. Col. Rec.,* IX, 118–19.
[128] To Captain Schlosser (Philadelphia), Feb. 6, 1764, Gage MSS.
[129] To Captain Phillips, Jan. 20, 1765, *loc. cit.*
[130] From Governor Sharpe, Sept. 6, 1765; from Governor Franklin, Sept. 14, 1765; to Franklin, Sept. 16, 1765; and to Sharpe, Sept. 16, 1765, *loc. cit.*
[131] Sept. 16, 1765, *loc. cit.*

lished, the Stamp Act disturbances in New York and Massachusetts passed by without a definite call for military assistance. In the latter province Governor Bernard did, in fact, appeal to the commander in chief for aid, but the order was countermanded before General Gage's plan for the dispatch of a force from Halifax could be accomplished.[132] In New York no formal requisition for troops was made. Lieutenant Governor Colden gave to General Gage, on one occasion, an oral hint that military aid might prove useful; to this Gage replied by letter that time was of the essence if such a requisition were in contemplation, and further declared:

It's needless for me to tell you, that the Military can do nothing by themselves; but must act wholy and solely in obedience to the Civil Power. I can do nothing but by Requisition of that Power, and when Troops are granted agreeable to such Requisition they are no longer under my command, or can the officers do anything with their Men, but what the Civil Magistrate shall command . . . when People go into open Rebellion . . . then other Measures are taken.[133]

Meanwhile, orders were issued for the marching of contingents from the forces stationed in the province of Quebec and along the western frontier to points of concentration at Albany and in Pennsylvania that they might be in a position to supply effective aid when requested.[134] In his instructions to General Burton at Montreal, Gage observed that as long as the tumults in New York remained in the mob stage he would not intercede unless requisitioned, but if "it increases to Arms it's Rebellion, . . . and particularly belongs to me to be active in suppressing it." [135] And he expressed to the Secretary of State his wish for a "legal pretence" for collecting all the troops into one body in order to "Check in some Measure the audacious Threats of taking Arms." [136]

At this juncture, but too late to be of use in the current disturbances, an order in council was sent to each of the governors and to the commander in chief that in view of the situation in Boston and elsewhere relative to the execution of the Stamp Act, the governors were to use all legal means to preserve peace, and, failing this, to

[132] Channing, ed., *Barrington-Bernard Correspondence*, pp. 229–38.
[133] Aug. 31, 1765, New York Historical Society, *Collections*, 1923, pp. 57–58.
[134] To Conway, Dec. 21, 1765, *Gage Corr.*, I, 77.
[135] Nov. 5, 1765, Gage MSS.   [136] Jan. 16, 1766, *Gage Corr.*, I, 82.

call on the commanders in chief of the army and the fleet for assistance.[137] Thus, additional authority was supplied for the use of the
military power. Pursuant to this order, therefore, Gage sent new
general orders to the commanders of all regiments, posts, and detachments in North America to honor all requisitions from governors and to pay strict obedience to their commands.[138] At the same
time he dispatched to the commanders detailed instructions as
to their conduct when such requisitions were presented.[139] The
prompt acquiescence of the commander in chief to the request of
the governor of New York for troops to quell riots in Dutchess and
Albany counties in 1766 led to effective results.[140] It is significant
that in Gage's instructions, which accompanied the governor's
requisition, the commanding officer was cautioned "not to be led
out of this Government into that of Massachusetts without having
the proper officers of the province you shall act in, with you." [141]
The action of the commanding officer in East Florida in sending a
detachment, at Governor Grant's request, to quell an insurrection
among the settlers was approved.[142] And the officer in command in
Nova Scotia was authorized to act at the behest of Governor Franklin if aid were called for to put the laws into force.[143] But the request of Governor Penn for the use of British forces to remove the
Connecticut settlers in Pennsylvania was refused on the ground
that there was involved in that instance a dispute concerning prop-

137 Oct. 23, 1765, *Acts of the Privy Council, Colonial,* IV, 733. On the following day
the governors were instructed to make proper requisition for military aid. Connecticut
Historical Society, *Collections,* XVII, 363.

138 Jan. 15, 1766, Emmet Collection, New York Public Library.

139 Based on an instruction from the War Office, Oct. 24, 1765. *Gage Corr.,* II, 47,
note 30. See letter to Bradstreet, Jan. 15, 1766, embodying the same instruction. He
added, however, that in case of open rebellion the independent initiative of the commanding officer for its suppression was sufficient. Force Transcripts, Library of Congress.

140 To Moore, June 19, 1766, Gage MSS; to Conway, June 24 and July 15, 1766, and
to Richmond, Aug. 26, 1766, *Gage Corr.,* I, 95, 99, 102–3.

141 To Captain Clarke, July 23, 1766, Gage MSS. But if the troops were fired upon
and any soldier wounded or killed, the rioters were to be pursued "without any Distinction of Government, or further aid of magistrates," Aug. 4, 1766, *loc. cit.* The
analogy between this situation and the subsequent practice under the Constitution of
the United States with regard to the use of Federal troops within the states is suggestive.

142 To Major Whitmore, Oct. 10, 1768, *loc. cit.*

143 To Lt. Col. Templar, Feb. 5, 1770, *loc. cit.*

erty, and the general believed that it would be "highly improper for the King's Troops to interfere."[144]

Affairs in Boston in 1768 focused attention in a new way on the use of British soldiers in support of public order. In response to an appeal for military aid from the newly established Board of Customs Commissioners resident in Massachusetts,[145] Gage replied according to the usual formula that he would be glad to comply, but that application must first be made through the governor as the appropriate authority, and that he had heard nothing from Governor Bernard.[146] A few days later he informed Bernard of his correspondence with the Customs Commissioners, and added that since no letter of requisition had been received from the governor he had not ordered troops into the province, as he did not "think it proper to order any of His Majesty's Forces to march for the sole purpose of quelling a Riot, unless required . . . by the civil power."[147] But he assured the governor that he would stand by for such a call. Such a requisition, however, was never made.

Entirely apart from Governor Bernard's personal desire to dodge the responsibility and thus to avoid popular fury for the presence of regular troops in his province, he was constitutionally inhibited from exercising the usual prerogative of a colonial governor with respect to calling in outside aid. In this, as in other matters, the assent of the provincial council was necessary, and that body unanimously refused to permit such a request.[148] But there was no legal impediment to quartering troops on Massachusetts, and no barrier to the issuance of instructions by the home government directly to General Gage to transfer to Boston whatever number of troops he deemed necessary in the public interest. Orders were therefore transmitted to the commander in chief for the placement of at least one regiment in Boston, to be supplemented by two additional regiments from Ireland.[149] In executing his instructions, Gage sought from Governor Bernard, through an aide-de-camp,

[144] To Penn, April 15, 1770, *loc. cit.* Gage's position in this affair was approved by the Secretary of State. *Gage Corr.,* II, 105.
[145] June 15, 1768, Gage MSS.　　　　　[146] June 21, 1768, *loc. cit.*
[147] June 24, 1768, *loc. cit.*
[148] Channing, ed., *Barrington-Bernard Corr.,* pp. 167–70.
[149] From Hillsborough, June 8 and July 30, 1768, *Gage Corr.,* II, 68–69, 72–73.

information respecting the number of soldiers desired,[150] and dispatched at the same time orders to the commanding officer at Halifax to embark the Fourteenth regiment for Boston.[151] In this regard, the positive orders of the commander in chief were in line with his previous instructions.

The officer Commanding the Troops ordered into your government, is informed, that he is sent thither to strengthen the hands of Government in the Province of Massachusett's Bay, enforce a due Obedience to the Laws, and protect and support the Civil Magistrates in the preservation of the public Peace, and to the Officers of the Revenue in the Execution of their Duty, and is directed to give every legal Assistance to the Civil Magistrates in the preservation of the public Peace, and to the Officers of the Revenue in the Execution of the Laws of Trade and Revenue. The Use that shall be made of the Troops to effect these Purposes I am to leave to the Direction, and Management of the Civil Power.[152]

Henceforth, until the forcible evacuation of 1775, the province of Massachusetts was not free of regular troops. The full story of those fateful years cannot here be retold—the story of the presence in Boston for a time of Gage himself, of the difficulties over quartering and the quarrel regarding Castle William, of the appointment of a commanding officer in Massachusetts with the rank of brigadier general, of the continuous sparring for tactical advantage between magistrates and officers—though it is relevant to emphasize that, despite the utmost caution taken by the commander in chief and his subordinates to preserve peace between soldiers and citizenry, there was an inescapable conflict between the two. The presence of the soldiers was resented and deplored and was provocative of too many incidents which reflected on both sides.

The growing ascendancy of the military power was viewed as encroaching upon the liberties of the colonies and as subtracting from the prerogatives of other branches of the government. When there should have been an active spirit of coöperation between the military and civil establishments in the royal colonies, misunderstanding too frequently barred the way to effective action. This was particularly true with respect to the question of the command of

150 To Captain Shireff, Aug. 31, 1768, Gage MSS.
151 To Colonel Dalrymple, Aug. 31, 1768, *loc. cit.*
152 To Bernard, Sept. 12, 1768, *loc. cit.*

the troops within a given province, which involved a fundamental principle—the right to give marching orders and the administration of the King's barracks in the provinces. The language of the governors' commissions did indeed appear to bring both the civil and military officials within their jurisdiction, and each naturally sought to interpret his commission to his own advantage.[153] Interminable confusion, approaching chaos in some instances, followed such an interpretation, and had it not been modified by orders from home, the authority of the commander in chief would have been completely ineffective. Early in 1765, however, the Secretary at War prepared an instruction designed to clarify the supreme military commission with special reference to the issues in dispute. The new order stipulated that in the absence of the commander in chief from any one of the provinces, and for want of specific orders from him, the governor was empowered to issue commands for the marching of detachments, and these commands must be obeyed. Such orders should be reported at once to the commander in chief, however, and when the latter was present in the province his orders only were to be obeyed. But the details of regimental duties were in no instance to be interfered with by the governor.[154]

General Gage, of course, took care that orders were conveniently lodged with his subordinates respecting all details of the command so as to afford as little excuse as possible for the assumption of any latent power by the governor. "You will receive from the Adjutant General, His Majesty's Orders respecting the Powers of the Civil Governors, to which you will pay obedience, Observing always, That My Orders to you . . . are *Specifick, Absolute,* and *Supreme,*" ran a typical letter.[155] On the other hand, he was equally careful to forbid his commanders to interfere with the civil power. On one occasion, among many, he reprimanded an officer in the province of Quebec for meddling with the civil administration. "I can't but highly disapprove of your intermeddling with Civil mat-

---

[153] The development of the controversy is described in some detail, for one colony, in Carter, "Brit. Admin. in W. Fla.," *Miss. Valley Hist. Rev.,* IV, 330–35. See also the account of the controversy between the commander in chief and the governors of New York, *infra,* pp. 217–18, 220.

[154] Ellis to Halifax, Feb. 7, 1765, *Docs. Rel. Col. Hist. N.Y.,* VII, 704; Halifax to Gage, Feb. 9, 1765, *Gage Corr.,* II, 23.

[155] To Major Farmer (Mobile), April 17, 1765, Gage MSS.

ters, or doing anything that might disturb or disgust any part of the Civil Government." [156]

Nevertheless the controversy never abated, and was even brought to the floor of Parliament, where the question was several times posed in extensive debates over the extent, and even the legality, of the military commission within the individual colonies.[157] The discussion in question served to call forth an opinion of the attorney and solicitor general, which not only supported previous interpretations of the home government respecting the relative powers of the governors and the commander in chief, but apparently also tended to exclude any power over troops by the former, the military clauses in the governors' commissions being viewed as touching only provincial forces.[158]

One method of avoiding disputes over the command was by conferring upon a ranking military officer a commission as governor. This was done in the provinces of Quebec and Nova Scotia, an action which proved to be a great relief to the commander in chief.[159] But the real test in this regard came when General Gage was commissioned as governor of Massachusetts in 1774. The background and the motives were so entirely different in the latter instance, however, that the effect on the relations of the colonies and mother country was disastrous.

With respect to other powers of the military office, we observe that it was especially deputed to aid in the enforcement of the trade laws. In an order in council of October 4, 1763, relating to the enforcement of the commercial system, the Secretary of State was directed to convey instructions to that end to the commander of the forces.[160] The latter in turn dispatched a circular letter to officers in command of posts in all the provinces ordering them

to strictly charge and require the Several Officers under your Command, to give their assistance upon all proper occasions, in preventing . . . illicit trade, and to make such a disposition of the Forces under your

---

[156] To Major Browne (Montreal), Sept. 9, 1765, *loc. cit.*

[157] *Parliamentary History,* XVI, 999; XVII, 299–300; William Samuel Johnson to Trumbull, May 21, 1770, Mass. Hist. Soc., *Collections,* 5th ser., IX, 434–44.

[158] May 16, 1770, Gage MSS. For other references see *Gage Corr.,* II, 111–12.

[159] To Barrington, Aug. 27, 1766, *ibid.,* p. 368.

[160] *Acts Privy Council, Col.,* IV, 509; Halifax to Amherst, Oct. 11, 1763, *Gage Corr.,* II, 3.

Command as will be most Serviceable in suppressing those dangerous practices, and protecting the Officers of the Revenue from the Violence of desperate and lawless Persons, who shall attempt to resist the due Execution of the Laws.[161]

Any enumeration of the powers of the commander in chief cannot exclude such items as the control of the navy on the interior lakes; [162] or the command of the colonial militia when called by the governor in support of the regular forces; [163] or the not infrequent interference with the packet service and the mail service generally; [164] or his possession of copies of the governors' instructions.[165]

There were, however, other functions of the military office which acquired significance equal to if not greater than the significance of the powers which have been catalogued in the foregoing narrative. The office in question was an important and powerful one; and it was the chief connecting link between the colonies and the home government. This was well brought out in a dispatch from Secretary of State Shelburne to General Gage in 1766, wherein it was asserted that

an extensive and Confidential knowledge of the Intentions of Government cannot be so properly entrusted to any of His Majesty's Servants in America, as to the Commander-in-Chief of His Forces, who by the Nature of His Commission and his Trust, holds by equal Ties to all the Provinces and watches over the Safety of the Whole.

Shelburne then set forth three heads of inquiry to which he desired the commander in chief to give his utmost attention and concerning which he was to transmit home from time to time all the information which he could gather, at the same time embodying his own opinions.[166] The establishment of a proper system for the management of Indians and their trade, the disposition of the troops in North America, and the reduction of expenses of royal administration in the colonies and the raising of a fund to defray these expenses were the questions which the commanding general

[161] Dec. 1, 1763, Gage MSS.   [162] *Gage Corr.,* II, 63, 85, 106.
[163] Gage to Governor Sharpe, April 4, 1764, Gage MSS.
[164] Maturin to Alexander Colden, April 15, 1765, and Gage to Colden, Sept. 26, 1768 and July 7, 1770, *loc. cit.*
[165] Halifax to Gage, May 12, 1764, *Gage Corr.,* II, 13.
[166] Dec. 11, 1766, *ibid.,* p. 48.

was charged to study. In a series of replies, Gage went meticulously into detail on each point.[167] This central agency became, therefore, an officially recognized source of information and opinion with reference to the proper policies to be formulated and enforced.

This significant recognition of the importance of the military office is maintained throughout the entire period, regardless of changes of personnel of the officers of government at home. Its central location in the old colonies, with active lines of communication radiating from New York to each colony on the seaboard, to the newly created provinces, to the remotest parts of the Indian country, to the insular colonies, and to the Spanish province of Louisiana enabled the commander in chief, in the course of his correspondence, to compile a vast mass of information on a wide variety of subjects, especially concerning the defense and integrity of the Empire. And so, pursuant to sequential instructions, General Gage transmitted a succession of opinions, based upon a multiplicity of facts in his possession, on such questions as the condition of American commerce and industry, the causes and remedies of colonial discontent, the character of provincial governments, disputes between military and civil departments, relations with France and Spain, the treatment of alien subjects, the abandonment of western posts and forts and the concentration of troops in the east, the best method of maintaining the military posts, the establishment of colonies in the unorganized area, land grants, and the rum trade.[168]

It cannot be assumed, of course, that the advice with which the commander in chief often accompanied his dispatches was always transmuted into policies to be executed. In fact it is plain enough that his recommendations, while always accorded the highest respect at home, were not fully embodied either in legislation, as in the case of the Mutiny Act, or in plans respecting such problems as the concentration of troops. That the home government leaned more heavily on his office as a reliable source of information than on that of any other agency then in America is nevertheless evident; and to that extent, apart from all other considerations, this

[167] Feb. 22, April 3, 4, 5, and 28, 1767, *ibid.*, I, 111–32, 135–37.

[168] Notable reviews and opinions regarding forts and posts, including the concentration of troops, Indian trade, and the creation of new colonies, are found in *Gage Corr.*, I, 121–24, 175–79, 274–81; II, 318–24, 349–52, 392–95, 449–50, 477–78.

office occupied more than an incidental place in the period.

Attention has already been called to the similarity, in this period, to certain earlier proposals for a commander in chief over all the colonies. Unification on some basis had always been an object of British policy, but plans for a formal union on either a voluntary or a prerogative basis had been abandoned. Conditions in North America, stemming partly from the enlargement of the Empire in 1763, nevertheless seemed to compel some form of imperial unity. The practical expedient of continuing the military establishment which prevailed during the late war was therefore adopted. Throughout the colonial empire of dissimilar elements was to be observed a cohesive force: each of the various parts touched at some point this strong arm of the British service to a greater degree than ever before.

The failure of this policy of integration may be attributed to several factors. We observe the fears of Americans, who viewed the ever-present redcoat as a symbol of tyranny. They were not mistaken when they sensed the growing power of the military branch of government, which was becoming more and more evident as revolutionary disorders increased. Cause and effect in this regard followed in rapid succession. Divided councils at home, with alternate ventures at plans of coercion and "appeasement," did not make for stable administration. The power of the commander in chief was too often immobilized by an insufficiency of funds and men and by the too frequently contradictory purposes of the government; and the power of the governors, already on the wane,[169] made little contribution to his support through active coöperation. The sands of ordinary methods of adjustment were fast running out by 1774.

[169] See pp. 214–68, *infra*.

The Royal Governors in the Middle and Southern Colonies on the Eve Of the Revolution: a Study in Imperial Personnel ⬥ LOUISE B. DUNBAR

BEFORE THE American Revolution the royal governorship in British North America was generally regarded by the home authorities as the best available link between the mother country and the colonies, as the substitution of royal appointees for governors otherwise chosen in eight of the colonies [1] and their introduction at the outset in several newly organized governments clearly indicate.[2] Excellent studies are available on the institutional aspects of the royal governors,[3] but relatively little has been done to delineate their characters and careers.[4] A comprehensive study of them would include the chief executives of Nova Scotia, Quebec, the Floridas, and Britain's island possessions, as well as those appointed to preside over the eight royal provinces which joined in supporting the Declaration of Independence. The present study deals with

[1] Virginia, New Hampshire, New York, Massachusetts, New Jersey, North Carolina, South Carolina, and Georgia.

[2] Notably, Quebec and the two Floridas.

[3] For example, Greene, *The Provincial Governor in the English Colonies of North America;* Dickerson, *American Colonial Government, 1696–1765;* L. W. Labaree, *Royal Government in America;* Pargellis, *Lord Loudoun in North America;* and Flippin, *The Royal Government in Virginia, 1624–1775.*

[4] The royal governors make numerous appearances in Osgood's seven volumes on *The American Colonies* and in other historical accounts of the colonial period. Nevins, in *The American States during and after the Revolution,* chaps. i–iii, *passim,* swiftly reviews the last years of the provincial governors. The *Dictionary of American Biography* and *Dictionary of National Biography* contain accounts of many of the governors. (For the most part, data in these reference works concerning their early lives will not be repeated in the present essay.) See Labaree's treatise on "The Early Careers of the Royal Governors" in *Essays in Colonial History Presented to Charles McLean Andrews by His Students,* and his bibliographical note on "Biographies of Governors" in *Royal Government in America,* pp. 467–68.

the governors of the six royal provinces in the middle and southern sections on the eve of the Revolution. Due to space limitations it omits the governors of quasi-royal Massachusetts and royal New Hampshire, whose roles in the opening scenes of the American Revolution have often been described.

New York, British military headquarters for North America during most of this period, is the best vantage point from which to begin a survey of the colonial scene, for the commander in chief, watching "equally over the safety of the whole," kept in touch with the governors of the various colonies to an extent unmatched by any other official on this side of the Atlantic.[5]

The royal governor of New York in 1763 was Major General Robert Monckton, best known to Commander in Chief Amherst for his military services in both Europe and America, although he had been lieutenant governor of Nova Scotia before his appointment to New York, March 20, 1761.[6] In November, 1761, Monckton set forth from New York to command the land forces attacking the French in the West Indies. Victorious in the islands, he returned to his province the following June, but left it in June, 1763,[7] "much regretted" and "universally esteemd" because his conduct had been "so upright generous and benevolent" (according to a prominent New Yorker's statement in a letter to former Governor Sir Charles Hardy).[8] Monckton subsequently received military promotion and appointments to offices in the British Isles and became a member of Parliament.[9] He continued to show some

[5] See Shelbourne to Gage, Dec. 11, 1766, C. E. Carter, ed., *Correspondence of General Thomas Gage* (2 vols., New Haven, 1931, 1933, henceforth cited as *Gage Corr.*), II, 48. For a treatment by Dr. Carter of the commander in chief's relations with the governors see *supra*, pp. 193–210. See also Carter, "The Significance of the Military Office in America, 1763," in *Amer. Hist. Rev.*, XXVIII (1923), 475–88. For New York as "the Capital Province" see Evarts B. Greene, "New York and the Old Empire," in A. C. Flick, ed., *History of the State of New York* (10 vols., New York, 1933–37), Vol. III, chap. iv.

[6] J. C. Webster, ed., *The Journal of Jeffery Amherst* (Toronto, 1931), pp. 3, 274; *D.A.B.*, XIII, 83–84; *D.N.B.*, XXXVIII, 165–67. For Amherst as commander in chief see *D.A.B.*, I, 257; *D.N.B.*, I, 357–59; J. C. Long, *Lord Jeffery Amherst, a Soldier of the King* (New York, 1933), p. 79.

[7] Webster, *op. cit.*, p. 275; Long, *op. cit.*, pp. 153, 160; *D.N.B.*, XXXVIII, 167.

[8] Dated June 11, 1763, in *Letter Book of John Watts, Merchant and Councillor*, New York Historical Society, *Collections*, LXI (New York, 1928), 146–47. Sir Charles, a high ranking naval officer, who coöperated with Amherst at Louisbourg in 1758, was governor of New York, 1755–57. See *D.N.B.*, XXIV, 352–53.

[9] *D.A.B.*, XIII, 84; *D.N.B.*, XXXVIII, 167.

interest in American affairs, judging by his correspondence with Americans.[10]

When Amherst's successor, Thomas Gage (temporarily governor, then lieutenant governor of Montreal), arrived in New York, November 16, 1763,[11] he found Lieutenant Governor Colden serving as acting governor. Cadwallader Colden was British-born, but by long residence a New Yorker. Public-spirited, politically alert, intellectually versatile, the "most learned man of colonial New York," Colden served several times as acting governor between 1760 and 1776. He was disliked by many New Yorkers because of his stubborn support of the viceregal office in local controversies concerning the tenure of judges, appeals from provincial courts, the breakup of large land grants in the Indian country, and the enforcement of the Acts of Trade during those difficult years when British efforts to increase the authority of royal governors, interrupted by the French and Indian War, were renewed through strict instructions from England. Colden, who would have put the Stamp Act into force if he had received adequate support from other branches of the government, was burned in effigy and suffered some property losses at the hands of the Stamp Act rioters.[12]

Despite Colden's unpopularity, suggested by John Watts's words to former Governor Monckton—"Somebody must come over, we shall never live in peace here again under this old Gentleman" [13]— it was not until November 15, 1765, after the Stamp Act was supposed to become operative, that Monckton's successor arrived. He was the recently knighted Sir Henry Moore. A Jamaican by birth

[10] *Letter Book of John Watts, passim.*

[11] See Webster, *op. cit.*, p. 254; *Gage Corr.*, I, 1, 20; II, 7–8; *D.A.B.*, VII, 87–88; *D.N.B.*, XX, 355–57.

[12] See *infra*, pp. 274–77; also *D.A.B.*, IV, 286–87; *D.N.B.*, XI, 260–61; A. Keys, *Cadwallader Colden: a Representative Eighteenth Century Official* (New York, 1906); *Letter Book of John Watts*, pp. 147, 219, 309, 315, 326, 334; Flick, *op. cit.*, III, 4, 38–40, 88, 121 (Colden as a medical practitioner), 124–25 (Colden as a philosopher), 134–36, 175, 186–87; Dickerson, *op. cit.*, pp. 205–6, 279–80; C. L. Becker, *The History of Political Parties in the Province of New York, 1760–1776* (Madison, 1909), p. 295. For Colden's own words see *The Colden Letter Books*, New York Historical Society, *Collections*, Vols. IX, X (New York, 1877, 1878); *The Letters and Papers of Cadwallader Colden* (9 vols., *Collections*, Vols. L–LVI, LXVII–LXVIII, 1918–23, 1937), especially Vols. VI, VII, IX. General Gage was scrupulously opposed to the use of the military forces without official request for aid from the civil authorities, and most of those entrusted with official responsibility were anxious to avoid clashes between the troops and the people.

[13] Feb. 23, 1765, *Letter Book of John Watts*, p. 334.

(his family, for two generations, had lived in the West Indies), he had served in Jamaica as assemblyman, councilor, secretary of the province, and, eventually, lieutenant governor and acting governor. He had suppressed a dangerous insurrection of Jamaican slaves, thereby winning wide acclaim. Confronted in New York with something akin to an insurrection of the King's New York subjects, he made no vigorous efforts to secure the enforcement of the Stamp Act. The consignment of stamps which arrived with him was lodged in the City Hall along with the previous supply, to reassure the people that they would not be used. Moore was acclaimed by the populace when his opposition to the enforcement of the Stamp Act became apparent, and he participated, in one case under embarrassing circumstances, in local celebrations of the Stamp Act repeal.[14]

Moore's relations with the commander in chief reached an open break in 1768, which Gage reported thus to Barrington and Amherst:

The Dispute between S^r H: Moore and myself, may indeed be termed silly. I had foreseen it comeing on for above two Years, but found means to avoid it, tho' much condemned for so doing by most People here. It was at length put so Home to me, tho' upon the most trifling occasion [because "Sir Henry Moore thought, that a proper distinction was not made between a number of Ladies engaged in a Country Dance"], I could not help answering. Which I found myself the more obliged to do, as I perceived there was a Doubt amongst some of the Officers, whether they should obey me. To clear their doubts . . . forced me to publish the Kings Orders. . . . S^r H: Moore alone would not understand them, and proceeded to his Council, and from thence to the Minister.

While seeking in his official account to make light of this friction, Gage, writing to Amherst, expressed his anxiety lest "the Ministers from not Knowing the real cause of such mighty bustle, should take it up in a serious light." Gage continued:

I must confess that it would pique me horridly, to have any alteration whatever, in my Orders and Instructions, on account of a Country Dance. It is often with some difficulty, and using management too, that I carry

<hr>

[14] *D.N.B.*, XXXVIII, pp. 354–55; *D.A.B.*, XIII, 126–27; *Gage Corr.*, II, 304; Flick, *op. cit.*, III, 195, 199–200; Labaree, *op. cit.*, p. 91.

on the King's Business, with some people, as my Commission stands: if it is lowered, I shall not be able to do it at all.

On the other hand, according to Gage, the governor had written to the Secretary of State

that he has so little Power in his hands it is necessary to keep up Appearances of Authority as much as possible, and if there was any Person superior to himself, it would take away the Respect due to the King's Governor; and alledging many Reasons, why the Commander in Chief's Commission should be lowered, and his own raised.[15]

Governor Moore, however, stood firmly by his instructions on the enforcement of the Quartering Act, and was reinforced by the act of Parliament of 1767 suspending the New York legislature from passing other laws until it satisfactorily supplied the troops in New York. The eventual compliance may, perhaps, be accredited more to a conservative reaction in New York politics than to the governor's efforts. Moore sympathized with the New Yorkers in their currency shortage and tried to secure royal approbation of a new paper-money act, despite the Parliamentary prohibition in 1764.[16] He was also interested in land operations and became a member of the Illinois Land Company.[17] He continued as governor until his death in New York, September 11, 1769, apparently fairly well liked by all parties.[18]

Francis Bernard, in 1768, desiring a transfer from the governorship of Massachusetts (unless he could be "quieted" there "with an adequate Salary"), wrote that he might "gratefully accept" the governorship of New York "if it was to become vacant and be offered" to him. Comparing New York with Massachusetts, he declared:

They are both . . . liable to be harrast by the Spirit of Jealousy of and Opposition to Government which prevails in both. . . . But . . . in N York that Spirit actuates Men of Rank and Ability, in Massachusets it works only with Men of Middling or low Rank; in the Latter the Gov[r]

---

15 Gage to Amherst, March 19, 1768, and Gage to Barrington, March 28 and Sept. 10, 1768, *Gage Corr.*, II, 456–57, 487. For the relatively weak position of governor compared with assembly in New York see Flick, *op. cit.*, II, 386–87; III, 147–48, 173–80, 136–37.

16 Flick, *op. cit.*, III, 201–4.

17 T. P. Abernethy, *Western Lands and the American Revolution* (New York, 1937), pp. 30, 34.

18 *D.A.B.*, XIII, 126; *D.N.B.*, XXXVIII, 355.

has the generality of respectable Men on his Side; in the Former they are more generally against Government. . . . It appears to me that the Administration of N York is more difficult than that of Mass^tts. . . .[19]

After Moore's death Lieutenant Governor Colden took over the executive responsibilities, only to earn a sharp rebuke from Lord Hillsborough, Secretary of State for the colonies, for assuring the New Yorkers that the duties *"without Distinction"* imposed by the Revenue Act of 1767 would probably be taken off at the ensuing session of Parliament. He was later reprimanded on other counts, though having "erred from real good intention." [20] Opposition to providing supplies for British troops in New York found expression in "an infamous libel" against the assembly and governor by a "Son of Liberty" identified as Alexander McDougall. Arrested and imprisoned, McDougall dramatized himself and his cause along lines popularized in England by John Wilkes, thus further defying Colden and British authority.[21]

As the nonimportation tactics, except against tea, were discontinued in New York, once the Townshend duties other than the tea tax were abolished by Parliament in 1770, that province was congratulated on "the salutary reconciliation effected by the people in this province" by the new royal governor, John Murray, Earl of Dunmore, who arrived in October, 1770. Well connected in England, twice elected a representative peer of Scotland, Dunmore was a man whose appointment seemed complimentary to New York. His announcement that he was not permitted to accept a salary grant from the New York assembly, since his salary was to be paid from duties collected in America, aroused no serious opposition. In December, Dunmore was ordered to Virginia.[22] His reluctance to obey is partly accounted for by his acquisition of large land holdings in New York, where he planned to settle Scot-

[19] E. Channing and A. C. Coolidge, eds., *The Barrington-Bernard Correspondence . . . 1760–1770* (Cambridge, 1912), pp. 141–42.

[20] *Documents Relative to the Colonial History of the State of New York* (15 vols., Albany, 1853–83), VIII, 201, 205, 215; *Colden Papers,* IX, 219.

[21] *Docs. Rel. Col. Hist. N.Y.,* VIII, 208. See also *infra,* p. 283.

[22] A. M. Schlesinger, *The Colonial Merchants and the American Revolution, 1763–1776* (New York, 1918), pp. 92, 223; Flick, *op. cit.,* III, 217–19; *D.A.B.,* V, 519–20; *D.N.B.,* XXXIX, 388; E. H. Roberts, *New York* (2 vols., Boston, 1892), II, 382; *Docs. Rel. Col. Hist. N.Y.,* VIII, 223, 249–50, 300; L. W. Labaree, ed., *Royal Instructions to British Colonial Governors, 1670–1776* (2 vols., New York, 1935), pp. 805, 808.

tish emigrants,[23] and his departure was regretted in New York, where he had entertained lavishly and won popularity with the favored classes.[24]

Dunmore's successor, William Tryon, having long sought to transfer to New York from his post in North Carolina (where, as lieutenant governor and governor since 1765, he had been confronted by many difficulties, including the armed uprising of the Regulators which he put down with a heavy hand),[25] was gratified by the appointment at last. Well received in New York as an experienced and able executive, Tryon expressed his "ardent desire to coöperate" with the New Yorkers for the "honor and dignity of his Majesty's Government, and . . . the real felicity" of a loyal people. The New Yorkers coöperated with him in local improvements, such as founding the New York Hospital, advancing education, upholding religion, improving the militia, and organizing Tryon County in the Mohawk country, where the governor acquired large holdings. After the governor's house in Fort George was burned, December 29, 1773, nearly costing the life of "Miss Tryon," £5,000 was voted to cover his losses.[26]

In February, 1772, Commander in Chief Gage feared that the "Contest for Pre-eminence" was to be revived, due to "some Opinion or Advice, Col° [Governor] Tryon had received from Lieut Governor Colden." Reassured by Barrington that Tryon "had not troubled Lord Hillsborough" with this, Gage dismissed it thus: "I suspected that the old Lieutenant Governor had set him upon it, the Old Gentleman th'o Eighty five Years old, does not dislike a little Controversy, which he has been engaged in for the greatest part of his life." [27]

[23] J. Sullivan, ed., *The Papers of Sir William Johnson* (9 vols., Albany, 1921–39), VIII, 192. "He [Dunmore] still I am told indulges the delusive hope of being reinstated in this his favourite Government," wrote Goldsbrow Banyar to Sir William, July 18, 1771.

[24] *D.A.B.*, V, 520. But contrast reports in Virginia of drunken pranks supposedly engaged in by Dunmore in New York. *William and Mary College Quarterly*, 1st ser., V, 156.

[25] *D.A.B.*, XIX, 25–27; *D.N.B.*, LVII, 276–77; M. D. L. Haywood, *Governor William Tryon and His Administration in the Province of North Carolina, 1765–1771* (Raleigh, 1903), p. 113. See *infra*, p. 252.

[26] Roberts, *op. cit.*, II, 382–83; *D.N.B.*, LVII, 276.

[27] *Gage Corr.*, II, 598–99, 611.

Tryon departed to England on leave in April, 1774, accompanied by many expressions of the New Yorkers' good will. He not only kept in mind problems concerning the New York–New Hampshire boundary line and Mohawk country land grants, but advocated to Lord Dartmouth, Secretary of State for the colonies, a conciliatory attitude toward the Americans.[28] In New York "the Old Gentleman," again acting governor, sought to preserve peace. When Tryon returned, Colden retired for the last time to his Long Island farm, where he lived long enough to hear of the Declaration of Independence, in which the New York patriot leaders took a somewhat reluctant part, and to see the shift of the scene of military operations from New England to his own province.[29]

Governor Tryon realized before his return from England in 1775 that war had begun. By an oft-noted coincidence the royal governor arrived at Sandy Hook the very day that George Washington passed through the city to take command of the American forces besieging the British under General Gage in Boston. Washington was greeted cautiously by the New York provincial congress; Tryon was welcomed by the city officials and numerous prominent citizens.[30] The Revolution progressed slowly in his province, and it was not until autumn that he was forced to seek refuge on a British ship in the harbor. Refusing to consider his flight as an abdication, he still attempted to participate in the government. In an address to the people of New York in March, 1776, he urged the acceptance of Lord North's conciliatory proposals, and as late as January, 1776, issued writs for a new election. Tryon not only took an active part in the war but was suspected of participation in a plot to kidnap or kill General Washington, a plot which might have been suggested by his own earlier appre-

[28] *D.A.B.,* XIX, 26; *D.N.B.,* LVII, 276; Roberts, *op. cit.,* II, 387.
[29] Flick, *op. cit.,* II, 244. By 1774 Colden was convinced that Dunmore was seeking to have him "removed from being Lt Govr of the Province," but wrote to Dartmouth of his confidence that "at this late stage of a Life, through which [he had] allways been devoted to his Majesty's Service," he would not be "dismissed without sufficient Reason." N.Y. Hist. Soc., *Collections,* LVI, 221–22. Dunmore was bringing suit against Colden "for half the Salary and Perquisites of Government . . . from the Death of Sir H. Moore, to the Day of Ld Dunmore's arrival" in New York. *Ibid.,* LVI, 220. See also *D.A.B.,* IV, 287; Roberts, *op. cit.,* II, 405.
[30] Nevins, *op. cit.,* p. 87; Roberts, *op. cit.,* II, 404–5.

hensions that royal governors might be seized by the rebels as hostages.[31]

New Jersey, unlike New York, underwent no change of royal governors during the period in question. Before 1763, General Amherst, as commander in chief, had come into contact with several New Jersey governors, the first being Francis Bernard (1757–60),[32] who enjoyed governing New Jersey because of "the Health and Beauty of the Country; the good disposition of the people," and "the free and easy Way of life" permitted him, but who, to provide for his increasing family, sought a more profitable post and welcomed a transfer to Massachusetts Bay. In thanking his patron, Barrington, for his "kind and Earnest Care" in securing this transfer, Bernard declared:

. . . Your Lordship must not be surprised if some years hence when I can better afford to perfer ease and pleasure to profit, I shall trouble your Lordship to get me sent back to Amboy: which I suppose will allways be an easier task than the present has been; as competitors for governments are, in General, more attentive to the income than the Situation.

Less than nine years later (June and October, 1768), after unforeseen difficulties in Massachusetts, Bernard asked to be removed from his New England post. He had "rather return" to his "old Government of New Jersey with a Salary of 1,500£ a Year . . . than go to a Southern or West indian Government (Barbadoes excepted) of twice or thrice the Value." He suggested that the New Jersey governor might be advanced elsewhere and the salary in New Jersey be increased for himself in a second term,[33] but to no avail.

Thomas Boone, Bernard's successor in New Jersey (1760–61), was transferred to South Carolina.[34] He was followed by Josiah Hardy, brother of New York's former governor, Sir Charles Hardy,

[31] Roberts, *op. cit.*, II, 404–5, 407–8; Flick, *op. cit.*, III, 248, 257, 262, 265, 337–38; Rupert Hughes, *George Washington, the Rebel and the Patriot, 1762–1777* (New York, 1927), pp. 392–96. For Tryon's grim tribute to the "General confederacy" and the Americans' determination "never [to] receive parliamentary Taxation," see *Docs. Rel. Col. Hist. N.Y.*, VIII, 589.

[32] *D.A.B.*, II, 221–22; *D.N.B.*, IV, 380–81.

[33] *Barrington-Bernard Correspondence*, pp. 4, 7, 9–10, 162, 181–82.

[34] *Archives of the State of New Jersey*, 1st ser., IX (Newark, 1885), 234–307 (relate to Boone's administration).

the admiral, but he was recalled to England in 1762 "as a necessary example" of a governor who had violated his instructions. As a matter of fact he had done nothing worse than to renew the commissions of three judges with good behavior tenure rather than to require these judges to serve at the pleasure of the King, subject to recall at any time. His action was in line with precedents which earlier had evoked merely reprimands from England.[35] Widespread sympathy for the disciplined governor was expressed by John Watts, prominent New York businessman, writing in December, 1762, to Josiah's seafaring brother: "You cannot think how all orders of people are chagrind at such a violent step, especially taking in the rank of the Successor, which seems to be a Burlesque on all Government, if it is not treason to say so, when such high Personages have thought fit to do it." Six months later Watts expressed to Sir Charles a belief that Josiah's political fortunes might be mending, since his actions were then viewed more dispassionately than "when the Storm first arose," for, "barring too great an easiness of Temper which seems to proceed from a Disposition to oblige, his Conduct certainly was very unexceptionable and so much to the Satisfaction of the Province, that it truely parted from him with great regret." The easygoing nature of this ill-fated governor is further suggested by Watts's confidential wish that the intentions of Hardy, who was still lingering in America in August, 1763, "were a little more animated in the Execution," and his conclusion that ". . . he should have been bred at Sea to have got a little more D— in him as Sailors say, which is become as necessary in our Voyage thro' this political Life (I cant call it natural) as Shoes to a Mans Feet or a Cockade to a Soldier." [36]

Hardy's successor, whose appointment appeared to Watts as "a Burlesque on all Government," was William Franklin,[37] son of the famous Philadelphian. Franklin's appointment came "like a Thunder Clap (without any warning)" to most people in England as

[35] *Ibid.*, 259, 262–63, 270–76, 316. For sketch of Hardy see *ibid.*, pp. 316–17n; for Hardy's administration, pp. 308–83; on recall, 346–47, 349–51, 361–62, 379–80; Dickerson, *American Colonial Government*, pp. 152–53.

[36] *Letter Book of John Watts*, pp. 103, 146, 171–72; *N.J. Archives*, 1st ser., XXIV (*Newspaper Extracts*), 238, 241.

[37] *D.A.B.*, VI, 600–601; *N.J. Archives*, 1st ser., IX, 369–71n. For Franklin's administration see *ibid.*, IX, 383–643; X (entire volume).

well as in America.[38] He may have received it as a mark of personal favor to himself from the Earl of Bute,[39] but such a distinction bestowed upon young Franklin was expected to attach the famous "Electrical Doctor" more closely to the British government. Watts's comments on young Franklin's appointment, exceeded in virulence by John Penn's enraged astonishment,[40] were perhaps not representative of public opinion. Certainly Franklin was given a cordial public reception, and he remained in office until dispossessed by the Revolutionists in 1776.[41] Perhaps his years of close contact with his astute and diplomatic father, whom he resembled in affability and ease of manner, were sufficient to disarm such hostility as existed. William Franklin had in his youth and through his father's influence secured an appointment as clerk of the Pennsylvania assembly. He gained some executive experience as postmaster at Philadelphia and general post office comptroller. His studies at the Middle Temple and his position as a barrister [42] in England doubtless gave him some prestige upon his return to America. His honorary M.A. from Oxford [43] should have gratified a province proud of its own recently established college.

Of more practical importance was Governor Franklin's participation in land deals, intercolonial in scale. Having done what he could to send New Jersey reinforcements to quell the Indian uprising of 1763,[44] he became interested in George Croghan's schemes to secure Indian lands as indemnification for the "Suffering Traders." [45] Undertaking in 1766 to engage such men as Sir William Johnson, William Franklin, Joseph Galloway, John Baynton, and the Whartons in land schemes and the organization of a colony in the Illinois country, Croghan enclosed for Johnson's approval "the

[38] *Letter Book of John Watts*, p. 102. Compare John Penn's letter to the Earl of Stirling, Sept. 3, 1762, in W. A. Duer, *The Life of William Alexander, Earl of Stirling, . . . with Selections from His Correspondence*, New Jersey Historical Society, *Collections*, II, 70.

[39] *D.A.B.*, VI, 601.	[40] See note 38.

[41] *N.J. Archives*, 1st ser., XXIV, 146–54; Carl Van Doren, *Benjamin Franklin* (New York, 1938), p. 304.

[42] *Ibid.*, pp. 164, 181, 198, 201, 212, 228–30, 246–53, 259, 263, 272, 275–78, 280–81, 283–84, 287, 291, 379–80, 398–99; *D.A.B.*, VI, 601.

[43] Van Doren, *op. cit.*, p. 300.

[44] *N.J. Archives*, 1st ser., IX, 392–93, 398–401; XXIV, 275–79, 359, 540–41.

[45] W. Franklin to B. Franklin, Dec. 17, 1765, *N.J. Archives*, 1st ser., IX, 521–24; also A. T. Volwiler, *George Croghan and the Westward Movement, 1741–1782* (Cleveland, 1926), pp. 265–67.

preposeals Drawn up by Governer franklin." Wrote Croghan, "the Sooner your honour Considers this plan and Writes to Governor franklin the Beter as one half of England is Now Land Mad and Every body there has thire Eys fixt on this Cuntry." Croghan was sure that Benjamin Franklin, in England, could "be of service in this affair," and Governor Franklin wrote hopefully of his proposals in a letter to his father, April 30, 1766.[46] When the Illinois country venture was blighted by the unfriendly attitude of Hillsborough, appointed Secretary of State for the colonies in 1768, William Franklin was ready to seek profits elsewhere, having joined the Indiana Company which took over the claims of the "Suffering Traders." He was present at the making of the Treaty of Fort Stanwix, and, with other members of the Burlington Company of which he was the active head, he secured an interest in lands on the New York frontier.[47] Early in 1771 Governor Franklin declared that he had reasons to regret his attendance at the treaty-making at Fort Stanwix. Finding his New York land venture unprofitable, he referred complainingly to "that cursed Business of the Otago Tract," which eventually involved him in heavy losses. But on at least one occasion he resentfully refused a proposal to sell his share in the Grand Ohio Company. Doubtless for a few years he looked forward to acquiring a great landed estate which he might hand down to his natural son, William Temple Franklin, in accord with Benjamin Franklin's suggestion.[48]

Plans for a new colony on the Ohio, eventually referred to as Vandalia, led to the merging of the Indiana Company in the Grand Ohio Company (1769). In December, 1772, Franklin received an informal assurance from his New Jersey friend, "Lord" Stirling, recently returned from Williamsburg, that rival land claimants in Virginia had been reconciled by promises safeguarding their interests and hence would not oppose the plan for the new colony.

[46] *The Papers of Sir William Johnson,* V, 128–29; C. W. Alvord and C. E. Carter, eds., *Illinois Historical Collections,* Vol. XI, *The New Regime, 1765–1767* (Springfield, 1916), pp. 221–22, 643; C. W. Alvord, *The Mississippi Valley in British Politics* (Cleveland, 1917), I, 356.

[47] *Ibid.,* I, 212; II, 43–44, 75; Volwiler, *op. cit.,* pp. 264, 266–78, 281–82; *Illinois Historical Collections,* XI, 468; XVI, 183–204, 540; Ruth Higgins, *Expansion in New York with Special Reference to the Eighteenth Century* (Columbus, 1931), p. 84.

[48] *N.J. Archives,* 1st ser., X, 228; Volwiler, *op. cit.,* pp. 282, 329–32; T. P. Abernethy, *Western Lands and the American Revolution* (New York, London, 1937), p. 52.

But the chief justice of New Jersey, in October, 1772, wrote to Hillsborough, though perhaps with prejudice, that the general sentiment in both New York and New Jersey was unfavorable to the proposals for a new colony [49] in the West, and that Franklin was taking an unpopular stand in championing such schemes and was foolishly espousing the cause of the dishonest treasurer of New Jersey whom the assembly was seeking to have removed, although "in other respects" the province was "in perfect tranquility." [50] Within the next two years Governor Franklin, with others of his company, was becoming disheartened, as well he might when his father, now out of favor in England, no longer could assist the enterprise and apparently lost faith in its success. After the outbreak of the Revolutionary War, William Franklin and his father, on opposite sides in political strife, continued correspondence with reference to salvaging something from their western land operations. The older Franklin, no longer a member of the company, was proxy for his son in 1776 in efforts to safeguard William's interests.[51] But the governor's future financial security was to be dependent upon grants to the loyalists from the British government.

As governor, Franklin coöperated in plans for the improvement of roads, communications, and agriculture—maintaining something of a model farm himself—and for some degree of prison reform. In conformity to his instructions, though somewhat reluctantly, he prevented the enactment of popular bills for emitting paper currency.[52] Although New Jersey was less a center of opposition to the unpopular trade and revenue measures than were her neighbors, whose large port towns had more at stake and numbered more restless artisans and laborers in their population,[53] the frequent dependence of the commander in chief upon New Jersey's conveniently located quartering facilities might have become a very serious problem, endangering public peace, without the

[49] Volwiler, *op. cit.*, pp. 270–77; Abernethy, *op. cit.*, p. 77.

[50] *N.J. Archives*, 1st ser., X, 379–81.

[51] Volwiler, *op. cit.*, pp. 286, 316; Van Doren, *op. cit.*, p. 399, chap. xvii, and pp. 542–43 (based on Abernethy, *op. cit.*, pp. 146–47).

[52] *D.A.B.*, VI, 601; L. Q. C. Elmer, *The Constitution and Government of . . . New Jersey with Biographical Sketches of the Governors . . . 1776 to 1845* (Newark, 1872), pp. 50–56; *N.J. Archives*, 1st ser., IX, 485–86; X, 48–50, 99–101, 113, 150–52.

[53] Nevins, *op. cit.*, p. 44.

good temper manifested in the frequent exchanges of notes between Gage and Franklin.[54]

Unable to secure complete legislative compliance with the British Quartering Act, Governor Franklin accepted what he could get for the King's troops. Reprimanded for such compromises by the Secretary of State for the colonies, he retorted vigorously, asserting that the New Jersey governor had none of the customary perquisites, such as "the Granting of the King's Lands," but that with a "Salary . . . much inferior to that of any other of the King's Governors" he was subject to the unusual expense of having "to meet the Assembly alternately," the province having "Two Seats of Government." Despite all proper and possible "Frugality and Oeconomy" he was unable to "save any Thing out of" his income unless he should "live in a Manner that would disgrace His Majesty's Commission," which he refused to do. Franklin had never known of benefits resulting from "that Experiment frequently tried by Governors" of dissolving their assemblies in cases of noncompliance. He charged that

the Succeeding Assembly has been either the same Men or worse; for as their Dissolution is generally on some popular Point, it only serves to increase their Popularity. . . . There are but very few of them that put any Value on their Seats, for they cost them Nothing, and their Attendance on the Business of the Publick is frequently productive of Inconvenience to their private Affairs, and seldom proves of any Advantage of them. The Governor of this Province has no other Means of influencing them but by his Prudence and Management, for he has not a Post . . . in his Gift that is worth any of their Acceptance, they being chiefly Men of independent Fortunes. . . .[55]

On June 1, 1774, Franklin wrote to Gage expressing "great Pleasure" at the return of the commander in chief from a visit to England and "very hearty Congratulations" on his "Appointment to the Government of the Massachusset's Bay." [56] Little more than a year later, after the disastrous experience of the troops whom Gage had sent out to confiscate American munitions at Concord,

[54] These are included in the Gage Papers at the William L. Clements Library, Ann Arbor, Mich., as are numerous items of correspondence between Gage and other governors.

[55] *N.J. Archives*, 1st ser., X, 64–95, especially pp. 82–94.   [56] Gage MSS.

Franklin reported to Secretary Dartmouth that, "Ever since that unfortunate Affair at Lexington, the Colonies [had] been in the utmost Commotion. The People . . . not contented to wait for the Determinations of the Continental Congress," were "continually holding County Committees and Provincial Conventions in every Colony." A convention had "been sitting at Trenton for about a Fortnight past" and was said to have resolved on providing "a Body of Militia in this Province . . . ready for immediate Service."[57]

A few days later, writing to Gage, Franklin reviewed his own efforts to persuade the New Jersey assembly to give favorable attention to conciliatory propositions from "His Majesty and the Parliament . . . on just and honourable Terms," but admitted that he did not "as yet see, among the present Leaders of the People, the least Symptom of a Disposition to promote conciliatory Measures." He noted the news of the military plans and activities of the Americans and their "general Congress" and called attention to the fact that there was no place in New Jersey "to which the Officers and Friends of Government . . . might resort in case of need for Protection." It was "publickly said, and generally believed, that in case the King's Troops should engage the American Army, or take any of the American Generals Prisoners," it was "intended immediately to seize on all the Governors and other principal Officers, and make them Hostages." While confessing that "at present we only live . . . upon Sufferance, nor is it in our Power to mend our Situation," Franklin believed that many friends of government would "shew themselves if they had a Chance of doing it with any Safety." He regretted that there were not "proper Persons appointed on each Side duely authorized to meet and form some Plan for accomodating the present unhappy Difference and preventing the like in the future," for he saw "no Difficulties in it but what might be easily surmounted if once People [could] be brought together heartily disposed for the Purpose."[58] Doubtless he believed that the royal governors could be helpful at such a peace meeting.[59]

57 Letter dated June 5, 1775, *N.J. Archives,* 1st ser., X, 603.
58 June 20, 1775, Gage MSS.
59 See B. Franklin to W. Franklin, Sept. 7, 1774, *N.J. Archives,* 1st ser., X, 495.

The governor's father, residing in London as a colonial agent, had written to him in October, 1773:

You are a thorough government man, which I do not wonder at, nor do I aim at converting you. I only wish you to act uprightly and steadily, avoiding that duplicity which, in Hutchinson, adds contempt to indignation. If you can promote the prosperity of your people, and leave them happier than you found them, whatever your political principles are, your memory will be honored.[60]

Joseph Galloway, long a political associate of Benjamin Franklin and trusted business friend of William,[61] shared the following reminiscence of 1775 with his fellow loyalist exile, Hutchinson:

. . . the Doctor's natural son, the Gov[r] of New Jersey, had told Galloway that his father had avoided any conversation with him upon the subject of the colonies; but suspecting his father's intention, the son said to him, he hoped, if he designed to set the Colonies in a flame, he would take care to run away by the light of it: that soon after, Galloway and the two Franklyns met together, and the glass having gone about freely, the Doctor, at a late hour, opened himself, and declared in favour of measures for attaining to Independence:—exclaimed against the corruption and dissipation of the Kingdom, and signified his opinion, that from the strength of Opposition, the want of union in the Ministry, the great resources in the Colonies, they would finally prevail. He urged Galloway to come into the Congress again; and from that time, united in the closest connection with Adams, broke off from Galloway. . . .[62]

Probably this was the closest Doctor Franklin ever came to seeking to convert to the American cause his son, the royal governor.

In June, 1776, the New Jersey provincial congress ordered Governor Franklin's arrest as "an enemy to the liberties of this Country." After being kept in custody for many months, chiefly in Connecticut, he was exchanged and allowed to join other refugees in New York, where he served for a time as president of the Board of Associated Loyalists, and he left his native land for England in 1782.[63]

[60] B. Franklin to W. Franklin, Oct. 6, 1773, J. Bigelow, ed., *The Complete Works of Benjamin Franklin* (10 vols., 1887–88), V, 241; Van Doren, *op. cit.*, p. 480.

[61] Galloway to W. Franklin, Sept. 6, 1767, *Illinois Historical Collections*, XVI, 8–9; Van Doren, *op. cit.*, pp. 364, 564.

[62] P. O. Hutchinson, ed., *The Diary and Letters of His Excellency Thomas Hutchinson* (Boston, 1886), II, 237–38. Compare Van Doren, *op. cit.*, pp. 527–28, 608, 718, 726.

[63] *N.J. Archives*, 1st ser., IX, 371, 720; Van Doren, *op. cit.*, pp. 549, 691; *D.A.B.*, VI, 601.

Having reviewed the royal governors with whom commanders in chief Amherst and Gage had to deal in New York and New Jersey, the provinces most closely associated with the military headquarters during most of our period, we may turn our attention to the royal provinces to the southward, beginning with Virginia, whose titular governor, in 1763, was Sir Jeffrey Amherst himself. Although a Virginia newspaper might wishfully report, in January, 1760, that "we hear that his Ex. Gen'l Amherst intends to pay a visit to his governm't (of Virg'a) this winter," Amherst did not favor the province with his presence, but regarded his governorship as a well-deserved sinecure. Several years after his return to England, Amherst evinced considerable indignation when he was ordered to go out to Virginia or relinquish his post.[64] There were precedents on his side, for the Old Dominion's governors had been habitually absentees, drawing part of the salary and receiving other financial returns while a resident lieutenant governor presided over Virginia's affairs. This practice had been criticized by Lord Halifax in 1754, upon the death of the Earl of Albemarle, absentee governor since 1737. Seeking to improve the colonial administration, Halifax called attention to "the inexpediency of any longer suffering the government of Virginia to remain a sinecure," and argued that the Virginians' complaints at being ruled by a substitute when they paid a considerable salary to a governor were the more valid because Virginia was "the only province in North America who have granted a permanent revenue to the crown for the support of government." Virginia's complaint, "so justly grounded," had "been constantly used by the other provinces as an argument in support of their . . . refusal to pass revenue laws of the same sort." Confronted as they then were by great danger from French and Indian attacks, the Virginians had "more than a common right to be well governed and by the person they pay." Halifax urged the appointment of "a man of quality, a military man, and a sensible and honest man. . . ."[65]

Robert Dinwiddie, Virginia's lieutenant governor in 1754,

[64] Long, *op. cit.*, pp. 122, 150, 197, 200–205, 207–15; *Virginia Magazine of History and Biography* (to be cited henceforth as *Virginia Historical Magazine*), XVI, 207; Webster, *op. cit.*, p. 21.

[65] Halifax to Newcastle, British Museum Additional Manuscripts, 32737, f. 505, quoted by Dickerson, *American Colonial Government*, pp. 151–52, note 338.

hoped that His Majesty might "think proper" to keep the governorship "open a few years" so that "the Salary w'd reimburse a
very great Expense" he had "been at in the Publick Service these
last two Years." [66] Actually no successor to Albemarle, resident or
otherwise, was appointed before Lord Loudoun was given the
post in 1756. Since Loudoun, in addition to his military authority,
was entrusted with some degree of supervision over the colonies
as a whole, he may have deserved the governor's title and a share
of the governor's salary in at least one colony. Encumbered with
his heavy military responsibilities during two of the most critical
years of the French and Indian War, Loudoun did not visit Virginia.[67] Amherst succeeded Loudoun as governor, and, Dinwiddie
having been "permitted to quit that Command on Account of his
Infirmities," was succeeded as lieutenant governor by Francis
Fauquier,[68] who arrived in the province in June, 1758, and served
there for the next ten years.[69]

Fauquier, an appreciative protégé of Lord Halifax, was a fellow
of the Royal Society and much interested in science and philosophy, and thus found congenial friends in a colonial capital which
was also a college town. Jefferson called Fauquier "the ablest man
who had ever filled" the office of royal governor of Virginia, and
years later paid tribute to the instructive conversations at Fauquier's table. His recollections may be contrasted with the charge
that "dice rattled, cards appeared, money in immense sums was
lost and won" when Fauquier mingled socially with the rich
planters.[70]

Fauquier was said to be one of the few governors who "never
would be prevailed upon to countenance" trade with the French

[66] *D.A.B.*, V, 316–17; R. A. Brock, ed., *The Official Records of Robert Dinwiddie, Lieutenant-Governor of Virginia, 1751–1758* (Virginia Historical Society, *Collections*, new ser., 2 vols., III–IV, Richmond, 1883–84), I, vii–xix; II, 3.

[67] See "Virginia" in Index of Pargellis, *op. cit.*; *D.N.B.*, VIII, 376.

[68] Order in Council, Jan. 27, 1758, C.O. 5/1329. *Dinwiddie Papers*, II, 580, 600. Con-trast Flippin, *op. cit.*, p. 143.

[69] *D.A.B.*, VI, 301; *D.N.B.*, XVIII, 249–50; *Virginia Historical Magazine*, XVI, 209. John Blair wrote to the Lords of Trade, June 20, 1758, of "the great satisfaction" he found in "our truly worthy Lieut[t] Governour and his Lady and Son," and hoped they would "all prove publick Blessings to this Country."

[70] *William and Mary College Quarterly*, 1st ser., VIII, 159n, 172, 177; XVI, 22; XXIV, 221; 2d ser., XVI, 566, 579n; P. L. Ford, ed., *The Writings of Thomas Jefferson* (10 vols., New York, 1892–99), I, 3, 4; G. Morgan, *The True Patrick Henry* (Philadelphia, 1907), p. 79.

West Indies—that is, trade with the enemy—during the French and Indian War.[71] He assisted as best he could in continuing Virginia's military coöperation with the British in that war, but after 1758 the chief war activities were geographically remote from Virginia and the Old Dominion took relatively little active part in them. When William Byrd, commander of the Virginia forces following Washington's resignation, sought to turn in his commission due to his "mind's being poisoned by the advice of young and hasty counsellors," Fauquier wrote him: "I have the Satisfaction to think that when more years have roll'd over your Head, and the Influence of Passions . . . give way to the Dictates of cool Reflection, you will see and acknowledge, that tho' a new acquaintance, I have acted the part of an old Friend." Fauquier joined Lieutenant Governor William Bull, of South Carolina, in attempting to secure the rescue from the Indians of the garrison of Fort Loudoun, and helped to end the Cherokee War.[72]

In 1763, Fauquier attended the southern Indian congress in Georgia, leaving President Blair in charge of the Virginia government. Soon after his return from Augusta he received a request from Amherst for five hundred Virginians "to act in Concert with his Majestys Forces on the British Establishment, to bring the northern Indians to Reason,"—a requisition repeated by Gage after succeeding Amherst as commander in chief. Reporting to Gage (January 28, 1764) the assembly's noncompliance with the requisition, Fauquier promised to do all in his power "to assist his Majesty's Forces in carrying on the Good of the common Cause" by stationing the Militia (which, by law, he could not order out of the Province) in such positions as would best cover the march of the royal troops or keep open communications "without exposing our own Settlements to fresh Insults from the Indians." If the cessation of hostilities should be accompanied by a congress with the northern Indians, Fauquier recommended that Gage "and the governors appointed to hold such Congress" should give due consideration to some persons from Virginia "legaly settled on

[71] Andrew Burnaby, *Burnaby's Travels through North America* (reprinted from 3d ed. of 1798, with notes by R. R. Wilson, New York, 1904), pp. 128–29. Compare Fauquier to Lords of Trade, C.O. 5/1330, pp. 539–41.
[72] *Virginia Historical Magazine*, VII, 444; XXXVI, 10–12; XXXVII, 302–5; enclosure in Fauquier's letter to the Lords of Trade, April 14, 1759, C.O. 5/1329.

some of the Branches of the . . . Missisipi" who had gone there with the double encouragement of a royal instruction to the Virginia governor and the approval of the Virginia assembly. Fauquier thought Gage "the most fit person to be apprized of all these Circumstances."[73]

Writing to Gage in April, Fauquier expressed surprise at "not receiving the Letter of Requisition of Troops from his Majestys Secretary of State, along with the rest of his Majestys Governors." Although "of Opinion it [had] been mislaid," he added, "But some Gentlemen of his Majestys Council differ from me, and think; that my Employment of the Militia of the Colony, having given such Satisfaction at home, as to merit his Majestys most gracious Approbation of my Endeavors to promote his Service, I was designedly pass'd over, and left to my self to protect the Country this Summer in the same manner I did the last." He believed he could "not have procured" success for this requisition, "especially as the Merchants of great Brittain [were] not yet satisfied with their Situation in relation to the Treasury Notes of this Colony; more of wch must have been emitted to pay for the Levy, money and Clothing of new raised Troops." According to Fauquier, "this Consideration was the sole Obstacle to the Assemblys complying" with Gage's request.[74]

Receiving complaints against Virginia's Colonel Stephen, Fauquier wrote to Gage in September, 1764, that he believed the complaints prejudiced and ill-grounded, but promised to "sift into the Truth of each Charge," and, should he see cause, to "remove Colonel Stephen from all Command." A few months later, when the Indian uprising was virtually ended, Fauquier expressed thanks to Gage, in behalf of Virginia, "for the happy Conclusion of a troublesome War conducted under [Gage's] orders."[75]

Although Fauquier had approved the Virginians' Twopenny Act (passed during his first year in the province) and showed sympathy with their desire for paper money,[76] he seemed unaware of the Americans' forthcoming opposition to British taxation meas-

[73] Fauquier to Board of Trade, Feb. 15, 1764, C.O. 5/1330; Fauquier to Gage, Jan. 28, 1764, and enclosure (Address of Virginia Assembly), Gage MSS.

[74] Fauquier to Gage, April 9, 1764, *loc. cit.*   [75] Sept. 1, 1764; Jan. 26, 1765, *loc. cit.*

[76] *William and Mary College Quarterly*, 1st ser., XVI, 24; XIX, 24–25; XXII, 10–11; 2d ser., XI, 22–23; *Virginia Historical Magazine*, XVIII, 215; C.O. 5/1329.

ures, remarking in a letter to Gage, January 26, 1765: "When the Taxes to be levied on this Continent for the Support of the 10,000 Men to be kept for the Defence of it, are settled and regularly paid by the people, I imagine This Colony will apply for their Share of the protection as they will pay their Share of the Expence." In that case he advocated the mouth of the Kanawha as the most proper place for a garrison in "this Colony, to the southward of Fort Pitt." Were Gage to agree in this opinion, Fauquier declared he should be obliged to him to represent it favorably to the King's ministers, "as the Opinion of the Commander in chief of his Majestys Forces in these parts . . . I am confident would have more Weight, than the opinion of any Governor of a single Colony, Who may be supposed to be partial to the people over whom he presides." [77]

Within six months Lieutenant Governor Fauquier was ruefully admitting to Gage that the "Conduct of the Inhabitants" of the Virginia frontiers in killing Indians was "outragious." He had "taken every Step in the power of the Government to bring the Offenders to Justice; by offering large Rewards for the apprehending and convicting any of them." Two of the offenders had been imprisoned but forcibly freed. "The Paxton Boys of Pennsylvania" had "sent Messages offering their Assistance . . . for they publickly say no Man shall suffer for the Murder of a Savage." Fauquier planned, if he could convict any of the slayers, "to invite some of the Cherokees to see the execution of Justice on them," and in this way prevailed upon the Indians to restrain their young men from taking revenge till they heard further from him.[78]

Fauquier dissolved the assembly because of their anti-Stamp Act resolutions, preventing the appointment of Virginia delegates to the Stamp Act Congress. He wrote,

In the course of the debates I have heard that very indecent language was used by a M[r]. Henry a young lawyer who had not been a month a

---

[77] Fauquier to Gage, Gage MSS, Jan. 26, 1765. Contrast *Journals of the House of Burgesses, 1758–1761*, p. xix.

[78] At this time he was progressing with his project of having the assembly provide for the appointment of public commissioners to enter the Indian trade. This experiment, similar to that under the South Carolina Act, was to be first tried at "the big Island on Holston River." Gage MSS, July 8, 1765.

Member of the House; who carried all the young Members with him; so that I hope I am authorised in saying there is cause at least to doubt whether this would have been the sense of the Colony if more of their Representatives had done their duty by attending to the end of the Session.

Shortly before the Stamp Act was supposed to become operative, an excited "concourse of people," which Fauquier said he would have called a "mob" if he had not known "that it was chiefly . . . composed of gentlemen of property in the Colony," assembled in Williamsburg and demanded that George Mercer, custodian of the stamps, resign before November 1. Fauquier accorded Mercer some moral support, apparently insufficient, for the resignation was forthcoming on October 31.[79]

The replacement of Dinwiddie by Fauquier was unfavorable to the Ohio Company. Fauquier seemed relatively indifferent to the land speculators, handicapped by rivalry among themselves, outside competition, uncertainties as to the interpretation of the Royal Proclamation of 1763, delays in the extinguishing of Indian claims, and "encroachments" of unauthorized settlers. Possibly Fauquier showed some slight favoritism to the Ohio Company's rival, the Loyal Company, in 1766, but he was dead before the making of the Treaty of Fort Stanwix, in which Virginia's representatives were two men outside the Ohio Company appointed by Acting Governor Blair.[80]

During the last two years of Fauquier's life, Commander in Chief Gage had numerous occasions to exhort Fauquier to put an end to the encroachments of his people on Indian lands. Gage forwarded to Fauquier a copy of some extracts of an abstract from George Croghan's journal under date of May 22, 1766, as follows:

. . . if Some Effectual Measures are not Speedily taken to remove those People Settled on *Red Stone Creek,* till a Boundary can be properly Settled as proposed, and the Governors pursue Vigorous Measures to deter the Frontier Inhabitants from Murdring Indians, which pass *to and from War* against their Natural Enemys, the Consequence may be

---

[79] *Journals of the House of Burgesses, 1761–1765,* pp. lxviii–lxx.
[80] Abernethy, *Western Lands and the American Revolution,* pp. 10–12, 60–61, 63; Dickerson, *American Colonial Government,* pp. 345–46.

dreadful, and we Involved in all the Calamity of another General War.

Gage wrote to Fauquier,

You will best know what is most proper to be done on such Occasions. I can only offer you every Assistance in my Power that you may have Occasion for, either to apprehend and secure the Murtherers, or to drive the Settlers off any Lands belonging to the Indians which they may have taken possession of in Your Province.

The next spring Gage reinforced his protests, enclosing an "Extract of a Letter . . . from Sir William Johnson concerning the People from Virginia Seating themselves at Red Stone Creek Cheat River etca on Lands belonging to the Indians, and I understand claimed as part of the Territory of Your Government." He offered "any Number of Men you shall require to drive the Settlers away. . . ." His letter, dated April 19, did not reach Fauquier till the second of August. Fauquier's reply was delayed by a "long and dangerous fitt of Illness" until September 25, when he agreed with Gage's view that "nothing but a military force" would remove the trespassers, and pessimistically added, "in this I can give you no assistance whatever, being fully convinced that the Militia which is the only force I have in my hands, would stand by these unlawful Settlers, rather than act against them." In December Gage reiterated his warnings that a rupture with the Indians was close at hand unless the offending "frontier people, chiefly . . . those of Virginia," were removed from the Indians' lands. He applied to Fauquier and the other "Governors of the Provinces immediately interested . . . to devise some effectual Measures to remove these lawless settlers," and repeated his readiness to send "a Sufficient No. of Troops" whenever Fauquier should acquaint him "that Civil Officers properly authorised" would call for them.

In January Fauquier wrote that he had convened the assembly for March 31 but he did not see "what Steps they can take to bring these notorious Offenders . . . to Justice." He thanked Gage for his kind solicitude for his health and congratulations on his recovery, but concluded, "I cannot say I am yet well and possibly am too old ever to have it in my power to say so." Within three months President Blair's letter to Gage, April 25, began with a reference to "the Death of our late Worthy Governor . . . on the 3^d Ult." [81] Blair had laid Gage's letter of December 7 before the assembly "in the most pressing Terms," but

they did not think it necessary or practicable to raise . . . Forces against those stragling Invaders of the Lands now Assigned to the Indians, but which his late Majesty had encouraged our Seating on the Branches of the Missisippi by a remission of Quit-Rents for ten Years and several Grants by patents have been duly made and Quit Rents since paid 'til the late proclamation in favour of the Indians. This Affair our late Governor had fully represented, but no Answer yet. He stopt granting any more Lands but waited Instructions about those Grants already made.[82]

Fauquier's death was much regretted in Virginia. His will, soon afterward proved at a York County court, may serve as a final commentary on his character. In addition to bequests to his family, his political patron, and his friends, he gave "one hundred and fifty Pounds sterling" to his cook, partly because of "the great Oeconomy with which she conducted the Expenses of my kitchen during my residence at Williamsburg as his Majesty's Lieutenant Governor, when it was in her power to have defrauded me of several Hundred Pounds." He hoped he had been a "Merciful Master" to his slaves, directed that they be given a chance to choose their new master, and expressed his distaste for the institution of slavery. He offered his body for post-mortem examination in case this would be helpful in determining for the benefit of others the nature of his fatal illness, and requested that he be buried "without any vain Funeral Pomp and as little expence as Decency can . . . permit, Funeral Obsequies as it has long appeared to me being contrary to the Spirit of the Religion of our Blessed Saviour." [83]

Far to the north, Francis Bernard in Boston was calculating the advantages of various governorships compared with his own uneasy situation in Massachusetts. In February, 1768, he wrote, "Virginia being a Lt Government would be no advancement." His noble patron, Barrington, on May 9 expressed a contrary opinion: "Lord

---

[81] Enclosure in Gage to Fauquier, July 2, 1766; correspondence between Gage and Fauquier, July 2, 1766; April 19, Sept. 25, and Dec. 7, 1767; Jan. 28, 1768; Blair to Gage, April 25, 1768, all in Gage MSS.

[82] Blair to Gage, April 25, 1768, *loc. cit.*

[83] *William and Mary College Quarterly*, 1st ser., VIII, 29, 172–77.

Hillsborough conceives it to be the same as a Government in point of Rank as the Governor never resides, and that in point of value it is better than what you have: In ease and comfort it is infinitely preferable." Barrington believed that there was "no Government in America which if vacant" Bernard might not have "with the greatest ease," and added: "but at present there is nothing to be disposed of but the Lieut. Government of Virginia. This I am authorised to offer you, with or without the Title of Baronet."

In August Barrington had to inform Bernard that other arrangements had been made for Virginia:

The Representations of that Colony to the King and Parliament shew such an alarming disposition there, that it was thought necessary a *Governor* and a man of great distinction should reside there. Sir Jeffrey Amherst declining to go to America in that capacity, Lord Botetourt has been appointed in his room, a man every way fit for the business he has undertaken.[84]

Horace Walpole saw Botetourt in London in August, 1768,

like Patience on a monument, smiling in grief. He is totally ruined, and quite charmed. Yet I heartily pity him. To Virginia he cannot be indifferent: he must turn their heads somehow or other. If his graces do not captivate them, he will enrage them to fury; for I take all his *douceur* to be enamelled on iron.

Junius stigmatized Botetourt as a "cringing, bowing, fawning, sword-bearing" courtier, and ridiculed the claim that a resident governor was needed. Thomas Jefferson's characterization, many years later, accords with Barrington's rather than with Walpole's or Junius's views: "Lord Bottetourt's great respectability, his character for integrity, and his general popularity, would have enabled him to embarrass the measures of the patriots exceedingly. His death was, therefore, a fortunate event for the cause of the Revolution." [85]

In May, 1769, resplendent in light red and gold, Norbonne Berkeley, Baron de Botetourt, rode forth in his state coach, to at-

[84] *Barrington-Bernard Correspondence*, pp. 142, 154, 163–64, 175.

[85] Mrs. P. Toynbee, ed., *The Letters of Horace Walpole* (16 vols., Oxford, 1903–5), VII, 210; J. Wade, ed., *Junius* (2 vols., London, 1865, 1868), I, 10; II, 201, 206–9, 212–13; Ford, ed., *The Writings of Thomas Jefferson*, X, 330n. Compare *William and Mary College Quarterly*, 1st ser., V, 165, XIX, 226; *Virginia Historical Magazine*, XV, 348.

tend the opening of a new assembly. His slow speech, broken by pauses, reminded some of the spectators of the speech of King George himself. Within a fortnight Botetourt dissolved the assembly for passing spirited resolutions against British ministerial measures. "Gentlemen," he said, "I have heard of your resolves, and I augur ill of their effect. You have made it my duty to dissolve you, and you are dissolved accordingly." But according to a contemporary Virginian, this had "not lessened him" in the esteem of the assembly, "for they suppose he was obliged to do so; he is universally esteemed here for his great assiduity in his office, condescension, good nature and true Politeness." [86] Governor Botetourt may have pleased Hillsborough by promoting a new Indian boundary for Virginia that was expected to be detrimental to Thomas Walpole and his fellow land speculators. Indications are not lacking that he coöperated in a friendly understanding between the Virginians' Loyal Company and the Walpole Company and discouraged the aspirations of the Virginians' Ohio Company.[87]

Botetourt seldom clashed with Virginia's political leaders and seems to have been popular in his province. He lived in viceregal elegance in the Governor's Palace, but could jovially unbend, as on one fine August evening when the Blairs and their guests silenced their singing when a solitary wayfarer, as Anne Blair described the episode,

stopt to listen to our enchanting Notes. . . . The invader . . . call'd out in a most rapturous Voice, Charming! Charming! proceed for God sake, or I go Home directly—no sooner were these words utter'd, than all as with one consent sprung from their Seats, and the Air eccho'd with "pray, Walk in my Lord"; No—indeed, he would not, he would set on the Step's too; so after a few ha, ha's, and being told what we all knew—that it was a delightfull Evening, at his desire we strew'd the way over with Flowers etc., etc., till a full half hour was elaps'd, when all retir'd to their respective Homes.

Governor Botetourt was a patron of William and Mary College, bestowing medals to be awarded annually for excellence in natural philosophy, mathematics, and classical learning. He met his death, in October, 1770, with philosophic composure, if we may accept

[86] *D.A.B.*, II, 468; *William and Mary College Quarterly*, 1st ser., V, 166; XIII, 87–88; XVI, 30; *Tyler's Quarterly Magazine*, III, 291.
[87] Abernethy, *op. cit.*, pp. 70–71, 77; *Tyler's Quarterly Magazine*, VII, 227–30.

the following tale. An admiring friend, Robert Carter Nicholas, Virginia's treasurer, had remarked to Botetourt that one "so sound in . . . nature . . . and so much beloved" and having "so many good things about him" should be "very unwilling to die." On his deathbed Botetourt sent for Nicholas, and told him that he wished his friend to see that he resigned "these good things . . . with as much composure" as he had enjoyed them. After a splendid funeral he was buried in a vault in the college chapel. A memorial statue of his lordship, made in London by order of the Virginia assembly, today lends a quaint touch of eighteenth-century dignity to a prominent section of the William and Mary College campus.[88] Colonel Landon Carter wrote of the late governor:

He was, anecdotes say, pitched upon to be the agent of a dirty tyranni-cal ministry, but his virtues resisted such employment, and he became the instrument of a dawning happiness, and had he lived, we should have been so; for through his active and exemplary rule order every-where revived out of that confusion that our dissipation and indolence had thrown us into.[89]

Lord Dunmore, reluctant to leave New York, did not arrive in Virginia until the fall of 1771.[90] In keeping with his ambition to acquire great landholdings in America for himself and his family, he encouraged westward expansion.[91] In 1772, disregarding in-structions from England, he assented to an act of the Virginia as-sembly creating by a division of Botetourt County the new western county of Fincastle for the regulation and protection of the in-

[88] *Ibid.*, XI, 76; *William and Mary College Quarterly,* 1st ser., III, 144; V, 165–71; XVI, 33, 178; for his generosity to "the College of Nassau Hall, at Princeton," *ibid.*, VIII, 33; XIII, 235; *Virginia Historical Magazine,* VI, 132–33; *Tyler's Quarterly Maga-zine,* I, 143; III, 106–26; IV, 65; VI, 30.

[89] *William and Mary College Quarterly,* 1st ser., XIII, 52. Compare *Virginia His-torical Magazine,* XLV, 161. On Botetourt's death elderly John Blair, twice acting Governor of Virginia, resigned as president of the council rather than act as gov-ernor again. *D.A.B.,* II, 337. His successor, William Nelson, took charge until Lord Dunmore arrived. Nelson disappointed Hillsborough by refusing to assert himself "as an opponent to Mr. Walpole and his associates," although he did advocate the claims of the Loyal Company, the old Ohio Company, and other Virginians, most of whom, it appears, had received some reassuring promises from Walpole Company spokes-men. *Virginia Historical Magazine,* XXXIII, 189; *Tyler's Quarterly Magazine,* VII, 230; Abernethy, *op. cit.,* pp. 49–50, 72; Alvord, *The Mississippi Valley in British Politics,* II, 115.

[90] *Journals of the House of Burgesses, 1770–1772,* p. xxvi.

[91] Alvord, *op. cit.,* II, 181 *et seq.*

creasing population in that region. In 1773 he visited Pittsburgh, involved in the Virginia-Pennsylvania boundary dispute. He requested for himself 100,000 acres in the West, quitrent-free. It seems that he undertook to grant patents under the land bounty provisions of the Proclamation of 1763, encouraged, perhaps, by reports that the Walpole or Vandalia Company projects, which he had disapproved before leaving New York, were declining in England. Pennsylvania's creation of a new western county to include Pittsburgh was countered in October, 1773, by an order from Dunmore and his council establishing the District of West Augusta in the disputed area.[92] Fort Pitt, evacuated in 1772 by British troops, was manned by Virginia's supporters and renamed Fort Dunmore. The frontier was on the verge of war between the Virginians and Pennsylvanians. Dunmore refused to evacuate the contested territory, being encouraged by the Croghan faction's coöperation and also, perhaps, by contacts with the land-seeking Dartmouth. In May a *modus vivendi* with Pennsylvania was established.[93]

Meanwhile, in April, 1774, "Dunmore's War" with the Indians had begun, for many Virginians were eager to settle to the westward, while numerous Indians, especially the Shawnee, were determined to reserve the region for hunting grounds. With reference to Kentucky settlement, Dunmore has been termed "the ally, and to some extent the victim, of several groups of land-hungry Virginians." It appears probable that the governor was associated with the land speculator, John Connolly, in deals concerning Kentucky. After word came of fighting in Kentucky the governor sought military aid from the house of burgesses, which authorized him to use the militia. Dunmore set forth to take the lead, probably desiring to see the Kentucky lands. Advancing by way of Pittsburgh, he delayed offensive operations, presumably hoping that the Indians would consent to a negotiated peace, and was not present at the major engagement of the war, the Battle

[92] Abernethy, *op. cit.*, 83, 87, 94; *D.A.B.*, V. 520; Alvord, *op. cit.*, II, 185, 188–89; Flippin, *op. cit.*, p. 144; *Journals of the House of Burgesses, 1770–1772*, p. xxvi.

[93] *D.A.B.*, V, 520; Dunmore to Gage, June 11, 1774, Gage MSS; Abernethy, *op. cit.*, pp. 89, 96–97, 109. See *William and Mary College Quarterly*, 1st ser., XIV, 183, for Landon Carter's terse, "Ld. Dunmore wants 1200 men to fight the Pennsylvanians. Id rather save them for Boston a great deal."

of Point Pleasant.[94] The tradition has survived that Dunmore knew that the Indians were to attack the advance expedition, and that he made no effort to reinforce the Virginians because he secretly hoped for their destruction." [95] Soon after this the Indians were ready to make peace and an informal treaty was agreed to at Camp Charlotte, where Dunmore arranged for a meeting with the Indians the following spring to agree to definitive peace terms.[96] But the spring of 1775 found Dunmore enmeshed in difficulties with enemies—or potential enemies—in Williamsburg, capital of a province on the verge of revolution.

Dunmore had sought an exchange of governments with Tryon before leaving New York, since he had expected that "residence in that country [Virginia] where there is little or no society," without his family, assuming they could not live there because of the climate, would be "so tiresome" that he could not be certain that he "should be able to stay there any time." But during his first year in Virginia and part of his second, he manifested a desire to maintain friendly relations with the house of burgesses.[97] In requesting a land grant, he declared such a gift "will be a means of my ingratiating myself very much with the people of this colony, as it will show by my desire of acquiring an interest in this particular country that my attachment to New York did not proceed from any dislike to this." [98] His liking for his New York situation and desire to remain there were known in Virginia before his arrival in Williamsburg, and probably put him at a disadvantage with the Virginians at the outset of his new administration.[99]

In March, 1773, Dunmore dissolved the assembly as punishment for their proposal for organizing intercolonial committees of corre-

[94] Alvord, *op. cit.*, II, 187, 189–92; *William and Mary College Quarterly*, 1st ser., XXII, 232; 2d ser., V, 159–65; X, 52–54; XI, 304–6; R. G. Thwaites and L. P. Kellogg, eds., *Documentary History of Dunmore's War* (Madison, 1905), pp. xi–xv, xvii, xix–xxiii; Abernethy, *op. cit.*, pp. 99, 107, 111–12.

[95] *Virginia Historical Magazine*, IX, 402–7; *William and Mary College Quarterly*, 1st ser., XXII, 232; *ibid.*, 2d ser., IX, 171; and information from Dr. Lucretia Ilsley, based on recent conversations with residents of West Virginia. Contrast Alvord, *op. cit.*, II, 192–94; *William and Mary College Quarterly*, 1st ser., XXVII, 231–32; L. P. Kellogg on Dunmore, *D.A.B.*, V, 520; *Documentary History of Dunmore's War*, pp. xxiv–xxv.

[96] Alvord, *op. cit.*, II, 192; *Documentary History of Dunmore's War*, pp. xxi–xxiii.
[97] *D.A.B.*, V, 520.   [98] Flippin, *op. cit.*, pp. 143–44.
[99] *William and Mary College Quarterly*, 1st ser., V, 156, 168.

spondence to facilitate expression of grievances against the mother country. In May, 1774, he administered a similar reproof after the assembly had set aside June 1, when the Boston Port Bill was to become operative, "as a day of fasting, humiliation and prayer." [100] Meanwhile Lady Charlotte Dunmore had arrived, with her children, "Lord Fincastle, the Honorable Alexander and John Murray, and the Ladies Catherine, Augusta, and Susan." The birth in the province of another daughter of the Dunmores seems to have called forth local congratulations and rejoicing which somehow gave rise to that daughter's belief, in later years, that in being christened "Virginia" she was made the "God Daughter" of the province, and that the assembly had undertaken to provide for her a sum of £100,000 upon her coming of age. No official record was found to justify her claims.[101]

Dunmore's attitude toward revolutionary trends appears in his correspondence with Commander in Chief Gage. In a cordial and confident letter, June 11, 1774, he congratulated Gage on his appointment as governor of Massachusetts, predicting a "change of conduct in the Bostonians" which would soon demonstrate how "judicious" His Majesty's choice had been. He continued:

. . . as you justly observe my good friends the Virginians have shown themselves a little to High spirited by a late resolution but I realy hope, and beleive, they were taken by surprise and I realy think that most of them repent sincerely for what they did; as the Indians are most certainly broke out and murdered a good number of our People on the Banks of the Ohio, all our thoughts must now be turned that way. . . .

He wrote with satisfaction of the rebuilding of Fort Pitt and its renaming in honor of himself and had no doubt but that he and the militia would "soon be able to give a pretty good account" of the Indians despite the formidable numbers of the latter.

The changes which followed, in Massachusetts and Virginia, as every schoolboy knows, were not of a nature to make pleasant news to royal governors. Some references to them in the Dunmore-Gage correspondence follow. Wrote Dunmore (May 1, 1775): "We have just now received from Boston the inclosed Hand Bill [presenting in exciting terms an account of the fighting at Lexington],

[100] *Ibid.*, 1st ser., XIV, 214; XIX, 236–37, 239.
[101] *Ibid.*, 1st ser., XXIV, 85–101; 2d ser., IX, 166.

not one word of which I suppose is true." A few days later (May 9) the commander in chief was transmitting to Lord Dunmore "a faithfull Narrative" of "the unfortunate Affair that happened in this Province, on the 19th last Month," after "finding that the most injurious and exaggerated Accounts" of it had "been spread universally." On May 15 Gage expressed his concern at hearing there had been "such Insurrections" in Virginia and authorized Dunmore to order some specified military assistance from St. Augustine and the island of Providence, but confessed: "I am sorry the Hostile State of this Province will not allow me to give your Lordship such Assistance as I could wish. . . ."

Meanwhile (May 1) Dunmore had dispatched to Gage an account of the active resentment of the Virginians at his having removed the powder from the Williamsburg magazine to a man-of-war for safekeeping and requested help:

Two or three Hundred Men or even one Hundred would probably prevent my being driven out of the Government, and enable me to maintain an entrenched Post on the bank of one of the Rivers under the Protection of the Guns of a Man of War, till I receive orders from Home, and by displaying the Kings Standard perhaps our Numbers might be increased . . . but without some appearance of force to protect the first who venture to me, I despair of receiving any assistance from the Country.

From headquarters on "The Fowey in York river the 17th of June 1775," Dunmore reported to Gage a lull in hostile activities after an armed party had extorted £330 sterling from the receiver general in retaliation for the removal of the powder. He had urged decorous consideration of "the Plan of Reconciliation held out . . . by Parliament." The assembly had rejected all overtures in the "most unequivocal terms of Independence" and contrived to "find reasons for being continually in a posture of war." No wonder Dunmore, "entirely deprived of all authority and defenceless in Williamsburg," had decided to retire to a man-of-war! There he suggested to Admiral Graves "that it might be Serviceable to employ Small vessels . . . along the Coast, for keeping up a communication between the different Governors and Servants of the Crown in America for the general utility . . . of the Service. . . ." To this proposal Gage (July 26) replied: "Your Lordships Observation . . . would . . . be of great use, but the Admiral Complains he has not Ships enough to guard the Coast as he could wish." Gage was "sorry to hear" that Dunmore's province was "in such Confusion," but added:

but not one seems in a better situation than Another, and Government can never recover itself, but by using determined Measures, I have no hopes at present of any Accommodation, the Congress Appear to have too much power, and too little Inclination, . . . and it Appeared very plainly, that taxation, was not the point, but a total Independency.

Under the heading "The William in Elizabeth River by Norfolk 22. August 1775," Dunmore acknowledged dispatches from Gage "by Captain Cooper who arrived here on the 11th . . . in Company with the other Officers of the 14th." He was sorry to inform Gage that the Virginians continued "in their Rebellious practices," had "voted in their Convention ten thousand Troops," and were "to emit paper Money for the payment of them." Dunmore believed that if he had "an authority to raise one or more Regiments" he would "not only have an opportunity of encouraging" the many persons "Sincerely well affected" but also would have "the farther Advantage of enfeebling the operations of His Majesties Enemies by . . . preventing them from joining which otherwise by Arguments interest and want of employment they may be induced to do." He would, of course, need outside aid for financing such operations, and he requested Gage to send him such arms and ammunition as he could spare. He was about to dispatch a vessel for "the remainder of the 14th. Regiment now at Augustine," and hoped that Gage could spare him "the few recruits that belong to that Regiment now at Boston." [102]

Lord Dunmore introduced to Gage, by letter, "Mr John Connolly" who had served ably as major in the expedition against the Ohio Indians in 1774, and who, under orders from the Virginia governor, had recently "held a Treaty with a part of the Six Nations Shawanese and Delaware Indians" at Fort Dunmore "in such a manner as to leave them perfectly desirous to espouse the Interest of his Majesty, as their Common Father." But the general assembly also had been making advances to the Indians, which Dunmore feared might "prove but too successful" unless he should be "soon

[102] Gage MSS.

empowered to counteract their measures." [103] In his reply Gage regretted his own inability to assist Dunmore "with Men, Money, Arms, or Ammunition," none of which he could spare, but did not doubt but that the "Government" would "gladly defray" Dunmore's expense in "raising Provincial Troops," should such troops be forthcoming. Even the "Remainder of the 14th Regiment at S[t] Augustine" would not be available for Dunmore's use unless they could be relieved by three companies long since ordered from Pensacola, of whose arrival he had received no word. Gage further explained the situation thus:

I would willingly send your Lordship a Transport, but at present . . . they are gon various ways in search of Subsistence for the Garrison . . . ; I have had Applications from other Provinces Similar to your Lordships, but never have been able to Comply with them; as you have lately sent a Vessel home, and I suppose Represented your Situation I hope you will soon from thence have the Assistance you want, and which I am very sorry is not in my Power to give you, for I am not supplied in the manner your Lordship may imagine.

He was "glad to see" by an address Lord Dunmore had enclosed that there were "yet some Loyal People in Virginia, tho' beyond the Mountains." A hint of Gage's approval of Dunmore's proposal to secure Indians as allies appears in the following:

M[r] Connolly has mentioned to me a plan of certain Operations he has settled with your Lordship, the particulars of which I cannot be any Judge of at this distance, but will give your Lordship every aid in my power towards putting them in Execution, in Order to which I Inclose Your Lordship Letters to the Officers Commanding at the Detroit and at Illinois, and likewise to the Indian Agent M[c] Kee, which you will please make such use of as you may think proper, I have likewise wrote to General Carleton, and to M[r] Guy Johnson Superintendent of Indian Affairs to do their Utmost to facilitate your Plan.

I send your Lordship some proposals made to me by Major Connolly respecting these matters, with my Answer thereto, by which your Lordship will see, how far it is in my Power to aid and assist you.[104]

But Gage himself soon left America, recalled by a government ill-pleased with his management of affairs in Massachusetts, where, since 1774, he had served as royal governor, relieving Hutchinson,

---

[103] *Loc. cit.* (not dated; endorsed as received Sept. 6, answered Sept. 10). Contrast the impression given in *Documentary History of Dunmore's War*, p. xxiii.
[104] Sept. 10. 1775, Gage MSS.

who had taken charge of the government following Bernard's withdrawal in 1769. Dunmore remained in America long enough to become anathema to the patriots because of his avowed intention of rallying Negroes as well as Indians to the royal standard, and because of his connection with the burning of Norfolk.[105] Years later, after the United States had become an independent nation, Dunmore for nearly a decade held the post of governor of the Bahamas. But his greatest chance for fame and fortune had been ruined by the American Revolution.

In North Carolina, three governors in succession represented the King during the 1760s and 1770s. The second, William Tryon, we have already met as last pre-Revolutionary governor of New York; his predecessor in North Carolina was Arthur Dobbs; his successor Josiah Martin. Dobbs's activities before his coming to America belie the charge that his abilities "hardly attained the rank of mediocrity." High sheriff of Antrim, member of the Irish Parliament, and engineer in chief and surveyor general of Ireland, he thought and wrote on problems of trade, agriculture, land tenures, and government, with special reference to his native island. He became a conspicuous advocate of the search for a northwest passage to the Pacific, thereby defying the Hudson's Bay Company, whose policies he condemned as obstructionist. Although the expeditions which he sponsored had terminated without success before 1750, his interest continued. As late as July, 1763, in expressing rejoicing at the recent "Glorious Acquisition" from the French, he declared: "I have nothing to wish for but the opening the Trade to Hudsons Bay and discovery of the passage to the Western American Ocean, which I have labour'd to obtain these thirty Years, and then I should die in peace." For many years he was interested in the improvement of trade relations between the British Isles and America, and, having made large land purchases in North Carolina, he was personally concerned with the welfare of that province and sharply critical of Governor Johnston, whose successor he became by virtue of a royal commission issued early in 1753.

Although cordially received in his province upon his arrival late in 1754, he became unpopular on both sides of the Atlantic. Per-

---

[105] *William and Mary College Quarterly,* 1st ser., XV, 18–19; 2d ser., IX, 173; XIII, 218–24; XX, 176, 178, 180, 184–85; XXII, 258.

haps he was too old (well past sixty) [106] to be transplanted to a new world; perhaps he was too stubborn and arbitrary. Despite his advice to Lord Loudoun that the North Carolinian assemblies must be "led and not drove," [107] he quarreled with the representative body over the location of the seat of government, the tenure of judges, the appointment and pay of a public printer, the choice of a colonial agent, and the representation of new counties.[108] Ardently patriotic and strongly anti-Catholic, he could write, at a depressing period of the French and Indian War: "I have still a great Confidence in Providence, that God will not give up his protestant Church and the Cause of Liberty; he may correct and chastise the Colonies for their Neglect of his Service, but all will end well against Popish Superstition and French Tyranny." [109] He scolded the provincials for not making greater sacrifices to promote the war against the "insatiable perfidious Enemy," France, and her Catholic ally, Spain.[110] In turn he was reproached by the North Carolinians for not having secured what they considered an adequate parliamentary reimbursement for their war services.[111]

Dobbs's efforts to strengthen the Established Church in a province where its voluntary supporters were relatively few incurred much enmity among dissenters, without securing unanimous approbation within the fold. While one S.P.G. missionary, after Dobbs died, described him as "Our worthy Governor Mr Dobbs . . . a great Patron of Religion," [112] another, James Moir, who had incurred "the Displeasure of the Venerable Society for being so free with Governour Dobbs his Character," declared himself not

---

[106] *D.A.B.*, V, 336–37; *D.N.B.*, XV, 130–32; H. Williamson, *The History of North Carolina* (2 vols., Philadelphia, 1812), II, 85; Dobbs to Egremont, July 17, 1763, C.O. 5/310; C. L. Raper, *North Carolina: a Study in English Colonial Government* (New York, 1904), pp. 51, 53–59; C.O. 5/324, pp. 189–90, 340.

[107] See Dobbs to Loudoun, Oct. 22, 1756, LO 2064, Loudoun Papers, Henry E. Huntington Library, San Marino, California. The Loudoun items are cited with the permission of the Huntington Library.

[108] Raper, *op. cit.*, p. 91; Williamson, *op. cit.*, II, 96–104; J. H. Wheeler, *Historical Sketches of North Carolina* (2 vols. in one, Philadelphia, 1851), I, 47; Dickerson, *op. cit.*, p. 255.

[109] Dobbs to Loudoun, Sept. 7, 1756, LO 1722, Loudoun Papers; Dobbs to William Pitt, Oct. 31, 1759, in W. L. Saunders, ed., *The Colonial Records of North Carolina* (10 vols., Raleigh, 1886–90), VI, 64–65; V, 220–21.

[110] For example, see C.O. 5/310, pp. 47–48.   [111] Williamson, *op. cit.*, II, 104–5.

[112] Daniel Earl to Dr. Burton, April 13, 1765, Library of Congress Transcripts of British Manuscripts, Society for the Propagation of the Gospel in Foreign Parts, London, Letters Received, Series B, Vol. V, No. 109.

"the only one in the Province that has a most contemptible Opinion both of his Morals and Politicks," and added, "as far as I can hear the News of his Death were received with the greatest Joy throughout the Province." [113] Perhaps the marriage of the aged governor to a young girl in her teens is a clue to part of this criticism, while the ambitions of Dobbs's office-seeking kinsmen may account for part of the criticism of the governor's "Politicks." [114]

Dobbs, himself a "Corresponding Member" of the S.P.G., scathingly criticized some of the clergy, including his critic, James Moir,[115] and urged the appointment of "two Bishops at least for this Continent, or Clergymen with Episcopal powers . . . with a Power of Suspension and Degradation of the Clergy for Immoralities or Heresies, or for neglect of their Cures," and "a Power of inflicting mild Censures and Discipline upon the Laity . . . where dissolute and profligate." He also urged the establishment of parish schools "to educate Youth in Christian principles." [116]

To criticism from political opponents Dobbs responded fretfully, so that "the dignified officer was sunk into a peevish disputant." Complaints against him were forwarded to England through the assembly's London agent, but did not result in his recall. Instead he received permission at his own request to return home for his health's sake.[117] William Tryon, a British military officer with friends at court, was appointed lieutenant governor; he arrived in the autumn of 1764 to relieve Dobbs, but the old governor lingered in North Carolina until removed by death in March, 1765.[118] Tryon's report to Lord Halifax, April 2, read as follows:

Last Thursday Governor Dobbs, retired from the Strife and Cares of this World. Two days before his Death he was busily employed in packing up his Books, for his Passage to England. His Physician had no other means to prevent his fatiguing himself, than by telling him he

---

[113] Letter dated April 10, 1765, *loc. cit.,* No. 165.

[114] *D.A.B.,* V, 337; *D.N.B.,* XV, 132; Wheeler, *op. cit.,* I, 46.

[115] Dobbs to S.P.G. Secretary, March 29, 1764, *loc. cit.,* p. 284.

[116] Dobbs to S.P.G. Secretary, March 30, 1762, *loc. cit.,* pp. 280–81.

[117] *D.A.B.,* V, 337; M. Del. Haywood, *Governor William Tryon,* p. 113; Williamson, *op. cit.,* II, 115.

[118] *D.A.B.,* XIX, 25-27; Haywood, *op. cit.* (based on a conviction "that history has dealt too harshly with the memory of Governor Tryon"), Preface and pp. 13–15; Raper, *op. cit.,* pp. 60–61.

had better prepare himself for a much longer Voyage. I have got into my possession the Seal of the Province and many Public Papers, the Orders and Instructions from your Lordship shall be obeyed with all possible Dispatch. As My Patron my Lord, I hope you will allow me to call on your Lordships Goodness, to forward His Majesties Most Gracious promise to appoint me governor to this Province.[119]

Tryon's administration as lieutenant governor and governor [120] began in times that would have been auspicious had Dobbs's expectations regarding them, shortly before his death, been fulfilled.[121] But before the end of 1765 new problems had arisen and popular opposition to the Stamp Act had been made manifest in North Carolina. Governor Tryon adopted conciliatory tactics. Ill though he was with a prolonged attack of "Seasoning" fever, he entertained at his home near Brunswick "near Fifty" merchants and gentlemen of the Cape Fear region in order to communicate his sentiments to them. Declaring that he had come to North Carolina "with no other view than to serve it," he frankly avoided discussing the right or wrong of parliamentary taxation of the colonies, but spoke persuasively of the expediency of obeying the Stamp Act and offered to pay personally the stamp duties required for official papers for the issue of which he was entitled to receive fees. His offer was refused, as his guests were reluctant to permit the operation of any part of an act which was "a direct Opening and Inlet for Slavery," but the refusal was accompanied by a grateful expression of confidence in his sincerity and a belief that his influence and fortune would support any efforts he might make in England in behalf of North Carolina.[122]

Tryon wrote to Lord Conway (December 26, 1765) explaining his belief that "the Operation of the Stamp Duty in All its parts" was "Impracticable" and telling why he had made "Proposals for the Ease, and conveniency of the People" and why he had endeavoured "to reconcile them to this Act of Parliament." [123] His attempt to conciliate a militia muster by a friendly bribe of beer

---

119 "Inclosure in N° 6. F.," C.O. 5/310; *N.C. Col. Rec.,* VI, 1321.

120 His appointment as governor was proclaimed in December, 1765. Haywood, *op. cit.,* p. 17; Raper, *op. cit.,* p. 60.

121 Dobbs to Gage, March 11, 1765, Gage MSS.

122 Haywood, *op. cit.,* pp. 17, 32–36; Tryon to Conway, Dec. 26, 1765, and enclosure, C.O. 5/310, *N.C. Col. Rec.,* VII, 127–31.

123 C.O. 5/310.

and barbecued ox was thwarted by the militiamen, and he, in turn, contemptuously rejected a military guard offered by a local committee. His shrewd management in preventing a meeting of the assembly during the Stamp Act agitation did not aid his popularity. But news of the repeal of the Stamp Act was soon followed by a reconciliation between the governor and the assembly, whose good will was manifested by appropriations for an imposing government house or "Governor's Palace" at Newbern. This mansion came to be viewed with pride by some and condemned by others as laying an unwarrantable tax burden on the impoverished province.[124]

The palace furnished a congenial setting not only for the governor but for his lady, who asserted herself upon the scene more insistently than did most wives of British officials in America. Perhaps the dower of thirty thousand pounds she is said to have brought to Captain Tryon at their marriage in 1757 emboldened her to claim a vested interest in the Tryon political fortunes, which she tried to advance by her feminine charms. Some admired her as "a very sensible Woman, and indeed what you call a Learned one"; others, no doubt, would have agreed with the vivacious Anne Blair, who tried to avoid "this fine accomplish'd Lady" when she and Governor Tryon were guests in Williamsburg because "we heard she took no notice of the Ladies." Wrote Anne: "They say she rules the Roost, it is a pity, I like her Husband vastly"; and added, "they have a little Girl with them that is equealy to be pitied. . . ."[125]

Tryon was "not a bigot." He won the gratitude of the Presbyterians by his support of the Church Act of 1766 extending to their ministers the right (previously the Anglican clergy's monopoly) to perform marriage services; he gave financial aid to the Lutherans; he pleased the Moravians by a friendly visit to Wachovia; he praised the preaching of George Whitefield. Tryon became an active member of the S.P.G., and was lauded by one of its missionaries as "by his

124 Wheeler, *op. cit.*, I, 40–42, 45–46, 53–54, 62–66, 68; W. S. Robertson, ed., *The Diary of Francisco de Miranda* (New York, 1928), pp. 5–6 and illustration facing p. 6; Haywood, *op. cit.*, pp. 66–67.

125 *Ibid.*, p. 12; *D.A.B.*, XIX, 25 (for the probability that she helped to secure the lieutenant governorship for her husband); *Virginia Historical Magazine*, X, 180; *William and Mary College Quarterly*, 1st ser., XVI, 175–76. For a description of a more pleasing impression made by Mrs. Tryon, see J. H. Clewell, *History of Wachovia* (New York, 1902), pp. 99–101.

inclination as well as by his office . . . the Patron and nursing father of the Church." He encouraged education and recommended the establishment of a school in the back country settlements.[126]

Tryon won favor locally by attending, though with too costly a retinue, a conference for running the Cherokee boundary line, and by his opposition to Lord Charles Greville Montagu's plan for adjusting the line between the Carolinas, as well as by his disposition to avoid clashes with the assembly.[127] Historians disagree about his claim to fame or blame for his treatment of the Regulators, climaxed by his suppression of them at the Battle of the Alamance. It is difficult to judge the sincerity of his promise in the earlier stages of the conflict to protect the back country settlers from extortion if they would present their grievances in decent form and pay their taxes; [128] certainly he was harsh in resorting to armed force against them. As the campaign was drawing to a close, Tryon received word of his appointment to the governorship of New York, a post much desired by him and, no doubt, by his lady.[129]

Though praised and defended by some North Carolinians,[130] Tryon was followed to his new province by the caustic and sustained invective of "Atticus" (Judge Maurice Moore), who dubbed him a "dull, yet willing instrument, in the hands of the British ministry," with "ministerial approbation . . . the first wish of [his] heart." Though conceding that Tryon's "private virtues" might have enabled him to live "serviceable" to his country and "reputable" to himself, "Atticus," in closing, declared to Tryon: ". . . when, with every disqualifying circumstance, you took upon

---

[126] Williamson, *op. cit.*, II, 118; Haywood, *op. cit.*, pp. 18–28; Clewell, *op. cit.*, pp. 98–102; N.C. Col. Rec., VII, 520; IX, 5. Compare S.P.G., B5, No. 166, p. 261. Letters from Governor Tryon to the secretary of the S.P.G. are printed in the *Colonial Records*.

[127] Haywood, *op. cit.*, pp. 56–57, 59; Wheeler, *op. cit.*, I, 54; Williamson, *op. cit.*, II, 162–63.

[128] Contrast Haywood, *op. cit.*, chaps. vi–vii, pp. 140–48, *passim;* Wheeler, *op. cit.*, I, pp. 55–60. See J. S. Bassett, "The Regulators of North Carolina," in Amer. Hist. Assn., *Annual Report . . . for . . . 1894* (Washington, 1895), pp. 141–212; Haywood, *op. cit.*, pp. 92–93, 98; Raper, *op. cit.*, p. 63.

[129] See Haywood, *op. cit.*, pp. 193–94. For Tryon's refusal to exchange governments with Dunmore, who wished to remain in New York, see *Docs. Rel. Col. Hist. N.Y.,* VIII, 278.

[130] For criticisms of Tryon in the *Massachusetts Spy* and the spirited retorts of his indignant admirers, see Haywood, *op. cit.*, pp. 151–53; for expressions of regret at his departure, see N.C. Col. Rec., IX, 5, 9.

you the government of a province, though you gratified your ambition, you made a sacrifice of yourself." According to "Atticus," Tryon was "too much of the soldier, and too little of the philosopher" to "bear to be told" of his faults "with temper," so these criticisms would "be more serviceable to the province of New York, than useful or entertaining to its governor." [131] Gage had kept in touch with Tryon during the North Carolina disturbance and had readily responded to the latter's call for military supplies. Rejoicing in the suppression of the Regulators, Gage wrote to Barrington (August 6, 1771) as follows:

Colonel Tryon has since taken the Reins of this Province, and it is astonishing that very few of the Bodies who have Addressed him, mention his Success in Carolina, it is not I am convinced that most of them do not Sincerely rejoice in it, but they are carefull not to take any Step that might put their popularity, in Danger. Some of the Boston Papers abuse him openly in the Language of Billingsgate. Your Lordship sees the Seeds of Anarchy and Licentiousness, are thick Sown through the Colonies, I hope they will not ripen in our Days.[132]

Since George Mercer of Virginia, commissioned lieutenant governor of North Carolina in 1768, was not in the latter province at the time of Tryon's departure for New York, the president of the council, James Hasell, served as governor pro tempore until the new chief executive, Josiah Martin, like Tryon, an army officer, arrived from England by way of New York where, delayed by illness, he had an interview with Tryon.[133]

Martin visited the Regulators' country in the summer of 1772, and his indignation toward the insurgents was "converted to pity." Thus he coöperated with the more lenient element in the province, urged the home government to pardon all the offenders not already granted mercy, and indirectly contributed to the rallying of nearly all the Regulators to the loyalist side when the province rebelled

---

[131] Reprinted in Haywood, *op. cit.*, pp. 155–64; see also Raper, *op. cit.*, pp. 64–65.

[132] *Gage Corr.*, I, 298–99; II, 134, 583, 586–87. Goldsbrow Banyar wrote of Tryon (July 18, 1771), "His Fame was loudly proclaimed by all our Advices from North Carolina and if a Judgment can be formed from the little observation as yet in my Power to have made, Experience will confirm the good opinion we have received of him from Persons of Distinction in the Government he so lately left. He is sensible affable and of a most engaging Address. . . ." *Sir William Johnson Papers*, VIII, 192.

[133] Haywood, *op. cit.*, pp. 60, 190–91; *D.A.B.*, XII, 343; Raper, *op. cit.*, pp. 65–66; *N.C. Col. Rec.*, IX, 16–17.

against the King. Martin has been accused of being jealous toward his predecessor, and well might he have been, for the assembly, passing over his head, forwarded a petition to the King through "his Excellency William Tryon, Esquire," described by them as "the present Governor of New York who happily for this Country for many years presided over it," and requested that Tryon "would accept of this important Trust as testimony of the great affection this Colony bears him, and the entire confidence they repose in him." Martin rose above the intended insult, comforted by the thought that these "evil dispositions" toward himself had drawn upon his friend, Governor Tryon, "a compliment and mark of confidence, to which his services in this country so greatly entitle him." [134]

Martin stubbornly resisted the colonists' demands for a law embodying the right of foreign attachment and opposed the assembly's plan for the appointment and tenure of judges. A deadlock developed during which the courts were closed for many months. He also clashed with the assembly over the power of removing the master of the public school in Newbern, undertaking to defend the recent incumbent, a protégé of the S.P.G. With the development of revolutionary tendencies, Martin was baffled by the ingenious methods by which the representative assembly resolved itself upon occasion into a provincial convention in defiance of his orders. Eventually he took a defensive stand at the governor's palace, but his cannon were dragged away by the provincials and he sought refuge at Fort Johnston and later on a British war vessel in Cape Fear River, from which he issued his last proclamation, August 8, 1775. Disheartened by the loyalists' defeat at Moore's Creek Bridge, he departed from North Carolina with the British fleet en route to attack Charleston in the spring of 1776.[135]

William Henry Lyttelton, governor of South Carolina, 1756–60, accepted promotion to the governorship of Jamaica, leaving a native son of the province, William Bull, lieutenant governor (1759–75),

---

[134] *Ibid.*, pp. 330, 787, 800; Haywood, *op. cit.*, pp. 191–92; Williamson, *op. cit.*, II, 163.

[135] Raper, *op. cit.*, pp. 66–67, 69; Williamson, *op. cit.*, II, 167–69; Nevins, *op. cit.*, pp. 17–18, 77–78; *Memoir of the Life of Josiah Quincy, Junior, of Massachusetts Bay . . . by His Son, Josiah Quincy* (Boston, 1875), p. 93.

to terminate with British military aid a dangerous Indian war. This service Bull, who had already been active in public life for more than thirty years, ably performed, and in many other ways he served his province well during the five periods totaling nearly nine years in which he was acting governor. Though loyal, popular, and rich, he was passed over in appointments to the governorship.[136] His official superiors were (1) Thomas Pownall (ordered to South Carolina when superseded by Bernard in Massachusetts in 1760), who resigned without visiting his new post; (2) Thomas Boone (1761–64); (3) Lord Charles Greville Montagu (1766–73), during whose northern trip (May to October, 1768) and visit to England (1769–71) Bull administered the government; and (4) Lord William Campbell (1775–76).[137]

Boone, related to the Boone family early established in the Carolinas, was a property holder in the southern province and was residing there when appointed to the New Jersey governorship in 1759. On his return to Charleston as governor of South Carolina, December 22, 1761, he was cordially welcomed by townspeople, militia, assembly members, councilors, and officials. His knowledge of local conditions, his reputed popularity in his New Jersey post, and his "well-known" ability and uprightness were good auspices for a successful administration.[138] Unfortunately he soon forced a quarrel over the operation of the election laws, thereby running afoul of Christopher Gadsden, and interfered in the confidential correspondence between the provincial agent and the Commons house of assembly. The Commons refused to have anything to do with him during the greater part of the two years before he finally took advantage of a leave of absence to go to England. On his departure he administered a final shock to the province by taking with him "a lady . . . not his wife." The Board of Trade to some extent sided with the province by reporting that Boone had "been

---

136 *D.A.B.*, III, 252–53: XI, 538–39: E. McCrady, *The History of South Carolina under the Royal Government, 1719–1776* (New York, 1899), pp. 345, 708–9, 800. Bull had found time, in his youth, to study medicine in Leyden and he became the first native-born American to receive a medical degree.

137 *D.A.B.*, III, 464–65: XV, 161–63: McCrady, *op. cit.*, pp. 345, 800.

138 McCrady, *op. cit.*, pp. 353–55, 800. See Charleston item in *New York Mercury*, March 3, 1760 (quoted in *N.J. Archives*, 1st ser., XX, 412), for mention of Boone's "very large estate" in South Carolina.

actuated by a degree of passion and resentment inconsistent with good policy and unsuitable to the dignity of his situation." [139]

Young Montagu and his lady arrived at Charleston after the animosities of the Stamp Act controversy had been "washed down" with Acting Governor Bull's wine at an "elegant entertainment" and was greeted with elaborate demonstrations of loyalty.[140] His popularity survived long enough to assure his election to the presidency of the Charleston Library Society for 1768–69, but he was not reëlected the following year. It appears that in his visit to the northern colonies he conferred with Governor Bernard of Massachusetts, who encouraged him to prevent the South Carolinians from reinforcing the Massachusetts and Virginia protests against unpopular parliamentary enactments. His attitude toward the back country settlers was shortsighted and unsympathetic. Before departing for England on leave in 1769, he was vexed by his inability to persuade the assembly to comply with General Gage's requests for the quartering of British troops in Charleston. He returned to Charleston in 1771 in bad health and, it has been charged, in bad temper,[141] although Acting Governor Habersham of Georgia found Lord and Lady Montagu "very agreeable and easy Guests" during their five days in Savannah in March of that year.[142] Becoming involved in disputes with the Commons House, especially over its claim to control provincial finances, he called the assembly to Beaufort, an unsuitable location some seventy-five miles from Charleston; then, chagrined at the full attendance, prorogued them back to Charleston. Georgia's acting governor was disturbed by these actions of Montagu,

. . . because if he has not Orders [from England], for this Porceedure, which I do not suppose, I must think it a wrong Measure, and will lay the Foundations of perhaps a serious Breach between him and the People. . . . I think Lord Charles an easy, polite and Agreeable Gentleman, and from the little personal Acquaintance, I have with him, I I am induced to wish his Conduct may be proper and wise. . . .

[139] Smith, *South Carolina as a Royal Province*, pp. 340–46; McCrady, *op. cit.*, pp. 355–63, 365, 371.

[140] *Ibid.*, pp. 587–88. For Bull's second term as acting governor see Smith, *op. cit.*, pp. 349–57; for Montagu's administration, *ibid.*, pp. 357–66, 379–85.

[141] McCrady, *op. cit.*, pp. 592–94, 607–8, 617–19, 694.

[142] Habersham to Governor Wright, March 28, 1772, Georgia Historical Society, *Collections*, VI (Savannah, 1904), 171.

The South Carolina Commons censured Montagu and recommended that their London agent seek his recall. In 1773, in response to a summons from England, his Lordship departed, to the accompaniment of numerous polite attentions, but followed by few regrets.[143]

Lieutenant Governor Bull for a fifth time shouldered the burdens of government. Probably no other royal executive was as nearly successful in warding off open rebellion against British rule and in retaining the good will of his people. But his unwillingness to use stern words and tactics was bitterly criticized by his Georgia neighbor, Governor Wright, who wrote Lord Dartmouth, August 24, 1774:

. . . now again my Lord, as in the time of the Stamp Act, I am to be Reflected upon and abused for opposing the Licentiousness of the People and its thrown out *"Why should our Governor do so and so, when the People in Carolina have gone Greater Lengths than we have and the Governor has not taken any notice of it.*

Bull's elevation to the governorship probably would have been the most popular move the home authorities could have made at this time with reference to South Carolina,[144] but, after a long delay, a new resident governor arrived—Lord William Campbell, third brother of the Duke of Argyle and husband of a South Carolina heiress, now transferred to Charleston from the governorship of Nova Scotia. He could do little or nothing to reëstablish royal authority, although materially, at least, his new province had less cause for complaint against England than had any other of the thirteen that joined in the American Revolution.[145]

The youthful province of Georgia, made royal in 1752, had re-

[143] McCrady, *op. cit.,* pp. 694–705; letter dated Sept. 13, 1772, Georgia Historical Society, *Collections,* VI, 210–11.

[144] Georgia Historical Society, *Collections,* IIIa (Savannah, 1873), 180; McCrady, *op. cit.,* pp. 708–9, 795–96, 800.

[145] *Ibid.,* pp. 709, 796; *D.A.B.,* III, 464–65; Smith, *op. cit.,* pp. 385, 402. Campbell did not come to his new government till two years after his appointment. J. B. Brebner, *The Neutral Yankees of Nova Scotia* (New York, 1937), p. 100, refers to Campbell as "by courtesy Lord William Campbell." Campbell had arrived in his northern province in 1766, "a relatively honest, ingenuous, and generous ex-officer of the East India Company's service" and was for a time "a babe in the hands of the Haligonians" *(ibid.,* p. 225); later he made "rather fumbling but stubborn efforts to do what he esteemed his duty to the British Government," and so asserted himself against selfish policies of the local oligarchy that its leaders sought his recall *(ibid.,* p. 241).

ceived her first royal governor in 1755.[146] James Wright, third and last royal executive head of Georgia, served from 1761 to 1776 and from 1779 to near the end of the Revolutionary War. Son of an outstanding chief justice of South Carolina and himself attorney general and subsequently London agent for that province, he resigned the latter post to accept appointment as lieutenant governor of Georgia in 1760, and the following year was advanced to the governorship.[147] Wright's constant loyalty to the Crown and his support of royal prerogative invests with noteworthy sincerity his references to royalty in a talk with some of the Creek Indians early in 1763. Telling them that "the good old King" had died since a former Indian conference, he continued:

> . . . but I have received Instructions . . . from the young King . . . his Subjects spread all over the World, and if ever so remote he will always like a true Father give them Protection. . . . He loves to be at Peace with all Mankind making it his invariable Rule to do as he would be done by.[148]

Wright followed a policy of appeasement toward the Indians, well aware of the military weakness of his province. He secured for Georgia the important Indian congress of November, 1763, attended by Fauquier, Dobbs, and Boone, governors of Virginia, North Carolina, and South Carolina, respectively, and by Indian Superintendent Stuart. The resulting Augusta Treaty served well in preventing a renewal of any very serious strife with the southern Indians. Wright, himself a large landholder, was much interested in territorial expansion. By August, 1774, Commander in Chief Gage, in Boston, was reporting to Lord Dartmouth of Wright that "he is intent upon settling the New Lands and has demanded a Body of Troops to Garrison a Number of Posts for the Protection of the Settlers, but I cannot at present comply with his Request, of which I have acquainted him." [149]

146 For Georgia's first two governors, Reynolds and Ellis, see E. M. Coulter, *A Short History of Georgia* (Chapel Hill, 1933), pp. 78–83; *D.A.B.*, VI, 104–5; XV, 518; *D.N.B.*, XVII, 278–79; XLVIII, 59.

147 *D.N.B.*, LXIII, 107–9; Coulter, *op. cit.*, p. 83; W. B. Stevens, *A History of Georgia*, II (Philadelphia, 1859), 18; A. D. Candler, ed., *The Colonial Records of Georgia*, VIII (Atlanta, 1907), 628.

148 *Ga. Col. Rec.*, IX, 13.

149 Coulter, *op. cit.*, pp. 84, 86, 92–94; Georgia Historical Society, *Collections*, VI, 6; *Gage Corr.*, I, 368–69.

During the Stamp Act troubles Governor Wright maintained his position with dignity and even secured a partial enforcement of the act in the clearing of vessels. "We are here in the utmost confusion," wrote Habersham in January, 1766, "and our honest Governor, who will not submit an Inch to the phrenzy of an unthinking Multitude, is laboring Night and day to prevent the worst Consequences." Wright expounded to the council and assembly "and a Number of People" the letter of the Secretary of State, October 24, 1765, "respecting the Riots committed in the American Provinces on Account of the Stamp Act," and pointed out "the very dangerous Tendency of such unwarrantable and outrageous Proceedings." [150] His consistent, outspoken concern for law and order and his unswerving loyalty to superiors in England complicated his relations with the assertive provincial leaders of Georgia.

Tension was relieved by Wright's absence on leave, July, 1771, to February, 1773. Reading between the lines of the letters of James Habersham, president of the council and acting governor while Wright was absent, one suspects that Wright was aware of his unpopularity and deeply hurt by it. Writing to a business friend in London, Habersham loyally declared:

You cannot think more highly, of Governor Wright than I do. During his Administration here, I had the Honor of an Intimate acquaintance with him, and from my own Knowledge can attest the goodness and uprightness of his Heart, and I am persuaded, that every cool and dispassionate man must join me in Sentiment, and that his Enemies, if he *really* has any here, which I almost doubt, because he gave no Occasion, that I know of, to make anyone so, will at some future day be ashamed to be thought so.

Early in 1772 Habersham again paid tribute to the absent Wright, for after reporting that for the present "all Parties" seemed "Contented" with his own administration, he concluded, "I am persuaded, that on cool recollection, they must and *do* think you the best Governor, that ever Georgia has had, or probably may have in our Day." [151]

The tone of Habersham's letter "to Mrs Wright in London" (March 31, 1764) testifies to the affectionate esteem in which the

[150] Coulter, *op. cit.*, pp. 101–2; Georgia Historical Society, *Collections*, VI, 56; *Ga. Col. Rec.*, IX, 470.

[151] Georgia Historical Society, *Collections*, VI, 6, 144, 153, 155–56, 165.

governor and his family were held by their Georgia friends. Not suspecting the tragic truth that Mrs. Wright had never reached London, having been drowned on her homeward trip from Georgia, Habersham wrote, "I must own their seems to be a Vacuum in your House; and I can truly sympathize with the Governor in his present tho' temporary State of Widowhood." Later Habersham wrote of the tragedy as follows:

What a stroke is this to the poor gentleman? There are few such good wives, tender Mothers and affectionate Friends remaining! . . . You wou'd be surprised and pleased to see how magnanimous the Governor behaves—He appears to have a Friendship for and a Confidence in me, and therefore I have of late been as much with him as possible and I really feel so much with and for him, that I almost forget I have any Concerns of my own to attend to.[152]

Some details of Governor Wright's extensive interests as a land-owner and planter (he is reported to have owned eleven plantations and 523 slaves in 1771) are available in the Habersham correspondence, since Habersham served as attorney for Wright's private interests during the governor's absence, and show how fully Wright had identified himself with the economic interests of the province.[153] But Wright was reluctant to return from England, and probably considered resigning the Georgia governorship. Habersham, growing "old and infirm," found his public duties an "almost intolerable Load of Business." He had occasion to remind Wright in December, 1771, along the following lines:

In one of your . . . Letters you mentioned, that you did not know, but you could get me a Lieutenants Governor's Commission, which I made no reply to . . . , being entirely satisfyed . . . and I really want no Preferment otherwise than it may enable me to discharge my Duty in a Public Capacity with more weight and may give me more Influence. I mention this, as our Friend J.G. some time agoe told me, that a Person in high Office here said, that I was only Commander in Chief by Succession, and by no particular Favour from the Crown. This carried a Reflection I need not point out.

By the spring of 1772 the acting governor had to report a renewal of troubles with the Commons House centering in their denial of "His Majesty's just, undoubted and indisputable Right [through

<hr>

[152] *Ibid.*, pp. 21, 27.   [153] *Ibid.*, p. 6.

his Governor] to negative a Speaker and their Folly in attempting to violate our happy Constitution," troubles similar to those that had annoyed Wright before his departure and likely to greet him on his return.[154] By May, 1772, Habersham was seeking to coax Wright to return for "six, nine, or twelve Months," offering him the Habersham house so that he "need not bring over any Furniture" "or plague" himself "with House–keeping." Referring to Wright's apparent surprise that the acting governor "should complain of being so much hurryed with Business" when he "had nothing to do but A.B.C, common Business," Habersham replied,

You had been long practised in the usual Business, that necessarily arises in Government, and every thing was plain and easy to you. It is not so with me, for conscious of my falling far very far short of your Abilities, I act, in every step I take with doubt and fear. You say you grow old, but I feel I do so, and while you was here, I scarcely knew any one, who enjoyed a better state of Health, which is not my Case. . . ."

Wright, in London, suffered a "dangerous Illness." This led Habersham to write to a London correspondent: "I think he [Wright] ought to return to Georgia for the recovery of his Health . . . and I think I have heard him say, he never had his Health better, than in Georgia." Again, "If Govr Wright was here, and left to persue such Measures, as he might think proper, I believe he would effect our Wishes" with regard to "the Creeks joining in the Cession of the Lands, which the Cherokees have given up," knowing Wright's interest in the consummation of certain Indian cessions in Georgia not yet completed or approved by the King.[155]

By this time Habersham, apprehensive that "the Example of the Assembly of Carolina" had "infatuated" the people of Georgia, reluctantly dissolved his assembly. In August, 1772, he was able to write: "I begin to think, that we shall have the Pleasure of seeing Governor Wright in Georgia about Christmas next, but of this he does not speak with any Degree of Certainty, and therefore I cannot do it, altho' its my private Opinion, he will return." The governor did return in February, 1773, as Sir James Wright, for he

[154] *Ibid.*, pp. 156, 160, 169, 171, 174, 182, 197, 200, 209. For a brief biography of Habersham see *D.A.B.*, VIII, 68–70; Georgia Historical Society, *Collections*, VI, 5–7. See also Coulter, *op. cit.*, p. 106.

[155] Georgia Historical Society, *Collections*, VI, 182, 196–97.

had been created a baronet late in 1772.[156] Local conditions he soon found "most Disagreeable" to one who wished "to Support Law Government and Good order and to discharge his Duty with Honor and integrity." [157] In the governmental crisis of 1768 he had declared: "I presume that the Authority of the British Parliament must be full and compleat or does not operate at all and that the Power of the British Parliament does extend to America is a point I never doubted or heard disputed till the Affair of the Stamp Act." Reiterating his earlier view on the evils involved in breaking away from England, he asserted that "if America could be or was to become Independent of the Mother Country; from that Day you might date the Foundation of your Ruin and Misery." [158]

In August, 1774, Wright declared that "the Licentious Spirit in America" had gone so far "that neither Coercive or Lenient measures will settle matters and restore any tolerable Degree of Cordiality and Harmony with the Mother Country." He blamed this in part upon "the Countenance and Encouragement" accorded the insubordinate Americans by many persons in Great Britain, but sensed, also, something of the significance of the vitality and growth of the colonies. Thus he pointed out to Lord Dartmouth that "things and circumstances in America have increased so fast, and . . . so amazingly exceeded what at the first Settling and Planting the Colonies could Possibly have been Supposed or expected, and America is now become, or Indisputably ere long will be, such a vast, Powerfull and opulent Country or Dominion" that "it may be found advisable to settle the Line with respect to *Taxation etc.* by some new mode or Constitution." Otherwise, "however matters may be got over at present . . . the Flame will only be *smothered for a time* and break out again at some future day *with more Violence.*"

Despite his American birth and background, Wright did not urge constitutional change out of sympathy for the colonial viewpoint, but rather in order "that Great Britain may receive that benefit and advantage which She has a Right to expect from the Colonies." He emphatically asserted that ". . . if any alteration

[156] *Ibid.*, pp. 6, 197, 200; *D.N.B.*, LXIII, 108.
[157] Wright to Lord Dartmouth, Aug. 24, 1774, Georgia Historical Society, *Collections,* IIIa, 182.
[158] *Ga. Col. Rec.*, XIV (Atlanta, 1907), 657-58.

should be thought of, Yet Previous to any thing of this kind intire Submission and obedience to the Sovreignty of Great Britain and Satisfaction for all Private Damages and Injuries ought to be exacted and fully Complied with in and by all the Colonies." [159]

Through warnings, pleas, and propaganda, and by use of the remnants of executive authority still conceded to him, Governor Wright contributed to the relative tardiness of Georgia in organizing resistance to British control. But by August, 1774, it appeared to him that Georgia was characterized by "Nothing but Jealousies Rancour and ill Blood . . . and everything unhinged and Running into . . . Confusion." [160] He let the home authorities know that he desired military aid, and in January, 1775, Dartmouth transmitted to Gage the King's command "to send a Detachment of . . . not less than 100 Men and Officers in proportion to Savannah." On the fateful nineteenth of April Gage acknowledged this command and reported to Dartmouth that he had "sent to the care of Sʳ James Wright" the required order to the commanding officer at St. Augustine.[161] Wright did not use the order, but explained to Dartmouth in June, 1775, that "altho' an 100 men 12 or 15 months" before might have been helpful to him, the situation had changed in the past six weeks and the number of soldiers offered was "so small" that sending for them "would answer no good purpose but might inflame the whole Province." He indicated that he had discussed with his council Georgia's need for defenses against an insurrection and mentioned proposals for securing at least five hundred troops, two war sloops or "one sloop and an armed Schooner" (although the governor himself thought schooners so small as to be "of very little use"), and for erecting a fort and barracks on the common.[162] We must reject, in the light of Gage's inability to meet similar requests from other governors, the assertion that substantial aid would have been dispatched to Governor Wright but for the fact that urgent appeals which Wright addressed to Gage and to Admiral Graves were intercepted in

[159] Georgia Historical Society, *Collections,* IIIa, 181–82.
[160] *Ibid.,* p. 182. For Georgia's entry into the Revolution see Amanda Johnson's "Georgia: from Colony to Commonwealth (1774–1777)," in *Georgia Historical Quarterly,* XVI, 253–73.
[161] *Gage Corr.,* I, 395; II, 183.
[162] Georgia Historical Society, *Collections,* IIIa, 187.

Charleston, where substitute dispatches, reporting Georgia quiet, were forwarded "in the original envelopes." [163]

In June "the Liberty Folks" staged various demonstrations, while persons loyal to the King found it "most prudent to waive opposition and remain quiet." "Why should they expose their lives and properties to the resentment of the people when no support or protection [was] given them by Government?" By June 17, Wright gloomily asserted: "Law and Government" in Savannah "as elsewhere seems now nearly at an end," although the courts and the ports were not yet closed. The Georgians had entered into the Association and Wright foresaw that "whatever is agreed upon by the Continental Congress, will undoubtedly be adopted and carried into execution here." [164]

When a well-attended provincial congress convened in Savannah early in July [165] and preparations of the Georgians for armed strife progressed with aid from South Carolina, Wright confessed himself "a mere Nominal Governor," now that "the Powers of Government" were wrested out of his hands and "Law and Government . . . nearly if not quite annihilated." Soon he was repeating a former request for leave to return to England. Habersham, who had served as acting governor during Wright's former leave of absence, had "gone to Philadelphia for the recovery of his Health," and Wright in a letter to Dartmouth, July 10, stated: "I begin to think a King's Governor has little or no business here." [166] Meanwhile he had acceded to a request from the provincial congress that he "Appoint a day of Fasting and Prayer . . . That a happy reconciliation may soon take Place between America and the Parent State, And that under the Auspicious Reign of His Majesty and his Descendants both Countrys may remain United, Virtuous, Free and happy untill time shall be no more." The governor's ardent wish for "the Ends proposed" had overcome his objections to co-operating with an unconstitutional assembly.[167] As for Habersham, he had declared before his death in New Jersey, August 28, 1775:

. . . I would not chuse to live here longer, than we are in a State of proper Subordination to, and under the protection of Great Britain,

[163] Stevens, *op. cit.*, II, 102–3; Coulter, *op. cit.*, p. 112, partially accepts this.
[164] Coulter, *op. cit.*, pp. 106, 113; Georgia Historical Society, *Collections*, IIIa, 183.
[165] Nevins, *op. cit.*, p. 84; Georgia Historical Society, *Collections*, IIIa, 192.
[166] *Ibid.*, pp. 192, 195.　　　　　[167] *Ibid.*, p. 193.

altho' I cannot altogether approve of the steps she has lately taken, and do most cordially wish that a permanent Line of Government was drawn, and persued, by the Mother and her Children. . . .[168]

Wright, futilely requesting permission to return to England, hung on as best he could in the province. He could not avoid being apprehensive of personal danger. As he explained to Dartmouth:

> Your Lordship cannot possibly conceive the dangerous consequences of suffering the Governor's letters to be made public and it is just hanging them out and exposing them to the resentment of an enraged people who are ready to tear any man to pieces who writes anything contrary to their opinions or in opposition to their measures or schemes.[169]

Yet later, when accused of giving a prejudicial account of the province, he found the council friendly to his refutations of the charge. His relations with the Lower House of Assembly reached an impasse in the spring and summer of 1775. Though reluctant to give up hope of "Conciliatory Measures," Wright by autumn was lamenting that "His Majesty's firm Resolution that the most vigorous Efforts Should be made both by Sea and Land, to reduce his Rebellious Subjects to Obedience" had not been put into action sooner; at the same time he was attempting to strengthen the governor's power through his manner of filling vacancies in the council.[170]

At the end of the year Wright still believed that the arrival of royal troops might rally the loyal elements of South Carolina and Georgia, although the chances for such a development probably would decrease markedly with further delay. He showed a friendly interest in the plight of his fellow governor, Lord William Campbell of South Carolina, who appeared to be cut off from communication with England. Perhaps it was a strain of the South Carolinian aristocrat in Wright that prompted him to send Dartmouth the following report regarding Georgia:

> In this Province . . . we are more unhappily Circumstanced, than in any other, for there are very few, Men of real Abilities, Gentlemen or Men of Property in their Tribunals.
> The Parochial Committee are a Parcel of the Lowest People Chiefly Carpenters, Shoemakers, Blacksmiths etc. with a Few at their Head in

---

[168] *Ibid.*, VI, 236.   [169] *Ibid.*, IIIa, 184.   [170] *Ibid.*, pp. 196–98, 200, 219, 221–22.

the General Committee and Council of Safety, there are Some better Sort of Men and Some Merchants and Planters but many of the Inferior Class, and it is really Terrible my Lord that Such People Should be Suffered to Overturn the Civil Government and most arbitrarily determine upon, and Sport with Other Mens Lives Libertys and Propertys.[171]

Early in January, 1776, writing privately to Dartmouth, Wright reverted to his belief that with "Proper Support and Assistance . . . Numbers would Join the Kings Standard, but no Troops, no Money, no Orders, or Instructions and a Wild Multitude gathering fast, what can any Man do in such a Situation?" He continued: "not so much as a Ship of War of any kind and the Neighbouring Province at the same time threatning Vengeance against the Friends of Government and to Send 1000 Men to assist the Liberty People, if they want Assistance, all these things My Lord are really *too much.*" Wright's public letter to Dartmouth of this same date (January 3) reported that "the Americans . . . Elate with Success, and having met with what they call no Opposition, tho they have been Declared Rebels by Parliament 12 Months ago, now Say Great Britain Cannot reduce them." [172] Fifteen days later, by order of the patriots' Council of Safety, Sir James Wright was placed under arrest by Joseph Habersham apparently to prevent him from coöperating with a British force which had arrived at Tybee. Violating his parole, he fled from Savannah February 11, but from his place of refuge, His Majesty's ship *Scarborough,* he soon sought to quench rebellion by the following message addressed to his council:

My regard for the province is such that I cannot avoid . . . exhorting the people to save themselves and their posterity from that total ruin . . . which, although they may not, yet I most clearly see at the threshold of their doors; and I cannot leave them without again warning them, in the most earnest and friendly manner, to desist from their present plans and resolutions . . . if they will enable me to do it, I will, as far as I can, . . . endeavor to obtain, for them full pardon . . . for all past crimes and offences. . . . But let things happen as they may, be it remembered, that I this day, in the King's name, offer the people of Georgia the olive branch; that most . . . inestimable blessing, the return of peace and happiness to them and their posterity.[173]

---

171 *Ibid.,* pp. 225, 228. 172 *Ibid.,* pp. 229–31.
173 Stevens, *History of Georgia,* II, 127–29, 131–32.

The consideration uppermost in his mind was the plight of "the Kings Officers and friends to Government Some seized upon and kept Prisoners and others hiding and obliged to desert their familys and Property . . . and Some threatened to be Shot whenever met with." He also was concerned about his own property, "a Considerable part" of which already had been "seized upon" as early as March, 1776. He bluntly criticized the sending to Georgia of any "Kings Ships or Troops . . . untill *their* was *sufficient* to reduce the Rebels *at once*," [174] and thus may have been playing for time in his February peace plea.

Nearly three and a half years later, royal rule in Georgia having been partially restored by military conquest,[175] Governor Wright returned and resumed his interrupted operations, until another reversal of military fortunes made possible a close blockade of the city of Savannah where Wright, about the middle of June, 1782, received royal orders to evacuate the province.[176] Subsequently, in recognition of "his situation, age, activity, and zeal, as well as abilities and large property," the American loyalists chose Wright as president of their board to press claims for indemnities from the British government, and the parliamentary commissioners adjudged him "to have lost real and personal property to the value of £33,702, and his office of Governor, value £1,000 per annum." [177]

Most of the very last royal governors in the revolting colonies suffered large property losses; none of them lost their lives because of the American Revolution. These facts possess a peculiar significance seldom recognized. The home authorities in every instance examined in this study chose as governor a man who on some count could be expected to win acceptance among the provincials, a man with military standing, some degree of prestige, with notable connections in Great Britain or America, or even some useful governmental experience. These appointees, generally well received upon their arrival in the colonies, identified themselves in varying degrees with the life of their people, especially the more influential classes. Like other men of wealth or position they had much to lose if discontent with the existing government should take the form of

---

[174] Georgia Historical Society, *Collections,* IIIa, 234.
[175] *Ibid.,* p. 254; Stevens, *op. cit.,* II, 185; *D.N.B.,* LXIII, 108–9.
[176] Stevens, *op. cit.,* II, 322.   [177] *Ibid.,* p. 350.

armed insurrection. Though schooled in authoritarian traditions they were sufficiently practical and intelligent to sense the advantage of a peaceable settlement, had the officials in England to whom they must defer countenanced or promoted such measures. Burdened by conventional responsibilities devolving upon His Majesty's representatives in America, and often intent on private investments and business speculations, the royal governors had little leisure or desire for meditation on constitutional reform, nor were they idealistically or sacrificially devoted to the existing system.

The colonial leaders realized that the royal governors, who sought to check their ambitions and repress their activities, were merely agents, not principals, in the British imperial system. This made possible an absence of vindictiveness toward representatives of the old regime, unusual in revolution. Heads did not roll; instead, the royal governors were at best treated with continued deference and at worst subjected to petty insults or temporary imprisonment until they departed from the scene, incidental casualties in the collapse of the Old Empire.

The Sons of Liberty

In New York ~~~ HERBERT M. MORAIS

THE AMERICAN Revolution was due in no small measure to the effective revolutionary agitation carried on by the Sons of Liberty. Directed with consummate skill by a resolute and capable group of radical leaders and supported mainly by mechanics, artisans, and day laborers, this organization mobilized the popular discontent of the time. Abhorring all kinds of privilege, it stood and struggled for the transfer of power from the aristocratic minority to the democratic majority. In its fight against "inveterate Enemies" at home and abroad, it used every conceivable weapon at its command to galvanize the masses into action. It organized demonstrations, forced the resignation of recalcitrant officials, circulated petitions, and distributed handbills. At no time did it hesitate to use force to fight force; in fact, on more than one occasion, it translated into direct action the current Whig theory of the sovereignty of the people without, however, restricting the term people to the rich and the wellborn.

As an agency of revolutionary agitation, the Sons of Liberty made its appearance in the latter part of 1765. Though its origins are still obscure, it seems to have arisen in some colonies out of previously existing organizations which were composed largely of dissident elements. For example, as early as 1755 some "true Sons of righteous Liberty" formed a political club in Connecticut for the purpose of defending civil and religious freedom. In all probability, this body was later revived as the Connecticut associates of the Sons of Liberty.[1] Similarly, a group of New Yorkers organized a Whig Club in 1752, which held regular weekly meetings and drank toasts to "the immortal memory" of Oliver Cromwell and

[1] J. H. Trumbull, "Sons of Liberty in 1755," *The New Englander*, XXXV, 308, 311; W. C. Abbott, *New York in the American Revolution* (New York, 1929), p. 41.

John Hampden. Some of its leaders were later connected with the New York Liberty Boys.[2]

Apparently appearing first in eastern Connecticut, the Sons of Liberty rapidly spread to Massachusetts and New York. Within a short time, associated bodies could be found in almost all of the American colonies. Unfortunately, however, these societies functioned practically as independent entities, an organizational defect which the revolutionary leadership in New York attempted to remedy by proposing that "a Congress of the Sons of Liberty [be held] in order to form a general plan to be pursued by the whole. . . ."[3] Since nothing was ever done about this proposal, the Sons of Liberty continued to operate as a loosely organized association whose sole connecting link was the local committee of correspondence.

The New York society played a particularly important part in the activities of the association as a whole. This was due not only to its strategic position as the central post from which communications were dispatched northeastward and southward, but also to the intrinsic merit of a leadership capable of giving direction to the movement. Besides being important to the body as a whole, the Sons of Liberty in New York was typical of it. Thus, a treatment of the New York organization should provide an insight into the functioning of other associated bodies. It is the writer's intention, as it was that of Dawson so many years ago, to give to the Sons of Liberty "a portion of that respect which has been too long directed toward other and less worthy objects."[4]

Making its appearance in New York City during the fall of 1765, the Sons of Liberty almost immediately became a political force to be reckoned with. At a mass meeting held on October 31, five of its leading members—Isaac Sears, John Lamb, Gershom Mott, William Wiley, and Thomas Robinson—were appointed to serve as an

---

[2] H. B. Dawson, *Westchester County, New York, during the American Revolution* (Morrisania, New York, 1886), p. 40; T. Jones, *History of New York during the Revolutionary War* (New York, 1879), I, 6; Abbott, *op. cit.*, p. 44. In his *History of Political Parties in the Province of New York, 1760–1776* (Madison, 1909), C. L. Becker, however, contends that the Sons of Liberty was not a continuation of the Whig Club (p. 49).

[3] Letter to the Boston Sons of Liberty, April 2, 1766, Lamb Papers, New York Historical Society.

[4] H. B. Dawson, *The Sons of Liberty in New York* (Poughkeepsie, 1859), p. 8.

intercolonial committee of correspondence. Thereafter, the influence of the Sons of Liberty grew so steadily that by the beginning of 1766 it was strong enough to abandon its initial secrecy and to declare its intentions publicly. From then on, local newspapers announced the time and place of its regular meetings, together with information concerning the business transacted and the resolutions adopted.[5]

Other towns in the province organized associated bodies. Albany had one in January, 1766, Oyster Bay and Huntington in February, White Plains in March, and Fishkill in April.[6] These associations were connected with the New York society by committees of correspondence which frequently expressed a willingness to carry out their brethren's commands "on any Matter." [7] Resolutions adopted at town meetings also were exchanged. On one occasion, the people of Huntington informed the New York Liberty Boys that they proposed to enjoy the "Privileges of every free born Englishman, *of being taxed by none, but by Representatives of his own chusing, of being tried by none, but his fellows in a Jury.*" [8]

The New York committee of correspondence also received communications from associated bodies in other colonies. These it sometimes relayed to New England and to the South. The letters it received often praised the splendid work it was doing, work which at times was responsible for the establishment of new associations like those in New Jersey at Upper Freehold and Woodbridge.[9] Frequently, the New York committee sent letters calculated to advance the formation of a continental union. In February, 1766, the Boston Sons of Liberty were reported as "Delighted at" the prospect.[10] Some two months later, the official New York committee, appointed in October, 1765, and made up entirely of Liberty Boys, sent a letter to Baltimore with a proposal for colonial unity and a

[5] For example, see *The New-York Gazette; or, The Weekly Post-Boy,* Jan. 9, Feb. 9, 1766; *The New-York Mercury,* Jan. 27, Feb. 10, 17, March 21, 1766.

[6] *The New-York Gazette; or, The Weekly Post-Boy,* Jan. 23, March 6, May 15, 1766; letter addressed to the Sons of Liberty in White Plains, April 3, 1766, Lamb Papers.

[7] See the letter of the Albany Sons of Liberty to the New York Sons of Liberty, Jan. 15, 1766, Lamb Papers.

[8] Feb. 24, 1766, *loc. cit.*

[9] *The New-York Gazette; or, The Weekly Post-Boy,* March 6, 1766; Becker, *op. cit.,* p. 47*n.*

[10] Letter of Feb. 17, 1766, from a Providence Son of Liberty, Lamb Papers.

request that the communication be dispatched southward as quickly as possible, "for we know not how soon we may be put to the test by that pack of infernal rascals, Grenville and his minions." [11] When the Sons of Liberty were finally "put to the test," they might well have congratulated themselves upon having contributed their share to the introduction of the celebrated committees of correspondence which European revolutionaries were later to imitate.

The proposal for a continental union arose partly out of a desire to coördinate the activities of those military establishments connected with the Sons of Liberty. In the early part of 1766 the Connecticut association was reputed to have had ten thousand men under arms, and Massachusetts and New Hampshire, forty thousand.[12] How many men the New York Liberty Boys could have mustered at this time is problematic; however, on the basis of the number participating in demonstrations of one kind or another, it can be assumed that large numbers would have answered the call. Determined not to be enslaved "by any power on earth; without opposing force to force," the New York society undoubtedly possessed an armed militia, as was evidenced by its readiness to fight the landing of British troops in March, 1766.[13] On this occasion, as well as on others, armed Liberty Boys could safely rely upon the people at large for active support.

That such a situation prevailed was not at all accidental. It was based on the fact that the Sons of Liberty in New York was essentially a lower-class organization.[14] Though mechanics, artisans, and day laborers made up the bulk of its membership, merchants and lawyers furnished it with the necessary leadership. An investigation of all names appearing on communications dispatched to and by the New York Sons of Liberty, together with all others mentioned

[11] As quoted in I. Q. Leake, *Memoir of the Life and Times of General John Lamb* (Albany, 1850), p. 19.

[12] Letter of Feb. 17, 1766, Lamb Papers; G. D. Scull, ed., *Montresor Journals*, New York Historical Society, *Collections* (1881; hereafter referred to as *Montresor*), p. 355 (March 24, 1766); L. H. Gipson, *Jared Ingersoll* (New Haven, 1920), p. 156.

[13] *Montresor*, p. 353, entry of March 18, 1766. See also Lamb Papers, letter of Feb. 20, 1766, to the Connecticut Sons of Liberty.

[14] Abbott, *op. cit.*, p. 43. See also R. V. Harlow, "The Causes of the Revolution in New York" in A. C. Flick, ed., *A History of the State of New York* (10 vols., New York, 1933-37), III, 196-97.

in biographical accounts and local histories, was made by the writer in an attempt to find out the social groups from which the leadership was drawn. Some thirty-eight names were found, of whom eighteen later became the subjects of biographical sketches. Of these eighteen, eleven were merchants—Joseph Allicocke, John Lamb, Edward Laight, Francis Lewis, Alexander McDougall, Charles Nicoll, Daniel Phoenix, Isaac Sears, John Thurman, Jr.,[15] Marinus Willett, and Jacobus Van Zandt; [16] four were lawyers— Egbert Benson, John Sloss Hobart, William Livingston, and John Morin Scott,[17] one, Leonard Lispenard, was a wealthy landholder and merchant; [18] one, Thomas Young, was a physician; [19] and another, Abraham Brasher, was a writer of popular ballads and might have been a mechanic by trade.[20]

In this group of eighteen the popularly acknowledged leaders were at first William Livingston and John Morin Scott, whose moderate policies were very soon replaced by the radical program of Sears, Lamb, and Allicocke. These three were later joined by McDougall and Willett. All five of these men were practical-minded merchants, master political strategists, opposed to compromise. Four of them began their careers in working-class or artisan surroundings; McDougall was the son of a milkman; Willett worked as a cabinetmaker; Sears was a privateer; and Lamb made mathematical instruments. All four eventually became prosperous merchants. Nevertheless, their devotion to the cause involved heavy sacrifices—in the case of McDougall and Sears, imprisonment, and for the latter, loss of position, as he was removed from his post as inspector of potash.

[15] Thurman took an active part in the Sons of Liberty during the Stamp Act agitation but later found himself out of sympathy with its radical leaders. By 1774 he was bitterly opposing the latter. See J. A. Stevens, *Colonial New York, Sketches Historical and Biographical* (New York, 1867), pp. 165–66.

[16] *Ibid.*, pp. 119, 141–42, 153–55, 160–61, 166–67; *Dictionary of American Biography,* X, 555–56; XII, 21–22; XVI, 539; XX, 244.

[17] *Ibid.*, II, 204; IX, 95; XI, 325–26; XVI, 495.

[18] Lispenard was undoubtedly a Son of Liberty. On this point see Stevens, *op. cit.,* p. 143.

[19] During the Stamp Act agitation, Young was a member of the committee of correspondence of the Albany Sons of Liberty. He moved to Boston in 1766. For his life see *D.A.B.*, XX, 635.

[20] Brasher was a member of the Committee of Mechanics organized in 1774. For his life, consult *Appleton's Cyclopaedia of American Biography, I,* 360.

Their ability as revolutionary leaders was clearly demonstrated during the Stamp Act disturbances. With great adroitness, they prepared the unenfranchised for battle. In the latter part of October, 1765, two thousand people were marshaled to prevent the landing of stamps. This hostile demonstration frightened the British officials, who waited until nightfall, after the crowd had dispersed, before taking the stamps ashore. Immediately, placards were posted warning the "first Man that either distributes or makes use of Stampt Paper . . . [to] take care of his House, Person and Effects." One day before the enforcement of the obnoxious law, that is, on October 31, a meeting attended by tradesmen, mechanics, sailors, and laborers was held to warn the British government abroad and some wavering merchants at home that the people intended to see that the Stamp Act was disobeyed.[21]

The next day a gigantic demonstration got under way. In a letter addressed to Lieutenant Governor Colden and posted at the Coffee House, an anonymous writer warned that official not "to fire on the town" unless he wanted "to die a matir to [his] own villainy and be hanged . . . as a memento to all wicked governors." In the meantime a great number of people poured into the city from the countryside.[22] These countryfolk, joined by four hundred to five hundred seamen, three hundred carpenters, and a host of others, marched through the streets to the fort where the stamps were kept. All along the line of march, the demonstrators conducted themselves in an orderly and disciplined fashion in accordance with the instructions of their leaders. Once at the fort, the question arose whether to take it or not. Had the crowd so willed, considering its numbers, of whom many were experienced in military matters, it might very likely have taken the fort, but instead it contented itself with informing the garrison that it intended to pull down the home of Major James, a British officer, who on a previous occasion had made the provocative remark that he would "cram the stamps down [the people's] throats with the end of his sword." Calling upon the major to defend his house, the demonstrators

21 E. B. O'Callaghan, ed., *Documents Relative to the Colonial History of the State of New York* (Albany, 1856), VII, 770; *Montresor*, p. 336 (Oct. 23, 1765); Dawson, *Sons of Liberty in New York*, p. 88.

22 This fact is, however, denied by Colden. See *Docs. Rel. Col. Hist. N.Y.*, VII, 774 (Colden to Conway, Nov. 9, 1765); *Colden Papers*, III, 301–7.

then proceeded to the home of the unhappy officer, "knocked it down," and victoriously carried off the colors of the Royal Regiment.[23] The great demonstration of November 1 was immediately followed by others. Sears and the Liberty Boys were determined to force the government to give up the stamps. Upon the advice of General Gage, the council, and conservative merchants, Colden eventually did so. The "detestable paper" was then turned over to a guard of forty militiamen, thirty-five of whom later voted to burn it." [24]

Having gained one victory, the New York Liberty Boys marched forward to a second, the resignation of stamp agents. On November 30, 1765, a number of gentlemen decided to visit McEvers, stamp collector in the New York area, to find out whether he intended to continue in office. A few days later the terrified McEvers, in the presence of Sears and Allicocke, resigned his post.[25] Meanwhile, Hood, a Maryland stamp master who had fled to New York and had been promised protection by Colden, was visited by some hundred Liberty Boys. He hastily resigned his office and took the required oath of sincerity before Justice Smith. The Liberty Boys then returned in triumph; on the flag which they carried were inscribed the words "Liberty, Property, No Stamps." They were later thanked for their work by the Sons of Liberty in Baltimore, who assured them that Hood had fled "from the just resentment of his injured countrymen." [26] The followers of Sears were likewise responsible for the resignation of DeLancey, inspector and stamp distributor for Canada and Nova Scotia. According to Weyman's *New-York Gazette* for December 2, 1765, DeLancey's retirement "gain'd him great Applause and entirely restored him the Esteem

23 *The New-York Gazette; or, The Weekly Post-Boy,* Nov. 7, 1765; Weyman's *New-York Gazette,* Nov. 25, 1765; *New York City during the American Revolution: a Collection of Original Papers* (New York, 1861), pp. 42–49 (contains some erroneous information); *Montresor,* p. 337; *Docs. Rel. Col. Hist. N.Y.,* VII, 771, 775, 792; Dawson, *Sons of Liberty in New York,* pp. 89–97; and M. J. Lamb, *History of the City of New York* (New York, 1877), I, 726–28.

24 *Montresor,* p. 343 (Dec. 21, 1765).

25 Weyman's *New-York Gazette,* Dec. 9, 1765. For McEvers's letter of resignation, see *Docs. Rel. Col. Hist. N.Y.,* VII, 761.

26 As quoted in Leake, *op. cit.,* p. 22n; H. Onderdonk, *Queens County in Olden Times* (Jamaica, 1865), p. 38; *Montresor,* p. 340 (Nov. 28, 1765). See also *The New-York Gazette; or, The Weekly Post-Boy,* Nov. 21, 1765, for the so-called "Last Speech, Confession, and Dying Words of Z. H. Esq., St..p M....r of the province of M......d."

of the Publick." Some time later Lamb went to Philadelphia and there with the aid of the Heart and Hand Fire Company forced the resignation of Hughes, the last stamp collector in America.

The Albany Liberty Boys were not far behind their associates in New York. On January 4, 1766, they held a meeting at which the charge was made that a number of their fellow citizens had applied for "Deputations in the Stamp Office. . . ." A resolution was passed to require all those named to appear immediately. All came except a Mr. Hansen, "who being waited on at his Home, gave under Oath immediate and ample Satisfaction, that he neither had applied nor never would accept" such a post. A few days later four hundred Liberty Boys marched to the home of Van Schaack, another prospective stamp collector. When he could not be found, they proceeded to "pull his house down." On the very next day Van Schaack hurried to a meeting of the Sons of Liberty and duly promised that he would neither apply for nor accept the post of stamp master. Thereupon he was cheered by the gathering and, according to report, "genteely conducted to his Lodging." [27]

In the meantime, the New York Liberty Boys pressed their fight on other fronts. In a petition to the assembly, delivered to the clerk of the house by an employee of his who, in turn, had received it from an unknown person, that body was requested to take away "as much money from the Lieu^t Governor's Sallery as will Repare the fort," to repeal the Gunning Law so that "thare will be a Good Militia but not before," and to consider the Building Act. The house was warned not to "take this petition ill" and not to be "so Conceited as to Say or think that other People know nothing about Government. . . ." In conclusion, the assembly was informed that "Oppressions of your make . . . make us *Sons of Liberty*. . . ." [28]

As a result of these activities the New York society began to function as an extralegal body with all of the powers and attributes of government. As early as December 8, 1765, the somewhat alarmist Montresor, a British officer stationed in New York, noted in his *Journal* that the "Sons of Liberty, as they term themselves, were openly defying powers, office and all authority. . . ." He ended his

[27] *The New-York Gazette; or, The Weekly Post-Boy*, Jan. 23; Weyman's *New-York Gazette*, Jan. 20, 27; *The New-York Mercury*, Jan. 27, 1766.

[28] E. B. O'Callaghan, ed., *Documentary History of the State of New York* (Albany, 1850), III, 299–300 (hereafter referred to as *Doc. Hist. N.Y.*).

lament with the ominous words "sole rulers." [29] Although this observation was undoubtedly an exaggeration, it nevertheless contained an element of truth. During the Stamp Act agitation, the
Sons of Liberty took matters into their own hands, and in the
absence of an effective counter-organization, exercised broad extralegal powers. For example, in February, 1766, a number of Liberty
Boys, headed by Sears and Allicocke, marched in broad daylight to
the homes of two well-known merchants suspected of having used
stamp paper. The merchants were seized and brought back to a
meeting where they promised never to use stamps again. Even more
significant than this was the occurrence which took place a month
later, when a committee of the Sons of Liberty, consisting of the
indefatigable Sears and Allicocke, boarded a British warship to demand the surrender of an officer accused of having made certain
derogatory remarks. When Gage, the commander in chief, inter-
ceded on behalf of the officer and even threatened to move troops
into the city, the Liberty Boys prepared to fight. In the meantime,
news arrived that Colonel Putnam was ready to come to their aid
with ten thousand armed men from Connecticut. A clash was prevented only by the arrival of news (later shown to be false) that
the Stamp Act had been repealed.[30]

The Sons of Liberty opposed not only the authority of a government three thousand miles away but also the domination of "respectable and substantial merchants" in America. The business
recession under way in the fall of 1765 was accelerated by the stop-
page of foreign trade resultant from the refusal of shippers to employ stamped paper for clearances, bills of lading, and governor's
passes. Merchants withheld payments in order to prevent remit-
tances from going to the mother country. The cessation of foreign
trade affected retail business and brought about unemployment.
Mechanics, artisans, and day laborers favored the resumption of
business without stamps. They therefore requested the Sons of
Liberty to act. The result was the calling of a meeting the "great
Design" of which "was to put Business in Motion again . . . with-

[29] *Montresor,* p. 348.
[30] *The New-York Mercury,* Feb. 17, 1766; *Montresor,* pp. 349, 353–55 (Feb. 14, March
19, and 24, 1766); Leake, *op. cit.,* p. 24; J. A. Stevens, "The Part of New-York in the
Stamp Act Troubles, 1761–68," in J. G. Wilson, *The Memorial History of the City of
New York* (New York, 1892), II, 375, 376; Abbott, *op. cit.,* p. 65.

out Stamps." A resolution to this effect was offered, but some of the leading merchants of the city, "Persons not Privy to the Design," were able to direct the meeting into much safer channels. Not wishing to submit to the "arrogant dictation" implicit in the resolution, they introduced another which was eventually passed. This motion, though calling for the repeal of the Stamp Act and of other obnoxious measures, contained "nothing to remove the present Obstructions on Business, and therefore not the Thing most wanted." [31]

This meeting, held on November 26, 1765, was very significant, for it clearly revealed the existence of two contending forces within the Revolutionary movement. One represented the right wing of the Revolution and consisted mainly of conservative merchants, men who gradually came to support the idea of independence but only with the proviso that state power be confined to them; the other, the left wing of the Revolution, consisted chiefly of the artisan democracy which, though favoring separation from England, nevertheless hoped to see established in America a government which would be responsive to the people at large. From the very beginning these two forces fought to direct the movement: during the Stamp Act agitation, the fight flared up not only outside but inside the organization of the Sons of Liberty. That dissension prevailed even in this organization was reflected in a notice that appeared on December 26, 1765, in *The New-York Gazette; or, The Weekly Post-Boy*. "The Sons of Liberty," so the announcement ran, "desire their Brethren will be ready at a Call, when the Common Good, the only thing to which they are attentive, requires them again to exert themselves. . . . Meanwhile let all Divisions cease." Discord did not come to an end, however, without a struggle. The battle lines were sharply drawn; the conservatives were led by John Morin Scott and William Livingston, the radicals by Isaac Sears and John Lamb. The issue involved a question not only of tactics—reliance upon petitions and theoretical arguments as against the use of direct action—but also of orientation—the

[31] *The New-York Gazette; or, The Weekly Post-Boy*, Nov. 28, 1765; Flick, *op. cit.*, III, 198; Dawson, *The Sons of Liberty*, p. 111; Virginia Harrington, *The New York Merchant on the Eve of the Revolution* (New York, 1935), pp. 329–31; Becker, *op. cit.*, p. 36.

introduction of policies designed to advance the class interests of merchants as opposed to the adoption of measures calculated to better the condition of the rank and file of the people. The struggle resulted in a decisive victory for the radicals. From then on, the Sons of Liberty became the voice of the artisan democracy.

The "levelling" tendencies which characterized the activities of the New York Liberty Boys undoubtedly encouraged the rise of a similar trend in the countryside. As early as November, 1765, settlers on the Philipse estate refused to submit to eviction proceedings and boldly urged all tenants to meet and reinstate those already evicted. By the early part of 1766, agrarian disturbances were widespread. The Westchester tenants of Van Cortlandt refused to pay rent unless their insecurity of tenure was replaced by a fee absolute. The movement spread to Dutchess County, where, under the leadership of Pendergrast, Munroe, and Finch, small farmers did not hesitate to use direct action to achieve their ends. By the middle of the year, there were seventeen hundred antirenters under arms at Poughkeepsie and three hundred more at Pawling. Within a short time, however, Pendergrast and seven other leaders were captured and the force of "the great Rebellion" was broken.[32]

From the viewpoint of the artisan class, it was most unfortunate that the Liberty Boys did not actively associate themselves with the country "levellers" and thereby forge an alliance between the urban masses and the rural tenantry. The basis for such a union was already there—a common enemy, that is, the royal government and those behind it, as well as joint participation in the November 1 demonstration against the Stamp Act.[33] With Pendergrast and his followers keenly aware of their kinship to the Sons of Liberty, it should not have been difficult for them to have established such

[32] It is interesting to note in this connection that John Morin Scott was one of the judges to condemn Pendergrast to death. However, it should be observed that by this time Scott, a wealthy lawyer and large landholder, was no longer connected with the active leadership of the Sons of Liberty, having already been replaced by others of more radical views.

[33] The effect of the November 1 demonstration upon the country people participating in it was suggested by a writer in *The New-York Gazette; or, The Weekly Post-Boy* for November 7, 1765: ". . . great numbers came from the Country and Parts adjacent . . . Some returned Home satisfied with our Firmness, determin'd to maintain their Freedom in their respective Places of Residence, and assist us, if their Assistance should be necessary."

an alliance. That the Liberty Boys failed to take the initiative in 1766 was indeed a grave mistake.[34]

While the Sons of Liberty were missing this golden opportunity to unite the urban masses and the rural tenantry, the Stamp Act was being repealed. In March and in April, two false reports were circulated. When authentic word of the repeal reached New York on May 20, 1766, hundreds of newsboys ran through the streets shouting "No more Shin Shams." The next day, bells rang, twenty-one guns were fired, and the Governor was congratulated by a committee representing the Sons of Liberty. On May 24, the Albany Liberty Boys sent a letter to their New York associates expressing "elation at the return of our Guardian genius Dear Liberty." Two days later, the Sons of Liberty in New York "most cordially [saluted] and [congratulated] all their American Brethren on this glorious and happy Event." On June 19, a notice appeared in the local press urging the people "to write Letters of Thanks to all those illustrious Personages who have so zealously exerted themselves in both Houses of Parliament, in obtaining the Repeal of the Stamp Act." [35]

Meanwhile, a liberty pole was erected to commemorate the event. In August, 1766, it was cut down by some British soldiers. The Sons of Liberty immediately called a protest meeting, some two to three thousand people attended, and an explanation was demanded. While the meeting was in progress, British soldiers fired into the crowd and wounded several people. The incident ended with the Liberty Boys refusing to allow British troops to patrol the streets and with the building of another pole.[36]

About a month before the August disturbances, the unsympathetic Montresor was busily engaged in burying the remains of the Sons of Liberty. He recorded with much gusto on July 16, 1766, that it was no longer holding its customary meetings or being talked

[34] For information about the antirent movement the writer is indebted to the work of a colleague, Irving Mark, the manuscript of whose forthcoming dissertation on the subject he has had the good fortune to see. *Montresor* has many references to the country "levellers." See pp. 361–62, 363, 366, 375–76, 384.

[35] Letter of May 24, 1766, from the Albany Sons of Liberty, Lamb Papers; *The New-York Mercury,* May 26, 1766; *Montresor,* p. 368; *The New-York Gazette; or, The Weekly Post-Boy,* June 19, 1766.

[36] *Montresor,* pp. 382–84 (Aug. 11, 12, 17, and 18, 1766); Leake, *op. cit.,* pp. 32–33; Moore to the Duke of Richmond, *Docs. Rel. Col. Hist. N.Y.,* VII, 867–68.

about. Some two weeks later, Nicholas Ray, a wealthy American patriot, in a letter from London, mentioned the dissolution of the Sons of Liberty and, after acknowledging its influence upon events in England, suggested the formation of a Liberty Club by ten or twenty of its leading members. The new society was to hold meetings regularly and to celebrate annually the repeal of the Stamp Act.[37] Although the Sons of Liberty seems to have disappeared as a formal organization during the summer of 1766,[38] its leading members nevertheless continued to carry on its former activities. Until its public reappearance in the fall of 1773, old agitators like Sears and Lamb and new ones like McDougall and Willett were occupied in supervising the distribution of handbills, the organization of demonstrations, and the inspection of nonimportation agreements.

The circulation of leaflets inspired by the Liberty Boys was a source of great irritation to the royal government in New York during the period under consideration. For example, in December, 1767, Governor Moore issued a proclamation against the printing and secret distribution of "sundry seditious Papers." As an illustration, he gave one written by "Pro Patria." This writer reminded his countrymen of the "glorious stand for Liberty" taken by them in 1765 against "a Set of Miscreants under the Name of Stamp Masters." He went on to warn his readers that a new "set . . . may soon make their Appearance amongst [them] in order to execute their detestable Office. It is therefore hoped that every Votary of that celestial Goddess Liberty, will hold themselves in Readiness to give them a proper Welcome; Rouse, my Countrymen, Rouse!"[39] The governor offered a reward of fifty pounds to any person disclosing the identity of "Pro Patria." In December, 1769, another leaflet appeared under the signature of "A Son of Liberty" and addressed "To the Betrayed Inhabitants of the City and Colony of New

[37] July 28, 1766, Lamb Papers.
[38] The writer agrees with Becker that "it is impossible to say whether there was a formal dissolution or not." *Op. cit.*, p. 48. The disappearance of the Sons of Liberty is predicated not only upon the material given above (Montresor's observation and Ray's statement), but also upon the absence of all references to it in the Lamb collection (Lamb was apparently the secretary of the body) from May 24, 1766, to May 11, 1770. See letter of May 24, 1766, from the Albany Sons of Liberty and of May 11, 1770, to a Son of Liberty in Philadelphia, Lamb Papers.
[39] O'Callaghan, *Doc. Hist N.Y.*, III, 316.

York." The handbill vigorously opposed an assembly measure providing for the granting of money to billet troops, reminded its
readers of Massachusetts's refusal to do so, and warned them that
for New York to do one thing and Massachusetts another was to
play into the hands of the British ministry, which hoped to rule the
colonies by dividing them. Urging his countrymen to imitate "the
brave Bostonians," the author called upon the people to hold a
meeting, after which they were told to "go in a body to [their as-
sembly] members and insist on their joining with the minority to
oppose the bill. . . ." If this failed, they were advised to appoint a
committee to draw up a memorial which was to be sent to the
speakers of all colonial assemblies and "to the friends of our cause
in England. . . ." [40] In accordance with the suggestion contained
in the handbill, some fourteen hundred people met.[41] Lamb, the
principal speaker, asked them whether they approved or disapproved of the action of the assembly. When the response was in the
negative, a committee, headed by Lamb and consisting of such
other prominent Liberty Boys as Sears, McDougall, and Van Zandt,
was appointed to wait upon the assembly. This the committee did,
but all to no avail. In fact, the legislature passed a resolution con-
demning "the Author or Authors Aiders and Abettors" of the
handbill, which they castigated "as a false, seditious and infamous
Libel," and requested the lieutenant governor to offer a reward for
the apprehension of the person or persons involved.[42]

The legislature's challenge was immediately accepted by the
Liberty Boys. Another handbill, this time signed "Legion," appeared and called upon the people to meet in order "to avert the
Destructive Consequences of the late base inglorious Conduct of
our General Assembly." The house, taking the paper under consideration, directed the lieutenant governor to offer a reward to anyone disclosing the identity of "Legion." [43] A friend of McDougall,

[40] *Ibid.*, pp. 317–18, 320.

[41] Colden claimed that the newspapers were exaggerating the size of the meetings
which were held by "the sons of liberty, as they call themselves." "People in general,"
he continued, "especially they of property, are aware of the dangerous consequences
of such notions and mobbish proceedings." *Colden Papers*, IV, 131 (letter of Jan. 6,
1770, to Hillsborough).

[42] O'Callaghan, *Doc. Hist. N.Y.*, III, 321; Lamb, *op. cit.*, I, 745; Leake, *op. cit.*, pp.
51–52; W. Dunlap, *A History of New York for Schools* (New York, 1837), I, 129.

[43] O'Callaghan, *op. cit.*, III, 322–23.

Benjamin Young Prime, was accused of having written the "obnoxious" handbill. In a letter to Dr. Tappan of Esopus (now Kingston) he told of the threats made against him by the "respectable" party of the Right which once before had declared its intention of giving him "a Damnation Drubbing and Imprisonment. . . ." [44] In the meantime, Lamb was charged with being the author not only of the "Legion" handbill, but also of the previous one. On December 20, 1769, he was brought before the assembly, and on the following day he was examined. He was accompanied by a number of leading Liberty Boys who declared that if Lamb was implicated in the matter, they were, too. With no definite evidence having been found against him, he was discharged.

About two months later, another prominent Liberty Boy, McDougall, was accused of having written the leaflet addressed "To the Betrayed Inhabitants of the City and Colony of New York." He was arraigned and, refusing to give the necessary bail, was imprisoned. Overnight he became a hero; crowds came to see him and newspapers announced his every move. Possessing "great Presence of mind," McDougall turned things to his own advantage and practically accused his accusers. His courageous stand won him the admiration of Sears and Lamb, who at first felt suspicious of him because of his lukewarm position during the Stamp Act agitation. He was defended by John Morin Scott before a grand jury composed of the most "respectable, opulent, and substantial gentlemen in the city." On his way to court, he was attended by some two to three hundred people. Prominent lawyers like William Smith who held office under the Crown and who were requested to assist the prosecution refused to do so. With government witnesses disappearing, the case fell to the ground. Amid much rejoicing, the "Wilkes of America" was released from prison. Toward the end of the year, however, he was again brought up on the same charge, this time before the assembly. When he refused to answer questions put to him, he was cited for "high contempt" and again imprisoned.[45]

---

44 *N.Y. City during the Am. Rev. . . . Original Papers,* p. 51.

45 "A Letter upon McDougall's Commitment," William Smith Papers, Nos. 204-9, New York Public Library; *Colden Papers,* IV, 149, 153; O'Callaghan, *Doc. Hist. N.Y.,* III, 323n; Leake, *op. cit.,* pp. 60-63, 71-72; Lamb, *op. cit.,* I, 747; Jones, *op. cit.,* I, 24-30.

Just a short time before the celebrated McDougall case came up, armed clashes were taking place between British regulars and the citizenry. In January, 1770, three months before the Boston Massacre, a similar event occurred in New York when British troops cut down a liberty pole, set to work on it with saws, and deposited the pieces in front of the headquarters of the Sons of Liberty. This deliberate act of provocation was answered at a meeting of three thousand people who not only protested the destruction of the liberty pole but vigorously denounced as injurious to the working classes of the city the employment of British troops to replace native laborers. British regulars responded to this protest meeting by issuing a handbill assailing the Sons of Liberty as dangerous enemies of the community at large.[46] When some British soldiers attempted to post the leaflet, they were seized by Sears, Quackenbos, and other Liberty Boys. This action resulted in the battle of Golden Hill, with regular British troops fighting a thoroughly aroused people armed only with sticks wrenched from carts, chairs, and sleighs. The clash was followed by the death of one citizen and the wounding of several others. With the Liberty Boys determined to erect another pole, the authorities yielded. The new pole was inscribed "Liberty and Property." [47]

Events such as these were calculated to frighten well-to-do merchants who felt that sooner or later similar action would be taken against them. They therefore decided to dissociate themselves from those "lawless" elements connected with the Sons of Liberty. Consequently in March, 1770, they held their own banquet to commemorate the repeal of the Stamp Act. They entertained themselves by drinking toasts to "Trade and navigation and a speedy removal of their embarassments." [48] These toasts reflected the real sentiments of the mercantile classes in the early part of 1770. They were ready and willing to scrap the nonimportation agreement in order to further their private interests. The Sons of Liberty, on the other hand, opposed any relaxation of the nonimportation agreement. When a Boston merchant, Nathaniel Rogers, an enemy of nonimportation, appeared in New York, the Liberty Boys hanged

46 For the contents of the handbill see Dawson, *Sons of Liberty in N.Y.*, pp. 113–14n.
47 *The New-York Journal*, Jan. 8, Feb. 8, 1770; *Colden Papers*, IV, 135–49; Dawson, *Sons of Liberty in N.Y.*, pp. 112–17; Leake, *op. cit.*, pp. 54–59.
48 *The New-York Journal*, March 22, 1770.

him in effigy before a crowd of five thousand people. The terrified
Rogers hastily left the city. When it was reported that he was going
to Philadelphia, a letter was sent to the Sons of Liberty of that
town advising them to give him a similar reception.[49]

Although the Sons of Liberty was apparently not functioning as a
formal organization at this time, three years later it definitely was.
On November 29, 1773, a great number of "Inhabitants of all
Ranks," being "influenced from a regard to liberty, and disposed to
transmit to our posterity, those blessings of freedom, which our
ancestors have handed down to us; and to contribute to the support
of the common liberties of America, which are in danger to be
subverted," did "agree to associate together, under the name and
stile of the Sons of Liberty of New York." They promised to treat
as enemies anyone aiding or abetting the introduction of dutied
tea or buying or selling that commodity regardless of whether the
duty was paid in England or America, and all others having connections with such transgressors.[50]

During the Tea Act agitation, the Liberty Boys used their previous tactics to arouse the masses. In the first place, they waited
upon three duly appointed tea agents, all of whom expressed a
willingness to resign their posts because of the "general Opposition" to the sale of tea.[51] Secondly, they organized mass meetings
of which that of December 17 was typical. Called "on business of
the utmost Importance," [52] the meeting was attended by two thousand people, despite the inclement weather. John Lamb, the presiding officer, read letters from Boston and Philadelphia. This was
followed by the appointment of a committee of fifteen to correspond with other colonies on the subject of the tea duty. The
mayor then appeared and informed the crowd that the tea was
soon to be delivered. To his question, "Gentlemen, is this satisfactory to you?" the answer was: "No! No! No!" Two resolutions
were then passed, one opposing the landing of tea, the other ap-
proving the "spirited and patriotic Conduct of our Brethren, of the
City of Philadelphia, and the Town of Boston, in Support of the
common Liberties of America." [53] Thirdly, the Liberty Boys

[49] May 11, 1770, Lamb Papers.   [50] *The New-York Journal,* Dec. 16, 1773.
[51] *Ibid.,* Dec. 2, *The New-York Gazette; and The Weekly Mercury,* Dec. 6, 1773.
[52] See the announcement in *The New-York Journal,* Dec. 16, 1773.
[53] *Ibid.,* Dec. 23, 1773.

adopted the tried tactic of direct action. They organized a group of "Mohawks" to prevent the landing of dutied tea. They also warned all New York pilots against directing any tea-laden ships into the port. Yet despite these precautions two vessels carrying tea made their way to New York during the spring of 1774. One of them was returned before it was able to unload its cargo and the other had its tea dumped into the harbor by an infuriated crowd of people who had arrived ahead of the "Mohawks." [54]

While these events were taking place, the merchants were again coming to grips with the mechanics and workers. In fact, as early as December 21, 1773, four days after the Liberty Boys held their meeting, conservative men of property attempted to steer all future demonstrations into safe and sane channels. They circulated a petition pledging signers not to resort to force in opposing the importation of tea. Although compelled to abandon the project because of the excitement occasioned by the news of the Boston Tea Party, they nevertheless persisted in their course. They cautiously bode their time and patiently waited for the day of reckoning. In May, 1774, the conservative merchants felt themselves strong enough to challenge the artisan democracy. Having received news from Europe that the British government intended to close the port of Boston, they decided to hold a meeting of their own on Monday evening, May 16. Significantly enough, they did not invite the popular elements; nevertheless, the Liberty Boys attended the meeting. Their opponents presented resolutions calling for the appointment of a committee to correspond with neighboring colonies on the present crisis and for the nomination that evening of a committee to be approved later by the public, such committee to consist of fifty persons. The radical element readily accepted both committees, but wished the second to comprise twenty-five instead of fifty persons. The chairman, Isaac Low, put the question, and the motion to amend was defeated "by a great Majority." The committee finally chosen was composed mainly of conservatives. [55] The following day a meeting to approve the selection of the committee was announced for May 19 at one o'clock—a most inconvenient hour for employed mechanics and laborers and hence the best time

54 *Ibid.*, April 28, 1774; *Colden Papers,* IV, 241; Leake, *op. cit.,* pp. 82–84.
55 *American Archives,* 4th ser., I, 294; Dawson, *Westchester County,* pp. 8–10.

for shrewdly calculating merchants who were playing the political game for all it was worth. Despite this maneuvering, a large number of mechanics and laborers attended the meeting. The gathering was addressed by the merchant Low, who blandly told his hearers "to banish from their hearts all little party distinctions, feuds and animosities" since everyone present meant "the same thing," that is, to preserve their rights and liberties.[56] But the radicals could not be swayed by soothing words. After some discussion, one of their leaders, Francis Lewis, was added to the committee, and eventually two nonmembers of the committee, Joseph Allicocke and Thomas Pettit, were selected secretary and messenger respectively.

Yet despite these concessions the Liberty Boys regarded the Committee of Fifty-one with suspicion. And well they might, for about forty percent of the committee later became loyalists.[57] Small wonder that Colden assured the Earl of Dartmouth, in a letter dated June 1, 1774, that the Committee of Fifty-one was made up of some of the most prudent and considerate persons in New York! [58]

It was inevitable that the authority of a committee such as this would be defied by the Sons of Liberty. The New York radicals held meetings at which they denounced the Port Bill, took up subscriptions to help the suffering people of Boston, recommended a rigid nonimportation agreement, and organized another committee of correspondence to carry on the work. They also raised an issue long in the making, namely, the share of the unenfranchised masses in matters of public concern. To accomplish this, they organized a committee of mechanics, which, according to Abbott, "claimed equal rights for the classes hitherto excluded from voting." [59] This action was entirely in harmony with the progressive character of the Sons of Liberty, one of whose chief objectives was democratic reform. In fact, just about five years earlier, the New York Liberty Boys had waged a campaign for the use of ballots to make "the suffrage of the People for Places of Trust . . . con-

---

[56] *American Archives, loc. cit.; The New-York Gazette; and The Weekly Mercury,* May 23, 1774.

[57] Dawson states that 21 of the 51 became Loyalists, while Barck puts the figure at 19 (Dawson, *Westchester County,* p. 11*n*; Barck, *op. cit.,* p. 37).

[58] *Colden Papers,* IV, 253. See also Thomas Young to John Lamb, June 19, 1774, Lamb Papers.

[59] Abbott, *op. cit.,* p. 108.

ducive to the Preservation of Liberty. . . ." [60] The creation of the mechanics' committee was not only a step forward from the democratic viewpoint; it was also the answer of the Sons of Liberty to the Committee of Fifty-one, a body which was ready at best to compromise the Revolutionary movement and at worst to scuttle it entirely.

Prodded on by the pressure from below, the Committee of Fifty-one eventually proposed the calling of a Continental Congress to discuss the "deplorable Circumstances" occasioned by the Boston Port Bill and to secure the "Common Rights" of America. It suggested to "the Inhabitants of the City" that Low, Duane, Livingston, Alsop, and Jay be selected as delegates to the proposed congress. Owing to the powerful opposition of the Liberty Boys, the people refused to endorse this conservative slate. In the meantime, the Committee of Mechanics, which by now was in fact the Sons of Liberty, had nominated its own set of candidates, consisting of Low, Jay, Livingston, Lispenard, and McDougall. Later, however, it advised its followers to vote for the original slate of the Committee of Fifty-one on the assumption that the majority would be responsive to public pressure.[61]

With delegates elected to a Continental Congress, the Sons of Liberty realized an objective for which it had been fighting for almost a decade. Less than a year later news of Lexington and Concord reached New York. To the Liberty Boys the decisive moment had come. A city arsenal was accordingly taken and about "600 Muskets with Bayonets and Catrige boxes with each filled with Ball Catriges" seized. The arms were then distributed to "the most active of the Citizens who formed themselves into a Voluntary Corps and assumed the Government of the City." [62] Thereafter the armed citizenry took over all customhouses and public stores. Under the direction of Lamb and Sears all vessels in the harbor were detained. During the months of May and June groups of armed Liberty Boys clashed with British regulars; in fact, on one occasion, under the leadership of Willett, they were successful in

60 William Smith Papers: handbill dated December, 1769, No. 205.
61 Dawson, *Westchester County*, pp. 17, 23–26; Leake, *op. cit.*, p. 94.
62 *N.Y. City during the Am. Rev. . . . Original Papers*, pp. 54–55 (Col. Marinus Willett's narrative). See also F. L. Bronner, "Marinus Willett," *New York History*, XVII (July, 1936), 274.

preventing the movement of British troops to Boston. According to Abbott, these armed acts "were almost, if not quite, the last overt acts of the old Sons of Liberty before the Revolution proper." [63]

To the American Revolution the Liberty Boys contributed both officers and men. In the critical period they were still on the alert to detect the slightest sign of counterrevolutionary activity,[64] serving as a democratic leaven in the formative post-war society.

[63] Abbott, *op. cit.*, p. 143.

[64] In March, 1784, they held two meetings. At one they expressed their belief that the Tories were plotting to establish a monarchy; at the other they suggested a program of action involving the exile of all loyalists. S. I. Pomerantz, *New York, an American City, 1783–1803* (New York, 1938), pp. 82–83. A number of leaders among the Sons of Liberty purchased forfeited loyalist estates. See H. B. Yoshpe, *The Disposition of Loyalist Estates in the Southern District of the State of New York* (New York, 1939), pp. 29n., 30–32, 41, 42, 46, 58, 69–72. For the influence of the Liberty Boys on the Irish revolutionary movement see *infra*, pp. 337–38. It is interesting to note that on the eve of the Civil War an anonymous writer, in a pamphlet entitled *The "Sons of Liberty" in 1776 and 1856* (New York, 1856), p. 8, urged his countrymen to organize under the banner of Liberty and emulate their forefathers by overcoming the new tyranny of Slavery.

*E*liphalet Dyer: Connecticut

Revolutionist ~~~~ GEORGE C. GROCE, JR.

BEFORE there can be an adequate understanding of revolutionary movements there must be some knowledge of the lives of revolutionists. According to Van Tyne, "The culture, the dignity, the official rank, the inheritors of wealth tended to support the old order." [1] While he was forced to qualify this assertion with respect to the Virginia planters, it was his view that in New England the socially elect were "cold toward rebellion." To this generalization there are, however, numerous exceptions. It clearly was not applicable, to take one example, to Eliphalet Dyer. Perhaps a study of Dyer and his interests may indicate, in some degree, how so many Connecticut men of property and position chose to break with the parent country during the crucial years of the American Revolution.

In his prime, Eliphalet Dyer (1721–1807) of Windham, Conn., was, perhaps, as influential a leader as the colony could boast.[2] He held high office in the legislature of Connecticut, was emissary to England on a matter of far-reaching importance, served with more or less distinction in the Continental Congress for many years, was a judge of the Connecticut superior court, and was a person of assured social position throughout his life.

Eliphalet Dyer came of a substantial New England family. His

[1] C. H. Van Tyne, *The War of Independence: American Phase* (Boston, 1929), p. 31.
[2] Note, for example, that Dyer receives 132 lines in the Index to the Revolutionary series of the Connecticut Archives (the files of the Connecticut General Assembly) as compared to 120 lines for Roger Sherman. Dyer manuscripts are to be found at the Connecticut State Library, Connecticut Historical Society, Massachusetts Historical Society, New York Public Library, New York Historical Society, Historical Society of Pennsylvania, Library of Congress, and Huntington Library. The main printed sources are the *Susquehannah Company Papers* (Wilkes-Barre, 1930–33) and *Letters of Members of the Continental Congress* (Washington, 1921–36). Since there are some errors in the article on Dyer in the *Dictionary of American Biography,* the present essay may be regarded as a minor biographical contribution.

great-grandfather, Thomas Dyer, was an influential resident of Weymouth, Massachusetts. His father, Lieutenant Colonel Thomas Dyer, was a person of standing in his home community at Windham, Connecticut.[3] Born September 14, 1721, Eliphalet was reared in this "very handsome little town," [4] and may have received some early tutoring at the hands of Thomas Clap, who, after a pastorate at Windham, became a distinguished president of Yale College. At any rate, Dyer was ninth on a list of twenty-one graduates at Yale College in 1740.[5] After graduating he married Huldah, daughter of Colonel Jabez Bowen of Providence, R.I., and turned to the law as a life's profession. In this vocation he soon attained an enviable distinction.[6]

Dyer now embarked upon a threefold judicial, political, and military career. In 1746 he was appointed a justice of the peace for Windham; he continued in that office until 1762, at which time he received a higher office. Between 1747 and 1762 he served eleven sessions as one of Windham's two deputies to the Connecticut general assembly. In the latter year he was elected to the upper house or council. Upon his entrance into that body his service as justice of the peace for Windham terminated.

Dyer's military career is enigmatic. He became a captain of militia in 1745, a major in 1753, and a lieutenant colonel in September, 1755.[7] However, the only engagement in which he is said to have served prior to the latter date was long celebrated in local song and story. This was the "Battle of the Frogs" (1754) in a Windham pond. A panic caused by the croaking of frogs has long been a source of merriment at Dyer's expense.[8] However, in 1755 he took the field as lieutenant colonel in the third Connecticut regiment

---

[3] Cornelia C. Joy-Dyer, *Some Records of the Dyer Family* (New York, 1884), pp. 97–98.

[4] François Jean Chastellux, *Travels in North America* (New York, 1827), p. 26.

[5] *Biographical Sketches of the Graduates of Yale College* (New York, 1885–1912), 1st ser., p. 638.

[6] Vital statistics are from the *Records of the Dyer Family;* Dyer's professional prominence comes out clearly in the Connecticut Archives (hereafter cited as Conn. Archives) at the Connecticut State Library. See "Finance and Currency," IX, 104b.

[7] For Dyer's selection for civil and military offices see *Connecticut Colonial Records* (hereafter cited as *Conn. Col. Rec.*), IX, X, XI.

[8] Lilian Marsh Higbee, *Bacchus of Windham and the Frog Fight* (Willimantic, Conn., 1930), p. 19. Cf. Henry Barnard's remarks as quoted in Crofut's *Guide to the History . . . of Connecticut* (New Haven, 1937), p. 867.

sent against Crown Point. Whether he actually participated in any battle is not known. But he was present at Lake George as late as November and was mustered out of service on December 10 of the same year. There is no evidence that he played an important part in this famous but abortive expedition.[9]

Meantime, Dyer had been actively maturing a plan which was to absorb his attention for the better part of twenty years. During the 1750s a desire for expansion toward the frontiers was as prevalent in Connecticut as it was elsewhere in America. Some Connecticut Yankees were speculating in the wild lands of Vermont, while others, led by Dyer, determined to stake out a claim to lands westward of New York. The western limit of Connecticut under her royal charter of 1662 was the Pacific Ocean. Thus the speculators could contend that their claims lay within the boundaries of Connecticut.

On July 18, 1753, at Windham, Conn., the Susquehannah Company, with Dyer as one of the principal leaders, was organized to acquire lands along the Susquehanna River in Pennsylvania. John Henry Lydius, a Dutch trader of less than spotless reputation, secured from certain sachems of the Six Nations a deed to these lands. Although the validity of the Indian deed was open to question on a number of points, the company now made plans for settlement. In 1753 Dyer was sent to the Susquehanna with a committee to appraise the lands and to negotiate with the Indians. In May, 1755, the company petitioned the Connecticut general assembly for permission to apply to the Crown for a charter, and the permission was granted without the legislature's taking any position on the legality of the claims under the terms of the Connecticut charter. However, the outbreak of the French and Indian War put a temporary stop to the company's plans for expansion.[10] Meantime, Dyer had materially strengthened his political influence in the colony when in May, 1762, he was elected one of the twelve

9 *The Papers of Sir William Johnson* (Albany, 1922), II, 198, 259; Connecticut Historical Society, *Collections*, IX, 34, 269–71.

10 An admirable brief account of developments is in Julian P. Boyd, *The Susquehannah Company* (New Haven, 1935). A more complete treatment of the subject as well as a full presentation of the sources prior to June, 1772, may be found in Boyd, *The Susquehannah Company Papers* (Wilkes-Barre, 1930–34). Except when otherwise specified, the material on the company is based on sources in the latter volumes (hereafter cited as *Susq. Co. Papers*).

assistants who constituted the upper house or council of the Connecticut general assembly. His appearance there was a first harbinger of the ascendancy in Connecticut politics which the Susquehannah Company soon was to enjoy.[11]

As the Seven Years' War came to a close, the company renewed its plans for pacifying the Indians, settling the land, and securing a charter from the British government. In March, 1763, Dyer and Woodbridge went, well supplied with presents, to negotiate with the Indians at Johnson Hall, the estate of Sir William Johnson. But no Indians appeared. Undaunted, the company now voted to send Eliphalet Dyer to England to secure a royal charter. The salary of a hundred and fifty pounds a year plus expenses was attractive, and Dyer lived handsomely upon it. From England he wrote to Jared Ingersoll, "I make a point of it allmost every week to make my appearance att Court att St. James . . . present King, Queen, the Royal family, Nobility, Gentry etc. . . . att Church once a Week, at play near as often. I have seen often both Commedys and Tragedies, Operas, Oratorios, Burlettas, Balls and Ridottoes. . . ." He also attended the English law courts as well as the debates of the Lords and Commons.[12]

But the forthright Dyer was unaccustomed to the slow and devious ways of Whitehall. Nevertheless, for nearly a year he waited, making friends and distributing shares in the company to persons in the highest available stations, before making direct appeal to the Crown. At last, in July, 1764, he signed a petition to the King in council for a grant of the Indian lands purchased by the company. But in view of the strong position of the Pennsylvania proprietors as well as the Indian policy of the government, that petition was predestined to failure.[13]

Meantime, the Grenville program for stationing soldiers and collecting revenues in America was taking form. In April, 1764, Dyer explained to Jared Ingersoll that,

It seems determined to fix upon us a large Number of regular Troops under pretence for our Defence; but rather designed as a rod and Check over us, and are determined to raise a fund in America for their

---

[11] *Conn. Col. Rec.,* XIII, 3.
[12] "Ingersoll Papers," New Haven Colony Historical Society, *Papers,* IX, 289.
[13] *Susq. Co. Papers,* II, 292–96.

Support, at first by dutys on Trade as being the least alarming, a Stamp duty propos'd but for the present postpon'd, and a direct and possitive tax is not Scrupled and believe will be soon attempted . . . fear all the United Indeavors of the Colonys will not Avert the Impending blow.[14]

However fearful Dyer may have been of the results of the ministerial policy, it is clear that he, like Franklin, did not foresee the full measure of colonial resentment. In fact, Dyer, much to his subsequent chagrin and his enemies' enjoyment, actually secured a position as "Controller of the Custom House in New London to prevent the Salors running molasses, but found that would not do and . . . flung up that office . . . [to become] one of the Honorable Judges of our Superior Court." [15]

Though Dyer had returned to Windham as early as January, 1765, he had scarcely resumed his accustomed ways of living before news reached Connecticut that Parliament had placed a stamp tax on American deeds, bonds, licenses, leases, ships' papers, pamphlets, and newspapers. There were turbulent demonstrations in the towns of eastern Connecticut. Jared Ingersoll, the stamp distributor for the colony, was surrounded by a mob of horsemen and compelled to resign his office, while the general assembly met in extraordinary session to elect delegates for a general congress which was to meet at New York and frame united protests against the recent acts of Parliament.[16]

As senior delegate to the Stamp Act Congress, Dyer appears to have found his Susquehannah connections more of a liability than an asset. Naturally his interest in this land speculation could hardly win him Pennsylvania support. Thus, the most influential Connecticut delegate, so far as committee assignments were con-

[14] "Ingersoll Papers," pp. 290–91. Cf. letter of Dyer to Governor Fitch, Sept. 20, 1765, *Connecticut Courant;* Sept. 20, 1765, L. H. Gipson, *Jared Ingersoll* (New Haven, 1920), p. 119n.

[15] "Plain Facts," *Connecticut Courant*, Jan. 12, 1767, and *New London Gazette*, Jan. 23, 1767, quoted in *Susq. Co. Papers*, III, 247. The announcement of his comptroller's appointment appeared in the *Connecticut Courant*, Oct. 29, 1764, and is quoted in *Conn. Col. Rec.*, XII, 299n. For other documents relating to the appointment see Conn. Hist. Soc., *Collections*, XVIII, 351; I. Minus Hayes, *Calendar of Franklin Papers*, I, 47; S. Peters, *General History of Connecticut* (London, 1781), p. 347n. He was appointed superior court justice in May, 1766. *Conn. Col. Rec.*, XII, 455.

[16] For general accounts of these developments see Gipson, *Jared Ingersoll*, chap. vi, and Groce, *William Samuel Johnson* (New York, 1937), chap. iv.

cerned, was Dyer's lifelong friend William Samuel Johnson. However, when Congress finally drafted its resolves, Dyer did yeoman service in securing their acceptance by the Connecticut general assembly.[17]

For some in the colony November 1, 1765, was a calamitous date, but for Eliphalet Dyer it was a lucky day. Governor Fitch was required on pain of a heavy penalty to take an oath faithfully to enforce the provisions of the Stamp Act. When the governor called his council together to administer the oath, all but five of the assistants withdrew from the council chamber. Dyer declared:

I was the only one that then made a public declaration to the Governor and Council, that it was an oath in my opinion contrary to the oath the Govr and Council had before taken to maintain the rights etc. of the Colony, that it was an oath I myself could not in conscience take, neither could I be aiding, advising or assisting therein.[18]

In the events which followed, politics was mixed with patriotism. Two groups, largely centered in the eastern part of the colony, were eager to be rid of Governor Fitch. The New Light faction had originated during the "Great Awakening" and, because its members suffered under certain legal disabilities, had come to take an active part in the colony's political life. As early as 1759 they sought to unseat Governor Fitch and several of his councilors, but failed by a narrow margin. Moreover, because of his attitude to their company, the Susquehannah shareholders were eager to defeat Governor Fitch. The "respectable populace," who opposed Governor Fitch and who christened themselves "Sons of Liberty," staged demonstrations and held conclaves throughout eastern Connecticut.[19]

But support in the west was essential to success. There were about a thousand Episcopalian votes in the colony and these were centered largely in the west. In December, Dyer was writing to

---

[17] "Journal of the Stamp Act Congress," Hezekiah Niles, *Principles and Acts of the American Revolution* (New York, 1876), pp. 155–69; W. S. Johnson MS Journal at Columbia University and in the Bancroft Transcripts, New York Public Library; *Conn. Col. Rec.*, XII, 420.

[18] Dyer to W. S. Johnson, Dec. 8, 1765, Johnson MSS, Conn. Hist. Soc.

[19] These matters are discussed by the writer in *William Samuel Johnson*, pp. 59–67, and in "Benjamin Gale," *New England Quarterly*, X (1937), 699–707. Cf. Samuel A. Peters, *A General History of Connecticut*, pp. 96, 286, 289–90.

William Samuel Johnson, probably the most distinguished Anglican in the colony, minimizing the extent of the disorders occasioned by the "respectable populace" in the east and prophesying
Johnson's election to the council. Johnson replied promptly, suggesting that the group for which he spoke "co-operate" in the eastern "system" of voting; he even suggested supporting Dyer for
governor or deputy governor.[20] In May, 1766, Fitch and the four assistants who administered the Stamp Act oath were defeated, while
Johnson and three new assistants were elected. However, it was not
a clear-cut victory. True, the Susquehannah shareholders were rid
of a governor they disliked, but even so, New Lights, antistamp-
men, and even an Episcopalian shared the fruits of victory.

Dyer now prepared to move forward on three fronts. After declining to go to England as Connecticut's special agent in the Mohe-
gan Case, he had the pleasure of seeing that agency placed in June,
1766, in the skillful hands of his "Dear Brother [William] Samuel"
Johnson. Throughout the next five years Johnson acted as un-
official agent for the company in England, although not invariably
as the shareholders would have chosen. Nevertheless, the selection
of Johnson for the English mission must have seemed to Dyer like
a victory for himself and the company.[21]

Secondly, after the Indian boundary line was fixed by the terms
of the Treaty of Fort Stanwix, November 5, 1768, Dyer urged that
the company make immediate military occupation of the Susquehannah region. Although Dyer declined to assume command of
the forces, he did defend those settlers who, for their violent actions, became involved in the Pennsylvania courts.[22]

The third objective—that of having the colony assume and actively prosecute the company's claim to the western lands under
the "sea-to-sea" grant of the charter of 1662—could not be accomplished without control of the colony's government. Dyer and his
associates seem to have sought this control in May, 1769.[23] In No-

[20] Dyer to Johnson, Dec. 8, 1765, and Johnson to Dyer, Dec. 19, 1765, Johnson MSS,
Conn. Hist. Soc.

[21] On these points see Dyer's letter to Johnson of Dec. 8, 1765, cited above, and
William Samuel Johnson, pp. 68–69, 87–88, 112–13.

[22] Boyd's *Susquehannah Company* gives a clear general account. Cf. *Susq. Co. Papers*,
III, 100, 141, 155, 190, 197–98, *passim*.

[23] *Connecticut Courant*, May 19, 1769.

vember of the same year, after the death of Pitkin, it seemed certain that Trumbull and Dyer, both active Susquehannah men, would become governor and deputy governor. But, to Dyer's great mortification, Matthew Griswold was elected deputy governor, while Benjamin Gale, the most articulate and vitriolic opponent of the company, published a devastating *Letter to J. W. Esq.* denouncing the company and all its works. This publication Dyer answered in a diffuse but clear defense of the company's position, entitled *Remarks on Dr. Gale's Letter to J. W. Esq.*[24]

In 1770 the company suffered a temporary reverse when William Samuel Johnson, the agent for the colony, advised Governor Trumbull and Colonel Dyer that it would be highly inexpedient for the colony to assume the company's claims. In these views Johnson was fully sustained by his colleague, the "Omniscient" Richard Jackson.[25] Nevertheless, in the spring of 1771, the Connecticut legislature finally determined that the Wyoming Valley lay within the limits of Connecticut as defined by its charter. British counsel, to whom the claim was submitted for an advisory opinion, advised, after a hasty review of the case, that the colony had good legal right, but hinted that it was not prudent to press the claim. Thereupon the general assembly sent Dyer, Johnson, and Strong to Philadelphia, where they arrived on December 14, 1773, to negotiate with Governor Penn. But Penn refused to negotiate, and both colonies, in a wave of excitement, prepared for the coming contest.[26] After the incorporation of Wyoming as a Connecticut township in 1774, Dyer and Trumbull were said to have received every one of the five hundred votes.[27]

In Dyer's correspondence there was a growing tone of resentment toward the mother country. Along with the other judges, he dressed in homespun during the nonimportation movement following the Townshend Acts, and he roundly but cautiously denounced "every attempt to enslave this country."[28] As the greater

[24] See Joseph Chew to Sir William Johnson, Nov. 7, 1769, and Chew to W. S. Johnson, Dec. 9, 1769, *Susq. Co. Papers,* III, 195, for Dyer's disappointment. Both pamphlets are reprinted in *Susq. Co. Papers,* Dyer's in III, 247–68.

[25] *William Samuel Johnson,* pp. 87–88.

[26] *Ibid.,* pp. 112–13. For the commissioners' report see *Conn. Col. Rec.,* XV, 465–82.

[27] Boyd, *Susquehannah Company,* p. 39.

[28] Dyer to W. S. Johnson, March 10, 1769. Johnson MS, Conn. Hist. Soc.; Dyer to Johnson, Aug. 8, 1769, Bancroft Transcripts, New York Public Library.

struggle between the parent country and the colonies had come
to overshadow the lesser struggle between Connecticut and Pennsylvania, Dyer aligned himself with the radicals. His long and fruitless
residence in England, his leadership in an economic venture which
(without British intervention) seemed to promise much, his jealousy of Connecticut's privileges of self-government under her
charter of 1662, his fear of Parliamentary taxation, and his residence in the heart of Connecticut's most radical section made this
alignment all but inevitable.

Windham was indeed a hornet's nest of radicalism, and Dyer
was ever sensitive to the currents of public opinion. After the "Intolerable Acts" of 1774, when Parliament closed the port of Boston
and abridged Massachusetts's privileges of self-government, the
town meeting of Windham not only resolved that Parliament had
no right to tax the colonists but also declared that its freemen
would drink no tea. In June the resolves of Windham against the
Boston Port Bill and the military government of Massachusetts
were so extensive as to cover four folio pages.[29] Moreover, the
Windhamites, like the residents of neighboring towns, declared
with vigor that the colony should send delegates to a general congress.[30] On July 13, 1774, Eliphalet Dyer was the first-named of
four Connecticut delegates selected to represent Connecticut at the
first Continental Congress.[31]

The delegates reached Philadelphia on September 1 and set
about their deliberations. John Adams noted that Dyer spoke not
only "often and long" but also "heavily and clumsily." Dyer was
clearly aligned with the left wing in Congress, for before the end
of September he had declared for immediate and complete commercial boycott of Britain and had foretold that the English
"would not sheath the sword in order to execute their plan for
subdueing America." On October 26 he left Philadelphia to take
part in securing Connecticut's compliance with the resolutions of
Congress.[32]

When the second Continental Congress met, blood had been

[29] MS Resolves of the town of Windham, Conn., in the Boston Committee of
Correspondence MSS, New York Public Library.
[30] (New London) *Connecticut Gazette,* June 10, 17, 24, July 1, 8, 1774.
[31] *Conn. Col. Rec.,* XIV, 324.
[32] Burnett, *Letters of Members,* I, 67, 69–71; cf. *Journals of the Continental Congress,* I, 27.

shed and war was in progress. Dyer, who had been warned of the danger of proceeding by water and who, as he confessed, "had rather tarry a little longer before . . . [having] the honor of being hanged for my dear Country," set off for the second Congress in Silas Deane's "Leathern Conveniency." In proposing the journey Dyer had urged, "we can Chatt, we can sing, we can dispute everything, Scold and make friends again every half hour. . . ." [33] After arrival on May 10, Dyer remained almost constantly at Congress until the sixteenth of the following January. Certainly Dyer was not a leading member. John Adams characterized the Colonel as, "long-winded and round-about, obscure and cloudy, very talkative and very tedious, yet an honest, worthy man, means well and judges well." [34] Dyer was important rather as a member of a homogeneous and far from conservative New England group. By October he was convinced that the British were "bent upon . . . [American] destruction" and by November, 1775, he was said to favor a declaration of independence.[35]

Meantime he worked at fever heat collecting supplies, urging on this and encouraging that person or group to ever greater zeal. Even the Susquehannah Company, in the service of which "he had thrown away the prime of his life," he now subordinated to the larger interest of the country, warning the men at Wyoming that "a jarr between two colonies may be of almost fatal consequences to the whole." [36]

But despite Dyer's ardor in the cause of liberty, coupled with his efforts to secure jobs for his constituents [37] and his insistence that the seat of Congress be removed to Hartford, he was not re-elected to his post in October, 1775. Some say his defeat was occasioned by the machinations of a disgruntled Susquehannah faction, but Ezra Stiles believed the general assembly thought "Liberty most secure under frequent changes of Delegates." [38] At any rate

---

[33] Dyer to Deane, April 14, 1775, N.Y. Hist. Soc., *Collections*, XIX, 42–43.

[34] John Adams, "Diary," *Works* (Boston, 1850–56), II, 422–23.

[35] *Journals of the Continental Congress* (Library of Congress ed.), II, 482, 488.

[36] Burnett, *Letters of Members*, I, 172–73, 186, 286.

[37] Dyer to Samuel Adams, May 10, 1776, Adams MSS, New York Public Library; *Connecticut Naval Office* (New London, 1933), II, 265, 284; Dyer to Major General Schuyler, April 2, 1777, Emmett Collection, New York Public Library; Burnett, *Letters of Members*, I, 122–29, 168.

[38] N.Y. Hist. Soc., *Collections*, XVII, 92, 98–99; Ezra Stiles, *Literary Diary* (New York, 1901), I, 636.

Dyer "set off in a violent hurry" for home on January 20. His observations on the way home he communicated in a hitherto unpublished letter to Samuel Adams, dated at New Haven on January 28, 1776:

The Jerseys appear spirited. Animated principally by Ld Sterling . . . New York appears Poorly[?] and desolate you would scarce see any person as but few in the Streets Carts and Waggons all employ^d in Carrying out Goods and furniture the Men of Warr lying broad side against the Town and near the Wharfs sails bent and prepared at a moment's warning[.] their present consternation in New York arises from the Near approach of Gen^{ll} Lee with a formidable body of Connecticut Troops I believe of between 2 and 3 thousand Completely armed Cloathed and accoutred which give more terror to New York than all the Russians and Irish Catholicks Threatened to be sent over by the Tyrant of Great Britain. Their Convention sent out Embassadors etc Meet and Treat with Gen^{ll} Lee to delay him if possible until they could hear from Congress to whom they had sent an express as I understood in order to procure them to interdict Gen^{ll} Lee's March into New York if possible

I was surprised to find some few (who were professed Whigs there) much against Gen^{ll} Lee's coming at this season, when they have the gravest reason to believe the Ministerial Troops will soon get footing there and strongly fortifyed unless Gen^{ll} Lee with his spirited army should prevent by taking first possession and fortifying, which I suppose is his design, unless prevented by your Congress, which if done by them, I pronounce will loose the Confidence of New England who have the expedition much at heart, and esteem as their greatest security. How long shall York and their delegates obstruct Measures most salutary for this Country? I tarried but one night in New York found them much divided in sentiments . . . but my time was so short there that I am not able to determine on which side lies the Majority.

On Thursday I arrived at the Confines of New England where the scene was Immediately changed[.] one heart one mind one spirit seem^d to animate[.] the whole country appear^d all in arms Company after Company in succession in the road well cloathed for a winter campaign well armed and accoutred; at Stamford the town was full of Soldiers, Number of Gentⁿ of the first figure and family, . . . young Gentlemen of fortune and fashion placing themselves in the Ranks All chearful but decent placing the Highest Confidence in their Gen^{ll} [Dyer talked to General Lee, the commander, who] is amazed at the spirit of the people and that he was able by the sound of a Horn in a few days, not more than 8 or ten, to have thousands flocking to his Standard and from only the Westward part of the Colony, is well armed and Cloathed and not one farthing money advanced either to officer or soldier. . . .

I long^d to have some Principal Gent^n of Philadelphia on the road with me to make their observations and see the amazing difference of the two countrys.

. . . Only beware of false brethren you have enemies but believe me your Friend etc. Eliph^t Dyer.[39]

By February 8, however, Dyer was at New London inspecting the colony's defenses, and before the end of the month he was urging that Samuel Adams coöperate in having the harbor made headquarters for the Continental navy.[40] In the spring he and William Williams, having been sent to Philadelphia to secure funds from Congress, received $166,666.66.[41] In June Dyer served as one of a Connecticut legislative committee to draft resolutions favorable to independence, but on July 4 Dyer was serving with the Committee of Safety at the "Lebanon War Office," and in August he was one of two delegates sent to confer with Washington on "every subject needful" to secure the country's independence. In December he represented Connecticut at a war conference held in Providence.[42]

The strenuous exertions of Dyer in behalf of the Revolutionary cause were recognized in October when he was reëlected to his old seat in Congress; but he declined on the ground of his own "ill health, as well as some others of my family." [43] Nevertheless, the following June he was back again in Congress. This time he served from June 27, 1777, to April 3, 1778, and from December 15, 1778, to April 6, 1779,[44] and, though punctilious in attendance, was on no important standing committee. His congressional service was characterized by zeal rather than by distinction. The minor committees on which he served dealt with military matters and supplies. For prosecuting the war he gave enthusiastic and consistent

[39] Samuel Adams MSS, New York Public Library.
[40] *Conn. Col. Rec.*, XV, 233; Conn. Hist. Soc., *Collections*, XXIII, 16; Dyer to Adams, Feb. 27, 1776, Adams MSS, New York Public Library.
[41] *Conn. Col. Rec.*, XV, 248; Conn. Archives, Revolution, XXI, pt. 2, 311a, b, 314; *Journals of the Continental Congress*, IV, 272.
[42] See *Public Records of the State of Connecticut* (Hartford, 1894–1922), I, 10, 10n, 120, 584–99, *passim*, for Dyer's public services; Force, *American Archives*, 5th ser., III, 776.
[43] Conn. Archives, Revolution, V, 122; Force, *op. cit.*, 5th ser., III, 475.
[44] Dates of congressional service are taken from Burnett's *Letters of Members of the Continental Congress*, I–VIII, *passim*.

support to Washington. In framing the Articles of Confederation
he favored the principle of one vote for each state, with congressional delegations varying from two to seven members.

In view of the Susquehannah question, it is significant that Dyer
opposed, and Pennsylvania supported, a precise definition, in the
Articles, of state boundaries. Moreover, Dyer was unwilling to
grant Congress the sole right of determining the western boundaries of states. The significance of the latter vote had, as we shall see,
some important consequences for Connecticut.[45]

As Dyer expressed it, he was "obliged to support himself and
family, to Expend a considerable part . . . [of his] real Estate"
because he was not paid for congressional service.[46] The death of a
son twenty-two years old, the serious illness of Mrs. Dyer, together
with the fatal illness of a second son, brought this period of congressional activity to a close on April 6, 1779.[47] From that date to
the middle of 1782 Dyer was occupied with state duties. He attended the council, sat upon the bench of the superior court, and
discharged a number of duties connected with prosecuting the war.
He participated in a convention at Hartford which recommended
that Congress be granted power to collect its requisitions on states
by using military force. It is not certain that he supported this
viewpoint, but it is clear that the movement of his mind was
toward a stronger Federal government.[48]

In June, 1782, when the Susquehannah question was once more
in the air, Dyer reappeared in Congress. Prior to November he
was primarily occupied with negotiations preliminary to a congressional court of arbitration which was to hear the conflicting
claims of Connecticut and Pennsylvania. First, Dyer suggested that
Connecticut reserve "a certain extent of territory beyond the
claims of Pennsylvania" in case the people of the former state
"should be so unfortunate as to lose their cause with Pennsylvania." Then, on November 12, he set off for Trenton, where the

[45] *Journals of the Continental Congress*, VIII–IX, *passim*.
[46] Conn. Archives, Revolution, XXI, 32a.
[47] Dyer to David Trumbull, Sept. 19, 1778, Emmet MSS, New York Public Library;
Gravestone inscriptions of the two sons reproduced, *New England Historical and
Genealogical Register*, LXXI (1917), 183.
[48] Conn. Archives, Revolution, XIX, 282, *Conn. State Rec.*, II, 562; Edmund C.
Burnett, *Catholic Historical Review*, XXIV (1938), 18; cf. Conn. Archives, Miscellaneous, III, 214.

court was to be held.[49] There were many days of preliminary negotiation before hearings began. On one occasion General Joseph
Reed, an agent for Pennsylvania, asserted that Dyer "speaks twenty
times a day, and scarcely ever finishes one sentence completely."
On the day that Dyer was to present his main argument to the
court, Reed observed, "we expect much amusement, though little
information; perhaps we may be surprised, as indeed we shall be,
if he argues with ability or judgment." [50] Whatever may have been
the quality of the arguments by Dyer and Connecticut's two other
attorneys, jurisdiction over the Susquehannah territory was unanimously awarded to Pennsylvania. In the long run, however, Connecticut did make a reserve of territory (known as the Western
Reserve), but this was secured during the incumbency of Dyer's
friend and successor in Congress, William Samuel Johnson.[51]

Wearied by long years in Congress, Dyer was, by May of 1783,
determined to return to his home and family in Connecticut. Since
his election as assistant in 1762 and his appointment to the bench
of the superior court in 1766 he had been an incumbent of both
offices. However, in May, 1784, he was dropped from membership
in the council since that office was now declared incompatible with
his judicial position.[52] After becoming chief judge of the court,
receiving an honorary LL.D. from Yale, and trying fruitlessly for
several years to secure an increase in salary, he retired from the
bench in 1793.[53] Prior to this, however, Dyer had served as one of
the members of the convention at Hartford which ratified the
Federal Constitution in January of 1789.[54]

During his last years Dyer lived in comfort at the old home in

[49] Burnett, *Letters of Members of the Continental Congress*, VI, 368, 376–77; "Trumbull Papers," Mass. Hist. Soc., *Collections*, 7th ser., III, 376, 387–94, 398, 400–401. For
details of Dyer's congressional work in 1783, see Madison's *Writings*.

[50] W. B. Reed, *Joseph Reed* (Philadelphia, 1847), II, 388–89.

[51] For the proceedings of the court see *Journals of the Continental Congress*, XXIV,
6–32, and for subsequent developments see *William Samuel Johnson*, pp. 115–17,
123–27.

[52] Stiles, *Literary Diary*, III, 120.

[53] *Ibid.*, p. 281; Conn. Archives, Miscellaneous, III, 300, 304, 305d. See Z. Swift, *A
System of the Laws of . . . Connecticut* (Windham, Conn., 1795), I, 93–94, for a
statement of the court's jurisdiction and duties. For the end of Dyer's term see Dwight
Loomis and J. G. Calhoun, *Judicial and Civil History of Connecticut* (Boston, 1895),
p. 138.

[54] B. C. Steiner, "Connecticut's Ratification of the Federal Constitution," American
Antiquarian Society, *Proceedings*, n. s., XXV (1915), 124–25.

Windham, cared for after Mrs. Dyer's death in 1800 [55] by his three Negro servants.[56] On May 13, 1807, the end came. In an obituary praising Dyer for "his highly useful talents, and the faithful and nonorable discharge of his important duties" it was asserted that: "He was one of those illustrious patriots (whose names will live in the annals of our nation to all posterity) who signed the *Declaration of Independence*." [57] However, neither has his name lived in the "annals of our nation," nor, through a trick of fortune, did he sign the Declaration of Independence. Nonetheless, while it is true that the Susquehannah cause, in which Dyer spent so many years of fruitless effort, was a failure, who can doubt that his interest in the company quickened his zeal for the "cause of liberty"? Through his strenuous efforts in behalf of the Revolutionary movement, in and out of Congress, as well as through his support of a stronger Federal union Dyer left his deepest and most lasting impression on American institutions.

[55] Her epitaph is printed in *New England Historical and Genealogical Record,* LXXI, 183.

[56] See Dyer's MS will at the Connecticut State Library.

[57] *Connecticut Courant,* May 27, 1807. There is a three-quarter-length portrait (50 by 40 inches) at the Connecticut Historical Society. There is a reproduction of the painting as the frontispiece of the *Susq. Co. Papers,* Vol. I.

The Patriot Newspaper and
The American Revolution

~~~~ SIDNEY I. POMERANTZ

THE IMPORTANCE of newspaper propaganda in the creation of certain desired emotional attitudes and behavior patterns needs no elaboration; [1] but the role of the newspaper in the shaping of historic events calls for further study.[2] This is true of the period of the American Revolution, for which there is no dearth of primary sources, though only within recent years have competent studies appeared.[3] The loyalists counted heavily on newspaper propaganda, as did their opponents; but in this study merely a limited phase of this activity will be examined—the patriot newspaper in the New York–New Jersey area during the actual period of hostilities. Though restricted in scope, the value of such a specialized inquiry rests on the fact that the patriot printers of these two states had the twofold task of meeting the challenge of Tory propaganda emanating from the British-held city of New York and of operating in a region of great strategic importance.

[1] On the subject of propaganda see H. Alpert, "Operational Definitions in Sociology," *American Sociological Review*, III (1938), 855–61; P. G. Davidson, "Whig Propagandists of the American Revolution," *American Historical Review*, XXXIX (1934), 422n; H. D. Lasswell, *Propaganda Technique in the World War* (London and New York, 1927); R. H. Lutz, "Studies of World War Propaganda, 1914–1933," *Journal of Modern History*, V (1933), 497; L. W. Doob, *Propaganda: Its Psychology and Technique* (New York, 1935), chaps. xvii, xviii; two articles in *The Public Opinion Quarterly*, III (1939): S. I. Hayakawa, "General Semantics and Propaganda," pp. 197 *et seq.*, and P. H. Odegard, "Social Dynamics and Public Opinion," pp. 239 *et seq.*

[2] M. E. Curti, "Public Opinion and the Study of History," *The Public Opinion Quarterly*, I (1937), pp. 84–87.

[3] A. M. Schlesinger, "The Colonial Newspaper and the Stamp Act," *New England Quarterly*, VIII (1935), 63–83; *idem*, "Politics, Propaganda, and the Philadelphia Press, 1767–1770," *Pennsylvania Magazine of History and Biography*, LX (1936), pp. 309–22; *idem*, "Propaganda and the Boston Newspaper Press," Colonial Society of Massachusetts, *Publications*, XXXII (1937), pp. 396–416; P. G. Davidson, "Revolutionary Propaganda in New England, New York, and Pennsylvania, 1763–1776," University of Chicago, Abstracts of Theses, *Humanistic Series*, VII (1928–29), 239–42; *idem*, "Whig Propagandists of the American Revolution," *Amer. Hist. Rev.*, XXXIX, 442–53.

American independence was achieved by military victory, but the extent to which wartime newspaper enterprise contributed to that ultimate triumph of arms opens up a fruitful field for speculation.[4]

The radical colonial leadership that welcomed an armed rebel-lion against British authority was not unaware of the success of the newspaper in furthering its objectives. "It was by the means of Newspapers," wrote the Whig John Holt, printer-editor of the *New-York Journal,* to Samuel Adams, in January, 1776, "that we receiv'd and spread the Notice of the tyrannical Designs formed against America, and kindled a Spirit that has been sufficient to repel them." [5] Nor was contemporary loyalist opinion ignorant of the essential accuracy of this view, for Ambrose Serle, who had for a time conducted the Tory *New-York Gazette and Mercury,* wrote to the Earl of Dartmouth that same year attributing "the present Commotion," in part, to "this popular Engine." [6] These conclusions are amply supported by the evidence adduced in sev-eral revealing studies.[7] When war broke out, therefore, the expec-tation was certain that the newspaper would be utilized to promote the fortunes of the belligerents.

Of the thirty-six papers in the colonies at the opening of the eventful year 1775, only three were in New York City.[8] There were no others in the province of New York or in the neighboring col-ony of New Jersey; but the journals of Hugh Gaine, John Holt,

[4] M. E. Curti, *Peace or War; the American Struggle, 1636–1936* (New York, 1936), p. 22. For some interesting observations on the press and modern warfare see K. Mar-tin, "The Influence of the Press," *The Political Quarterly,* I (1930), 157–78; E. J. Ridg-way, *The Relation of the Press to Social Unrest* (New York, 1907), pp. 30–31.

[5] Holt to Adams, Jan. 29, 1776, Samuel Adams Papers, New York Public Library; also in V. H. Paltsits, "John Holt—Printer and Postmaster. Some Facts and Documents Relating to His Career," N.Y. Pub. Lib., *Bulletin,* XXIV (1920), 494.

[6] Ambrose Serle to the Earl of Dartmouth, Nov. 26, 1776, in B. F. Stevens, compiler, *Facsimiles of Manuscripts in European Archives Relating to America, 1773–1783* (London, 1889–98), No. 2046.

[7] See the articles by Schlesinger and Davidson cited in note 3, *supra;* also M. C. Tyler, *Literary History of the American Revolution* (New York and London, 1897), II, 8–9; J. C. Miller, *Sam Adams: Pioneer of Propaganda* (Boston, 1936), pp. 136, 239; C. A. Duniway, *The Development of the Freedom of the Press in Massachusetts* (New York, 1906), chap. viii; M. Kraus, *Intercolonial Aspects of American Culture on the Eve of the Revolution* (New York, 1928), p. 91; E. Channing, *A History of the United States* (New York, 1910), II, 489; B. Faÿ, *Notes on the American Press at the End of the Eighteenth Century* (New York, 1927); H. Hastings, ed., *Public Papers of George Clinton* (New York and Albany, 1899–1914), I, 61–62; S. N. D. North, *The Newspaper and Periodical Press* (Washington, U.S. Census Office, 1884), p. 23.

[8] I. Thomas, *History of Printing in America* (Albany, 1874), II, 8.

and James Rivington exerted a wide influence and reflected three sharply defined groups of opinion regarding the controversy with the mother country. Holt's Whiggism was beyond question; Rivington's conservatism was equally well known; and Gaine wavered between the two horns of the political dilemma until war forced a decision upon him.

Of the three New York printer-editors, Gaine had been longest in the publishing field, his newspaper dating back to 1752.[9] An Anglican in religion, affiliated with the court party in politics, and a beneficiary of provincial and city printing contracts,[10] Gaine's self-interest should have been a sufficient motive for boldly espousing the royal cause; but he had not always been subservient to authority,[11] and as the tension increased, he drifted toward the radical position. When in the spring of 1775 Lieutenant Governor Colden approached Gaine about publishing General Thomas Gage's version of the Lexington and Concord incidents, the printer at first showed reluctance and then categorically refused to do so.[12] Instead of questioning Gaine's loyalism, Colden was inclined to place the responsibility for this attitude on Hancock and Adams, who were at that time in New York. Whatever influence the radical New Englanders may have exerted on Gaine, other facts would seem to indicate that he was then on their side anyway.

The columns of his paper gave good publicity to the proceedings of Revolutionary committees and the Continental Congress, referred contemptuously to "the ministerial army," and ridiculed the enemies "to the Liberties of America." [13] Finally, despite the British victory on Long Island, Gaine, early in September, 1776, joined the patriots and, to avoid the King's troops already pre-

[9] C. S. Brigham, "Bibliography of American Newspapers, 1690–1820," American Antiquarian Society, *Proceedings*, n. s., XXVII (1917), 423.

[10] V. H. Paltsits, "Hugh Gaine," *Dictionary of American Biography*, VII, 91–92; W. G. Bleyer, *Main Currents in the History of American Journalism* (Boston, 1927), p. 97; Thomas, *op. cit.*, I, 301; C. R. Hildeburn, *Sketches of Printers and Printing in Colonial New York* (New York, 1895), pp. 76–79; C. Evans, *American Bibliography*. . . . (Chicago, 1903–34), V, 453.

[11] Thomas, *op. cit.*, II, 109–10; Bleyer, *op. cit.*, p. 97.

[12] Colden to Gage, May 31, 1775, in *Letterbooks, 1760–1775* (N.Y. Hist. Soc., *Collections, Pub. Fund Ser.*, IX, X, 1876–77), II, 414.

[13] *N.Y. Gazette and Weekly Mercury*, Oct., 1775–Sept., 1776, *passim;* also cf. P. L. Ford, *The Journals of Hugh Gaine, Printer* (New York, 1902), I, 51–53; O. T. Barck, Jr., *New York City during the War for Independence* (New York, 1931), p. 146.

paring to take New York City, transferred his paper across the
Hudson to Newark "in East New-Jersey." Here, from September
21 to November 2, *The New-York Gazette and Weekly Mercury*
appeared.[14] Precisely what the circumstances or considerations
were that prompted Gaine to return to New York are not known.[15]
There was no intimation in the Newark issue for November 2 that
it was the last in that town. However, this much is certain: Gaine
was concerned about "the great and uncommon expence attending the carrying on business at this juncture." Whatever his motives, on November 11 the *Gazette and Weekly Mercury* once more
came out in New York City under his direction. While Gaine had
been in Newark, the British had appropriated the name of his
paper for a weekly conducted by Ambrose Serle. When Gaine returned, Serle relinquished this paper to him. Serle later wrote to
the Earl of Dartmouth suggesting that the Crown subsidize papers
in the various colonies in view of the "incredible Influence" the
existing journals wielded among "the great Bulk of the People." [16]

Once Gaine had decided to throw in his lot with the loyalists, he
lost no time in energetically supporting the British cause. Thus,
in his paper for November 11, he denounced "the Absurdities and
Falsehoods with which the Leaders of the present Rebellion endeavour to keep up the Spirits and Opposition of their deluded
Followers." In the trying years of journalistic strife that followed,
he reiterated or elaborated on this theme, now and then singling
out a particular patriot politician, editor, or newspaper to receive
the full force of his indignation.[17] The Whigs, for their part, were
prompt to reply to the abuse heaped upon them by what Holt, in
1777, referred to as "Lord and General Howe's" gazette, and
pounced on any item the inaccuracy of which was sufficiently glar-

14 *N.Y. Gazette and Weekly Mercury* (Newark), Oct. 12, 1776.

15 For some conjectures as to Gaine's motives in forsaking the American cause, see
Ford, *op. cit.*, I, 55; G. H. Payne, *History of Journalism in the United States* (New
York and London, 1920), p. 127; A. M. Lee, "Pioneer American Daily in 1783," *Editor
and Publisher*, March 10, 1934, p. 37; L. Sabine, *Biographical Sketches of Loyalists
of the American Revolution* (Boston, 1864), I, 451–52; Hildeburn, *op. cit.*, pp. 74–75;
Thomas, *op. cit.*, II, 109.

16 Serle to the Earl of Dartmouth, Nov. 26, 1776, in Stevens, *Facsimiles*, No. 2046.
This interesting letter is reprinted in full in Ford, *op. cit.*, I, 57–58, and in part in
Bleyer, *op. cit.*, p. 93, and Payne, *op. cit.*, pp. 120–21.

17 See, for example, *N.Y. Mercury and Gazette*, March 10, April 14, 1777; March 20,
1780.

ing to afford opportunity for satirical comment.[18] But if the patriot printers looked with suspicion on Gaine's paper, they, nevertheless, read it regularly, as did American political and military leaders seeking helpful information.[19] Nor were the columns of this Tory journal irrevocably closed to news emanating from patriot sources, for occasional extracts from Whig papers were published, often without any supplementary qualifying comment.[20]

Fourteen years after Gaine's initial newspaper venture, John Holt, a Virginian, with important family connections and a long experience in printing and publishing, established the *New-York Journal*.[21] Previous to the launching of this paper, Holt had won a reputation for militancy in opposing enforcement of the Stamp Act, and the subsequent policy of his journal justified the expectations of his radical well-wishers.[22] John Adams called him "the Liberty printer," [23] a reference quite descriptive of his interests and activities. Holt greeted William Goddard's efforts to found a "Constitutional Post Office" system free of British surveillance, and early in May, 1775, hailed the demise of the royal postal organization, "which has long been an engine in the hands of the *British* ministry to promote their schemes of enslaving the Colonies and destroying the *English* Constitution." With his printing shop already a unit in this system, Holt called on the New York delegation to the Continental Congress to press for his official appointment as postmaster for the province, citing his opposition to British tyranny and to the resulting obstructions to the sale and distribution of his newspapers by the royal postal officials.[24] But

18 *N.Y. Journal,* July 14, 1777; June 1, 1778. Ford, *op. cit.,* II, vi, calls attention to many discrepancies between Gaine's diary jottings and his newspaper stories.

19 Cf. letters in Force, ed., *American Archives* (Washington, 1837–53), 5th ser., III, 1153, 1490; *Public Papers of George Clinton,* VII, 360, 362; Stevens, *Facsimiles,* No. 848.

20 See, for example, *N.Y. Gazette and Mercury,* March 8, 1779.

21 Paltsits, "John Holt—Printer and Postmaster," N.Y. Pub. Lib., *Bulletin,* XXIV (1920), 483–86; *idem,* "John Holt," *D.A.B.,* IX, 180–81; F. Hudson, *Journalism in the United States, 1690–1872* (New York, 1873), pp. 121–22; Hildeburn, *op. cit.,* pp. 89, 92; Thomas, *op. cit.,* I, 303, II, 116; Brigham, "Bibliography of American Newspapers," Am. Antiquarian Soc., *Proceedings,* n. s., XXVII (1917), 263.

22 Schlesinger, "The Colonial Newspaper and the Stamp Act," *New England Quarterly,* VIII (1935), 69, 71, 75, 82, 83.

23 Diary of John Adams, Aug. 25, 1774, in *Public Papers of George Clinton,* I, 97. Adams was then in New York City.

24 *N.Y. Journal,* May 4, June 1, 15, 1775; *American Archives,* 4th ser., II, 537.

Ebenezer Hazard was chosen instead, a disappointing circumstance, which failed, however, to cool Holt's ardor for the patriot cause [25] or dampen his interest in the postal service, improvement of which he considered so essential to newspaper publishing.[26] Moreover, the Provincial Congress began to award him printing work, giving him an economic stake in the Revolution.[27]

The inexorable progress of the war forced Holt, as it had Gaine, to seek refuge outside of the city of New York. The patriot printer found a haven in Connecticut after putting out his last paper in New York at the end of August, 1776, but returned to the state when the committee of safety offered him £200 annually to act as state printer on condition, however, that he publish a weekly newspaper.[28] This he undertook to do.[29] On July 7, 1777, the *New-York Journal,* which "for ten months past" had been "overwhelmed and sunk, in a sea of tyrannic violence and rapine," as its publisher put it, appeared once again, this time from Holt's new printing shop near the Kingston (Esopus) courthouse. In the first issue Holt promised that he would exert himself as before "to a defence and support of American rights and freedom" and solicited the coöperation of the public and the state in facilitating the expeditious transmission of news to his office. Moreover, as his paper was "printed under the patronage of the state," he bespoke the aid of members of the legislature in securing subscriptions.[30]

Three months later Holt was on the move once more, his official printing and publishing activities disrupted by the British attack on Kingston. It was the proud boast of the English that the place had been "reduced to ashes"; it was Holt's sad lament, however,

---

[25] A. G. Vermilye, "The Early New York Post Office," *Magazine of American History,* XIII (1885), 117, 119; *The Constitutional Gazette,* Oct. 21, 28, 1775; W. E. Rich, *History of the United States Post Office to the Year 1829* (Cambridge, Mass., 1924), pp. 48, 49.

[26] Holt to Adams, Jan. 29, 1776, in Samuel Adams Papers; also in Paltsits, "John Holt—Printer and Postmaster," pp. 490–95.

[27] *Journals of the Provincial Congress . . . of New-York, 1775–1777* (Albany, 1842), I, 303 (Feb. 16, 1776).

[28] *Ibid.,* pp. 750 (Dec. 12, 1776), 793 (Jan. 31, 1777); John Holt to James Duane, March 7, 1778, in Duane Papers, Vol. IV, No. 115, N.Y. Hist. Soc.

[29] *Loc. cit.;* John Holt to the New York assembly, Feb. 13, 1778, in Emmet Collection, No. 10994, N.Y. Pub. Lib.; also in Paltsits, "John Holt—Printer and Postmaster," pp. 495–96.

[30] *N.Y. Journal,* July 7, 1777.

that only one-sixth of his possessions were saved.[31] With £200 received from the state, plus some borrowed funds, he went to Poughkeepsie to take up his work again. Financial difficulties, prior assembly printing, and lack of help prevented him, however, from reviving his weekly until May 11, 1778, seven months after its temporary suspension at Kingston.[32] The "Printer to the State of New-York," as Holt was now described on the masthead of his journal, explained that a scarcity of paper compelled him to reduce the size of his weekly from four to two pages and that the irregularity of the postal service put it up to the subscribers to get their copies. These deficiencies were but two of the many that continued to plague his newspaper to the end of the war. His paper supply was so low in the summer of 1779 that he wondered whether to issue the weekly at all, as it was necessary to curtail its contents to "the most material events." [33]

Another serious handicap to newspaper publication was the fluctuation in prices resulting from the depreciation of the paper currency. To meet this situation, Holt fixed the cost of a subscription at the pre-war rate of three shillings a quarter (thirteen weeks) and stood ready to accept, on the basis of pre-war purchasing power, farm produce or other commodities in quantities of equivalent value. This he was willing to do despite his complaint that expenses were ten times as great as before the war; but he felt that such an exchange arrangement, if generally adopted, would discourage the depreciation of "our paper currency." Inflationary prices not only hampered subscription payments but made printing costs, both for labor and materials, prohibitive.[34] Nevertheless, Holt struggled along until mid-August, 1780, when he gave notice that the failure of many subscribers to pay for their papers "and other discouragements" made discontinuance of the journal im-

[31] Typescript notation in N.Y. Pub. Lib. copy, *New York Senate Journal, 1777–1779,* in Rare Book Room; *Public Papers of George Clinton,* II, 457–58n; Holt to the New York assembly, Feb. 13, 1778, Emmet Coll., No. 10994, or Paltsits, "John Holt—Printer and Postmaster," pp. 495–96.

[32] *Loc. cit.;* Holt to Duane, March 7, 1778, in Duane Papers, Vol. IV, No. 115; *New York Assembly Journal, 1777–1778,* pp. 16, 27, 69 (March 5, 1778), 109, 125; *N.Y. Journal,* May 11, 1778.

[33] *Ibid.,* Aug. 16, 1779.

[34] *Ibid.,* May 10, 1779; Sept. 18, 1780; also cf. Oct. 6, 1777; John Holt to George Clinton, April 15, 1780, in *Pub. Papers of George Clinton,* V, 624–25.

minent. Three months later "the difficulty and expence" of obtaining paper forced publication to stop.[35]

Nine months later, on July 30, 1781, the *New-York Journal* was revived, Holt requesting prepayment of subscriptions, for, said he, "experience has abundantly convinced him, and all the news Printers on the Continent, of the impropriety of publishing newspapers or Advertisements on trust." But it was not long before arrears began to pile up once more, and neither threats of suspension nor warnings of legal proceedings against delinquent customers had any effect.[36] On January 6, 1782, for the fourth time since the beginning of the war, the *Journal* was discontinued, in this instance to permit Holt to devote all his time to bringing out the state laws.

Even by comtemporary standards the *New-York Journal* was hardly an attractive weekly. The type was so small as to arouse complaint; but the editor justified its use because of the limited paper supply and the demand for "the greatest quantity of intelligence." While the exigencies of war cut down on the customary length of contributions, these continued to be unduly extended. News and other items were reprinted from patriot journals throughout the country, and foreign and Tory papers were also drawn upon, though there seems to have been some difficulty in obtaining copies of the latter.[37] Legislative enactments were given preference over all other copy, and, on occasion, news was sometimes entirely omitted to make room for the publication of statutes. As for the quantity of news available, that was dependent on the success with which the postriders eluded capture by the enemy or interception by highwaymen,[38] the state of the weather,[39] and the family affairs of the printer.[40] The distribution of newspapers was a precarious problem. Postal facilities were hardly adequate; but even more serious was the fact that the postriders carried papers simply as a courtesy, no regular mailing privileges being accorded

[35] *N.Y. Journal*, Aug. 14, Nov. 6, 1780; cf. Brigham, "Bibliography of American Newspapers" (April, 1918), p. 90; *N.Y. Assembly Journal, 1781*, pp. 27, 28 (Feb. 15, 17).
[36] *N.Y. Journal*, Aug. 13, Oct. 22, Dec. 3, 1781.   [37] *Ibid.*, Nov. 8, 1779.
[38] *Ibid.*, Nov. 22, Dec. 6, 1779; Sept. 17, 1781.
[39] *Ibid.*, Jan. 10, 24, 1780. Subscriptions fell off sharply during the winter, as there was "seldom much news." See, for example, "A Printer's Lament," *ibid.*, Feb. 28, 1780.
[40] *Ibid.*, Sept. 14, 1778.

newspaper deliveries. Holt sought to impress on Samuel Adams the necessity for remedying this situation; [41] but throughout hostilities complaint continued, and when Holt suspended his paper in January, 1782, he urged "such regulations in the Post-Office, as will make it that public conveniency, which was the original design of its institution, and which a free people have a right to require it to be made." [42]

In the light of all the heartbreaking difficulties he encountered in putting out the *Journal*, Holt's editorial policy is especially noteworthy. For over three years, he declared in November, 1780,

he . . . faithfully endeavoured, not only to give his readers such intelligence as it most concerned them to receive, but upon all occasions, so far as the . . . limits of his paper would admit, to inculcate such principles, moral, political and religious, as he conceived, had the most direct and powerful tendency to promote public and private happiness.[43]

For his news columns, he announced in August, 1777, he wished authentic, firsthand accounts from authoritative sources, and regretted that such reports had not always been available, even if they dealt with American reverses, for "it is . . . much the safest, to know the reality of our circumstances, that we may make provision and exert ourselves proportionately." [44] However, Holt was not always at liberty to print without restriction military intelligence that had been forwarded to him.[45] On the other hand, he did not hesitate to repudiate news reports, no matter how favorable to the American side, that proved to be inaccurate. Thus, in the fall of 1779, he acknowledged that he was "much concerned and ashamed at the part he has (tho' innocently) had in propagating falsehoods, thro' a paper devoutly consecrated to truth," and reaffirmed his determination to trust only the accounts of "official authority." [46] The following year he again apologized for unintentional inaccuracies, maintaining that the poor postal facilities occasioned "the circulation of a thousand falsehoods" and that the

[41] Holt to Samuel Adams, Jan. 29, 1776, in Samuel Adams Papers; also in Paltsits, "John Holt—Printer and Postmaster," p. 494.

[42] *N.Y. Journal*, Nov. 23, 1778; Jan. 24, May 29, 1780; Aug. 13, 1781; Jan. 6, 1782.

[43] *Ibid.*, Nov. 6, 1780. [44] *Ibid.*, Aug. 18, 1777; cf. *ibid.*, Sept. 11, 1780.

[45] Holt to George Clinton, April 15, 1780, in *Pub. Papers of George Clinton*, V, 626, 633.

[46] *N.Y. Journal*, Sept. 6, 1779; cf. *ibid.*, Aug. 30, 1779.

impatience of the public for news encouraged "inventions and conjectures." [47]

In other ways Holt displayed notable professional integrity. When demand was made that he reveal the name of one of his contributors, he said he would do so only on "apparent necessity or good reason," otherwise "it would be a great restraint upon the Freedom of the Press, and prevent many important public advantages of it." [48] Before publishing a letter criticizing another person, the editor would seek by preliminary inquiry to substantiate the justice of the charges.[49] He scrupulously sought to avoid printing contributions that gave uncalled-for offense to others; [50] and he stopped publication of an advertisement which he believed to be false.[51]

Judged in connection with his position as a patriot leader, Holt's publishing standards and independent spirit are not surprising. He was no servile printer, but an influential participant in the struggle for independence. His revolutionary ardor was genuine and his personal and property sacrifices were considerable. He was in regular communication with civil and military officials, and his sound advice was apparently well received.[52] He had an excellent understanding of the technique of propaganda, as is revealed by his ruthless analysis of the motives and methods of the Tory press, excerpts from which he occasionally published, usually cautioning his readers that loyalist news was "selected, modeled or fabricated, to suit" the British designs.[53]

In reprinting from Gaine's paper several items of foreign news favorable to the American cause, Holt reminded his public "that TRUTH is not the object intended for, or to be expected from" the Tory papers, which abounded in fabrication, additions, and omissions, "in order to give . . . the intended colouring," so as "to keep up the spirits of their party, and discourage their opposers"; and he expressed little "confidence in any of their reports, even when they happen to be true." [54] But he published them, never-

[47] *Ibid.*, Aug. 7, 28, 1780.   [48] *Ibid.*, Jan. 25, 1779.   [49] *Ibid.*, May 8, 1780.
[50] *Ibid.*, May 15, 1780.   [51] *Ibid.*, Aug. 17, 24, 1778.
[52] *Independent Gazette, or N.Y. Journal Revived,* Jan. 15, 1784; *Pub. Papers of George Clinton,* IV, 547–48; V, 624–26.
[53] *N.Y. Journal,* March 1, 1779.
[54] *Ibid.*, March 6, 1780; also cf. *ibid.*, May 25, 1778.

theless, generally to refute them. Proclamations addressed by the British to the Americans were reprinted, followed by editorial criticism; and Tory news that was palpably inaccurate inspired virulent denunciation of "a most tyrannical, cruel and rancorous enemy, long practised in all the arts of treachery, deceit and false-hood" seeking "to reduce the inhabitants of America, to a state of absolute slavery, under the government of an arbitrary tyrant." [55] Sometimes an "atrocity story," too horrible to be true, was repub-lished from its Tory source without any comment, as was done with the report that two deserters from the Continental army were caught and crucified on a special machine in Dutchess County.[56] Thus, Holt systematically sought to undermine the integrity of the opposition press, a task in which he was aided by correspond-ents who with great care laid bare the "lying and misrepresenta-tions" of the enemy journalists.[57] At the same time, he endeavored to present the patriot side of events "in the best dress" and exerted himself to secure as wide publicity as possible for the proceedings and activities of the American Congress.[58]

Probably more successful than either Holt or Gaine as a news-paper publisher was James Rivington, scion of a London printing firm, and a comparative newcomer in the city.[59] In the spring of 1773 he began publication of *Rivington's New-York Gazetteer; or the Connecticut, New-Jersey, Hudson's River, and Quebec Weekly Advertiser*. Pretentious as this name was, the circulation of the paper seemed to warrant it, for by October, 1774, its editor boasted a weekly impression of 3,600 copies, widely distributed in America and Europe. So promising an achievement for so young a paper could not but influence Rivington "to do ample justice to

---

[55] *Ibid.*, May 8, 1780.   [56] *Ibid.*, June 1, 1778.

[57] See, for example, "O," in *N.Y. Journal*, Sept. 15, 1777, and his strictures on the Tory printers of New York City, whom he characterized as "servants of the servants of the abandoned servile profligate ministry of an infatuated tyrannical Prince."

[58] George Clinton to James Clinton, May 2, 1779; John Holt to George Clinton, April 15, 1780, in *Pub. Papers of George Clinton*, IV, 791; V, 623–26.

[59] For details of Rivington's publishing and bookselling career before coming to New York see S. Rivington, *The Publishing Family of Rivington* (London, 1919), pp. 42, 45; Thomas, *op. cit.*, I, 306, 307; Hudson, *op. cit.*, p. 132; Hildeburn, *op. cit.*, pp. 105 *et seq.*; Paltsits, "James Rivington," *D.A.B.*, XV, 637–38; Sabine, *op. cit.*, II, 215–19; G. H. Sargent, "James Rivington, The Tory Printer," *Americana Collector*, II (1926), 337.

all opinions in the unhappy dispute with the mother country." [60]
There is no reason to doubt the sincerity of his effort to refrain
from partisanship at this time. In November, for example, he
wrote to the Bradfords, Philadelphia printers, urging them to send
him "some of any new pamphlets published on either side of the
dispute." [61] But the radical strategists were intolerant of such a
position and willingly endorsed a movement of intimidation designed either to silence Rivington or to win him over to their
point of view. Toward the end of 1774 action was taken to bar the
New-York Gazetteer from South Carolina, and a boycott of the
paper and its advertisers was advocated in Connecticut.[62]

By March of the following year the committees of inspection for
Newport, Rhode Island, and Freehold, New Jersey, also resolved
to boycott Rivington, accusing him of printing "glaring falsehoods" in his pamphlets and newspapers, which were "dirty, scandalous, and traitorous performances." Curiously enough, the Newport committee invoked "the freedom of the press" in justification
of its stand, defining that concept as the "diffusion of liberal sentiments on the administration of Government." [63] That same month
Rivington clashed with the New York City committee of observation over an account of its proceedings, but promised to be more
accurate thereafter.[64] Nevertheless, the tide of indignation against
him mounted steadily, perhaps not without justification, for
though Rivington raised the cry of persecution, there was on its
way to him a commission as "His Majesty's Printer" for the province of New York, carrying with it an annual subsidy of £100,
payable from January 1 of that year.[65]

[60] *N.Y. Gazetteer*, Oct. 13, 1774. The subsequent widespread boycott movement
against this newspaper would appear to indicate that Rivington's circulation claims
were not entirely inspired by a desire for advertising patronage.

[61] James Rivington to Messrs. Bradford, Nov. 17, 1774, in Rivington Miscellaneous
MSS, N.Y. Hist. Soc.; also cf. Rivington to Bradford, Jan. 28, 1775, *ibid.*; H. B. Dawson,
Westchester County, N.Y., during the American Revolution (Morrisania, N.Y., 1886),
p. 127.

[62] The Friends of America to the Committee of Observation for . . . Hartford,
Conn., Dec. 5, 1774, in James Rivington Papers, N.Y. Pub. Lib.; also in Misc. MSS,
"F," N.Y. Hist. Soc.

[63] *American Archives*, 4th ser., II, 12–13, 36–37; also cf. resolutions of the freeholders and other inhabitants of New Windsor, N.Y., March 14, 1775, to boycott
Rivington until he repents, *ibid.*, p. 133.

[64] *Ibid.*, pp. 50–51.

[65] Secretary Pownall to James Rivington, April 5, 1775, in E. B. O'Callaghan, *Doc.
Rel. Col. Hist. N.Y.* (Albany, 1857), VIII, 568; *American Archives*, 4th ser., II, 51.

In mid-April Rivington was hung in effigy in New Brunswick, New Jersey, "merely," as he explained, "for acting consistent with his profession as a free printer." Printing a cartoon of himself hanging from a tree,[66] he denounced the participants in the incident as "some of the lower class of inhabitants," "little, flabby, piddling politicians," "snarling curs," "the very dregs of the city," incidentally paying his respects to "the pediculous Committee at Freehold." Having rid himself of these epithets, Rivington proceeded to reaffirm his policy of publishing the views of "all parties," and maintained that the newspaper was a public institution, and that in England he had been taught to consider the "liberty of the press" as "the great security of freedom." He contended that "his enemies make liberty the prostituted pretence of their illiberal persecution of him" while "their aim is to establish a most cruel tyranny"; and he concluded by praising "the good old laws and constitution, under which we have so long been a happy people." [67] Twist and turn as he would, the "freedom of the press" had now become too thin a cloak to hide Rivington's true sympathies. Though his *Gazetteer* still advertised for sale "the several pamphlets on the Whig and Tory side," [68] a more forthright pronouncement as to his attitude was essential if he wished to remove the stigma of loyalism. This was made two weeks later when Rivington expressed himself as friendly "to the Liberties of this Continent," regretted that his publishing activities had "given great offence," and promised that it would not happen in the future.[69]

Yet those who espoused the radical cause did not stay the mob of vengeance, which, ignoring this protestation of patriotism, vented its spleen on Rivington six days later, forcing him to seek protection on board a British warship. "His crime," wrote Cadwallader Colden to Lord Dartmouth, "is only the Liberty of his

[66] Neither cartoons nor caricatures appeared in the patriot newspapers of New York and New Jersey during the war, though the printers probably appreciated the propaganda value of such illustrations. Cf. William Murrell, *A History of American Graphic Humor* (New York, 1933-38), I, 4, 11-12, 28; Isabel S. Johnson, "Cartoons," *The Public Opinion Quarterly*, I (1937), p. 3.

[67] *N.Y. Gazetteer*, April 20, 1775.

[68] *Loc. cit.;* Hildeburn, *op. cit.*, p. 117, holds that the greater number of pamphlets from Rivington's press in 1775 favored the Tory position. For a tentative check list of Rivington imprints, see Sargent, "A Bibliography of the Imprints of James Rivington," *Americana Collector*, II (1926), pp. 370 *et seq.*

[69] *N.Y. Gazetteer*, May 4, 1775.

Press." [70] With his property at stake and his life in danger, the distraught printer appealed first to the New York City committee of correspondence and then to the Continental Congress to permit him to resume his business. In a most humble petition, dated May 20, 1775, Rivington pleaded his case with moving eloquence, emphasizing that though he was an Englishman by birth he was an American by choice. Richard Henry Lee, corresponding with Gouverneur Morris about the case, thought Rivington "should be forgiven," as it was "not yet too late" for him "to exert his powers in defence of the liberty and just rights of a much injured Country." [71] The New York Provincial Congress, to whom the matter was finally referred by the Continental Congress, concurred in this view and, after exacting a solemn declaration from Rivington that he would scrupulously observe the Continental Association, guaranteed that he would not be molested in his publishing activities.[72]

Once more the *Gazetteer* appeared, its masthead announcing that it was "printed at" Rivington's "OPEN and UNINFLUENCED PRESS," but in mid-August this was omitted from the colophon.[73] What the specific provocation, if any, was is not apparent, but on November 23, about one hundred troopers from Connecticut, with Isaac Sears in the lead, rode into the city, confiscated Rivington's type, and smashed his press, thereby concluding a series of extralegal exploits. This incident, though probably countenanced by public opinion, stirred some of the city and provincial patriot leaders to resentment. In a request for the return of Rivington's type to its jurisdiction, the New York Provincial Congress cautioned Governor Trumbull of Connecticut that "the glory of the present contest for liberty" should "not be sullied by an attempt to restrain the freedom of the Press." [74] As for Rivington, this new

[70] Colden to Lord Dartmouth, June 7, 1775, in *Letterbooks*, II, 422.

[71] N.Y. State, Secretary of State, *Calendar of Historical MSS Relating to the War of the Revolution*. . . . (Albany, 1868), I, 88–89; *American Archives*, 4th ser., II, 726.

[72] *Ibid.*, I, 836–37, 899, 1284; also cf. E. C. Knight, comp., *New York in the Revolution as Colony and State*, Supplement, ed. by F. G. Mather (Albany, 1901), pp. 104–5, for some minor printing work performed by Rivington for the Provincial Congress.

[73] Cf. Thomas, *op. cit.*, II, 120; Evans, *American Bibliography*, V, 187, No. 14437.

[74] For newspaper comment and the legislative proceedings dealing with the destruction of Rivington's press, see J. Shannon, ed., *Manual of the Corporation of the City of New York, 1868*, pp. 813–27; also Thomas, *op. cit.*, I, 309, 310; II, 121; Dawson, *Westchester County*, pp. 128–31; C. Becker, *History of Political Parties in the Province of New York, 1760–1776* (Madison, 1910), pp. 245–46; E. F. De Lancey, ed., *Thomas*

display of force determined his course of action. He went to England for another press and in the fall of 1777 was back in New York where, as "Printer to the King's Most Excellent Majesty," he issued the *New-York Gazette,* changed within two months to *The Royal Gazette.* Perhaps an even more formidable journalistic adversary than Gaine now confronted the patriot editors,[75] and they lost no time in meeting the new challenge.[76]

In the trying years that followed Rivington was the object of patriot newspaper criticism that pictured him as a "lying printer," a "learned rogue," and a "varlet." [77] But he was no less sparing in his characterizations of the opposition, referring, for example, to Governor William Livingston of New Jersey as "pernicious" and "infernal." [78] Despite this animosity, reports "from the rebel papers" were reprinted in the *Royal Gazette* without comment, and one irate correspondent even complained that the Tory press was "stuffed with pro's and con's" on the issues of the war.[79] By 1782 there came a definite shift in editorial policy, the previous intransigent attitude giving way to a more conciliatory tone. In February of that year Rivington defended himself from an attack in the *Pennsylvania Packet,* at the same time admitting that ill-founded reports occasionally crept into his paper. Samuel Loudon, of the *New-York Packet,* reprinted this from the *Royal Gazette* with the observation: "There are some hopes of a bad man when he is ashamed of his villainy." [80] That August, Rivington went still further in his acknowledgment of "past errors," inspiring Loudon to conclude "that Satan, Rivington & Co. have thoughts of breaking up partnership." [81] Pleasing as these admissions must have been to the patriot editors, they nevertheless did not let the public forget

---

Jones' History of New York during the Revolutionary War (New York, 1879), I, 66, 561–68; II, 341–42.

[75] Ford, *op. cit.,* I, 62; Thomas, *op. cit.,* I, 310.

[76] Cf. F. L. Pattee, ed., *The Poems of Philip Freneau* (Princeton, N.J., 1902), II, 191. For the numerous instances in which Freneau made Rivington the butt of his satirical verse, see *ibid.,* pp. 116 *et seq.,* 120 *et seq.,* 124, 143 *et seq.,* 169 *et seq.,* 190 *et seq.,* 229 *et seq.*

[77] *N.Y. Journal,* Aug. 2, 1779; *N.J. Journal,* July 26, 1780.

[78] James Rivington to William Eden, March 27, 1780, in Stevens, *Facsimiles,* No. 725.

[79] *N.Y. Loyal Gazette,* Dec. 27, 1777; "Anglo-Americanus," in *N.Y. Royal Gazette,* June 23, 1779.

[80] *Ibid.,* Feb. 20, 1782; *N.Y. Packet,* March 14, 1782.

[81] *Ibid.,* Aug. 8, 1782; Thomas, *op. cit.,* II, 122–23; Pattee, *op. cit.,* 168–70.

Rivington's past record.[82] But the Tory printer was not disheartened by this persistent hounding, taking it all in good spirit.[83]

Between the outbreak of hostilities in the spring of 1775 and the adoption of the Declaration of Independence in the summer of 1776, two new papers made their appearance in the city of New York: John Anderson's *Constitutional Gazette* and Samuel Loudon's *Packet*. Anderson's newspaper came out in the summer of 1775 as a champion of the Whig cause.[84] Only eight by nine and a quarter inches in size, consisting of four pages, it sold for two coppers a single copy or ten shillings a year and was published twice a week, something of an innovation at the time. Distributed by news carriers, this journal claimed a circulation of about two thousand copies in and around New York City as well as "a considerable number" of country subscriptions. On the basis of these figures, it solicited advertisements at "half the price charged by others." [85] Anderson probably did not exaggerate the popularity of his sheet, for its contents apparently appealed to a wider group of readers than did its competitors, and the paper makes interesting reading even today. The British advance on New York, however, forced the suspension of the paper and disrupted Anderson's seemingly thriving publishing, bookselling, and stationery business "at Beekman's Slip." [86]

Loudon's *New-York Packet* commenced publication on January 4, 1776, after being well advertised in the other city papers.[87] It was undertaken, announced the publisher, "by the advice and promised literary assistance of a numerous circle of warm friends to our (at present much distressed) country," and he informed the

[82] See, for example, "Epigram Occasioned by the Title of Rivington's Royal Gazette Being Scarcely Legible," in *N.Y. Packet,* Feb. 21, 1782, and "Rivington's Last Will and Testament," *ibid.,* March 14, 1782.

[83] Pattee, *op. cit.,* II, 190; *N.Y. Packet,* Dec. 19, 1782.

[84] Brigham, "Bibliography of American Newspapers" (1917), p. 395; I. N. P. Stokes, *Iconography of Manhattan Island* (New York, 1915-28), II, 419; E. B. Greene and R. B. Morris, *Guide to the Sources for Early American History in the City of New York* (New York, 1929), p. 66; Thomas, *op. cit.,* II, 124; Hildeburn, *op. cit.,* 150.

[85] *The Constitutional Gazette,* Aug. 23, 1775; May 15, 1776.

[86] *Ibid.,* May 22, 1776; *N.Y. Journal,* Nov. 30, 1775; Hildeburn, *op. cit.,* 152-53.

[87] Brigham, "Bibliography of American Newspapers" (1917), p. 235; A. E. Peterson, "Samuel Loudon," *D.A.B.,* XI, 427-28; *Constitutional Gazette,* Dec. 20, 1775; *N.Y. Journal,* Dec. 21, 1775; Loudon to Dudley Woodbridge, March 29, 1776, in A. J. Wall, "Samuel Loudon: Merchant, Printer, and Patriot; with Some of His Letters," N.Y. Hist. Soc., *Bulletin,* VI (1922), 78.

public that the paper would be a "splendid" one, complete and accurate. Its comparatively handsome appearance did not belie these assurances.[88] Judging from the number of advertisements that filled its columns, the venture was a success from the start. Early in March, Loudon explained his editorial policy:

While the Printer intends to maintain the Liberty of the Press, by publishing decent Essays that may from time to time be sent to him, he begs leave to drop a caution to some of his correspondents, . . . to omit too strong and indecent expressions in their pieces. He is averse to publish such. They give offence to his readers. Do they help the grand American cause? Quite the reverse. Cool reasoning best suits important subjects. He requests writers on controversial subjects to send their names with their pieces, without which he will decline printing them. . . .[89]

But Loudon soon found his freedom as a printer circumscribed by the radicals, who objected to his publication of a pamphlet purporting to refute *Common Sense,* though he contended that "it was written with decency," and "did not express or even imply any disapprobation of the proceedings of the . . . Continental Congress or the glorious Cause, in defence of which Americans are spending their blood and treasure." It did, however, question the wisdom of a declaration of independence. Hailed before the committee of mechanics and then the general committee of inspection, Loudon finally promised to suppress the pamphlet, 1,500 copies of which had already been printed; but, despite this pledge, the mechanics seized "the whole impression" the night of March 19, and burned it. Asking that he be compensated for the resulting loss of some £150, Loudon warned the committee of safety to "secure the liberty of the Press," which was so much in danger that "America may fall a sacrifice to a more fatal despotism than that with which we are threatened." He never received any damages, however, the Provincial Congress disallowing the claim early that June.[90]

[88] *N.Y. Gazette and Mercury,* Jan. 15; *N.Y. Journal,* Feb. 1, 1776.
[89] *N.Y. Packet,* March 7, 1776.
[90] For the pertinent documents in this case see N.Y. State, *Calendar of Historical MSS Relating to the Revolution,* I, 273, 281; *American Archives,* 4th ser., V, 439–40, 1389, 1441–42; VI, 1393; *Journals of the Provincial Congress, etc., of New York,* I, 405–6; *N.Y. Packet,* April 11, 1776; also cf. Wall, "Samuel Loudon," 80; Becker, *op. cit.,* pp. 216, 228, 252; De Lancey, in *Jones' New York during the Revolutionary War,* I, 566–67.

Despite this incident, Loudon had not fallen from political grace, and he was led to expect printing work from the Provincial Congress.[91] With the British hammering at the gates of the city, he made preparations to leave, planning to resume printing at "Fish-Kills, where the Provincial Congress now reside." [92] In December, he came to an agreement with the committee of safety to publish the legislative acts and a weekly paper for one year at a compensation of £200, payment to commence once the newspaper appeared.[93] On January 16, 1777, he revived the *Packet* at Fishkill, publishing it there to the conclusion of the war.

Within a week after publication was resumed, Loudon once again offended official patriot sensibilities, this time by reprinting extracts from Gaine's journal. Though he informed the committee of safety that he had done so merely "to satisfy the curiosity of those who might wish to see what stuff was published at New-York," that body reminded him "that so long as you receive a pension from this House you are their servant." [94] The committee pardoned Loudon, but not long thereafter another patriot printer, John Holt, began to receive the favor of that body.[95] In February, Loudon wrote to John McKesson, secretary to the state constitutional convention, requesting his friendship in counteracting "idle criticism" of the *Packet,* and professed to be insulted because Holt had also been appointed an official printer.[96] That spring Loudon once more was upbraided for indiscreet publications in his paper. Commenting upon this, he wrote to John McKesson: "Pray, must I take upon me to alter or suppress intelligence sent me by gentlemen? . . . I do what I can to please, but I shall never consent to give up my judgment, to be modeled by others." [97]

Notwithstanding the vicissitudes of war, Loudon managed to get the *Packet* out with more or less regularity during the long struggle, successfully overcoming difficulties arising from the scarcity of

[91] S. Loudon to John McKesson, Aug. 13, 1776, in *Journals of the Provincial Congress* . . . , II, 283.

[92] *Ibid.;* notation on flyleaf, N.Y. Pub. Lib. file, *N.Y. Packet,* 1776; *N.Y. Gazette and Mercury,* Sept. 2, 1776.

[93] *Journals of the Provincial Congress* . . . , I, 750 (Dec. 12, 1776); De Lancey, in *Jones' New York* . . . , I, 568; Wall, "Samuel Loudon," pp. 83–84.

[94] *Journals of the Provincial Congress* . . . , I, 780–81 (Jan. 21, 22, 1777).

[95] *Ibid.,* I, 793 (Jan. 31, 1777).

[96] S. Loudon to John McKesson, Feb. 20, 1777, *ibid.,* II, 362.

[97] S. Loudon to John McKesson, May 24, 1777, *ibid.,* II, 445; also cf. *ibid.,* I, 481–82.

paper, the lack of skilled help, and the hazards of communication.[98] Efforts, instigated by the enemy, were made to disrupt the distribution of the *Packet* as well as other patriot papers; [99] and the British authorities discouraged the circulation outside of New York City of papers arriving from England, thus crippling a source of foreign news.[100] The problem of financing the *Packet* was a trying one. Expenses, Loudon complained in February, 1781, were very heavy and hard cash was scarce.[101] That summer he informed the public that "the price of his paper is not adequate to his charge in publishing it," and warned his customers that unless they paid their arrears he would cease publication.[102] In the fall he again announced that subscriptions must be paid promptly, for "the business cannot be carried on without ready cash." [103] Some of the *Packet's* readers were as much as five years in arrears at this time,[104] but nothing that the printer could say and no threats that he made seemed to have any effect.[105] Fortunately, Loudon had other sources of income, for not only did he do printing for the state, but he was the local postmaster, sold books and stationery, and ran a general mercantile establishment.[106]

Beset though he was with almost insuperable publishing difficulties, Loudon never relaxed his editorial standards, his disputes with the state authorities early in the war apparently having failed to dampen his independent ardor. News items, mostly dealing with foreign affairs, were reprinted from the Tory press. Inaccuracies were promptly acknowledged.[107] Rumors, however favorable, were made to wait for verification before being published as fact. When, for example, a report was current in the fall of 1781 that Minorca had been captured, Loudon, in referring to the rumor, observed that it "was propagated by a set of beings in the vicinage of New-

---

[98] *N.Y. Packet*, May 16, Aug. 1, 1776; July 1, 1779; Feb. 15, April 5, Sept. 13, Nov. 8, 1781; March 21, 1782; *Calendar of Historical MSS Relating to the Revolution*, I, 643.

[99] *N.Y. Packet*, June 7, 1781; July 18, 1782. On the other hand, Rivington complained that the "rebel leaders" sought to prevent the reading of Tory papers. *Royal Gazette*, Jan. 6, 1779.

[100] *N.Y. Packet*, Dec. 13, 1781.   [101] *Ibid.*, Feb. 22, 1781.

[102] *Ibid.*, Aug. 9, 1781.   [103] *Ibid.*, Oct. 25, 1781.

[104] *Ibid.*, Dec. 13, 1781.   [105] *Ibid.*, Nov. 21, 1782; Aug. 28, 1783.

[106] *Ibid.*, Sept. 24, 1778; Dec. 2, 1779; Oct. 25, 1781; Dec. 26, 1782; *Journals of the Provincial Congress . . .* , II, 387; notation in typescript, N.Y. Pub. Lib. copy, *N.Y. Senate Journal, 1777–1779*; Wall, "Samuel Loudon," pp. 81–82.

[107] See, for example, *N.Y. Packet*, Dec. 2, 1779.

burgh, called *Trunk Makers;* but as their manufacture is in bad repute with honest men, we return their cob-web news, and shall not publish it till it comes from better authority than theirs." [108] Contributions that might cause unjustifiable offense were carefully edited,[109] and some, especially those dealing unfairly with personalities, were omitted altogether.[110]

As the war continued, other newspapers were started, both on the loyalist and patriot sides. James Robertson established *The Royal American Gazette* in New York in January, 1777, and carried on publication for six years, being aided in his task by his brother Alexander and by two Tory printers from Boston.[111] In the middle of May, 1778, Robertson's paper was included in a plan to give the city a daily news service. Accordingly, his journal, as well as Rivington's, began semiweekly publication, the former coming out on Tuesdays and Thursdays, the latter on Wednesdays and Saturdays, while Gaine's paper appeared regularly on Mondays. With the launching, in September of the following year, of William Lewis's *New-York Mercury,* a weekly which was issued on Fridays, the city's residents were supplied with a newspaper six times a week, an arrangement which continued until the summer of 1783.[112] There was no love lost between the Robertsons and the opposition printers. Holt denounced *The Royal Gazette* as "a prostitute paper printed in New-York . . . under the inspection of British tyranny"; but he admitted, however, that its editors "may some times relate the truth," though one could "never be certain that they do so." [113] As for Lewis's *Mercury,* its editor was a rabid "rebel" baiter, who, "at the risk of his ears," as he explained, thundered against the patriots well into the spring of 1783.[114]

To meet the increased journalistic activity of the Tories, the patriots bestirred themselves to reënforce the efforts of Holt and

108 *Ibid.,* Oct. 25, 1781. 109 See, for example, *ibid.,* March 7, 1776.
110 *Pub. Papers of George Clinton,* VII, 259.
111 Brigham, "Bibliography of American Newspapers" (1917), pp. 489–90; Hildeburn, *op. cit.,* pp. 163–68.
112 Thomas, *op. cit.,* II, 123; Lee, "Pioneer American Daily in 1783," p. 11; Barck, *op. cit.,* p. 150.
113 *N.Y. Journal,* Feb. 15, 1779; also cf. *ibid.,* Aug. 31, 1778; and *N.Y. Packet,* Feb. 14, 1782, where Loudon said of the *Royal American Gazette,* "we cannot expect any thing but effusions of dirt from the miscreants who publish it."
114 Brigham, "Bibliography of American Newspapers" (1917), p. 458; Hildeburn, *op. cit.,* 168–70; *N.Y. Mercury,* June 16, 1780; April 6, 1783.

Loudon. In October, 1777, Governor William Livingston, of New Jersey, sent a message to the assembly urging support of a newspaper. Isaac Collins, previously royal printer for the colony and then state printer, expressed his willingness to assume the task of publication provided the legislature underwrote 700 subscriptions. This it consented to do, recognizing the fact that

a well-conducted Gazette would at any Time, but especially in the present Conjuncture, be of very essential Benefit to the good People of this State. The Enemy by their Emissaries, and the disaffected among ourselves, take all possible Pains to circulate, through the Country, their Papers and Hand bills filled with the grossest Falsehoods and Misrepresentations, and purposely calculated to abuse and mislead the People, while we are without the least available Means of defeating their mischievous Designs, by setting publick Events and Transactions in a true point of View.

Moreover, the assembly felt that such a journal would promote useful knowledge and manufacturing in the state.[115] For his part, Collins informed the public in the first number of his paper, December 5, 1777, that the advantages of publication were so obvious that it would be an impertinence to justify the appearance of a newspaper in the present "Crisis," which required "a quick Circulation of Intelligence . . . to all the American States."[116] *The New-Jersey Gazette,* as the new venture was called, was a pioneer undertaking in the state.[117] Founded at Burlington, the *Gazette* was removed to Trenton, where it resumed publication in March, 1778.[118]

Like the other patriot printers, Collins found himself confronted by many serious obstacles in publishing his weekly. Almost from the very outset, there was a shortage of paper, which necessitated limiting the number of subscriptions.[119] Experienced help was hard to get, even though promised "handsome wages" and exemption from actual military service.[120] The hazards of com-

---

[115] *N.J. General Assembly Proceedings, 1777,* pp. 7–8, 9 (Oct. 11, Nov. 5).

[116] *N.J. Gazette,* Dec. 5, 1777; also "Proposals for Printing by Subscription the New Jersey Gazette," bound in Vol. I, N.Y. Pub. Lib. file, *N.J. Gazette.*

[117] For the three previous newspapers published in New Jersey, none of which proved successful, see Brigham, "Bibliography of American Newspapers" (1916), pp. 415–16, 442, 458–59; also cf. newspaper clipping in Vol. I, N.Y. Pub. Lib. file, *N. J. Gazette;* Thomas, *op. cit.,* I, 316; II, 128, 130–31.

[118] *N.J. Gazette,* Feb. 25, 1778.   [119] *Ibid.,* April 23, 1778.

[120] *Ibid.,* Dec. 16, 1778; Aug. 11, 1779.

munication were a constant worry,[121] as were the possibilities of an invasion by the enemy.[122] Fluctuating prices proved a source of utmost discouragement. Arrears in subscription payments piled up at an alarming rate. In the summer of 1779, Collins complained of "very considerable Losses owing to the Depreciation of the Money, the increased price of Wages and every Article used in the Printing Business." [123] Advertisements, however, seem to have been plentiful and probably brought in some income.[124] But it would appear that the editor depended for his livelihood during the war not so much on the newspaper as on such collateral undertakings as job printing, bookselling, and the retailing of stationery, patent medicines, and general merchandise.[125]

In its editorial policy, the *New-Jersey Gazette* did not differ to any marked degree from the other Whig papers. The "falsehoods" of the loyalist press were effectively pilloried,[126] while, at the same time, items culled from this source were frankly acknowledged.[127] Contributions on the issues of the war filled the columns of this journal, for which Governor William Livingston, hiding behind various pseudonyms, was a steady writer.[128] Collins showed a scrupulous regard for maintaining a reputation for accuracy, rejecting items that were the least doubtful.[129] "Intemperate Effusions" were not wanted; [130] and exacting literary standards were enforced. One correspondent was informed that "the irony" in his piece "was not thought sufficiently pointed"; another was told that he needed "practice in writing." It was explained to a third that "the language" of his essay "being very *incorrect,* the method *confused,* and the object *more obscure,* it cannot be admitted in the *New-Jersey Gazette* until it has undergone a *thorough repair.*" [131]

[121] *Ibid.,* Dec. 20, 1780.   [122] *Ibid.,* June 24 (July 1), 1778.

[123] *Ibid.,* June 23, 1779; also cf. Nov. 25, Dec. 16, 1778; May 5, 1779; March 8, Aug. 30, 1780.

[124] *Ibid.,* Feb. 11, March 18, Sept. 2, 1778; March 3, May 5 (Supplements), 1779.

[125] *Ibid.,* July 29, 1778; May 30, 1781; Jan. 30, 1782.

[126] See, for example, *ibid.,* Dec. 4, 1782.

[127] See, for example, *ibid.,* April 8, Aug. 26, 1778; Jan. 13, 1779.

[128] *N.J. Archives,* 2d ser., II, vi; T. Sedgwick, *A Memoir of the Life of William Livingston . . .* (New York, 1833), pp. 248–49, 282; Davidson, "Whig Propagandists of the American Revolution," 446–47, 449.

[129] See, for example, *N.J. Gazette,* Feb. 23, 1780.

[130] *Ibid.,* Dec. 5, 1777; April 28, 1779.

[131] *Ibid.,* March 21, 1781; Nov. 6, 1782; also cf. Feb. 23, 1780.

A little over a year after the founding of Collins's *Gazette,* another patriot paper was born, Shepard Kollock's *New-Jersey Journal,* which came out in Chatham, February 16, 1779.[132] There is nothing in the first number of the *Journal* to indicate precisely what were the considerations that prompted its editor to establish it. However, when in 1781 he sought encouragement for *The Political Intelligencer,* which he issued two years later at New Brunswick,[133] Kollock stated that the paper was designed for public service as well as "for his own emolument." He went on to explain:

The *utility* of a *publick newspaper* is universally acknowledged; but at *no time* can it more gratify curiosity, or be so beneficial to the community, as in the *present* most interesting *contest* for the preservation of our *freedom,* and of every thing, indeed, estimable in this life, there being a variety of particulars which necessity requires should be communicated to the citizens of the state with all possible dispatch.[134]

Previous to his first newspaper venture, Kollock had been a lieutenant in the American army, from which he resigned, it would appear, in something of a huff.[135]

For Kollock, as for the others of his craft, the hardships of publishing were many, though not insurmountable. Paper was difficult to secure; the postriders were not as faithful in their deliveries as the editor might have wished; [136] and the financing of the *Journal* was precarious. In the summer of 1781, Kollock warned that arrears in subscription payments would compel him to suspend publication.[137] By the fall, he was threatening unpaid subscribers with dire, unnamed consequences.[138] These admonitions must have had

---

[132] Brigham, "Bibliography of American Newspapers" (1916), p. 418; *New Jersey Journal,* Feb. 16, 1779. A facsimile of this number was distributed as a souvenir supplement to the *Elizabeth Daily Journal,* Feb. 16, 1929.

[133] Brigham, "Bibliography of American Newspapers (1916), pp. 420, 434; G. H. Genzmer, "Shepard Kollock," *D.A.B.,* X, 493.

[134] *N.J. Journal,* Nov. 21, Dec. 12, 19, 26, 1781.

[135] Lieut. Shepard Kollock to Col. John Lamb(?), May 15, 1778, Lamb Papers, Box II, No. 35, N.Y. Hist. Soc.; but cf. Genzmer, "Shepard Kollock," p. 493; E. T. Hutchinson, "A Pioneer New Jersey Printer," N.J. Hist. Soc., *Proceedings,* LV (1937), 138–39, 141; A. L. Johnson, in *Elizabeth Daily Journal,* Feb. 16, 1929; unsigned article, *ibid.,* p. 97; J. M. Lee, *History of American Journalism* (Boston and New York, 1923), pp. 89–90.

[136] See, for example, *N.J. Journal,* Jan. 25, 1780; July 17, 1782.

[137] *Ibid.,* Aug. 15, 1781.   [138] *Ibid.,* Nov. 14, 1781.

some effect, for the paper continued to be issued to the end of the war.

Harassed though he was by publication difficulties, Kollock edited his paper with tact and dignity. He refused to permit one of his contributors, a voluminous and skillful writer, to precipitate "a theological dispute." [139] On another occasion, he informed a correspondent that his "satire" was "too poignant" and might "disturb that unanimity which is essential to our welfare at this stage of the war." [140] In the fall of 1780 he rejected "several pieces . . . which are too personal to appear in this paper." [141] Moreover, like his colleague, Isaac Collins, he was very much concerned about the literary quality of his journal; he frankly told one would-be poet: "In the Piece signed *The Miserable Life of a Tory*, we can discover neither rhime nor poetical beauty; such barbarism is unfit for this paper." [142]

Analyzing the wartime problems and activities of the patriot newspapers, the question arises as to precisely how valuable their publication proved in the struggle for independence. The printers themselves considered their efforts eminently successful. John Holt, for example, believed his paper "had some considerable effect in kindling that noble flame that has glowed in the breasts of his countrymen, raised them above their enemies and established their freedom on a permanent foundation." [143] Public officials, both civil and military, were equally certain that the newspapers were helpful to their cause, a conviction that was shared by the British authorities, who seemingly made attempts to stop the distribution of patriot journals. Contemporary confidence in the utility of the press resulted in the founding of new papers during the war, especially necessary because of the increased journalistic activity of the opposition.

Ample justification for the belief that the wartime newspapers were exceptionally serviceable is to be found in an evaluation of the extent to which the objectives of publication were achieved. By skillful refutation and counterattack, the Tory propaganda efforts were neutralized and the reliability of the loyalist editors was com-

---

139 See the printer's reply to "Eumenes," *ibid.*, July 4, 1781; and cf. an essay by "Eumenes," *ibid.*, April 25, 1781.
140 *Ibid.*, Nov. 14, 1781.   141 *Ibid.*, Nov. 8, 1780.   142 *Ibid.*, Dec. 26, 1781.
143 *Independent Gazette, or N.Y. Journal Revived*, Jan. 15, 1784.

pletely undermined. Every attempt was made to use the columns of the newspapers to arouse and maintain fighting morale, patriotic fervor, and national feeling. Contributions were so written as to attain these ends,[144] the patriot editors and their correspondents being highly versed in the art of indoctrination.[145] How effective these efforts were, it is, of course, difficult to ascertain precisely; but we do know that the civil and military leaders read the papers, and we have contemporary testimony that the "pieces in the public prints . . . produced the most agreeable feeling and encouraging prospects, in the minds of the virtuous part of our community." [146]

In other ways the newspapers served the American cause. Legislators, printers in other parts of the country, the clergy, and citizens generally relied on them for accurate and necessary information on public affairs,[147] the editors taking great pains to meet the demand for news of this sort.[148] Resolutions of public bodies, official messages and proclamations, and statutes were published regularly, often at the express order of the state legislatures.[149] Early in the war, the New York committee of safety directed Postmaster Ebenezer Hazard to send it "all those papers heretofore printed or which may hereafter be printed, and which contain the plans or forms of government . . . in the different States." [150] Moreover, the papers were especially helpful to the military. To the printing office there came reports about the movements of the enemy, and in the columns of the press there appeared notices on such army matters as recruiting, cancellation of furloughs, desertions, and requisitioning of supplies. Furthermore, the newspapers served as a forum for the discussion of the theoretical and practical problems involved in building the new state governments as well as a new

144 Cf. "N.R." in *N.Y. Journal,* April 4, 1781.
145 See, for example, "Philo-Patriae" on "Patriotism" in *N.Y. Journal,* Nov. 2, 1775; and "A True Patriot" in *N.J. Gazette,* March 17, 1779.
146 *Ibid.*
147 *Journals of the Provincial Congress . . . ,* I, 689, 694 (Oct. 25, 31, 1776).
148 *N.J. Gazette,* June 23, 1779; *N.Y. Journal,* July 14, 1777.
149 In replying to a complaint that the laws of the legislature took up too much newspaper space, Samuel Loudon reminded his correspondent "that the knowledge of the laws are peculiarly necessary, and useful to the inhabitants" and that "they are published by order of the legislature for" the people's benefit. *N.Y. Packet,* July 26, 1781. The New Jersey general assembly in 1778 ordered the printing of the Articles of Confederation for public consideration, *N.J. Gazette,* April 29, 1778.
150 *Journals of the Provincial Congress . . . ,* I, 689 (Oct. 25, 1776).

nation, a process going on concurrently with the military struggle. Essays on the means to preserve liberty in a republic, the limitations of congressional power, the education of youth, and like subjects were printed.[151] Controversies raged, among other matters, over an acceptable currency system, ways to halt profiteering and speculation, and the place of religion in the state.[152]

This utilization of the patriot newspapers for purposes much broader than those comprehended within the narrow sphere of propaganda activity contributed, in part, to the formulation of an editorial policy unique in a war-torn country. It is surprising to what an extent the Whig printers asserted their independence of outside pressure and showed their resentment of official interference. Considerations of political expediency, it would seem, should have barred many an item that was printed. Published criticisms of public officials and policies were remarkably outspoken.[153] For these American journalists liberty of the press was no mere theoretical concept even in wartime.[154] Equally significant was their scrupulous regard for the truth and accuracy of what they printed. Fully aware though they were of the fine art of persuasion by falsehood, the patriot editors valued their professional integrity too dearly to surrender it for the dubious advantages to be gained by the intentional distortion of events. No less noteworthy, considering the unsettled conditions of the period, was the determination with which these publishers adhered to what they considered acceptable standards of literary quality, showing no hesitation and the utmost frankness in rejecting contributions deemed stylistically faulty.

While this editorial policy was basically the outgrowth of the many-sided character of the services rendered by the patriot newspapers during the war, its adoption was occasioned by several other circumstances. The printer himself was an influential member of

151 See, for example, *N.Y. Journal*, Dec. 14, 1778; *N.Y. Packet*, July 12, 1781; *N.J. Journal*, April 25, 1781, Feb. 6, 1782.

152 *N.J. Gazette*, March 17, 1779; *N.Y. Journal*, March 1, 1779; *N.Y. Packet*, May 3, 1781.

153 See, for example, "A Tradesman of New Jersey" in *N.J. Gazette*, Oct. 28, 1778; "A Farmer" and "Quarter-master" in *N.Y. Journal*, Feb. 22, 1779; "A True Patriot" in *N.J. Gazette*, March 17, 1779; "Cincinnatus," *ibid.*, Oct. 27, 1779; *N.Y. Journal*, Jan. 31, 1780.

154 "Hampden" in *N.J. Gazette*, Dec. 29, 1778; but cf. Duniway, *op. cit.*, pp. 131–32.

the new Revolutionary society. His judgment was respected, and public officials sought his advice. He had a strong sense of his own responsibility as an editor, appreciated the power he wielded, and consciously endeavored to employ his talents for the public good.[155] He understood that in a war for independence, such as the Americans were waging, it was essential to pay more than just lip service to the principle of freedom.[156] His readers expected him to pursue a policy predicated on the liberty of expression. "The public papers," wrote one correspondent in the *New-Jersey Journal,* "are a channel by which every individual may convey his opinions and advice for the public good." [157] Without a free press, held another writer, there is no liberty.[158] A third warned American patriots "never" to "let the press be over awed either by public or private persons. Only let truth and decency be observed, and then . . . speak freely, write freely, of *all* men, and of *all* measures." [159] Still another rejoiced that the liberty of the press had been "secured so . . . that men can tell their grievances." [160] Finally, the fond hope that their papers would be a record for posterity may have been a contributory factor in actuating the patriot printers to pursue the sort of editorial policy that would redound to their credit. Samuel Loudon believed that the *New-York Packet* would be preserved "as a faithful Chronicle of its own time"; [161] and John Holt was no less certain that "newspapers which contain historical account of events, as they occur, at such an important æra as this, will be esteemed in after ages; they will increase in worth the older they grow, and every succeeding generation, will value them more than the former." [162]

The conclusion is warranted that the patriot newspaper editors contributed their share to the winning of American independence, but they did so while observing canons of journalistic conduct all too often forgotten in wartime.

155 See, for example, John Holt's address to the public, in *N.Y. Journal,* July 7, 1777; also *ibid.,* Sept. 25, 1780.
156 Cf. *N.J. Gazette,* Nov. 8, 1780; *N.J. Journal,* Jan. 10, 1781.
157 "Agricola" in *N.J. Journal,* April 20, 1779.
158 "Cincinnatus" in *N.J. Gazette,* Oct. 27, 1779; also cf. *ibid.,* March 17, 31, April 7, 14, 1779; *N.Y. Journal,* April 26, 1779.
159 "Bob-Centinel" in *N.Y. Journal,* Sept. 14, 1778, and *N.J. Gazette,* Oct. 7, 1778.
160 *N.Y. Packet,* April 25, 1782.   161 *N.Y. Journal,* Dec. 21, 1775.
162 *Ibid.,* July 14, 1777.

America and the
Irish Revolutionary Movement in the
Eighteenth Century ━━ MICHAEL KRAUS

BY ITS very existence, said Oliver Wendell Holmes, America is a standing threat to the absolutist governments of the Old World. The America of the eighteenth century was of less threatening aspect, but even then it held within itself the seeds of destruction for Europe's social structure. This does not mean, of course, that events in thirteen far-off colonies were the most important factor in breaking the crust that bounded European society. A changing industrial mechanism and an altered intellectual outlook that challenged respected and even revered mores were enough to disrupt a world. But the vague aspirations of Europeans toward a new universe were given solidity by the concrete appearance of the world of tomorrow in the thirteen colonies. The fortunes of the many thousands who had sailed from Europe to seek a new homeland, with all their fears and hopes, had become part of the stream of consciousness of those who were left behind. For those who missed the *Mayflower* there was at least the hope that on her return trip she would bring back some manifestation of that new spirit arising overseas—new wine to be poured into old bottles. It was the American Revolution which was the "chief factor in the collapse of the Georgian reaction." [1]

England, Scotland, Ireland, France, Belgium, the German states, the Netherlands, the Scandinavian countries, and others to the east and south, all in varying degrees felt the impact of distant events. John Adams was right when he said that a complete history of the

[1] In the preparation of the present study the author was aided by a grant from the Social Science Research Council. The quotation cited is from R. Coupland, *The American Revolution and the British Empire* (New York, 1930), p. 42.

American Revolution would be a "history of mankind during that epoch." [2] The American Revolution and its effects so faded into the more momentous French Revolution that the general student often overlooked the particular influence of America. Probably in no part of Europe were the effects of the American Revolution felt more immediately nor more deeply than in Ireland. Horace Walpole, who heard all and discreetly told some, wrote that "all Ireland is *America mad.*" It was added, "So is all the Continent." [3]

That Ireland was ready for this impulse which came from over the western waters was clearly apparent. Before the days of the Stamp Act the tide of Irish resentment against England had risen higher than that from America. The inspiration of Dean Swift, Molyneux, and, more particularly, Charles Lucas kept alive a discontent that needed little fueling. Molyneux's work, *Case of Ireland Being Bound by Acts of Parliament in England Stated* had a very wide circulation, and as for Swift's *Drapers Letters,* we are told that they were hawked about the streets of Dublin and that every literate man read them. Lucas, who was the editor of the *Freeman's Journal,* was charged with directing the activities of the merchants and traders whose representative he was in Parliament.[4]

Irishmen followed closely the unfolding of the new imperial policy in America after 1763. Letters against standing armies appeared fairly often in the press. One reader asked about a new law relating to the army in America and the billeting of troops on private families. This led him to raise queries as to the constitutional rights that Englishmen have when they go to the colonies. He asked whether such a law for the plantations would not be "a large stride towards enslaving us in the same manner at home? Whether our tamely submitting to fix such shackles on our fellow Subjects in America would not shew that we ourselves were ripe for the same in England?" [5] One rural reader queried whether the humiliation of America was "part of a plan of Humiliation nearer home?" [6] Sympathy was also expressed for American opposition to the proposed establishment of an episcopate. Another letter to the *Free-*

[2] *Works* (Boston, 1850–56), V, 491–96.

[3] Mrs. Paget Toynbee, *The Letters of Horace Walpole,* Vol. IX (June 25, 1776).

[4] Francis Plowden, *An Historical Review of the State of Ireland . . . to . . . 1801* (2 vols., London, 1803), I, 352, 390.

[5] *Freeman's Journal,* April 20, 23, 1765.   [6] *Ibid.,* Feb. 18, 1766.

man's Journal signed "An American" spoke of the right of the
colonial legislatures to tax themselves.[7]

The conflict between the colonies and England over the Stamp
Act was detailed at length in the Irish press, and of course the
American complaints against mercantile restrictions found a warm
response in Ireland. The same issues that were being aired in the
American papers were ventilated in the Irish too. Many essays on
constitutional liberties, attacks on general warrants, and proposals
for Parliamentary reform appeared in the press. Extracts were
printed of John Adams's *Dissertation on the Feudal and the Canon
Law,* and these emphasized the fact that it was the struggle against
temporal and spiritual tyranny that peopled America. To instill
more vigor into the Irish, this sentiment from Adams was quoted:
"The true source of our suffering [at England's hands] has been
our Timidity." [8] Other extracts reminded the reader that many
people in England still were attached to ideals of liberty, but the
real motive for printing portions from the work of Adams was to
marshal arguments against the Stamp Act and against violations of
the English constitution.[9]

The *Freeman's Journal* ran a series of articles on the subversion
of civil authority by the military, and in support printed a memorial drawn up by London merchants against alleged excesses of
the soldiery in the colonies.[10] Fear of an augmented military establishment haunted both the Americans and the Irish. One objector
to a bill for increasing the army pointed to outrages committed by
soldiers in America, London, Limerick, Drogheda, and Cork. Another writer was convinced that the move to increase the army was
proof of "a long-settled scheme for establishing Despotism in every
Part of the Kings Dominions." [11] Almost as if to underline these
fears came news of the Boston Massacre. The Independent Whigs
of Belfast alleged that the troops of the Twenty-ninth Regiment
concerned in the "massacre" had a profligate character which had
become manifest when they were quartered in Belfast.[12]

Charles Lucas (probably after consultation with Franklin, who
was then in Ireland) published a letter that he had written to the

[7] April 27, 1765.
[8] *Ibid.,* Dec. 7, 21, 1765.
[9] *Ibid.,* Jan. 11, 14, 1766.
[10] Jan. 18, 1766.
[11] *Ibid.,* Nov. 4, 1769; April 10, 1770.
[12] *Ibid.,* April 28, May 10, 1770.

committee on the Boston Massacre emphasizing the common plight
of America and Ireland. Irishmen had been forcibly deprived of
legal as well as natural rights. "What redress do you expect," he
asked James Bowdoin and Joseph Warren, "for grievances in
America, which are grown familiar in England, and almost the
established, the sole mode of government in Ireland?" "Usurpations" in England were spoken of along with "oppression" of America and "the heavy Yoke of Tyranny" in Ireland. Whigs in England and leaders in Ireland and America at this time all argued
that the King was being betrayed by his advisers.[13]

Disabilities in land tenancy were protested against and these
protests were given added emphasis by emigration to America. Advice was given to prospective emigrants who were reminded also
of the hardships and disadvantages of life overseas. In suggesting
certain areas for settlement it was observed that there were "no
voracious Landlords to extract from you the Fruits of your Industry." [14] Emigration reached figures which alarmed the upper
classes, and it was feared that manufactures would suffer and that
the landed interest might be ruined. It was emphasized that it was
not the "lower ranks" alone who went to the colonies; tradesmen,
skilled artisans, and manufacturers had gone too. The establishment of an extensive linen trade overseas would lessen the demand
for Irish linen, the great staple of the country, on which the landed
interest and manufactures depended. The linen trade was already
in a serious state.[15] At the time when Dublin had already gotten
word of the Boston Port Bill, a local paper stated, "There is above
an hundred gentlemen in this town, of known abilities and courage, who have taken passages for America." [16]

Lists of vessels with estimates of the numbers of people who
had sailed from Irish ports for America between 1769 and 1774
were published with a warning to the government. After noting
that 152 ships had gone with over 37,000 passengers, the writer
added his injunction, "Read this, Ye! Men in Power, and relieve
this oppressed, sinking and Betrayed nation. . . . Repeal the Bos-

[13] *Ibid.*, Sept. 17, 19, Oct. 22, 1771; J. Bennett Nolan, *Benjamin Franklin in Scotland and Ireland, 1759 and 1771* (Philadelphia, 1938), p. 148.
[14] Letter signed "An American," *Freeman's Journal*, July 16, 1772; see also *ibid.*,
Oct. 24, 1771.
[15] *Ibid.*, April 17, June 17, 1773.   [16] *Ibid.*, April 5, 1774.

ton Port Bill . . . Restore to the Middlesex Freeholders [Wilkes's constituents] their Birth-rights. Restore the Charter of Boston." He urged too, the abolition of useless offices and unmerited pensions. It was alleged that the Quebec Bill was dangerous to Ireland because Catholics would be encouraged to leave for Canada where their religion would be tolerated, thus leaving the lands of the lords depopulated.[17]

The Irish who feared for their own export trade followed closely American efforts to promote local manufactures. Colonial non-importation hurt Irish linen manufactures, and respectable members of the local community said they would not pay their rents unless the government changed its policies.[18] The press continued to feature long selections from American constitutional theorists. John Dickinson's *Letters from a Pennsylvania Farmer* were immediately reprinted in extracts applicable to Ireland's situation. Their popularity led to many more reprintings in later issues of the *Freeman's Journal.*[19] The conflict between the Massachusetts assembly and the governor was presented in detail in the same paper, and its readers kept on calling for more news of this type.[20] Americans, especially the Boston radicals who were regularly engaged in correspondence with Charles Lucas, saw to it that the Irish papers kept abreast of events in the colonies and were very pointed in prodding their sympathizers in Ireland. A writer from Philadelphia asserted that "the Body of the People on this Side are determined not to be the Subjects of Plunder and Rapacity to the Courtiers in England. Ireland may, if she chooses, so to continue." [21]

Radicals everywhere took note of the expulsion of Wilkes from Parliament, and some coupled that event with suppression in New England. Liberty was indivisible and its cause was held to be "one common cause." Irishmen learned that £1,500 had been sent from Charleston, S.C., to the London Society for Supporting the Bill of Rights, a radical group which championed the cause of America. On Wilkes's release from jail, jubilant diners in Dublin and Belfast toasted him along with "the Brave Americans." [22] A correspondent for a club devoted to political discussion contributed

17 *Ibid.,* July 2, 12, 1774.   18 *Ibid.,* Dec. 19, 1767; July 10, 1770.
19 Jan. 26, 1768; Feb. 2, Nov. 1, 12, 15, Dec. 3, *et seq.*   20 Aug 30, Sept. 3, 6, 17, 1768.
21 *Ibid.,* Jan. 3, 1769.   22 *Ibid.,* Feb. 10, April 19, 26, July 5, 1770.

some satirical resolutions to the press, including one reading, "That the Americans are a Turbulent and seditious People, and therefore ought be chastised, particularly the inhabitants of Boston, who have dared to rattle their chains louder than the Rest." Dubliners read with pride of Boston diners toasting "Dr. Lucas the Patriot of Ireland." [23]

Constitutional arguments heard in American legislative halls were also heard in the Irish Parliament. There too it was maintained that money bills could originate only in their own house of commons and that they had to be accepted unaltered.[24] Gervase Parker Bushe published a pamphlet on the subject of American taxation in which he argued that none of the colonists voted for representatives in the British Parliament and that they had the right to tax themselves in their own provincial assemblies.[25] In speaking of his pamphlet to Henry Grattan, Bushe said that it had "a very good invective against George Grenville, whom I hope you hate." [26] Bushe foresaw that, if the parliamentary system of taxation was established against America, Ireland would be at the mercy of England.

Dublin newspapers kept their readers informed about the progress of the opposition to English fiscal measures in America. Advertisements of prints satirizing the Stamp Act and its repeal appeared in Dublin periodicals.[27] In Ireland and in America there were Hearts of Oak Boys and Hearts of Steel Boys who were very effective in expressing discontent with the status quo. Steel Boys were said to have migrated en masse to America after being dispossessed of their lands.[28] News of celebrations by the Sons of Liberty in Boston was related for Irish readers, who joined enthusiastically (albeit vicariously) in such toasts as "The Sons of Liberty throughout the world" and "The Illustrious Patriots of the Kingdom of Ireland." [29] Irishmen, as well as Americans, found re-

[23] *Ibid.*, March 14, April 8, Oct. 19, 1769.
[24] *Debates Relative to the Affairs of Ireland, in the Years 1763 and 1764. Taken by a Military Officer* (2 vols., London, 1766).
[25] *Case of Great Britain and America Addressed to the King and Both Houses of Parliament* (2d ed., London, 1769), p. 2.
[26] Henry Grattan, *Memoirs of the Life and Times of the Rt. Hon. Henry Grattan* (5 vols., London, 1839–46), I, 136–37, 269.
[27] George Faulkner, *The Dublin Journal*, Dec. 31, 1765; Jan. 18, July 12, 1766.
[28] H. B. C. Pollard, *The Secret Societies of Ireland* (London, 1922), p. 10.
[29] John Ferrar, *The Limerick Chronicle*, Oct. 20, 1768.

lease for their libertarian sentiments in sending aid to the Corsican revolutionary Pascal Paoli.[30]

Dublin's Liberty Boys and other patriotic "Boys" were urged to be careful lest riotous acts bring new oppressive measures. Liberty Boys on both sides of the Atlantic seem to have been drawn from the same social stratum.[31] Irish readers kept track of the Sons of Liberty in New York, Boston, New Haven, and New Jersey, and they were informed too of the number of men in the colonies who were able to bear arms. It was said that the American colonies were united and would never submit "so long as they have the power of Resistance." [32]

All threats to liberty were carefully scrutinized by the *Freeman's Journal*. A "Letter . . . to be read by all Jurymen" on the subject of libel was printed, and the action of the American jury in declaring Zenger not guilty was held up as a noble example to be followed.[33] A vigorous campaign in favor of freedom of the press was carried on in succeeding issues of the paper which published a long story of the Zenger case, including the celebrated speech of the lawyer Andrew Hamilton in defense of Zenger.

By its more vital leadership America gave direction to Irish aims and the two movements were interlinked. Ireland, it must be remembered, was included in Grenville's new financial policies. An act in 1769 which raised the number of troops in Ireland from 12,000 to 15,000 at Irish expense was interpreted as enabling Britain to keep more troops in America "in order to crush the spirit of the colonies." [34] These words, uttered by a member of the Irish house of commons, reveal as clearly as words may the community of interests binding the American and Irish movements. When new taxes similar to the notorious Stamp Act were proposed for Ireland in 1773 the example of the Americans in opposition was urged upon the Irish. Patriots continually reminded their countrymen that everything that occurred in America was written "for our admonition." [35]

In Dublin a Society of Free Citizens was formed, and its membership was very much like the merchant groups in the American

[30] *Freeman's Journal*, Jan. 3, June 6, 1769.   [31] *Ibid.*, Sept. 10, 1763.
[32] *Ibid.*, Feb. 4, 11, March 11, April 19, 22, 1766.   [33] Feb. 21, 1764.
[34] Coupland, *op. cit.*, pp. 100–101.   [35] *Freeman's Journal*, June 10, Nov. 18, 1773.

colonies. It was organized in "support of the Trade, Commerce and Liberties of Ireland," and at its meetings toasts were tendered to the citizens of Boston. James Napper Tandy, later to be a revolutionary and exile in America, was president of the society.[36] When the Irish house of commons passed the Stamp Act, a meeting of the Society of Free Citizens toasted opposition to it and drank "To the Glorious Revolution of '88," adding "and may we never stand in need of another." A few days later came the news of a meeting in Faneuil Hall, Boston, to oppose the landing of the tea and of similar action by the New York Sons of Liberty. The *Freeman's Journal,* by far the most active periodical in opposition to the government, was claiming a country-wide circulation of "thousands" at this time. It ran a history of the constitutional debate between the American colonies and the mother country following the Stamp Act, with the obvious design of encouraging the Irish to work for repeal of their own.[37]

News soon arrived from New York of the proposal for a general congress of the colonies, and from then on the pages of the *Freeman's Journal* were filled with reports of American activities in support of common action. The paper was a forum in which the American cause was upheld and British ministerial policy bitterly criticized. Anyone reading the *Journal* from 1765 on could get a pretty clear idea of American political developments. Panegyrics on the Americans were mingled with news of protest meetings of merchants trading with North America who were suffering heavy losses.[38] The *Hibernian Magazine* from 1771 down through the end of the American Revolution gave much space to the events in the colonies. Though less radical than the *Freeman's Journal* its bias was pro-American. It was suggested that the American market for Irish linen might be closed after the war if the Irish Parliament went on record against the colonists. It was said also that American flour which has "hitherto kept down the price of provisions in this country" might no longer be sent over.[39]

Irish sympathizers with the colonists were assured that the Americans had splendid military ability and needed only a few

---

[36] *Ibid.,* Sept. 25, 1773; Oct. 9, 19, 22, 1774.
[37] *Ibid.,* Jan. 18, 29, Feb. 15, April 2, 23, 1774.   [38] *Ibid.,* Jan. 17, 1775.
[39] *Hibernian Magazine,* Oct., 1775, p. 610.

good general officers to lead them.[40] A civil war in America and a civil war in Ireland, it was hinted, would be too much for the administration to bear. The King was urged to be a king and to avoid the counsel of supporters of absolute monarchy; the careers of Charles I and James II were suggested as required study for George III. The theory of Locke and the practice of Americans were invoked as guides to the Irish. All free nations, it was asserted, have a right to be governed by measures "agreeable to the plurality of the people, from whom all political power is derived." "The Americans have exerted this right, and set us a noble example . . . to show ourselves men!" [41]

While continuing to speak in belligerent language, many of the respected citizens of Ireland, particularly the "solid" elements in Dublin and Belfast, were working to effect a reconciliation between Great Britain and the colonies. Sir Edward Newenham, friend of Franklin, was now president of the Society of Free Citizens, who toasted their "friends in America" and petitioned the King to bring to an end "the present horrid civil war." England was reminded of the almost impossible task of conquering the colonies, and just concessions on both sides were urged.[42] Portraits of American patriots were sold and poems commemorating their deeds were reprinted in Ireland. In Irish song Washington's defeat of the British was cheered.[43]

Paine's *Common Sense* was recognized as political dynamite and had its antagonists as well as defenders. In a number of installments the *Freeman's Journal* reprinted Paine's pamphlet. Three thousand citizens signed a petition in favor of the Americans, it reported, maintaining that "not one of them disapprove the sentiments contained in *Common Sense*." It was now claimed by Irish political theorists that the people have a right to depose a king who pursues a despotic course. The Declaration of Independence was but two months old when Irishmen were urging England to grant independence to the colonies and then to conclude an alliance with the latter against Spain, France, and others. This would retain for England the benefits of American commerce, and the greater Amer-

---

[40] *Freeman's Journal*, Feb. 23, April 6, 1775.
[41] *Ibid.*, March 9, April 6, May 13, 1775. [42] *Ibid.*, Jan. 16, July 18, 1776.
[43] G. L. Kittredge, in Colonial Society of Massachusetts, *Transactions*, XIII, 254–59.

ica became the more advantageous would her trade be for Great Britain.[44]

In keeping warm these sentiments of a common antipathy to England, the anger of thousands of Irish transplanted to America played its share. The memories of a wronged people were not cooled on the long ocean voyage and ten thousand people a year between 1772 and 1774 added their tales to those of the many thousands who had preceded them. Along with human freight these ships carried to America gunpowder and military stores that had been loaded at friendly Irish ports. Lord Harcourt was very much disturbed over these exports and said that the government intended to stop them.[45] Americans preyed upon British ships in their own waters; the American flag, writes Froude, "was seen daily fluttering in insolence from the Irish coast anywhere between Londonderry and Cork." [46] Irish seaports gave shelter and supplies to American privateers. Franklin, a familiar of Irish patriots, was only one of the American leaders who saw the wisdom of joining the discontents of the two peoples.[47] More official steps were taken when the Continental Congress drew up an address to Ireland asking for support. Help was not long in coming.

Ulstermen began to express opposition to the war and the viceroy was convinced that "Presbyterians in the North . . . in their Hearts [were] Americans." [48] Harcourt wrote to Lord North that the "infatuation" of the Presbyterians for the Americans would, however, carry them no farther than to supply the Revolutionaries clandestinely with materials of war. The Catholics in southern Ireland were said to be "in hourly expectation of assistance from France or Spain." [49] Irish sympathizers were encouraged by a like stand taken by the opposition in the British Parliament. In the summer of 1775 the municipality of Dublin voted its thanks to Lord Effingham, who had resigned his command rather than "draw his sword against the lives and liberties of his fellow subjects in America." Merchants addressed a letter of thanks to those legisla-

---

[44] *Freeman's Journal*, June 6, 25, July 11, 30, Sept. 7, 1776.
[45] Public Record Office, State Papers, Ireland, 63; 443 (Oct. 7, 1774).
[46] J. A. Froude, *The English in Ireland in the Eighteenth Century*, II, 197 *et seq.*
[47] Irish patriots used to visit Franklin in London. Nolan, *op. cit.*, p. 132.
[48] P.R.O., State Papers, Ireland, 63; 449 (No. 25a).
[49] E. W. Harcourt, ed., *The Harcourt Papers*, X, 196–97 (Oct. 21, 1776), 271.

tors who opposed the "American Restraining Bills." This address was printed in the papers and "produced a very strong sensation throughout the nation." [50]

The *Hibernian Journal, or Chronicle of Liberty* carried a number of items on America (including Boston's opposition to the tea tax), and one of its readers who had joined the emigrant movement attributed Irish emigration to the decline of her trade resulting from America's nonimportation agreement. America's cash, he believed, "seems to have been the source from whence our little circulating cash flowed." Like so many others of both moderate and radical sympathies, he tied together American, Irish, and English liberties. Dubliners were urged to protest to the throne, in "behalf of America and in Behalf of yourselves." [51]

So general was the opposition to the government, particularly among the poorer people, that it was very difficult to get army recruits for service in America. It was feared that the departure of so many troops to America would leave Ireland at the mercy of the White Boys, who were Catholic revolutionaries in the southern provinces.[52] Harcourt felt he had to act decisively to stifle the rising sympathy for America. In the military emergency confronting the government the Crown gave him permission to fill up the regiments remaining in Ireland with Irish recruits. At the same time Lord North reminded Harcourt that the refusal of the Americans to supply food for any part of the British Empire would increase the demands upon Ireland. The latter was expected to meet the needs of the army in America and the West Indies. North thought this would "raise the price of all provisions exceedingly, and may even render the supply of our own army and our own colonies precarious." An embargo was proposed on Irish exports to the rest of the world in order to save them for the exclusive use of the British Empire.[53]

The administration was not to be overawed by public opinion. When Parliamentary support was not easily forthcoming, time-honored devices such as bribery and the like were resorted to, but such characters as Sir Edward Newenham were not to be coerced.

[50] Plowden, *An Historical Review* (1803), I, 440n.
[51] *Hibernian Journal*, Jan. 7, 24, 31, 1774; April 12, 1775.
[52] *Ibid.*, May 29, 1775; *Freeman's Journal*, Aug. 15, 1775.
[53] *Harcourt Papers*, IX, 303 (Feb. 6, 1775), 366 (Oct. 15, 1775); X, 90 (Jan. 22, 1776).

Harcourt felt impelled to challenge the pro-American sentiment of the Irish, and through official pressure the Irish Parliament was at length induced to declare its abhorrence of the American rebellion. It also agreed to the withdrawal of 4,000 troops from Ireland for service in America, but it refused to have them replaced by German soldiers. These official actions did not mirror the true feelings of the Irish. "In spite of the sentiments of a large number of its people . . . [Ireland] was committed to an approval of the war by the votes of those who were by a fiction denominated the representatives of the nation." [54]

News of military hostilities overseas was followed eagerly by Irish readers. Items were presented in language highly colored in America's favor. The opening battles were described as "Butchery in America" and the eventual salvation of Ireland was thought to rest on "American Virtue." [55] The *Freeman's Journal* objected to the Americans being called "Rebels." The paper had great difficulty in procuring American news giving the colonial side of the war, but in time such items filtered through despite official interference.[56]

The *Freeman's Journal* carried on a running argument with the prominministerial organs which spoke of American cowardice and charged that colonials ran away rather than fight. The misfortune is, said that journal, that whenever it was judged advisable to attack the Americans, they did "incredible mischief . . . by their flight." The *Hibernian Magazine* printed an engraving of "a real American rifleman" (probably idealized) in answer to a burlesque portrait that had appeared in rival publications. Irishmen boasted that their kinsmen in the American army were largely responsible for the defeat of the English at Saratoga.[57]

The Irish Revolution was hardly behind the American in the course of its development. It brought about the amelioration of the penal code, the formation of the Irish Volunteers, and the modifications of the trade laws. It was charged that British officers did re-

[54] William Hunt, ed., *The Irish Parliament, 1775, from an Official and Contemporary Manuscript* (London, 1907), p. 81; Michael J. O'Brien, *A Hidden Phase of American History; Ireland's Part in America's Struggle for Liberty*, pp. 11–16, *passim.*

[55] *Hibernian Journal*, June 2, 1775.

[56] June 17, 1775, July 30, 1776. The Declaration of Independence was speedily reprinted in Ireland in the *Hibernian Journal*, Aug. 1, 1776, and *Freeman's Journal*, Aug. 20, 1776.

[57] *Freeman's Journal*, Aug. 31, 1776; *Hibernian Magazine*, April, 1776; 1778, p. 232.

cruiting among Catholics, promising them to relax the penal laws; but it was no easy task to get them to enlist for service overseas against Americans. Many of the Protestant Irish apparently believed that Catholics were less enthusiastic than they actually were in supporting the American cause. Naturally, Catholics were more immediately concerned in ameliorating their own evils than in remedying injustices done to America.[58] Removal of the penal laws against the Catholics was urged, and it was remarked that all kinds of religion had been encouraged in Pennsylvania and elsewhere with no disturbance to the body politic, but rather to the benefit of trade and agriculture. An Irish legislator said that the policy of repressing the Catholics would drive them to America.[59] British moves to make concessions to America, such as Lord North's proposals of 1778, stirred the Irish to demand similar treatment. It was pleaded that whatever privileges or advantages in trade were granted to the colonies should likewise be extended to Ireland. A resolution was adopted by the Irish house of commons asking that Ireland have the same liberty of trade with the colonies in America and in Africa that Great Britain herself enjoyed.[60]

America's ways were thought useful in Ireland too. The Irish were called upon to wear their own manufactures, and when shopkeepers were suspected of not abiding by the nonimportation agreements they were "after the American fashion" tarred and feathered.[61] A Dublin meeting in 1779 passed a nonimportation agreement and the Irish Volunteers, now numbering some 40,000, were threatening revolt if the trade laws were not relaxed.

The war had disastrous effects on Ireland's economy.[62] A petition signed by hundreds of people in Cork, 1779, expressed concern about their declining linen trade and protested against the war with America, which, it charged, was carried on in "the pursuit of

58 *Freeman's Journal*, Aug. 24, 31, 1775. See also J. A. Froude, *The English in Ireland in the Eighteenth Century*, II, 175n; O'Brien, *op. cit.*, pp. 40, 44–46, 47–49, 57–58.

59 *Freeman's Journal*, March 25, 1777; *Hibernian Magazine*, 1779, p. 55.

60 *The Journals of the House of Commons of the Kingdom of Ireland*, Vol. X, Pt. 1 (1779–82), p. 55 (Dec. 20, 1779).

61 *Magee's Weekly Packet*, Nov. 6, 1779; Plowden, *An Historical Review*, Vol. II, Pt. 1.

62 *The Speeches of the Rt. Hon. Henry Grattan*, ed. by his son (4 vols., London, 1822), I, 13–20 (Feb. 6, 1778).

an inexpedient, unnecessary and perhaps illegal, power of taxation." [63] Threats were made that if England persevered in a restrictive policy many more Irish would go to America, the part of the Empire on which the mother country could least depend. Those who would go were manufacturers who would transfer to America the woolen and linen manufactures "to the great prejudice of those trades in England, Scotland and Ireland." [64]

The lord lieutenant believed that Irish discontent was increasing, fomented, so he said, by French and American emissaries.[65] Franklin's propaganda sent from France certainly helped foment this discontent, as he shrewdly pointed to the less obvious disabilities experienced by Irishmen as well as their better-known complaints. He said Americans grieved with the Irish over "the load of oppressive pensions on your establishment," the many well-paid sinecures, and the privileged position of the military. He held out the promise that if England did not remove commercial restrictions on Ireland, "means will be found to establish your freedom in this respect." [66] Within a year laws were passed giving Ireland almost the same freedom of trade as that enjoyed by Britain. Americans naturally looked with enthusiasm upon any signs of discontent in the Empire and John Adams believed he saw so many in 1780 that it seemed to him that the "British empire [was] crumbling to pieces like a rope of sand." [67] Irishmen who spoke with Franklin were quick to express their "obligations to America" for their success in wresting concessions from England.[68]

Grattan, then the most distinguished figure in the Irish Parliament, again followed American precedent and challenged the right of the British Parliament to make laws for Ireland. On a later occasion he flung this challenge to his own people and to their English rulers:

[63] S.P., Ireland, 63; 443, Nos. 21, 22.

[64] *The Commercial Restraints of Ireland Considered in a Series of Letters to a Noble Lord* . . . (Dublin, 1779), pp. 215–16.

[65] *Memoirs of . . . Henry Grattan*, I, 345–46.

[66] P. L. Ford, ed., "Benjamin Franklin, an Address to the Good People of Ireland on Behalf of America, Oct. 4, 1778," *Winnowings in American History* (Brooklyn, N.Y., 1891).

[67] Francis Wharton, *The Revolutionary Diplomatic Correspondence of the United States* (Washington, 1889), III, 571–72.

[68] *Ibid.*, V, p. 511.

Before you decide on the practicability of being slaves forever look to America. . . . What you trample on in Europe will sting you in America. When America sends forth her ambassadors to . . . Europe and manifests to the world her independency and power do you imagine you will persuade Ireland to be satisfied with an English Parliament making laws for her?

Like his vigorous contemporary in England, Richard Price, Grattan spoke of America as "the only refuge of the liberties of mankind." [69] English reformers of the type of Price, Major Cartwright, and the Reverend Christopher Wyvil frequently tied together British, American, and Irish aspirations for social change. The example of Massachusetts in broadening the franchise was urged as worthy of emulation. Price said all Ireland should continue to exert pressure on England, and he believed that Catholics should be given equal voting rights with the Protestants as a way of breaking the hold of the aristocracy. [70]

The defeat of Cornwallis at Yorktown spurred on the Irish in their demands for political concessions; and in 1782 Britain was willing to satisfy them with grants of greater political autonomy. The Irish now had free trade and their Parliament enlarged powers, although still under English control. Well might Grattan say that "the American war was the Irish harvest." Once again, in 1785, Ireland likened her cause to America's. Pitt proposed that economic concessions be made to Ireland on condition that she support the imperial navy. The Irish believed themselves now to be in the situation in which the Americans were in 1765 when the latter had been asked to support armed forces. However, economic concessions were held out as a bait to win from the Irish their acceptance of Pitt's proposal, which the opposition of British businessmen was strong enough to defeat. So great was the wrath of the Irish patriots that talk of following the American example of revolt was outspoken. The formation in every county of Ireland of a Constitutional Society on the plan of England's was suggested, and

69 *Speeches of . . . Grattan*, I, 39 *et seq.* (Declaration of Irish Rights, April 19, 1780), 117–18, 183.
70 *A Collection of Letters . . . to the Volunteers of Ireland on the Subject of a Parliamentary Reform*, by the Earl of Effingham, Price, Cartwright, Jebb, and Wyvil (London, 1783), pp. 31–32, 80–81n.

it was proposed that a correspondence be maintained between them.[71]

Much political and economic discussion of the type familiar to America a score of years earlier was carried on in Ireland. A considerable number of provincial towns in Ireland had their first printing presses in the 1760s and '70s, founded undoubtedly under the spur of contemporary events.[72] In Ireland and in America, it was asserted, the press had had great influence in disseminating constitutional and legal knowledge among the people, and in both countries had been instrumental in overturning "assumed and illegitimate authority." [73]

One of the proposals made at this time, reminiscent of the earlier imperial outlines sketched by Franklin and Joseph Galloway, was called *Renovation without Violence Yet Possible* (Dublin, 1779). It suggested an imperial parliament, each portion of the Empire, including Ireland, to maintain its own legislature, to raise its own taxes as well as its quota for imperial expenses. Perfect free trade was to subsist among all parts of the Empire. Although there was to be a religious establishment, it was to be so liberal as to leave room for few dissenters; there was to be ample toleration. The political changes provided for lopping off the "rotten boroughs" in the house of commons to make room for new members.[74]

That international revolutionary, Tom Paine, had his many readers in Ireland too, and Wolfe Tone quoted him in support of political reform. In his view the events of 1782 granting greater freedom to Ireland were nothing for the Irish to cheer over, since Ireland's oppressors had lost none of their power. Arguing in behalf of the emancipation of Catholics in Ireland, he pointed to the example of America where "the Catholic and Protestant sit equally in Congress, without any contention arising, other than who shall

---

[71] Coupland, *op. cit.*, p. 147; *The Volunteers' Journal, or Irish Herald,* Oct. 15, 1783. England had a "Society for Constitutional Information," composed of people friendly to America.

[72] E. R. Dix, *A List of Irish Towns and the Dates of Earliest Printing in Each* (*Irish Bibliog. Pamphlets,* No. 6, Dublin, 1909).

[73] L. Macnally, *The Claims of Ireland and the Resolutions of the Volunteers Vindicated, on the Principles of Selden, Locke, Hooker, Burke, etc.* (London, 1782), pp. 11–12.

[74] H. R. Wagner, *Irish Economics: 1700–1783; a Bibliography with Notes* (London, 1907), p. 88.

serve his country best. So may it be in Ireland!" [75] Grattan likewise urged American experience in support of granting the franchise to the Catholics. He sought to weave the tangled Irish problems into the pattern of the familiar American situation and thus get the support of the liberals who had espoused America.[76] Irish patriots who were worried over their religious and civil difficulties believed that the Americans had revealed their true political genius in "not making religion a matter of state." [77]

The moment when fairly peaceful adjustments might have been made had passed by the middle of the 1780s. The French Revolution was to bring on another wave of reaction which submerged Wolfe Tone and the pitiful few with him. The years of desolation stretched on into the nineteenth century when American fortunes once again became intimately bound up with Irish misfortunes. The struggle of Ireland for economic and political emancipation continued to draw sustenance from America. The Yankee Club of Stewartstown, County Tyrone, Ireland, sent a note of congratulation to Washington at the close of the war. In reply, he hoped that good had come to Ireland from the success of the American Revolutionaries.[78] A sentimental reminder of Irish-American ties came from the South Carolina assembly after the Revolution. A loyalist petition had been sent to the legislature for the return of confiscated property; in restoring it the assembly was moved by the fact that the family was Irish and the son had served in the Volunteer Corps.[79] "The Volunteers of Ireland still live," said the exiled patriots, "they live across the Atlantic." Well might another Grattan have said, "The growth of America was the Irish harvest." [80]

[75] T. Wolfe Tone, *An Argument on Behalf of the Catholics of Ireland* (5th ed., Dublin, 1792), p. 16.

[76] *A Sketch of the Debates in . . . the Parliament of Ireland on the Roman Catholic Bill Passed in the Session of 1792* (Dublin, 1792), p. 12.

[77] Historical MSS Commission, *The MSS and Correspondence of James, First Earl of Charlemont* (1891), II, 9 (Nov. 16, 1784).

[78] *Massachusetts Centinel*, May 22, 1784; reprinted, Colonial Society of Massachusetts, *Transactions*, Vol. XIV.

[79] Hist. MSS Comm., *First Earl of Charlemont* (1891), II, 1 (Feb. 13, 1784).

[80] Society of United Irishmen of Dublin, *Proceedings* (Philadelphia, 1795), pp. 237–41. See some useful material in P. H. Bagenal, *The American Irish and Their Influence on Irish Politics* (London, 1882); deals mainly with the nineteenth century.

The Massachusetts Conservatives In the Critical Period ~~ ROBERT A. EAST

The deliberate and firm manner in which she [Massachusetts] has conducted her policy formed her laws regulated her finances and administered Justice since the peace . . . have given her a degree of respectability that every other State acknowledges.
NATHAN DANE to THOMAS DWIGHT, February 11, 1786

Time will make curious disclosures, and you, Sir, may be astonished to find the incendiaries who have fomented the discontents among the miserable insurgents of the Massachusetts, in a class of men least suspected.
MERCY WARREN to JOHN ADAMS, December, 1786

THE MOST publicized of the troubles encountered by an American state in the immediate post-Revolutionary years were the insurrections against the process of law in back-country Massachusetts in 1786. These were aggravated, however, by the conservative fiscal and social policies which were pursued in that state after 1780 and which eventually tended to break down of their own weight rather than because of radical opposition. The larger importance of the disturbances, moreover, is that they played into the hands of the strong nationalists, who used them as arguments to drive the more complacent of the Massachusetts conservatives, against their earlier desires and fears, into accepting a plan to reconsider the powers of the Federal union. The drift of conservative purpose and interest thus affords a study more revealing of the inner meaning of the so-called Critical Period in Massachusetts than do the activities per se of the "Reverend" Samuel Ely, the sturdy Captain Shays, and other colorful disturbers of the peace.[1]

[1] It is an interesting commentary upon the variety of historical interpretations existing for this period that, whereas modern writers place heavy emphasis upon such radical activities, George Bancroft, in his *History of the Formation of the Constitution of the United States of America* (2 vols., New York, 1882), gave only a half-page to the events of Shays's Rebellion, and merely spoke of the husbandmen supporting the rebels as being otherwise law-abiding citizens. It is my own feeling that it is the strength of the conservatives which has been underestimated, but my definition of a conservative is rather broad. This is permissible in the absence of anything like well-formed parties, but it should be compared with the interpretation in Anson E. Morse, *The Federalist Party in Massachusetts to the Year 1800* (Princeton, 1909), chaps. i–iii.

The term "conservative" is necessarily somewhat loosely used; for example, it obviously applied to far more persons at the time of Shays's Rebellion than it did on other, less alarming, occasions. Nevertheless the alignment of a number of solid citizens became sufficiently pronounced in Massachusetts politics during these years to make the expression feasible. They possessed no party organization worthy of the name, but their general agreement was evident in a sectional way; on a variety of questions in the middle eighties there was a more or less persistent geographical grouping of votes in the house of representatives which foreshadowed the division in the Federal constitutional ratifying convention of 1788. And behind this sectional façade there came to be a common understanding among conservatives as to what constituted fundamental objectives of good government: the enactment and proper administration of laws encouraging commerce, the payment of public and private debts, and the protection of property rights generally in the post-war society.

The reconditioned character of that society in its upper levels is a fact of the first importance for an understanding of subsequent developments. To certain enterprising inhabitants of seaboard Massachusetts the Revolution had given greater opportunities for gain (and consequent elevation in social position) than to persons in any other state. As a result of the heavy commercial activities carried on throughout most of the war years (stimulated by needs of both the continental and French forces) and the exciting opportunities in privateering, together with the removal as loyalists of many older merchants, a number of men of but small fortune in colonial times had been enabled to enter the big-business society of post-war Boston. Many persons were still wealthy from earlier times, but Thomas Russell, originally from Cambridge, was now Boston's greatest merchant; George Cabot and Stephen Higginson, originally from Beverly and Salem, were among her most important businessmen; and young James Swan, originally from Scotland, was representative of the speculator type which the war had encouraged. Such men were especially interested in political policies which would favor their commerce, encourage their newer business speculations, and protect their newly won wealth (or, as in the case of Swan, newly married wealth). They were also determined to retain the considerable measure of political influence in the state which many of them, especially those from Essex County, had seized in the early years of the war when they had successfully combatted the "levelling" tendencies of the period.[2]

Generally sympathetic with these highly self-confident and aggressive newcomers on the seaboard, and with the older merchants there, were other conservatives scattered throughout the state. Some of these were vestigial remains of a native aristocracy from colonial times, for example Colonel John Worthington of Springfield (represented in politics immediately after the war by his son-in-law, Thomas Dwight, and later by another son-in-law, Fisher Ames), and old Samuel Dexter of Dedham. The conservative tradition was carried on even in far-off Berkshire County by Theodore Sedgwick of Stockbridge, whose wife was a member of that Williams clan earlier known in western Massachusetts as the "Lords of the Valley." Men of similar temper were to be found especially in Connecticut River towns, though some of these, like the lawyer Caleb Strong, had become prominent only during the war and at times expressed, halfheartedly at least, popular sympathies.[3] Indeed the only interior county in which there seem to have been relatively few of these conservatives by birth or circumstance was Worcester: it was incorrigibly radical throughout the entire Critical Period, more uniformly so than either Hampshire or Berkshire.

It should be added immediately that defining a conservative on economic and social grounds alone is never wholly satisfactory. In the period under survey there were some interesting exceptions to the idea that principles are conditioned by material interests. Even "radical" members of the general court were necessarily property holders, as required by the constitution of 1780, and several of the more popular political leaders in the state were propertied persons. This was conspicuously true of John Hancock and was true to some extent of his principal political lieutenant, Thomas Cushing; also of James Warren of Plymouth, who was able to

2 Cf. my *Business Enterprise in the American Revolutionary Era* (New York, 1938), chaps. iii, ix, x.

3 Although a good conservative, Strong wrote Theodore Sedgwick from Boston, March 13, 1786, regarding proposals in the House of Representatives for a "Bull and Boar" act and other debt-easing measures, and commented, "The Difficulty is that many of the members from this part of the country [i. e., the seaboard] dont owe half as much as they are worth." Sedgwick Papers A, Massachusetts Historical Society.

acquire Thomas Hutchinson's old residence at Milton for a new home. From Marblehead came Elbridge Gerry, a successful war trader and heavy holder of government securities who further enhanced his fortune by a brilliant marriage with a New York heiress, but whose political career after the time he settled in Charlestown was not exactly orthodox. There was also something irregular about the conservatism of Dr. Charles Jarvis of Boston, well-fixed and usually found voting in the house with his conservative Boston colleagues, but a person not unwilling to stand on occasion as the people's friend. He was, perhaps, like the lawyer, James Sullivan of Groton, whose reputed influence with John Hancock on the question of a "tender" act in 1787 got him into a serious quarrel with Theodore Sedgwick.[4]

It should not be inferred from this that Governor Hancock's following was identical with the radical back-country element; the governor's popularity and actions contradict such a naïve assumption. Although he was distasteful to many of the Boston merchants, they found him voting with themselves in the house on several occasions in 1786. Hancock was, indeed, a patriot whose very name symbolized the entire Revolutionary cause to representatives of all types of his fellow citizens, and his election to the governorship as many times as he desired in the eighties was no indication of a "radical" state government, despite the insinuations of his enemies. He headed no party machine with a legislative program, and the important issues in the state had comparatively little connection with his personality.

To a greater degree on the question of a more vigorous union were there differences of opinion among the merchants and gentlemen of Massachusetts. All of them agreed that Congress needed additional power over commerce (since Massachusetts was heavily dependent upon a national market) and additional revenues to pay off the continental debt; but anything beyond this was strongly suspected by some as damaging to Massachusetts's peculiar interests and also to her pride. Sectional animosity toward southern aristocrats was already strongly pronounced, not only because of

---

[4] Sullivan wrote Sedgwick, Sept. 22, 1787, heatedly denying reports which he claimed Sedgwick was spreading, that Sullivan had influenced Hancock not to veto "what was commonly called the 'Tender Act.'" *Loc. cit.*

the latter's manners and habits but because it was widely feared in New England that the South would never consent to giving Congress the power to enact national trade laws. Some of the *nouveaux riches* in Massachusetts talked about the dangers of an "aristocratical" rule just as did their back-country opponents (who, paradoxically, regarded the *nouveaux riches* themselves as among the aristocrats). Not until the fear of a domestic insurrection had alarmed the least nationally minded of the conservatives into a conviction that the struggle for a stronger union was also a struggle against vicious democratic movements at home was an adequate solidarity of viewpoint achieved. Hoping for such an eventuality, several of the more pronounced nationalists were pleased to make political capital out of Shays's Rebellion, despite their gloomy statements as to its seriousness. It doubtless was such persons who were accused on several occasions—very vaguely, to be sure—of actually having stimulated the uprising for their own purposes, and of having "monarchical" ideas.

The foundation for a conservative regime had been well laid in the state constitution of 1780, a document declared ratified only by some forceful reasoning.[5] Primarily the work of John Adams, who combined hard sense with his Revolutionary enthusiasm, and to a lesser extent of the merchant James Bowdoin, this constitution established property requirements for voters and office holders, and these could be *increased* for the latter at the will of the legislature. It also created an executive with respectable powers, an independent judiciary, and other features characteristic of a "balanced" government. In the estimation of those who feared too direct a control of affairs by the people, all this was sound reasoning; and so, doubtless, in the estimation of the mercantile element was that constitutional provision which permitted the burden of taxation to be laid upon the polls and estates of the commonwealth. This fiscal provision, immediately put into execution, was not an innovation, but therein exactly lay the significance: new and extraordinary problems were to be met largely in the same old way.

There was at first some justification for an optimistic and conservative attitude on fiscal questions, since even Massachusetts

[5] Cf. S. E. Morison, "The Struggle over the Adoption of the Constitution of Massachusetts," Mass. Hist. Soc., *Proceedings*, L, *passim*.

354 The Massachusetts Conservatives

farmers had enjoyed considerable war prosperity until about 1780, and it was but natural that future difficulties should have been too readily discounted. In both 1780 and 1781 the large amounts of hard money and bills of exchange which the French forces put into circulation in Massachusetts lent an additional luster to an economy which was already declining in agriculture. Not only were the warring forces, so important as a market for produce, being steadily concentrated to the south, but there had been a sharp increase in the production of foodstuffs in the fertile valleys of the middle and southern states with whose productivity the relatively exhausted soil of Massachusetts was in sharp contrast. After a few happy years of rising prices for his produce, which had encouraged him to live high and go into debt, the New England farmer reverted to a condition of lower prices for his customarily scanty crops, though his situation did not become critical until after the war.[6]

Unaware of this imminent change, the Massachusetts general court entered upon a series of measures in 1780 and 1781 which not only provided for the collection of extremely heavy taxes but abolished all legal tenders except gold and silver, thus establishing hard money standards for the payment of private debts.[7] It also

[6] R. V. Harlow, "Economic Conditions in Massachusetts during the American Revolution," Colonial Society of Massachusetts, *Publications*, XX, speaks of agricultural conditions as worse by 1780, but the charts in Ruth Crandall, "Wholesale Commodity Prices in Boston during the Eighteenth Century," *Review of Economic Statistics*, XVI, indicate a temporary recovery of flour prices in 1782.

[7] Cf. *Acts and Laws of the Commonwealth of Massachusetts* (Boston, 1890–98), 1780, c. 3; 1781, c. 7. Included in these volumes are the *Resolves of the General Court of Massachusetts,* and the two are hereafter referred to as *Acts* and *Resolves.* Even the temporary "tender" act of July 3, 1782, *Acts,* 1782, c. 10, merely sought to retain fair money values in permitting the extension of cattle, lumber, and other things in payment of private debts. Its radical implications are probably overemphasized by J. S. Barry, *The History of Massachusetts: the Commonwealth Period* (Boston, 1857), p. 222. I cannot understand why it should have suspended many lawsuits, as he implies was the case, for this was permitted only when a creditor, having already commenced action at law, should be unwilling to receive such personal estate in payment. Barry drew heavily upon George R. Minot, *History of the Insurrections in Massachusetts in the Year MDCCLXXXVI* (Worcester, 1788), p. 15, *passim,* a stimulating work in which, however, Minot, clerk of the house, frequently put forth the fears of the extreme conservative element. But his own references to the fate of subsequent tender and paper money attempts should dispel the idea that the general court was seriously affected by radicalism in the early eighties. That this fact was not wholly unappreciated at the time is indicated by the writings of the conservative but level-headed Nathan Dane. Cf. Dane to Thomas Dwight, Feb. 11, 1786, in E. C. Burnett, ed., *Letters of Members of the Continental Congress* (8 vols., Washington, 1921–36), VIII, 303, *passim.*

continued the conservative paper money policy adopted early in the war, for Massachusetts had to some extent checked currency inflation after 1777 by consolidating her state debt into interest-bearing certificates. The policy of consolidation was now resumed, accompanied by no new issues of state currency.

Thus at this early date were inaugurated those conservative policies which alone can give a proper understanding of the critical fiscal situation existing after 1785. The starting point was the act of January 25, 1781, which repealed former acts delaying the redemption of Massachusetts securities until 1788 and 1789, because "Injustice must accrue to the Possessors of said securities, by being kept so long out of their money. . . ." [8] Following this lead, on February 17 and May 15, 1781, provision was made for the calling in (or consolidation) of £400,000 and £800,000 of state securities, to be replaced by certificates bearing compound interest and themselves to be redeemed in equal annual portions from 1785 to 1788. As a safeguard, it was further provided that, in case the general court should fail to make provision for prompt redemption on those dates, the state treasurer should automatically issue his tax warrants to the towns for the required amounts. Similarly, in March, 1783 (the last important act of this kind), further consolidation of state securities to the amount of £300,000 was ordered, with the same automatic provision for repayment in those later years. Meantime, on July 5, 1781, notes equaling £111,000 were authorized to replace soldiers' notes already overdue, and these were to be repaid in equal portions from 1784 to 1786, with the same automatic provision for taxes should the legislature fail to provide them. Such measures indicate the fiscal difficulties which the Massachusetts conservatives were laying up for themselves in the near future.

This program for the abrupt redemption of the state debt at a relatively early date would have been doubly shortsighted had it not been accompanied after 1780 by efforts to levy heavy taxes to meet annual interest on the debt and to pay the current costs of government and the requisitions called for by Congress. Such efforts were indeed sufficiently in evidence to indicate once again the conservative character of the new state order. The first specie tax

[8] The date of redemption was subsequently changed to 1786–89.

was called for in 1780. The next year the legislature laid a tax of £374,795, and in 1782 another of £291,482, to defray public charges, in addition to providing £200,000 for the Federal government.[9] Since these sums were derived from the ratable polls (i. e., male persons over sixteen years, though voters had to be at least twenty-one) to something between thirty-three and forty percent of the total amount (the remainder being collected on the estates), it is evident that the burden of taxes even in the years preceding the time when the state debt would have to be redeemed was very heavy on the lower income classes.

That revenue for current needs had already been demanded to the limit of collectability by 1783 is suggested in the absence of a general tax act that year. In 1784, however, £140,000 was levied for the payment of a portion of the soldier's notes come due,[10] and the treasurer was ordered to make interest payments on the state debt as well as a large sum on Federal requisitions (out of previous taxes, the collection of a small portion of which was suspended because of the new act).[11] An effort was also made to improve the general situation by a new valuation of property throughout the state, but since this was only slowly completed it was necessary in 1785 to repeal the automatic provision for laying those taxes necessary to redeem the first portion of the consolidated debt. That this did not indicate a reversal of conservative policy, however, is proved by the fact that a few months later, early in 1786, there was still enough response to the scoldings of Governor Bowdoin for the court to levy the extraordinary sum of £300,439, to meet current needs and also to make interest payments on the state debt and a heavy payment on Federal requisitions.[12] This must have been the measure which Stephen Higginson foretold in December, 1785, when he wrote encouragingly of the fiscal situation in Massachusetts:

[9] There is a short sketch of financial matters in this period by C. J. Bullock, "Historical Sketch of the Finances and Financial Policy of Massachusetts, 1780–1905," in American Economic Association, *Publications*, 3d ser., Vol. VIII. Cf. *Acts*, 1780, c. 43; 1781, c. 16, 28; 1782, c. 65.

[10] *Acts*, 1784, c. 25.   [11] *Ibid.*, c. 24, 25.

[12] *Acts*, 1785, c. 74. Note the conservative opinion of the court as expressed in a letter to Governor Bowdoin on Dec. 1, 1785, *Resolves*, 1785, Oct. Sess., c. 151; also the laws for speeding up the collection of taxes, etc., *Acts*, 1785, c. 46, 50, 70.

The character of Massachusetts stands high, and is rising; even in money matters, we are much more liberal [i. e., sound] than our neighbors—as a proof of this, I now inclose you a report made the last Session which calculated not only to provide amply for the Interest on the State Debt, but to reduce the principal—this report I have strong hopes will be adopted the next Session it being the general Sentiment that we can and ought gradually to reduce the Debt.[13]

But Higginson and the other conservatives were disappointed later in 1786 when the new court again discontinued redemption of the state debt, though it made a conditional grant of "supplementary funds" called for by Congress, to the disgust of country members. By that date even Rufus King had begun to wonder if direct taxation had not been carried too far; and Governor Bowdoin himself had been forced to admit something of the kind.[14]

Except for legislation relating to indirect taxation, these are the principal fiscal laws of Massachusetts in the early Critical Period. Despite the facts that in 1786 an enormous state debt, accompanied by heavy Federal obligations, still existed and that sums on old taxes were still uncollected, it is nevertheless true that the general policy pursued in the state after 1780 had been one of hard money, no paper currency, and heavy taxes—plainly not a record of "radical" financing but quite the contrary. The financial plight of the commonwealth was not due to a lack of conservatism in her legislature, but to an unfortunate plan for the abrupt and early redemption of an extraordinary debt, coupled with unfortunate conditions, especially after 1784, in both commerce and agriculture.

As distinguished from these direct, or "dry," taxes, there remained the duties and excises, forms of indirect taxation especially significant by reason of their close connection with commercial and industrial policies in both Massachusetts and the nation at large. Their role in the fiscal scheme, moreover, was one of increasing importance: they produced revenues of over £50,000 even in

[13] Higginson to John Adams, Dec. 30, 1785, "Letters of Stephen Higginson," American Historical Association, *Annual Report, 1896*, I, 732.

[14] Cf. King to John Adams, Oct. 3, 1786, in C. King, ed., *The Life and Correspondence of Rufus King* (4 vols., New York, 1894), I, 190; Governor Bowdoin to the general court, Oct. 20, 1785, *Resolves*, 1785, Oct. Sess., c. 2.

the bad business year of 1785, and the payment of interest on the state debt came to depend heavily upon them.

Although the excises and duties were so frequently revised or, as James Swan said, so often "eeked and repealed," as to indicate a rather tenuous character for any one of them, there was clearly a tendency between 1781 and 1786 to increase the rates on the importation or sale of teas and liquors in particular and of foreign and domestic manufactures in general. Invariably introduced by such phrases as "in order to do justice to the public creditors" or "to pay interest on the securities," these acts gradually established a widespread schedule of indirect taxation. On foreign importations a two and one-half percent duty was established in 1783 and raised to a five percent level two years later. The climax came in 1786—the period of Bowdoin's governorship and of the last successful effort by conservatives to levy heavy direct taxes—when there was a sharp increase on duties generally. Long before the three-year tenure of this act was ended, however, such extreme rates were reduced by the "radical" general court of 1787.[15] The year before a Worcester County convention at Leicester had complained, among other things, of the use of duties and excises for the benefit of security holders.[16]

However desirable the fiscal objective which inspired this type of legislation, the conservatives themselves were far from unanimously in favor of it. Not only were excises a question upon which conservatives from back country and seaboard sometimes differed, but on the seaboard itself duties were at once repugnant to merchants and welcome to security holders. To Theodore Sedgwick of Berkshire all of the commercial legislation of the May, 1785, session of the general court was undesirable. He thought that trade would be diverted and a spirit of smuggling introduced as a consequence, and significantly added, "I believe not a member from this county but will heartily join in a repeal." [17] In January, 1786, he reiterated his criticism, inquiring of a Boston merchant, "Pray

15 The principal laws dealing with this subject are in the *Acts,* 1781, c. 17; 1782, c. 33, 64; 1783, c. 12; 1784, c. 14, 17, 75; 1785, c. 17, 18; 1786, c. 28, 48, 49; 1787, c. 63.

16 Barry, *Massachusetts: the Commonwealth Period,* p. 225.

17 Sedgwick to Caleb Davis, Oct. 14, 1785, Caleb Davis Papers, 12b, Mass. Hist. Soc. Apparently his disapproval covered all commercial legislation, including that against Great Britain.

does the frenzy still remain respecting impost, excise, etc.?" [18] On the other hand, James Swan, who was always concerned about the well-being of commerce but who was also deeply interested in the future of public securities, strongly condemned the "mercantile interest" in 1786 because of its opposition to the collection of duties: no one, he vigorously wrote, would believe the arguments the merchants used.[19]

In this conflict between their own interests all that the Massachusetts conservatives could do was to acquiesce in a compromise policy: to continue to place the greatest emphasis upon direct taxation, but at the same time to give up any idea of an entirely free trade, except what could be carried on by smuggling and other indirect methods (such as Samuel Breck and Stephen Higginson testified took place); to acknowledge the need for some protection for home manufactures; and to continue the use of duty revenues for the benefit of the public creditors. An even more completely state-controlled economy might eventually have been sponsored by them had they not in the meantime, like the merchants of Rhode Island, come to recognize the greater necessity for a nationally controlled economy. It is significant in this connection that Rufus King expressed pretty complete disagreement in 1785 with the free trade ideas he found in Adam Smith's *Wealth of Nations*.[20]

This program of direct and indirect taxation was the more remarkable in Massachusetts during the early eighties not only because economic conditions tended to get worse but because it ran counter to the spirit of the whole Revolutionary generation, which was steeped in self-assertion against any vigorous fiscal measures. Confusion in local affairs had been a not infrequent spectacle in Massachusetts for years and, despite the establishment of a strong state government in 1780, it continued as a result of protest against these fiscal measures. In fact, the new constitution had recognized the legality of local gatherings to protest against undesirable legislation, and the right was promptly seized upon to the embarrassment of the new government itself. As early as March, 1781, Abner Holden, the speaker of the house of representatives, informed a

[18] Sedgwick to Caleb Davis, Jan. 31, 1786, Caleb Davis Papers, 13a.
[19] James Swan, *National Arithmetick; or Observations on the Finances of the Commonwealth of Massachusetts . . .* (Boston, 1786), p. 89.
[20] Cf. King to Elbridge Gerry, June 5, 1785, in King, *King*, I, 109.

Boston merchant friend of such a sad state of affairs in Worcester County:

I find afairs in the Countrey Rather Dissagreable Some peoples minds Inflamed by [E]Very Indirect Measure, persued by Some from Whom We might Justly Look for better things and those two Who know better then they practice; a Circular Letter has originated from the Respectable Town of Sutton Signed by Willis Hall and one other Gentleman by order of T[he] Town Calling upon all the Towns in the County Joyne in a County Convention to be Held att Worcester on a Sertain Day in this month to Remonstruate to the General Court against the Repeal of the Tender Act. . . .

Such alarming measures, he added, if continued would do more harm in a month than the British could do in a year. But he did not despair. There were "firm friends" in the country "as well as in the City" who would "Defend the Cause of America with Life and fortune." [21] He plainly identified "the Cause" with the suppression of such popular agitation, and identified independence from Great Britain with the triumph of the conservatives in civil affairs.

That Holden's optimism was well-founded was shortly afterwards proved by the conservative course of general legislation, as well as that dealing with taxation. It is true that in 1782 the conditions which made possible Sam Ely's brief career in Hampshire, together with the wise remonstrances of Joseph Hawley of Northampton,[22] moved the general court to make an investigation into the condition of unrest and to pass an act permitting debtors to extend cattle and produce in the payment of debts; but this relief, if such it may be called, was only temporary. In both 1783 and 1784 other laws were enacted which put more teeth into writs for the collection of debts, prescribed methods whereby both real and personal estates could be seized for debts, and reëstablished the old colonial statute providing for unlimited personal actions in law. About the only concessions made to the less fortunate members of society in 1784 and 1785 were that ancient one restraining the taking of "excessive usury" and an act which provided that an

[21] Holden to Caleb Davis, March 14, 1781, Caleb Davis Papers, 10a.
[22] Cf. Hawley to Ephraim Wright, April 16, 1782, in *American Historical Review*, XXXVI, 776–78.

attorney at law must have a good moral character and take an oath to tell no falsehoods unwittingly!

Even the year 1786 marked no very radical departure from established conservative policies, despite the solemn assertion of the general court in November that the late session was almost entirely given over to a consideration of the grievances of the people in "divers counties." It strove to cope with the situation by multiplying the law courts and enlarging their jurisdiction; by calling for an improvement in morals and manners, a return to principles of industry, of sobriety, and of fidelity in contracts; by asserting that both state and Federal securities could and must be paid, lest the history of the American Revolution be "blackened with the tale, that we refused to redeem the securities we had given to effect it. . . ." [23] Paper money was declared a ridiculous remedy, and the sole gesture toward easing the payment of taxes in specie was the permission for making substitutions with certain commodities, and the release of certain indigent persons.[24] An act to permit the use of any kind of property as a tender for debts for a period of eight months was also passed, but it was so modified and restrained as to be a mockery of relief.[25] Such measures as these were far from what the radicals desired. Meantime, debtors were writing in this fashion, as to Caleb Davis of Boston:

I have been informed that you are not contented with your security and want to com in to possession of the Estate Before the time set in the Deed is Expired. Sir you have all my living. I dont supose that it will Sel for so much by a great Sume as it would then but I have nothing more for you but my Body and that is a very poor one. . . . I and my Wife and Little Children must absolutely perish if they have no Bread over the winter. . . .[26]

There is no way of telling how genuine this particular protest may have been; the writer may have been a scoundrel, for all that is

[23] "An Address from the General Court to the People of the Commonwealth of Massachusetts," Nov. 14, 1786, *Acts and Resolves,* 1786.

[24] *Acts,* 1786, c. 39.

[25] *Ibid.,* c. 45, passed Nov. 15, 1786: "An Act for suspending the laws for the collection of private debts, under certain limitations." Its title is misleading. Even the payment of specie interest, if specifically provided for on earlier debts, was exempted from the provisions of this act. Cf. the remarks by Minot, *Insurrections in Massachusetts,* p. 60, as to the way the bill was amended to meet the objections of the conservatives.

[26] Joseph Remick of Eastham to Caleb Davis, July 27, 1785, Caleb Davis Papers, 12b.

known about him. But there was undoubtedly enough of such feeling abroad to account for an almost revolutionary change in the membership of the general court in 1787; had affairs continued longer under control of the legislature of 1786, according to a vigorous speaker in the constitutional ratifying convention, the state must have "run with blood."

The success of the conservatives as late as 1786 was due largely to their preponderant strength in the senate, which frequently overpowered the house, invariably in a conservative direction, as in the election of Governor Bowdoin in 1785. "Much bickering" between the two bodies was frequently remarked. It is readily understandable why the numerous county conventions of 1786 desired the abolition of the upper chamber. With a property qualification for membership there of either a £300 freehold or £600 in personal estate, no penniless agitator could secure entrance, no matter how great his popularity. When a bill was up in June, 1786, to make all kinds of property and state notes legal tender for debts, Caleb Strong could still feel confident that "the major part of the Senate will do right on all these Matters"; that there was no danger of the senate giving in on paper money.[27] In November Christopher Gore wrote encouragingly that the senate was still holding firm on tender laws and other proposals.[28] Not until 1787 or 1788 did such radicals as Captain Walter McFarland of Hopkinton, Phanuel Bishop of Rehoboth, and Jonathan Grant of Petersham appear in the senate, but in the former year even Suffolk returned Benjamin Austin, Jr. ("Old Honestus," the outspoken critic of lawyers), as senator over the merchant Thomas Dawes. However, it is probable that sectional animosities had always played some part in the deliberations of the upper house; even "esquires" were not above being influenced by prevailing sentiment in their communities.

Manifestation of popular feeling was much more frequent in the house of representatives, but even there a genuine upheaval did not take place until 1787. Although a premonition of dissent from conservative policies was suggested as early as 1783, when there was a large return of new members, this did not indicate a permanent

[27] Strong to Sedgwick, June (20?), 1786, Sedgwick Papers.
[28] Gore to King, Nov. 7, 1786, in King, *King*, I, 195. A highly modified "tender" act was actually passed a week later, but the senate was able to impose an eight months' limitation upon it. See note 25 *supra*.

trend. Samuel A. Otis of Boston could write in May, 1784, that "all" agreed that the new house that year was superior to the last.[29] Even in 1786 the house was not much enlarged, though there was a significant increase in the relative number of new members from Hampshire, Middlesex, and Worcester. Not until the following year did the turnover in membership rise sharply, accompanied by a great increase in the size of the house. With the exception of Hampshire, which apparently felt that it had already expressed itself sufficiently, every large county thus reacted in 1787, even seaboard Suffolk and Essex returning over fifty percent new members in that unsettled year. A decline in the relative number of members with the rank of "esquire" was also noticeable as early as 1786 for every large county except Suffolk, but this, too, became pronounced only in 1787. It should be remarked in this connection, however, that in all of the western counties except Hampshire there was a marked tendency from 1785 to 1787 to return more and more representatives with military titles to the house.[30] The responsibility of ex-army men for radical leadership in the legislature has never been fully appreciated, though their presence in mob gatherings has been frequently noticed.

More valuable for an understanding of the situation in the house is an analysis of the voting there on those few issues for which the ayes and nays were recorded between 1785 and 1788.[31]

[29] Samuel A. Otis to Theodore Sedgwick, May 31, 1784, Sedgwick Papers A.

[30] These statements are made on the basis of several analyses of membership lists in the house, as given annually in the *Acts and Resolves*. On the remarkable change in 1787, see Nathan Dane to Nathaniel Gorham, June 6, 1787, in Burnett, *Letters*, VIII, 604.

[31] The following generalizations are based upon a table made up of votes of the town representatives, grouped by counties. These votes, almost the only ones recorded for this period in the manuscript Journals of the House of Representatives, now in the Massachusetts Archives in the State House, include: (1) Whether to engross a bill imposing duties on licensed vellum, parchment, and paper, March 10, 1785. 65 yeas, 46 nays. (2) Whether to engross a bill granting to the United States a tax on the polls and estates of Massachusetts to operate as a supplementary fund to the Continental Impost, June 30, 1786. 65 yeas, 72 nays. (3) Whether it is consistent with the constitution to reduce the governor's salary, Oct. 19, 1786. 75 yeas, 47 nays. (4) Whether to engross a bill to suspend laws for the collection of debts, under certain limitations, Oct. 26, 1786. 69 yeas, 50 nays. (5) Whether to reconsider a vote empowering the supreme judicial court to try persons in any county who have been guilty of obstructing the law, inciting violence, etc., Nov. 8, 1786. 55 yeas, 66 nays. (6) Whether an engrossed bill for continuing an act suspending the laws for the collection of debts, under certain limitations, should pass to be enacted, Nov. 13, 1787. 116 yeas, 74 nays. (7) Whether to approve a committee report favoring the sale of western lands to Nathaniel Gorham and Oliver Phelps, March 31, 1788. 52 yeas, 40 nays.

It discloses the presence of serious sectional antagonisms even before the period of the greatest social disturbances, the principal division, with important modifications, being the familiar one of seaboard versus back country.

Thus Suffolk County was overwhelmingly in favor of collecting revenue on legal documents and other papers in 1785; it unanimously supported the granting of supplementary funds to Congress the next year; and in both 1786 and 1787 it was almost completely opposed to an alteration in the laws for the collection of private debts. However, it also appears that even in Suffolk there was nothing like unanimous support of Governor Bowdoin, as revealed in 1786 on the constitutional question involving the reduction of his salary. Essex County tended to follow Suffolk fairly closely, with one conspicuous exception. In both 1786 and 1787, on the question of collecting private debts Essex was almost evenly divided, this being a question upon which members from the country towns, like old Israel Hutchinson of Danvers (a pronounced "radical" on every possible occasion), acted with something like unity.

Standing halfway between the Boston viewpoint and that of the more radical western counties was Middlesex. Its voting was fairly evenly divided on all questions, except that it was strongly in favor of a broad jurisdiction for the supreme judicial court in trying the leaders of insurrections. This generally noncommittal attitude was not true of Hampshire County, however, except in the case of the indirect paper tax of 1785; otherwise, Hampshire displayed a definitely anti-Boston, anticonservative bias between 1785 and 1787. On most issues its attitude was similar to that of Berkshire County, except that it was more friendly than Berkshire to an alteration in laws for the collection of debts.

The acme of radicalism in the house, however, came from Worcester County. On every question except one, its representatives persistently opposed the seaboard interests—on questions of private debts, Federal funds, support of Bowdoin, and trial of the insurgents. Their opposition, moreover, was heavily felt, since the Worcester members seem to have been unusually prompt in attending the sessions of the court and in registering their votes almost en bloc. Regarding their attitude on land speculation—the one exception noted—it is interesting to observe that they were much more divided than usual, favoring Phelps's and Gorham's purchase in 1788 in about the same ratio as did the Suffolk members. Apparently there was in the back country as general approval of land speculation as there was in the metropolis. As for the lesser counties, their votes were so few as to call for only passing notice. Bristol was the most radical of these during the Critical Period (much more so than its subsequent vote in the Federal constitutional ratifying convention would suggest). In Maine the counties of Lincoln and Cumberland tended to follow the lead of Boston on all measures, but York revealed opposition colors in 1787 when it unanimously favored continuing an altered method for collecting debts.

Another way of analyzing these votes is to estimate the extent to which there was a connection between such sectional manifestations and those revealed in the Federal constitutional ratifying convention of 1788. If the vote of the Boston delegates may be regarded as a criterion of the "Federal" and conservative viewpoint between 1785 and 1788 (and the Boston delegates voted unanimously except for a single vote on one occasion), it is possible to estimate the degree of correlation throughout the state between the vote on any one of these issues and the vote on ratifying the Federal Constitution itself.

For example, on the vote of 1786 for granting supplementary funds to Congress, Boston voted solidly yea. From those other towns in the state which, like Boston, favored the ratification of the Constitution in 1788, there were 50 yeas cast in favor of the supplementary grant and only 23 nays. From those towns which opposed the ratification of the Constitution, however, there were only 7 yeas cast in favor of the supplementary grant, as opposed to 47 nays. In other words, 67 percent of the votes of "Federal" towns were cast on this issue as one would expect to find them, and 87 percent of the votes of the "anti-Federal" towns were cast as one would expect to find them. Such percentages, which may be labeled the "degree of expectancy," run fairly high on various issues between 1785 and 1788, ranging from 53 to 76 percent in case of the votes of the "Federal" towns, and from 61 to 87 percent in case of the "anti-Federal" towns. That the percentages were persistently higher in case of the "anti-Federal" towns is rather interesting, indicating that more of an effort was required in 1788 to whip up the proconstitutional vote than the anticonstitutional. However, the most important fact to be deduced from the above figures is that the alignment of opposing factions was fairly well drawn by March, 1785, if not earlier, and that it tended to increase.

It is therefore understandable why the extreme Massachusetts conservatives should have begun to despair as the year 1786 advanced. Despite their general control of legislation through control of the senate, sectional hostility in the house was increasingly pronounced, reflecting popular distemper, and the finances of the state were bogging down in a morass of poor administration and an impractical scheme for debt redemption. Conservative direction of state affairs had not solved even state problems, to say nothing of the Federal problems of debt repayment and commercial regulation. Some sort of stronger Federal government might be the answer to all these problems, especially since state and Federal finances had become so closely interwoven, but as to the exact nature of that government there was up to 1786 no agreement among the conservatives themselves.

A few persons had long since declared that a more vigorous central government would be desirable under any circumstances. Of these extreme nationalists, General Henry Knox was perhaps the chief spokesman. Others believed that a general revision of the Articles of Confederation was especially desirable for the benefit of commerce and the Federal creditors. Of these moderate nationalists, James Bowdoin was the leader, and his followers probably comprised the bulk of the mercantile element. A third group was made up of a few strong-minded but influential persons who were intensely jealous of the "rights" of Massachusetts and inclined to favor the establishment of a "northern confederation," since it seemed impossible to secure national commercial powers for Congress. Of such New England particularists, Theodore Sedgwick was representative. Lastly, there were those persons who were above all else devoted to the "principles of '76" in the sense that they continued to worry exceedingly about protecting individual "freedom" from any kind of "oppression" and who would reject any proposal for government which seemed to them to contravene that ideal. Of these doctrinaires, Elbridge Gerry was an excellent example.

There was, of course, much overlapping of types; likewise, a number of conservatives did not fit into these categories at all. Nathan Dane, whose conservatism was evinced by his dislike of "radicals" like Israel Hutchinson and by his being a favorite with the "wise men" of Essex, never seemed to get much disturbed by the dire forebodings of others. He took the attitude that one form of government was superior to another only in the manner of its administration. The mild nationalism of Dane and his kind simply reflected their confidence that conservative control in Massachusetts could be continued indefinitely, thus rendering them independent of the need for outside support. Speaking broadly, the success of the Federal movement in Massachusetts came to depend upon the disillusionment of such complacent persons, together with the fusion of all types of conservatives into an aggressive nationalistic front. It ultimately proved successful even without the support of either the extremely complacent or the "doctrinaires," but only after the timely domestic agitation of late 1786 and early 1787.

This movement in Massachusetts for a stronger union was early made evident in a variety of ways. On all of the questions of a Federal impost, a uniform commercial policy, commercial and legal reciprocity between the states, and the settlement of land claims, Massachusetts was in the early eighties already ahead of the other large states. With truth could her delegates to Congress claim that she was a "Federal" state, looked up to for leadership in Federal matters. Nevertheless, the national movement failed to develop there in the way one would expect from such beginnings. It almost proved abortive in 1785 and sank into a state of desuetude in the following year. The explanation of this curious reversal lay in part in the above-mentioned divisions among her conservative politicians, some of whom were deeply marked with New England particularism.

The need for greater Congressional authority had been recognized by many thoughtful persons almost as soon as the Articles of Confederation went into operation. The Boston lawyer, John Lowell, lamented late in 1782 the opposition made to the payment of Federal obligations, and the conflict between state and Continental authority; but he doubted if a new constitution would help much. Government was an organic growth and all that could be done was to "blunder on." [32] Such blundering consisted at that time of the struggle to secure the approval of every state for a five percent impost grant to Congress (which Massachusetts had finally acceded to in the previous May, but only by a majority of three in the house), and without which, men like Nathaniel Gorham were already saying, the Confederacy would dissolve.[33] Despite the approval of this measure by Massachusetts, several of her influential politicians continued to criticize the plan because of prejudice against Robert Morris, the Congressional financier. That the iconoclastic and somewhat radical James Warren should have been one of these was to be expected, for he was infected with the anti-Morris virus of earlier years; [34] but so was the merchant Stephen Higginson, who feared that the impost would increase the power of the financier. Higginson (whose private business was not connected with that of Morris, as was that of Thomas Russell and other Boston merchants) actually welcomed the "jealousies" and "Fears" which appeared in the legislature of 1783 against "the great man or his party." [35] This hypercritical attitude, which Higginson was to display on later occasions and with much less cause, was one of the reasons why modest proposals for Federal reform eventually had to be superseded by a thoroughgoing revolution in government. But perhaps this merely proves him to have been a wise man, after all.

As interest in a national commercial policy continued to grow with merchants everywhere (being well expressed in January, 1784, by an address from a group of Philadelphians to the Massachusetts mercantile element),[36] the conservative Massachusetts legislature

[32] Lowell to Benjamin Lincoln, Nov. 28, 1782, Misc. MSS, Mass. Hist. Soc.

[33] Gorham to Caleb Davis, Feb. 26, 1783, Caleb Davis Papers, 10a.

[34] Cf. *Warren-Adams Letters* (2 vols., Boston, 1917, 1925), II, 232, 236.

[35] Cf. Higginson to Samuel Adams, May 20, 1783, in Samuel Adams Papers, New York Public Library; Higginson to Theophilus Parsons, April, 1783, T. Parsons, *Memoir of Theophilus Parsons* (Boston, 1859), p. 457; Higginson to Arthur Lee, Oct. (?), 1783, "Letters to Higginson," pp. 711, 712.

[36] There is a copy of the address in the Society Collection of the Historical Society of Pennsylvania. An appreciation by a Boston merchant of what the Philadelphians were trying to do may be found in a letter of Jan. 19, 1784, to Thomas FitzSimons, in the John Codman, Jr., Letter Book in the Baker Library, Harvard University.

duly empowered Congress on July 1, 1784, to restrain for fifteen years all foreign commerce "not founded on principles of equality," should all the other states concur.[37] For similar reasons, the Boston merchants petitioned the general court a year later to instruct its delegates to impress upon Congress once again the need for commercial retaliation against the trade laws of Great Britain. The success of this petition to the court was great. Governor Bowdoin proceeded to take his courage in hand in May, 1785, and suggested a convention from all the states to consider the general powers needed by Congress. The general court, continuing in the "Federal" character which it had shown for several years past, not only endorsed the proposal and ordered its delegates to lay such a plan before Congress, but empowered the governor to address all of the states on the subject. More than that, it proceeded to ratify an alteration in the eighth article of the Confederation so that future Federal requisitions could be made on a population basis. As an example to the other states, it also made the trade laws of Massachusetts retaliatory against discriminatory nations (despite the opposition of certain "Country Gentlemen" and with not too much enthusiasm on the part of all merchants), and it repealed that portion of the last duty act which had denied to citizens of other states equal trade rights in Massachusetts without equal duties.[38] There was little more that the legislature could have done to aid the Federal cause.

Yet nothing came of these efforts. After a searching of hearts on the part of the Massachusetts delegates to Congress, they arrived at the alarming conclusion that the convention proposal might introduce dangers of "baleful aristocracies," standing armies, and possibly even "anarchy," if it should be applied and result in failure.[39] The three delegates, Dr. Samuel Holten, Elbridge Gerry, and Rufus King, were all good enough Federal men in their way, but the first two were still saturated with the Revolutionary doctrine of "no tyranny" and young King was probably under their influ-

[37] *Acts*, 1784, c. 15.

[38] Bowdoin's address of May 31 is in the *Resolves*, 1785. Cf. also *Acts*, 1785, c. 8, 16; *Resolves*, 1785, May Sess., c. 75, 77, 78, 134.

[39] Cf. letters of the delegates to Governor Bowdoin, Aug. 18 and Sept. 3, 1785, in King, *King*, I, 59–66. On Oct. 17, King wrote Caleb Davis that, in addition to what was said in these letters, there were "many reasons in favor of our Opinion which would be improper to have communicated." Caleb Davis Papers, 12b. Cf. also *infra*.

ence at the time, trying as he was to be agreeable to influential people. King's rather curious idea of the way to work for Federal trade laws was by "moderation and delay"; "too much precipitation may injure us," he thought.[40] It should be noted also that both King and Holten were in all probability feeling none too friendly toward the Massachusetts legislature in the summer of 1785. The former had heard that his fellow lawyers there had opposed his election to Congress; [41] and Dr. Holten had actually failed of reëlection in July, because of a technicality (so Governor Bowdoin earnestly assured him) or possibly because of certain unfriendly persons in the general court (as Holten himself believed, with the encouragement of Dr. William Gordon).[42]

At any rate, in August the Massachusetts delegates effectually spiked the convention idea by failing to submit it to Congress; and the general court was sufficiently on edge in the matter to approve of their rather dubious conduct by withdrawing the whole proposal in November. When the question was mentioned among conservatives in later months, it is striking how little enthusiasm some of them had for the plan. Nathan Dane was in favor of greater revenues for Congress, but he agreed entirely with the delegates in opposing the convention idea. It had been so ill-considered and hastily advanced, he thought, because of the widespread feeling that additional revenues had to be secured to pay the United States debt and because of the need for national commercial legislation. No doubt the Confederation needed some amending, "particularly as to the mode of suppressing revolts in the respective Governments," but no complete revision of the Articles of Confederation was justified, in his opinion. Its principles were "certainly good." [43] Of somewhat similar mind was Theodore Sedgwick, who believed that it would be to the interest of the northern states for Congress to have power to regulate trade

[40] King to Elbridge Gerry, May 1, 1785, in King, *King*, I, 93.
[41] April 11, 1785, *ibid.*, p. 88.
[42] Draft of letters of Bowdoin to Holten, July 16 and 28, 1785, in "Letters, 1780–88," Mass. Archives; also Holten to Bowdoin, Aug. 11, 1785, Bowdoin Papers, Mass. Hist. Soc.
[43] Dane to King, Oct. 8, 1785, in King, *King*, I, 67–70; Dane to Sedgwick, Oct. 26, 1785, Sedgwick Papers A; Dane to John Choate, Jan. 31, 1786, in Burnett, *Letters*, VIII, 293.

and to raise greater revenues, but who considered rewriting the Articles of Confederation quite another thing:

. . . can it be the wish of the general court to submit whether the great outlines of the federal constitution founded in democratical principles shall be subjected to a *chance of alteration?* and may not laying the subject open to free discussion give birth to new hopes of an aristocratical faction which every community possesses? [44]

That Sedgwick, like King and others, could still be writing at this date of "aristocratical" dangers is most interesting, for they were to think quite differently only a few months later when their power in Massachusetts seemed to be challenged from within.

Even in 1785, however, these men were really rationalizing to cover up their dislike of a stronger union with southerners, especially since they suspected the latter of not favoring the kind of a union in which Congress should have power to enact national commercial laws. King had written disparagingly, in October, of Massachusetts's recent commercial legislation; no doubt it showed a laudable willingness to make sacrifices for the common good, he admitted, but "care should be taken to well observe the extent of such sacrifices. . . ." A month later his fears were more fully revealed. Speaking of the need for giving commercial and other powers to Congress, he suggested that the seven eastern states, as a "subconfederation," might allow Congress to regulate trade for them uniformly, for he doubted if the southern states would "relinquish their partial, and unfederal, policy concerning commerce." But "if once a power is brought into existence under the authority of the States, who may generally revise the Confederation, farewell to the present Republican plan." [45]

Lest this sort of opinion be emphasized to the exclusion of that which was favorable to the idea of a convention, the attitude of the merchant Caleb Davis should be remarked. Writing favorably in March, 1786, of the forthcoming Annapolis meeting, Davis mentioned the fact that the Massachusetts delegates had considered the convention idea of the past year as a "dangerous measure," but

[44] Sedgwick to Caleb Davis, Jan. 31, 1786, Caleb Davis Papers, 13a.
[45] King to Caleb Davis, Oct. 17, Nov. 3, 1785, Caleb Davis Papers, 12b. Cf. also King to John Adams, Nov. 2, 1785, in King, *King*, I, 113.

he confessed that it had ever appeared to him as "the only alternative to Strengthen and Confirm the Federal Government." [46] The truth of the matter is that there already was at that time in Massachusetts, as there continued to be for three subsequent decades, a difference between the moderate New England federalism of the Davis-Bowdoin-Adams faction and the federalism of the Sedgwick-Cabot-Pickering particularists, the latter including Rufus King during the early part of his public career.

The year 1786 at first promised no better Federal results, but if anything the reverse. Although conservative unrest continued to grow over Federal securities and trade regulations, neither the situation in the general court nor domestic conditions generally had assumed such a character as to drive all conservatives into a greater appreciation of the Federal movement. Indeed, the idea of a northern confederacy was considered more and more as an alternative to a genuine national revival. By July, 1786, Massachusetts had so far relapsed from her national commercial leadership as to repeal her trade laws discriminating against discriminatory foreign nations, "for want of coöperation of our Sister States." [47] More serious was the sorry role which she played in (or, rather, out of) the Annapolis convention in September.

The increase of sectional feeling goes far to explain the "crisis of '86," as was demonstrated in Massachusetts early that year on the question of granting "Supplementary funds" to Congress for a period of twenty-five years. Although the general court, especially the senate, was well disposed in March, 1786 (fulfilling at that time other Federal requisitions of the previous September), because, as Nathan Dane said, in any embarrassment of the chest "we ourselves shall suffer most," [48] nevertheless it postponed making the supplementary grant until the next session. The strongest argument

[46] Davis to Nathan Dane, March 20, 1786, Dane Papers, Personal, Library of Congress.

[47] Even Nathaniel Gorham wrote Caleb Davis, June 16, 1786, favoring the repeal of this law which, he said, neither of them had been very fond of originally except for the possibility of the other states coöperating, and he added that one reason for repeal might be "toward restoring the Province of Main to good humor." Caleb Davis Papers, 13a.

[48] Dane to Jacob Wales, Jan. 31, 1786, Burnett, *Letters*, VIII, 297. This referred to the large interest which Massachusetts and most northern states had in the Federal debt, as southerners were fond of pointing out.

against it was the fear that many of the states were increasing in wealth and numbers much faster than Massachusetts, and "New States forming." [49] It was the same sort of apprehension which moved the Massachusetts delegates to Congress in 1786 to oppose the demands of the South and West on the Mississippi navigation question, thus contributing to the political stalemate in that year.

However exaggerated may have been James Monroe's suspicions that the eastern states, under the inspiration of the Massachusetts delegates, were actually holding secret meetings in New York that summer to discuss the advisability of dissolving the union,[50] it is a fact that sectional feeling was sufficiently pronounced to discourage coöperation even in attending the Annapolis commercial convention. For a number of the Massachusetts conservatives had long been convinced that nothing good could come from an idea originating with southern aristocrats. As Stephen Higginson insisted in 1785, there was great dissimilarity in the habits, manners, and commercial interests of the North and South. A lack of industry was also characteristic of certain of the southern delegates in Congress, according to Nathan Dane, who was correspondingly proud of the virtues of his own people.[51]

On the other hand, there were those conservatives who refused to take such notions too seriously, such as Nathaniel Gorham, who wanted Caleb Davis to support another proposal for a Federal convention in February, 1786, and to use his influence to have a Massachusetts delegation attend at Annapolis, "more especially as the overture comes from a Southern State." Since "we have Men among us who have sufficient Commercial Knowledge, but are somewhat antifederal in their opinions," he wrote, "you will therefore judge how necessary it is to send Men of good Federal ideas and that if they are not so they may overthrow the whole plan." [52] Gorham, like some of the other Massachusetts leaders, was particularly alarmed at this time by the paper money and narrow commercial policies being adopted by the state of New York, and also by the fact that New York was selling the best of the lands

[49] Caleb Davis to Nathan Dane, March 20, 1786, Dane Papers, Personal.
[50] Cf. Burnett, *Letters*, VIII, 424, 445.
[51] Cf. "Letters of Higginson," p. 728; Burnett, *Letters*, VIII, 282, 302.
[52] Gorham to Caleb Davis, Feb. 23, 1786, Caleb Davis Papers, 13a.

which Massachusetts claimed in that state, for he apparently already had an eye to land speculation there.

In equal measure did Governor Bowdoin welcome the idea of Massachusetts participating in the Annapolis meeting, and at his suggestion the general court duly appointed successive sets of delegates; but none of these even put in an appearance. Once again Rufus King tended to throw cold water on the proposition. Although he wrote rather favorably to John Adams of the proposed gathering at Annapolis, his letters to personal friends revealed a deep suspicion of what he thought were the real sentiments of the Virginians on national commercial powers: the proposal had not come from those persons "favorable to a commercial system common to all the States, but from those, who in opposition to such a general system have advocated the particular regulations of individual States." [53] And when it was all over, King had the ill grace to write Governor Bowdoin that its history "must be seriously painful" to friends of a good Federal government. His attitude was somewhat like that of Higginson (one of the delegates *in absentia*) who heaped scorn upon the motives of the "great Aristocrats" of the South, of whose ignorance on commercial matters he was certain.[54] In even more self-confident tone did Theodore Sedgwick criticize the Annapolis proposal, for he had "the most decisive evidence" that the original idea was simply to prevent larger powers (i. e., commercial powers) being given to Congress. His own sectional objectives became obvious as he continued his remarks:

It well becomes the eastern and middle States, who are in interest one, seriously to consider what advantages result to them from their connection with the Southern States. . . . No other substitute can be devised than that of contracting the limits of the confederacy to such as are natural and reasonable. . . .[55]

[53] Compare King to John Adams, May 5, 1786, in King, *King*, I, 173, with King to Jonathan Jackson, June 11, 1786, in Mass. Hist. Soc., *Proceedings*, XLIX, 86. At the last minute, however, King apparently favored attending.

[54] Cf. "Letters of Higginson," *loc. cit.*, p. 724. On June 15 Higginson had written Samuel Osgood of similar fears, saying with apparent satisfaction that the "competent" men in Boston refused to attend; but on July 22 he raised the question whether the meeting could not assist in increasing the power of Congress, saying that it must be done. Osgood Papers, I, N.Y. Hist. Soc.

[55] Sedgwick to Caleb Strong, Aug. 6, 1786, Burnett, *Letters*, VIII, 415, 416.

It is only fair to Massachusetts to point out that such sectional feeling was far from one-sided. Monroe, in turn, was equally certain that at Annapolis, "The Eastern men be assur'd mean it as leading further than the object originally comprehended." [56] And behind this particular question there had long existed a conviction that the New Englanders wanted to deprive the southern states of a free trade; that Massachusetts had enacted her trade law of 1785 against Great Britain "in hopes of drawing in the Southern States to come into the measure of prohibiting foreign Vessels from coming to our ports, by which means the Vessels from the Eastern States may obtain high Freights and keep down the price of our produce. . . ." [57]

Such deep-rooted antagonisms never were to be completely abandoned by extremists in either the North or the South, but they were obscured in Massachusetts late in 1786 by developments which at last persuaded some of the Massachusetts particularists that it was necessary to acquiesce in a new Federal movement as the last hope for order and honesty in government. One of those events in all probability was the crisis in public securities; the other, closely connected with it and developing with such rapidity that it shook the confidence of many a conservative in his own state government, was the outbreak of domestic insurrection.

The crisis in securities affected those of both Massachusetts and the Federal government, the former by the failure of the legislature to provide for the redemption of the huge state debt (the first payment on the greater part of which came due that year); the latter by the final breakdown in the Federal requisition system. The two types of securities were, moreover, closely related, both depending upon the degree of vigor with which town officials collected taxes; and in case the state taxes should not prove satisfactory, there was always danger that the entire revenue might be diverted away from the Federal chest.

Especially revealing on the developing fiscal crisis of 1786 was the experience of Nathaniel Appleton, the Federal Loan Office

[56] Monroe to Madison, Sept. 3, 1786, *ibid.*, VIII, 461.

[57] Thomas Farr of Charleston, S.C., to Caleb Davis, Feb. 8, 1786, Caleb Davis Papers, 13a. He goes on to say that patriotism has finally overcome such fears. Similar suspicions were frequently expressed in Congress by Richard Henry Lee of Virginia.

Commissioner in Massachusetts.[58] The work of this long-suffering gentleman (who had held office since 1775) was greatly increased that year by the Massachusetts tax act of March 23, which, by fulfilling certain Congressional requirements, enabled Appleton to begin issuing interest indents due since 1782 on those Loan Office and other debt certificates previously given out from his office. In return, Appleton was to receive back from the Massachusetts treasurer the state's share of the Federal requisition of September 27, 1785: one-third in specie and the remainder in Appleton's indents. That is, what was paid out as interest on the Federal debt was simply to be taxed back again as a Federal requisition.

Even this simple plan, however, failed to work out. Appleton paid out his indents freely enough—as much as $100,000 in some months of early 1786—but collection of the Federal tax, like that of the state, was so poorly executed as to yield almost nothing. Not until early 1788 did Appleton receive back an appreciable number of the indents he had issued, and then they were unaccompanied by specie, for the state had decided in the meantime that it needed the latter for itself!

Throughout 1786, therefore, Appleton's letters to the Board of Treasury in New York grew more and more woeful (and the securities, of course, of less and less value). The state treasurer simply could not pay him a cent. On July 18 Appleton asked that official what specie could be expected by October, but the treasurer was so discouraged that "he dont incline to mention any sum, he observed that not more than 20 Towns had yet made returns of assessments of the last Taxes." Appleton was moved to remark that "I have long apprehended that dry taxes as they are called with us Vizt on Polls and Estates can never support the Federal Treasury in credit." The state's condition was made worse because the treasurer had fallen into the vicious habit of selling his "due bills" (anticipations of taxes) at a great discount, thereby affording a fine speculation to such a person as Oliver Phelps of Granville.[59]

58 The following is based upon the letters of Appleton to the Board of Treasury, in his "Loan-Office Letter Book," June 1, 1785, to Aug. 14, 1791, Old Loans Records, National Archives.
59 There are several letters on this subject in 1787 and 1788 in the Oliver Phelps Papers, New York State Library. Phelps owed money to Samuel Osgood in 1787 which he had used for this business of speculating in tax collections. There is, perhaps, some

Despite this deplorable situation, the pressure of the Federal creditors upon Appleton was immense. Certificates were presented for interest indents in "floods"; he was "crowded" with business, even with the help of two clerks. In August all those who had applied in May had not yet been taken care of, and when the general court convened business increased because of the requests which its members brought with them. In December over a thousand persons were still waiting for their interest. Appleton commented sadly on November 18 that "from the demands made on the Office for Indents one would suppose that thé people intended to pay taxes but they have not yet begun." It was all topped off by the fall riots which "prevented a single Dollar being recd by the Treasurer on the new Tax." So long as these disturbances continued, the Board of Treasury need expect nothing, he wrote, for confidence in government was thereby destroyed.

If this unfortunate state of the public credit (thus intensified by the riots) did not change the minds of certain lukewarm nationalists, the riots themselves did. The experience of Theodore Sedgwick, who was actually threatened with bodily violence, was unique, but most persons of his social status were deeply alarmed by the prospect of a social revolution. The latent feelings of some conservatives for the settlement of their difficulties by forthright methods were at last given a pretext for expression, and the personal influence of persons like Alexander Hamilton (in the company of both Rufus King and George Cabot in New York City late in 1786) was doubtless used to convert the more stubborn particularists. The bulk of the conservatives, however, though long since well disposed toward a more authoritative Federal government, still went along with the extremists only in part.

The impact of the social crisis upon the thinking of such men as King and Sedgwick (both of whom had previously written of "aristocratical" dangers) is revealed in the expressions they began to use. King was moved to observe in October, 1786, that if, as it appeared, "the great Body of the people are, without Virtue, and

reason in this for the antifederal views of Phelps (as also in his land speculation hopes), and it is interesting that he took it for granted as late as December, 1787, that Osgood was an antifederalist also. Osgood was eventually influential in getting Phelps to leave the Massachusetts ratifying convention, one of the turning points in its history.

not governed by any internal restraints of Conscience, there is too much reason to fear that the Framers of our constitution and Laws, have proceeded on principles that do not exist. . . ." The next year, following the "radical" successes in elections to the general court, all he could hope was that the conservatives would be able to check "the madness of Democracy." [60] And Sedgwick wrote savagely in July, 1787, that

the natural effects of a pure democracy are already fully produced among us. A very large party in both branches of the legislature filled with a spirit of republican frenzy are now attempting the same objects by legislation, which their more manly brethren last winter would have procurred by arms. In both instances it is a war against virtue, talents and property carried on by the dregs and the scum of mankind.[61]

Even before this extreme language was expressed, however, there had existed an inchoate but threatening body of opinion in New England and elsewhere which held that all republican government was impracticable, and that even monarchy might be preferable. King and Sedgwick were plainly not among those so infected, but they could not help being aware of such opinions, for the atmosphere since the close of the war had been full of strange rumors centering around the idea that Federal reform could be secured only by "vigorous" action. Foreign observers remarked on the monarchical tendencies as being especially prevalent in New England; for, as George Mason of Virginia explained in early 1787, "the people of the Eastern States, setting out with more republican principles, have consequently been more disappointed than we have been." Years later James Monroe was to accuse Nathaniel Gorham of having been the gentleman who transmitted a letter in 1786, together with one from General Von Steuben, to Prince Henry of Prussia, sounding out the possibilities of establishing a limited monarchy in America.[62]

A suspicious attitude toward Gorham was apparently held by

60 King to Theodore Sedgwick, Oct. 22, 1786; June 10, 1787, Sedgwick Papers A.

61 Sedgwick to Nathan Dane, July 5, 1787, Sedgwick Papers.

62 On this whole subject see Louise B. Dunbar, "A Study of 'Monarchical' Tendencies in the United States from 1776 to 1801," University of Illinois, *Studies in the Social Sciences*, X, No. 1, chap. iv, and citations. This judicious study of a highly important and difficult subject has not yet been absorbed in histories of the period, but it must be reckoned with seriously henceforth. See also Burnett, *Letters*, VIII, 547*n*, 548*n*.

Rufus King at the time,[63] but his specific accusations were reserved for Von Steuben (a popular member of the Order of the Cincinnati, which King was severely criticizing at the very time that Alexander Hamilton and Nathaniel Gorham were celebrating with it in New York, and drinking toasts to a more powerful Congress). He declared the general to be an unscrupulous adventurer, and in November, 1786, accused him of "openly" justifying the conduct of the Massachusetts insurgents (among whom were many ex-army men) with the hope of serving as their leader—the first part of which accusation had some basis in truth.[64] It must have been the knowledge of such a situation as this which prompted Mercy Warren to assure John Adams in December, 1786, that "Time will make curious disclosures, and you, Sir, may be astonished to find the incendiaries who have fomented the discontents among the miserable insurgents of the Massachusetts, in a class of men least suspected." [65] The same charge was to be reiterated many years later in her *History of the American Revolution,* and it was supported by the contemporary statement of a conservative who identified one element among the insurgents as consisting of persons "who wished to carry popular measures to such extremes as to shew their absurdity, and demonstrate the necessity of lessening the democratick principles of the constitution." [66]

It seems paradoxical, however, to try to connect Von Steuben's monarchical ideas and his sympathy for the rioters with the new constitutional movement in Massachusetts, since his critic King himself soon became an ardent supporter of that constitutional movement. It seems paradoxical, yet it is doubly fascinating when the additional fact is considered that it was Von Steuben's dearest

---

63 Cf. King to Elbridge Gerry, June 4, 1786, *ibid.,* VIII, 382.

64 Cf. King to Gerry, Nov. 5, 1786, and inclosure, in King, *King,* I, 192–95. King accused Von Steuben of being the author of the "Bellisarius" article in the *New York Daily Advertiser* of Nov. 1, 1786, where the assembling of Federal troops in Massachusetts for use in the "Indian War" was cleverly unmasked. Proof of Von Steuben's authorship is found in John M. Palmer, *General Von Steuben* (New Haven, 1937), pp. 338, 339. For further remarks on the conduct of the general, who was also posing as a friend of republican government *even the day before he wrote Prince Henry of Prussia, suggesting the possibility of establishing a monarchy in America,* see *infra.*

65 Mercy Warren to John Adams, Dec., 1786, Mass. Hist. Soc., *Proceedings,* XLIV, 160. She was defending her husband against similar accusations.

66 Mercy Warren, *History of the American Revolution* (3 vols., Boston, 1805), III, 346; Minot, *Insurrections in Massachusetts,* p. 105, also pp. 62, 63.

friend, young Major "Billy" North, who consciously or unconsciously played an important role in the series of events, which, under the inspiration of General Henry Knox, led up to the *suppression* of Shays's revolt and the closely connected success of the constitutional movement.

There is still a mystery in much of this, even as regards the conduct of General Knox.[67] If he felt like his confidential correspondent, Stephen Higginson (who, despite his sectional bias, had believed as early as 1783 in the necessity of thoroughgoing constitutional reform, and like Rufus King had come to believe by 1786 that only a "common danger" would ever weld the states together), then Knox recognized the possibilities of advancing Federal reform as a result of the riots which appeared in Massachusetts in the summer and fall of 1786. Spreading the most alarming reports as to their character and goading "men of property" with fears of an impending social revolution, he sought financial support for energetic and secret measures for putting down the rioters with Federal troops, on the grounds that Congressional property was threatened, and for the larger purpose possibly of developing a community-of-interest point of view on Federal affairs.

This conduct of Knox is explained to some extent by his background. Born and bred a Massachusetts man, he had allied himself by marriage with a wealthy (and disapproving) conservative family, but had made a fine military record as one of Washington's most trusted generals during the Revolution. After the war he continued as a military figure, organized the Order of the Cincinnati, and left his circle of prominent Boston friends in 1785 to serve in New York as the Secretary of War of the United States. A strong nationalist, Knox had advocated constitutional reform in 1783, and had expressed his Federal feelings on the narrow con-

[67] It should be understood that in what follows I am not impugning the sincerity of Knox in being alarmed at the prospect of a social revolution in Massachusetts, but am suggesting that he, too, realized the potentialities in the situation for advancing the cause of a stronger Federal government. I cannot entirely agree, however, with the statement made by J. P. Warren, "The Confederation and Shays Rebellion," in the *American Historical Review*, XI, 56, that Knox "was accustomed to write very frankly to Washington" in these matters. See *infra*, note 89. But Dr. Warren admits that the severe interpretation which men like Knox put upon the aims of the rebellion was, in his opinion, "unjust to most of its participants." *Ibid.*, p. 42. Washington also received impassioned letters on the subject from Henry Lee and David Humphreys, from the former as early as Sept. 8, 1786. Both Humphreys and Knox used the word "neuter" in such letters.

duct of New York in early 1786 by saying with soldierly vigor, "every liberal good man is wishing New York in Hell." [68] He must have been fully aware of the potentialities of the ex-army men in "solving" certain state and Federal problems. In fact, Dr. William Eustis of Boston wrote him in detail in February, 1785, of how the soldiers might be thoroughly organized, and "by some well lined publications and applications to the state and to the Congress to obtain some special payments of interest or of principal in preference to the common holders of various species of public securities." And Eustis frankly added, "For myself I am free to acknowledge that I am governed by a desire to make better my public securities. . . ." [69] Perhaps he was aware of the fact that Knox himself was a securities holder.

Despite his enthusiasm for reform, Knox was loath to use military force to the extent of anything like a coup d'état. In February, 1787, he acknowledged that "much has been said about the influence of the Army being united with the influence of the other public creditors to procure a general system of Finance or permanent continental funds"; but added that "the influence of the army can only exist on one point, that to be sure is a sharp point, which I hope in God will never be directed but against the enemies of the liberties of America." The army should restrain itself, though he admitted that a point might be reached beyond which endurance could not go. [70] And Knox some months before had given a "gentle check" to Colonel Benjamin Tupper of Massachusetts for suggesting a government of "majesty" to be established through the instrumentality of the Cincinnati. [71] In holding these opinions, Tupper, who had recently returned from a surveying trip in Ohio, was like some of the other army men who were to settle shortly afterwards in that region. [72]

However reserved his written words on this question, the ac-

[68] Knox to Henry Jackson, April 23, 1786 (draft), Knox Papers, Vol. XVIII, Mass. Hist. Soc.

[69] Eustis to Knox, Feb. 13, 1785, Knox Papers, Vol. XVII.

[70] Knox to General McDougall, Feb. 21, 1787, Knox Papers, Vol. XIX. (This could not have been General Alexander McDougall, who had died the previous year.)

[71] Cf. Dunbar, *op. cit.*, p. 73.

[72] This characteristic of the early Ohio group (which was backed by Knox and several great securities speculators) is remarked upon by Dunbar, *op. cit.*, p. 74. In this connection it is perhaps worth pointing out that Captain Daniel Shays must have been well acquainted with the leader of the Ohio group, General Rufus Putnam, under whom he had served during the Revolution.

tions of Knox in the fall of 1786 certainly indicate his disposition to view the domestic troubles of Massachusetts as a national calamity which justified armed intervention by Congress. The early months of that year had been rightly filled with "crisis" talk about national affairs, and his friend Higginson had written in July of a possible "revolution" in the Bay State.[73] In such an atmosphere did Knox hurry to Springfield in the middle of September to survey the situation of the Federal arsenal there. He immediately began to report (even before the insurgents had gathered at Springfield, and again after their peaceful dispersal, without touching the arsenal, on September 26) [74] that the worst fears were about to be realized. Throughout October Knox made further reports to Congress and wrote letters to Washington and others, predicting a complete social and political revolution in Massachusetts, describing the threat of "armed tyranny" there, and relating other "melancholy information." [75] Bad as the disturbances in Massachusetts were (and frequently had been for fifteen years or so), he plainly made them out as calamitous, thereby helping to disturb Washington and others exceedingly and getting Congress in secret session to adopt a report recommending the requisitioning of Federal troops—ostensibly to be used against the Ohio Indians but really to be stationed in Massachusetts for use against the insurgents—and urging men of wealth to lend money to support the project. In pursuit of this plan, which apparently had been worked out with the Massachusetts leaders around October 1, Knox sent Major "Billy" North to Boston to aid in recruiting the Federal troops, under the command of Knox's closest friend, General Henry Jackson. The latter had written Knox on September 28 of the disturbances at Springfield and of Bowdoin's spirited address to the general court, and had concluded, "I pray to God something important will be the event." [76] To complete this curi-

[73] Cf. Higginson to John Adams, July, 1786, in "Letters of Higginson," pp. 740, 741.

[74] Cf. J. P. Warren, "The Confederation and Shays Rebellion," pp. 45, 46. He speaks of the dispersal of the insurgents led by Shays at Springfield on the 26th, as being accomplished by a "curious device." David Humphreys wrote Washington, Feb. 11, 1787, remarking on the poor leadership of the insurgents. "At an earlier period it was obviously in their power to have seized the public Magazine." Washington Papers, Library of Congress.

[75] Warren, *op. cit.*, pp. 45, 46; Burnett, *Letters,* VIII, 486· W. C. Ford, ed., *The Writings of Washington* (14 vols., New York, 1889–93), XI, 80–82.

[76] Jackson to Knox, Sept. 28, 1786, Knox Papers, Vol. XIX.

ous picture it is only necessary to add that it was from Major North's reports from Ohio in August that the "first explicit information" of a threatened Indian uprising had been heard; [77] that North had served under both Knox and Jackson during the Revolution; and, again, that North was the dearest friend of General Von Steuben, who was "openly" sympathizing with the Massachusetts insurgents! [78]

The only hitch in the plan was the want of money. Knox emphasized to Higginson on October 22 that "exertions must be made and something must be hazarded, by the rich." Higginson replied on November 12 in a most confidential manner:

Your Letter 22d ulto by Capt. North I recd—the measures proper, upon the view of a War with the *Indians* and the consequent Requisition of Congress, obtained very speedily and with more ease than I expected. you have in this case taken the best ground. the money wanted for the men will, I trust, be soon raised. the Treasurer has just opened his loan; and though monied men, like others, are more ready at profession than action, yet, I think their feelings and a regard to their beloved property will induce them to furnish what is immediately wanted. The present moment is very favorable to the forming further and necessary arrangements, for increasing the dignity and energy of government. what has been done, must be used as a Stock upon which the best Fruits are to be engrafted. the public mind is now in a fit state, and will shortly I think become more so, to come forward with a system competent to the great purpose of all civil arrangements, that of promoting and securing the happiness of Society. as far as I can be conducive to a right improvement of this disposition, so very favorable an opening shall not be lost.[79]

---

[77] This is a curious set of circumstances, but Warren, "The Confederation and Shays Rebellion," p. 55, dismisses it by saying, "When these officers wrote they could not possibly have foreseen any connection between their reports and civil commotions in Massachusetts." This begs the whole question. The "real" danger of an Indian uprising seems to me to be a very debatable proposition despite Dr. Warren's able documentation. The frontier was frequently full of such reports. The situation reminds one of what Edward Channing once wrote about "bleeding" Kansas. Furthermore, it required no prophet to predict trouble in Massachusetts. Witness Higginson's prediction in July of a possible "revolution," as noted above.

[78] Even if Von Steuben's attitude were wholly unconnected with any larger movement, there is still the possibility that he was being used by other men for concealed purposes. But in any case it is difficult to understand how his viewpoint could have been so different from "Billy" North's. It simply does not make sense, considering their close relations and also the degree of intimacy between Von Steuben and General Knox.

[79] Knox Papers, Vol. XIX. That this opportunistic attitude towards Shays's Rebellion was no secret is revealed by cynical comments in several newspapers in 1787, as

Two weeks later Higginson again wrote, complaining of the slowness of the subscription and stating that the fears of "our monied men" had subsided since Knox was in Boston. The news that Shays was on the march, he added, had again raised them and now promised better results. He also cited the recent action of the general court as mortifying, but predicted that this action, too, "will tend much to prepare the public mind, for transferring power from the individual Governments to the federal, and may facilitate those measures which We esteem essential to Our public happiness."

I am often disposed to think that we shall, in despite of our folly and timidity, become a respectable people. when from the Vices or Follies of our rulers we seem to be in danger of anarchy, some new Event turns up to avert the Evil and show us the necessity of abridging the power of the States to controul or impede the measures of the union. I never saw so great change in the public mind, on any occasion, as has lately appeared in this State as to the expediency of increasing the powers of Congress, not merely as to commercial objects, but generally—by the next summer I expect we shall here be prepared for any thing that is wise and fitting—Congress should be making the necessary arrangements for improving this disposition, when sufficiently increased, to right and valuable purposes. they must be prepared, not only to support a proper force in the field, but to consolidate the Several Governments into One, generally and efficient. but I am going too fast.[80]

General Jackson also complained of how poorly the loan went (papers for which were deposited at the various marine insurance offices), despite his efforts to "influence the rich." He thought that if only several of the merchants would take the business into their own hands it would go better.[81] Enthusiasm for a military foray, however, soon began to rise. Colonel Benjamin Hickborn wrote Knox on December 14, "I am afraid the Insurgents will be conquered too soon"; and the success of a similar loan to support the state troops to be used against Shays caused Jackson to observe in January that the people of Boston, of all classes, were as enthusias-

---

quoted by Dunbar, *op. cit.,* p. 80, and by Samuel B. Harding, *The Contest over the Ratification of the Federal Constitution in the State of Massachusetts* (New York, 1896), p. 13.

[80] Higginson to Knox, Nov. 25, 1786, Knox Papers, Vol. XIX.

[81] Jackson to Knox, Dec. 3, 11, 1786, *ibid.*

tic as in the year 1775, and "you remember how we used to enjoy ourselves in those happy days." [82]

Although this enthusiasm was largely for suppression of the insurgents by state rather than Federal troops, the fears which Knox had aroused and the plan for severe military repression which he had suggested were undoubtedly of the greatest importance in promoting the other scheme. Among those who had been from the first particularly impressed with his stratagem was at least one representative of a new but rapidly growing element in American society. That speculator-legislator-pamphleteer, James Swan, had addressed Knox on October 26 on a most interesting subject:

Being in town at Court I am agreeably saluted with the news of War being declared against the Indians. I hope in this declaration "Indians," is meant all who oppose the Dignity, Honour, and happiness of the United States, or of either of the States. I told you in State Street what my hopes were—little did I think the happy circumstance so near. Pray do I not trouble you, beyond even what the most sanguine friendship can warrant, when I beseech you to give me your advice as to my future conduct in buying or selling into the Continental funds? I have felt, I momently feel, the good effects of your former advice and friendship, as warmer—as swells my heart with a tumult of gratitude— at this moment I want it again—our State is distracted—I mind them not, as it effects the debt of the Union. . . .[83]

To this remarkable letter Knox replied in a somewhat vague manner. He was "highly flattered" by Swan's confidence, but added:

The funds were not [have not been] the object of my contemplation and therefore I am incompetent to form a judicious opinion respecting which species of them ought to have the preference. There are certain national maxims and habits of honer and faith essential to a confidence in the promises made by the public. You can determine whether these are possessed by the United States generally. I know that Congress are upright in their intentions. But [with?] the local legislatures convenience seems to be too much of a ruling principle. It has been an object with some of the states to have an apportionment of the national debt, as soon as this shall happen, the public creditors will be ruined because if the public debt is to be provided for at the pleasure of the local governments[?] they will never please to provide for it.

---

[82] Hickborn to Knox, Dec. 14, 1786; Jackson to Knox, Jan. 21, 1787, *ibid.*

[83] *Ibid.* The first two sentences only are quoted by Warren, "The Confederation and Shays Rebellion," p. 57, who thus ignores the fact of the conversation about "buying or selling into the Continental funds."

. . . In a great commotion which shall involve all that is dear to society you would not hesitate[?] the part you are to take— In this[?] case you and every person of Fortune must take a decisive and active part—neuter will not be tolerated— The principle of government must be supported or we shall experience the most [—] anarchy and all its attendent and consequent horrors.[84]

That Swan duly recognized his "part" when the crisis arose is proved by his service under General Lincoln in the January campaign against Shays. With him were other young conservatives, such as Harrison Gray Otis who had been commissioned in a Boston regiment raised the previous fall, the afore-mentioned securities holder, Dr. William Eustis, and even some of the older merchants, including Higginson himself.

The success of General Lincoln in raising a large loan from the merchants to support the state troops stands in contrast to the failure of Knox and Jackson to do the same for the Federal troops. There probably was doubt in the minds of the more moderate conservatives as to the desirability of the Knox maneuver, and Jackson complained from the first of a lack of coöperation on the part of the general court. Eventually Massachusetts was to help pay for what Federal troops were raised (and which, incidentally, never did march to the Ohio), but as early as October, 1786, certain country members of the court had laughed at the "danger" of an Indian war and declared that the whole scheme was simply one to raise a standing army; or, as Major North said, "The people here smell a rat. . . ."[85] Again, however, it must be emphasized that Knox and Jackson had contributed much to raising the fears which made the state campaign possible, although Bowdoin and his generally conservative legislature of 1786 had early evinced their intention to put down the rioters.[86]

84 Knox to Swan, Nov. 4, 1786, *ibid.* A draft and difficult to decipher. An "are" was apparently scratched out, and the "have not been" discarded in favor of "were not." Other parts of the letter appear to read to the effect that the rigorous events arising demand reform and that public creditors must postpone their expectations until tranquillity is restored. Meantime, lands appear to be the best security, etc.

85 Cf. Warren, "The Confederation and Shays Rebellion," p. 57.

86 On Oct. 4, 1786, even the Massachusetts House of Representatives had *unanimously* resolved its "greatest abhorrence of certain unwarrantable and outrageous proceedings in several counties"; and the next day it had *unanimously* approved of Governor Bowdoin's use of the militia to suppress proceedings against courts of law. Mass. House MS Journals. These facts make Knox's conduct all the more striking.

Even before Shays was utterly routed, the larger objectives of the extreme nationalists were being clarified in letters to each other, the general point of agreement being that bold measures for Federal reform were now expedient and that the Philadelphia convention in May was the place to apply them. Recognizing the favorable temper of the moment, Higginson wrote Knox on February 13, "You will endeavor no doubt to draw strong Arguments from the insurrection in this state in favour of an efficient General Government for the Union." And a few weeks before he had told General Lincoln, "We are here, preparing for matters more HARD TO MANAGE and MORE DANGEROUS than Shays and his party. But if you can give a decisive stroke to the latter, . . . we can more easily obtain the former." [87] Although many Federalists remained cynical—as did Jeremiah Wadsworth of Hartford who severely criticized Massachusetts in early January, 1787, because there were so few there who were "really in earnest to establish a new system" [88]—Knox and Higginson were once again outlining the method and voicing the spirit whereby a real revolution in national affairs might be achieved. No better proof of the foresight, determination, and apparently of the influence of these extremists can be found than in their amazing letters of January and February, 1787, three months before the Philadelphia meeting convened.

The earliest and most temperate of these was written to Washington by Knox on January 14.[89] Two weeks later, however, he expressed his private opinions with much more vigor and candor to Higginson. Speaking of the forthcoming convention, he voiced the hope that, although the meeting might not have been intended originally for radical reform, it might be turned to excellent purpose. He continued:

I have heard all that has been said about legal and illegal conventions. I confess I do not find the objections on this point so weighty as some

[87] Morse, *Federalist Party*, p. 42n, quoting from the *Boston Centinel*, Aug. 1, 1787.

[88] Wadsworth to Knox, Jan. 7, 1787, Knox Papers, Vol. XVII.

[89] Jared Sparks, ed., *Correspondence of the American Revolution; Being Letters of Eminent Men to George Washington* (4 vols., Boston, 1853), IV, 156 *et seq.* Evaluate the "frank" character of this letter by comparing it with that to Higginson, quoted in part immediately below. Note also Knox's references to armed force in the letter to Washington.

people do. Should the Convention agree on some continental constitution and propose the great outlines either through Congress or directly to their Constituents the respective Legislatures with a request that State conventions might be assembled for the sole purchase [purpose] of choosing delegates to a Continental Convention in order to confer and decide upon a general government, and to publish it for general observance, in the same manner as Congress formed, and decided upon the articles of confederation and perpetual union, would not this to all intents and purposes be a government derived from the people and assented to by them as much as they assented to the confederation? [90]

The broad sweeping character of the reform he proposed is impressive, though his anticipation of the details of ratification was inexact. Even these details, however, were accurately forecast by Higginson in his famous reply of February 8, in which he suggested the establishment of a truly sovereign Federal government by the more daring method of ratification by nine states only, preferably by conventions.[91] It was in keeping with the spirit expressed in such confidential communications that Nathaniel Gorham wrote Knox only a week later, "Sensible and bold men shall be chosen for the convention if I can have any influence in the business." [92]

Sensible and bold men were indeed required, but for different reasons by different persons. It was now the belief even of Elbridge Gerry, who had previously vacillated on Federal questions, that unless at Philadelphia "a system of Government is adopted by *Compact, Force* I expect will plant the Standard: for such an anarchy as now exists cannot last long. Gentlemen seem to be impressed with the necessity of establishing some efficient system and I hope it will secure us against domestic as well as Foreign Invasion." [93] Nor were his fears wholly imaginary, for distaste with republican government had grown in recent months to almost revolutionary lengths with a certain class of men in Massachusetts. One who was in a good position to judge wrote in January, 1787, that

[90] Knox to Higginson, Jan. 28, 1787, Knox Papers, Vol. XIX. If this is the source used in Francis S. Drake, *Life and Correspondence of Henry Knox* (Boston, 1873), pp. 93, 94, then the "legal and illegal conventions" portion was omitted there.

[91] Cf. "Letters of Higginson," pp. 745–50.

[92] Gorham to Knox, Feb. 18, 1787, Knox Papers, Vol. XIX.

[93] Gerry to Monroe, June 11, 1787, in W. C. Ford, ed., *Some Letters of Elbridge Gerry of Massachusetts, 1784–1807* (Brooklyn, 1896), pp. 8, 9.

"Mr King, Mr Sedgwick and several others (I believe I might say John Jay) who have been mortally opposed to the Cincinnati, now look with considerable confidence to that quarter for our political preservation." [94] But "force" was not what constituted the basis of Knox's fears, as he continued to write in May of the necessity for radical action at Philadelphia and not merely "a patch work"; for a strong government with "a Judicial to be formed on the highest principles of Independency." All this was necessary in his opinion because "a mad democracy sweeps away every moral and divine trait from the human character." [95]

Such language, as has been noted, was rendered the more vitriolic in Massachusetts in 1787 because of the increased radical character of the general court that year, a fact which probably as deeply alarmed the majority of the conservatives as did all of Shays's forays combined. Some of them, again including Nathan Dane, continued to look on the best side of a bad situation, and even the merchant Samuel Breck properly pointed out that the "riotous" element was still far from a majority. Conservative feeling was at least strong enough to put aside a paper-money proposal. Nevertheless it was only by the "good sense" of Dr. Jarvis of Boston that a complete country-seaboard break was averted during the May session, and the radical interest was sufficiently strong to force a compromise on the selection of a Congressional delegate. [96] Throughout the rest of the year the court was continually troubled with agitation for paper money, while "Some Genii" plead for "a Scale, others for Excise, others for land tax." [97] Another disconcerting feature for the conservatives was the fact that Hancock had again been elected governor—in the "greatest contest ever known of the occasion"— for they had little faith in his vetoes being cast in the right direction.

There was little in such a situation to reassure the public as to

[94] David Humphreys to Washington (private), Jan. 20, 1787, Washington Papers. He apparently had had occasion to talk with these men at the meeting of Massachusetts and New York delegates on the boundary question. Cf. the blunt statement in Minot, *Insurrections in Massachusetts*, pp. 62, 63.

[95] Knox to Mercy Warren, May 30, 1787, *Warren-Adams Letters*, II, 294–96.

[96] Samuel Breck to Knox, July 14, 1787, Knox Papers, Vol. XX; Christopher Gore to Rufus King, June 28, 1787, King, *King*, I, 226, 227.

[97] Samuel A. Otis to Theodore Sedgwick, Sept. 8, 1787, Sedgwick Papers A.

the value of Massachusetts securities; Henry Knox resolved to convert his into a land speculation in August, against the advice of Samuel Breck and the Boston brokers who anticipated a rise in all securities "from the appearance of the proposed Constitution being adopted." [98] Indeed, all hope of security holders, either state or Federal, had apparently come to rest upon the establishment of a new Federal system. Anticipation of this possibility was doubtless behind the reasoning of Stephen Higginson in January, 1787 (the time of his prophetic plan for constitutional ratification), when he had proposed a speculation in Loan Office certificates to Samuel Osgood.[99]

To such a degree of self-consciousness on all Federal questions had the Massachusetts conservatives come by late 1787, when the question of ratifying the Federal Constitution was before them. The general breakdown in the conservative policies inaugurated in the early eighties had been accompanied by a period of severe but timely domestic disturbances during which armed force, financed by a thoroughly propagandized seaboard, had dispersed the rioters but had not prevented a bitter reaction in state politics. Domestic reform, both political and fiscal, now seemed to have its last hope in Federal reform, as the extremists had long desired. Those conservatives who had formerly opposed the latter were now to make their choice of either going along in a far more comprehensive movement than they had ever anticipated or being dubbed followers of Shays, paper money advocates, and other opprobrious things.[100] Capitalizing upon local fears and antagonisms,

[98] Henry Jackson to Knox, Oct. 21, 1787, Knox Papers, Vol. XXI.

[99] Higginson to Samuel Osgood, Feb. 21, 1787, Osgood Papers, Vol. I. On the basis of some 3000 names of persons receiving interest indents and liquidated debt certificates on Federal securities in Massachusetts, 1785–88, it can be stated that most of the Boston members of the court during the Critical Period, and all but one or two of her delegates to the convention, were Federal security holders (including one "Samuel Adams, Esquire" of Boston), and there were other important persons scattered throughout the state for whom identity also seems certain. The fragmentary character of the record and the difficulty of exact identification of holders with members of the same name in the general court or in the ratifying convention of 1788 obviate more definitive conclusions. The issue is further confused as it would seem that country members of the general court often collected interest at the Boston Loan Office for neighbors back home. Libers 264, 266, 269, 270, 283, 285 (some of the names were checked against the later fragmentary Funding Subscription Records in Massachusetts, libers 286, 287, 288), Old Loans Records, National Archives.

[100] On the vituperative character of the Federalist campaign, cf. the remarks by Professor Charles Warren in the Mass. Hist. Soc., *Proceedings*, XLIV, 152 *et seq.*

the extremists had at last had their way, and they continued to have it during the period of the ratifying convention when, by close coöperation with their fellow conservatives, in the face of the untempered denunciation of all antifederalists, they achieved the near impossible.

Index

Abbott, W. C., quoted, 287

Absolutist governments, America a threat to, 332

Acadia, 142, 147

Accomac (Va.), writs of assistance issued at, 67, 71

Acts of Trade, 76, 216; effects on thirteen colonies, 3-39; *see also* Navigation Acts

Adams, Abigail, quoted, 130

Adams, John, 98, 307, 309; notes on Otis's speech, 43; quoted, 101, 332, 334; on Eliphalet Dyer, 298, 299; *Dissertation on the Feudal and the Canon Law*, 334; believed British Empire crumbling, 345; Massachusetts constitution of 1780 primarily the work of, 353

Adams, Samuel, 98; as advocate of price regulation, 106; letter from Eliphalet Dyer, 300 f.; Dyer urges coöperation to make New London base for the Continental Navy, 301; holder of Federal securities, 390n

Administration, centralized, attempts at, 173-75; in western country, 193-95

Africa, colonial trade with, 10

Agrarian disturbances, 279

Agriculture, condition in Massachusetts, 354, 357

Aix-la-Chapelle, Peace of, 157, 158 f., 160

Alamance, battle of the, 252

Albany (N.Y.), freemanship in, 82n; assize of bread, 84n; price regulation at, 93; committee of correspondence, 103, 133; punishment of profiteers, 128; Sons of Liberty, 271, 276, 280

Albany County (N.Y.), assizes, 125 f.

Albany plan of 1754, 174

Albemarle, William, Earl of, governor of Virginia, 230

Alleghenies, territory west of, *see* Reservation, Indian

Allen, William, chief justice, 59 ff., 63

Allicocke, Joseph, leader of the Sons of Liberty, 273 f., 275, 277, 287

Alsop, John, 288

Amazon River, 142

Amelot de Chaillou, Jean-Jacques, French foreign minister, 156

America, and the Irish revolutionary movement, 332-48

American balance of power and European diplomacy, 140-69

American colonies, England's desire for gain from, 30 f.; newspapers, 305-31

American Revolution, writs of assistance as a cause of, 40-75; and balance of colonial power, 162-69; formulation of French attitude toward, 162; Vergennes's policy toward, 164 ff.; cause of success of, 169; standing army one cause of, 170; relation of Sons of Liberty to, 269 ff.; conflict of motivating forces, 278; Connecticut men of wealth and influence in, 290

Americans, prod sympathizers in Ireland, 336; toasted in Ireland, 336

Ames, Fisher, 351

Amherst, Sir Jeffrey, 177; governor of Virginia, 230, 231; declines to reside in Virginia as governor, 238

Ammunition, exported from Ireland to America, 341

Anderson, John, *Constitutional Gazette*, 320

Anglo-French entente, 147

Anglo-Spanish declaration (1732), 146, 149 f.

Anglo-Spanish treaty (1750), 159

Anjou, Duc d', *see* Philip V

Annapolis convention, 122; commercial regulation, 371, 372, 373-75

Appleton, Nathaniel, administration of Federal Loan Office during fiscal crisis of 1786, 375-77

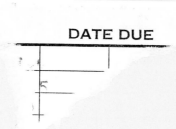
DATE DUE